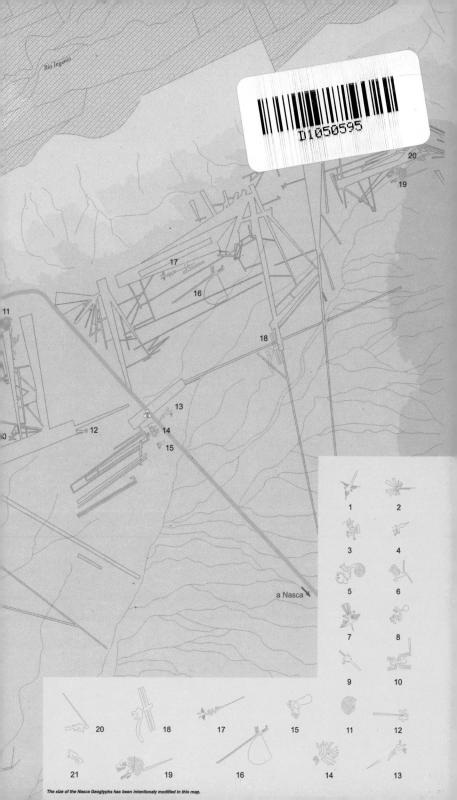

Rio Ingenio

D1050595

20

19

11

17

16

18

13

12

14

15

a Nasca

1

2

3

4

5

6

7

8

9

10

20 18 17 15 11 12

21 19 16 14 13

Editorial Team

Editors: Walter H. Wust, Germán Coronado
Text and photography: Walter H. Wust
Editing supervision: Celia Schaefer Revoredo
Translation from the Spanish: Laura Shannon, Arian Manchego
Surveying and cartographic documentation: Inside Perú
Design and preparation of cartography: Grupo Geo Graphos SRL
Assistance: Natali Wust, Pilar Marimón, Carlos Gutiérrez,
  Jorge Reynafarje
Digital pre-press: Gráfica Biblos S.A.

Advisors

The following specialists have provided advice for part three
of this guide:
  Rodolfo Hinostroza, on cuisine; Luis Millones,
  on Peruvian history and popular feasts; José Pinilla,
  on archeology, and Luis Enrique Tord, on art history.

Authors of Special Articles

Walter Alva *(Sipán);* Antonio Cisneros and Rodolfo Hinostroza
(Cuisine); Luis Millones *(Popular feasts);* Walter H. Wust
(Protected natural areas).

Correspondents

Daina d'Achille *(Arequipa),* Gerd Burmester *(Tumbes y Piura),* Sylvia
Morán *(Lima),* Mauricio Soldi *(Trujillo),* Alexander Funcke *(Iquitos),*
Aldo Tovar *(Ayacucho),* Mary Valdivieso *(Cajamarca)* y Luis Nieto
Degregori *(Cusco),* Claudia Echegaray *(Puerto Maldonado).*

Complementary photographs

Mylene d'Auriol, Alejandro Balaguer/Biósfera, Ricardo Balarezo,
Caretas, Cosas, Daniel Giannoni, Wilfredo Loayza/PEISA, Jaime
Marimón, Sengo Pérez/Biósfera, Luis Pilares, Heinz Plenge, Juan
Puelles, Carlos Sala, Michael Tweddle, Renzo Uccelli, Antonio
Valdivia, M. Valqui & C. Munn/Inka Natura.

Inca Guide to Peru:
Tourism Routes and Destinations
Second edition
© 2002, PEISA
  Promoción Editorial Inca S.A.
  Av. Dos de Mayo 1285, San Isidro
  Lima 27, Perú

ISBN: 9972-40-211-8

Legal Deposit N: 1501132002-0947

Printing: Gráfica Biblos S.A.

INCA GUIDE TO
PERU

TOURISM ROUTES AND DESTINATIONS

Contents

Preface 11
How to use this guide 12
To our readers 14
Abbreviations used in this guide................. 15
Acknowledgments 16

1 Perú

General information 18
Brief history 27
The royal tombs at Sipán, *Walter Alva* 37
Protected natural areas of Peru, *Walter H. Wust*....... 43
The principal protected natural areas in Peru ... 44
The great cuisine of Peru, *Rodolfo Hinostroza* 50
The realm of the raw, *Antonio Cisneros*.......... 57
The traditional feast, *Luis Millones* 59
Calendar of festivals 64

2 Useful Facts for the Traveler

Tourism services in Peru 70
Urban transport........................... 72
Peru by road 73
Peru by plane............................. 82
Peru by train 85
Peru by boat 87
General recommendations.................... 88

3 Destinations

Abancay.................................. 94
Andahuaylas 101
Arequipa 107
Ayacucho................................ 127
Cajamarca 141

Colca Canyon, the. 155
Cusco 172
Chachapoyas 203
Chanchamayo Valley, the. 212
Chiclayo 221
Huancavelica 232
Huancayo 238
Huánuco 249
Huaylas, Callejón de 258
Ica 277
Iquitos. 286
Lima 299
Machu Picchu 340
Manu, el 351
Nasca. 359
Paracas. 368
Piura 378
Pucallpa. 392
Puerto Maldonado. 399
Puno 406
Tacna. 423
Tarapoto 431
Tarma 438
Trujillo 444
Tumbes 459

4 Routes

North
1 Lima-Tumbes 470
2 Trujillo-Cajamarca 488
3 Chiclayo-Tarapoto 491
4 Lima-Callejón de Huaylas 495

Center
5 Lima-Huancayo 498
6 Lima-Valle de Chanchamayo 503
7 Lima-Pucallpa 506

South
8 Lima-Tacna 512
9 Huancayo-Ayacucho 527

10 Pisco~Abancay 529
11 Nasca~Cusco. 532
12 Arequipa~Cusco 534
13 Cusco~Puno 537
14 Cusco~Puerto Maldonado. 542
15 Cusco~Manu 545

5 Index

Index of place names 550
Index of maps 569
Index of photographs 570

6 Route Maps

6 Route Maps 579

Preface

The *Inca Guide to Peru* was conceived of as a complete source
of information for the visitor to Peru. The idea of creating the
guide grew from my innumerable trips through this vast territory,
a land of natural and cultural diversity that can always surprise
even the most seasoned traveler.
Beaches, deserts, mountains and
jungles, as well vestiges from the
pre-Hispanic and Colonial eras are
only a few of the attractions that
make any excursion in this country such a fascinating experience.

Walter H. Wust
(photo: *Cosas*)

To complete this ambitious proj-
ect, which now reaches its second
edition, a select group of professionals keep travelling permanen-
tly within Peru, taking notes and
photos of its routes and gathering
information on its main attractions. This new edition of the Inca
Guide to Peru is the result of this endless expedition, combined
with valuable input from many specialists, and is destined to
become a useful companion to travelers who set out on the adventure of visiting this wonderful country.

Have a good trip!

WALTER H. WUST / MITSUBISHI PERU
Editor
Inca Guide to Peru

How to Use This Guide

The *Inca Guide to Peru* is divided into six parts containing the following information:

1 Perú

Basic information on the country (surface area, population, climate, currency, telephone services, etc.), a synopsis of its history, and articles written by specialists on the following subjects: archeological excavations that brought to light the royal tombs at Sipán, protected natural areas of Peru, the country's cuisine and its traditional festivals. Also included are a calendar of feasts and holidays and a list of the most important protected natural areas in the country.

2 Useful Facts for the Traveler

This is information we suggest reading before beginning your trip: available services (hotels, restaurants and institutions providing assistance to tourists), how to get around in cities, and things to know before traveling by road, plane, train or river. The part includes a list of overland transport companies and their destinations, as well as other practical advice.

3 Destinations

The most complete information on thirty destinations in Peru and further excursions that you can make from them. To aid in scheduling your trip, each excursion has a symbol next to it indicating the time required:

>) = Up to half a day
> ○ = One full day
> ○) = More than one day

At the beginning of each destination, other symbols indicate the means of transport servicing it. Below these, a number indicates the map on which you can find the destination.

This part also includes a selection of hotels and restaurants, telephone numbers and other useful information, along with city maps and excursion maps for the more important destinations. The following symbols are used on both city and excursion maps:

CITY MAPS

++++++++	Railway
🚃	Railway station
▨▨▨▨▨	Pedestrian path
■	Cathedral
●	Church, convent
⌂	Lookout point

EXCURSION MAPS

◉	Provincial capital
●	District capital
○	Populated area
□	Archeological / ecological area
→	Point of reference between distances
38	Distance in kilometers
→→	Continuing road
▬▬	Paved road
▬▬	Unpaved (packed) dirt road
=	Bridge
++++++++	Railway

4 Routes

This part provides a detailed description of fifteen overland routes, along with access and detour maps for the principal cities of the country. In part six (Route Maps) there is a map for each route described here. Place names in bold type will help the traveler locate and follow the route on the map. Side roads and their destinations are described in smaller type.

Many places mentioned here are described in detail in part three (Destinations). You can quickly find these destination descriptions by checking the Index in part five.

5 Index

This is an alphabetical list of the places and maps that appear in this guide. Use this index first to find a place or map quickly.

6 Route Maps

This part contains a political and a physical map of Peru and twelve previously unpublished road maps (route maps) with detailed information on types of roads, points of interest, distances in segments, altitudes, police stations and control points, basic services (restaurants, hotels, service stations) and toll booths. Each road map has icons indicating its relation to other maps, an insert showing the area's location within the country, measures of scale, and the geographical north. Different shades of background color show the altitude in increments of 1 000 m.

To our Readers

By the time you consult this guide, some of its information on infrastructure and services may be outdated. Furthermore, involuntary errors are bound to slip into any work of this magnitude. To offer the best service possible, our field team will be constantly revising the *Inca Guide to Peru* and bringing it up to date.

We would greatly appreciate your letting us know of any error, omission or change in the information in this book. Contact the editors at:

Ediciones PEISA
Av. Dos de Mayo 1285, Lima 27
Tel (511) 221 5988
E-mail: peisa@terra.com.pe
          whwust@terra.com.pe

Abbreviations Used in this Guide

approx.	approximately	NW	northwest
Av.	avenida (avenue)	**of.**	oficina (office)
E	east	**p.**	page
Fri	Friday	**pop.**	population
Gral.	general	**Prolong.**	prolongación (extension)
h	hour		
Jr.	jirón (narrow street)	**Psje.**	pasaje (court)
kg	kilo	S	south
km	kilometer	**Sat**	Saturday
l	liter	SE	southeast
m	meter	**Sun**	Sunday
masl	meters above sea level	SW	southwest
		Tel	telephone
min	minute	**Thu**	Thursday
Mon	Monday	**Tue**	Tuesday
N	north	**Urb.**	urbanización (urbanization)
N.°	number		
n/n	no number	W	west
NE	northeast	**Wed**	Wednesday

Acknowledgments

The publishers would like to thank those who helped in the creation of this book, especially to:

Gerd y Karen Burmester
Alfonso Casabonne
Casa Hacienda San José
Angelita Cillóniz
Corporación Turística Amazónica
Familia Croquet
Anne Deverte
Luis Nieto Degregori
El Lago Resort
Golden Gate
Carlos Gonzales
Mirador de los Collaguas
Mitsubishi del Perú
Familia Orihuela
Guillermo y Eva Ostolaza
Giovanna Pollarolo
Profot
Puerto Palmeras Resort
Silvia Vallenas
Antonio y Anie Vellutino
Rudolf e Ivna von May
Paul Wright
Natali Wust

All the trips related to the production of this book were made on Mitsubishi vehicles.

PERU

Concerning the man-ners and customs that dis-tinguish the peoples of this fabulous kingdom

General Information

Basic Information

Coordinates	0°01'48" y 18°21'03" L.S.; 68°39'27" y 81°19'34,5" L.W.
Surface area	1 285 215,6km²
Territorial sea	200 miles
Capital	Lima
Estimated population	25,6 million inhabitants

Surface Area

Peru is located on the central west coast of South America. Its neighboring countries are: Ecuador and Colombia to the N; Chile to the S; Brazil and Bolivia to the E; and the Pacific Ocean to the W. It is the third largest country in South America, with a surface area of 1 285 215,6km^2 (larger than France, Spain, and Germany combined) distributed approximately in the following manner: 12% coastal territory, 28% Andean highlands and 60% Amazon jungle.

Population

Peru has a population of some 25,6 million inhabitants, 6,7 million of whom live in Lima, the capital city. The coastal strip is home to around 52% of the population; the Andean highlands, 36%; and the Amazon jungle, 12%. The inhabitants are primarily of *mestizo,* or mixed race, although a significant indigenous minority inhabits the southern Andes and the Amazon. Nearly 70% of Peruvians live in urban areas.

Geopolitical Division

Peru is divided into 24 departments, containing a total of 194 provinces, plus the constitutional province of Callao, the country's main port, located 14km from Lima.

For administrative purposes, the country has been divided into 13 large regions made up of one or more departments *(see political map).*

Government

Peru's government is democratic and based on the Constitution of 1993. The President leads the Executive branch and the Armed Forces and has a fifteen-member cabinet. Legislative power lies with the one-house, 120-member Congress of the Republic. The term of office is five years and voting is universal and mandatory for citizens between 18 and 60 years of age. Since July 2001, Alejandro Toledo rules the country. He has been elected as President for a five years period.

Geography

The country is divided into 3 large geographical regions: the coast, the Andes, and the Amazon jungle *(see physical map)*.

Costa

The western, or coastal zone is a narrow band of desert measuring 180km at its widest point, bathed by the Pacific ocean along 3 080km of cliffs and beaches.

Its mainly flat terrain (with highest elevations at 650masl, or 2 133ft), is dotted with nearly 50 oases, fertile river valleys formed by streams born high in the Andes and running into the ocean.

The volume of water in most of these rivers declines considerably during the dry season (from April to December).

Lima and other coastal cities are located in these valleys, where the country's greatest economic activities take place.

El Raspón Beach, Paracas.

Andes

The Andes mountains run north to south like a backbone through the territory of Peru. This range is the continental watershed, source of the rivers that flow either west to the Pacific Ocean or east to the Amazon River basin. Its steep, complex terrain is marked by narrow canyons, deep and fertile valleys, vast high plateaus, large navigable lakes and over 12 000 smaller lakes. Although the altitude of the range is generally between

3 000m and 4 000m (9 843ft and 13 124ft), it is possible to reach altitudes of 6 000m (19 686ft) in a short distance of 100km. Mount Huascarán (6 768m, or 22 206ft) is the highest mountain in Peru and the second highest in America.

Puna of Canchayllo, Junín.

Jungle

The Peruvian jungle is a region of lush vegetation due to the heavy rainfall it receives throughout the year. It has a softly undulating landscape. Beginning on the eastern slopes of the Andes, it is covered in tropical vegetation extending all the way across the Amazon plain. It contains extraordinary natural wealth and is a land of forests and winding rivers that are sometimes the only means of communication between its people. All jungle rivers flow into the Amazon River, the world's longest and widest river, with the greatest volume of water.

Jungle of Chanchamayo, Junín.

Climate

Because of its location in the southern tropics, Peru should have a warm, humid, and rainy climate. However, the Andes range, the high-pressure systems of the southern Pacific and the cold waters of the Humboldt current are the determining factors in its weather and give rise to a great variety of climates.

The coast, where it almost never rains, is characterized by dense fogs and soft drizzle between May and November, making you feel cold although the temperature might only be 14°C to 18°C (57°F to 64°F). During the summer (December to April) the humidity decreases and the sun shines brightly.

In the Andes and the jungle there is a dry season (May to October) with mostly sunny days and a rainy season (December to March) that is considered winter. While the Andes have a cold, dry climate, with an annual average temperature of 9ºC to 18ºC (48ºF to 64ºF), the jungle has a tropical climate with temperatures ranging from 26ºC to 40ºC (79ºF to 104ºF).

In the Andean valleys it is possible to find dry, temperate climates all year round, with only some rain during the summer.

Economy

Peru is a country with mining, agricultural, fishing, and forestry resources. Its principal exports are mineral (copper, zinc, gold, lead, and silver), crude petroleum and petroleum products, fishmeal, cotton, sugar, coffee, as well as some unconventional products such as hardwoods from the Amazon, asparagus, and achiote and cochineal for dyes. Based on rates of employment, the principal economic activities of the country are manufacturing (21,8%), agriculture (13%), and mining (9,1%).

Language

The official languages of Peru are Spanish, spoken by 73% of the population, and Quechua or *runasimi* spoken by 24% of Peruvians. Linguists recognize two distinct variants of Quechua within Peru: *huáihuash*, which predominates in central Peru, and *huámpuy*, spoken in the rest of the country. The majority of Quechua speakers are bilingual and speak Spanish as a second language, as do the Aymara people, whose language is spoken primarily on the southern Altiplano. There are also some 55 languages spoken in the Peruvian Amazon (including Asháninka, Aguaruna, and Machiguenga).

Religion

The official religion of Peru is the Roman Catholic faith, practiced fervently by close to 80% of Peruvians. However, there is

Palm Sunday in Ayacucho.

freedom of religion in the country and a marked variance in religious practices, particularly throughout the Andes and the jungle, where the people practice Catholicism in addition to their traditional beliefs generally related to worship of the Earth, called Pachamama, and natural phenomena.

Currency

Peru's official currency is the *nuevo sol*; its symbol is S/. The denominations in circulation are bills of 10, 20, 50, 100, and 200 *nuevos soles*; coins of 1, 2, and 5 *nuevos soles*; and coins of 5, 10, 20, and 50 *céntimos,* or hundredths of a *nuevo sol.*

Exchange

The foreign currency most readily exchanged in Peru for local money is the United States dollar (US$), commonly used in commercial transactions and in purchasing goods. Exchange offices abound in the larger cities. It is also possible to exchange dollars in downtown areas via street-corner moneychangers called *cambistas.* Hotels and credit card agencies can also exchange money, but do so at a lower rate. The exchange rate fluctuates weekly, but not enough to be significant. Peru does not limit the amount of money you can bring into the country.

Traveler's Checks

The use of traveler's checks is not widespread among Peru's commercial establishments. It may even be difficult to cash traveler's checks at some banks (count on a loss of 2% to 5% of the amount exchanged).

Money Transfers (*giros*)

These can be done at any bank. At least three days should be allowed for international transfers. National transfers should take only 24 hours or less to conclude. It is also possible to make cash withdrawals by charging them to a credit card.

Credit Cards

Banks are generally open to the public Monday through Friday, 9am to 6pm, and Saturday until noon (varying). They may be open fewer hours during summer months (January to March).

Banks

Generalmente los bancos atienden al público de lunes a viernes de 9 h a 18 h, y los sábados hasta el mediodía (con algunas variaciones). El horario de atención es ligeramente más corto durante los meses de verano.

Local Time

Peruvian time is five hours past Greenwich Mean Time and is similar to Eastern Standard Time in the United States (except when the U.S. goes on daylight savings time from April to October). In reference to other cities, when it is noon in Peru, it is 1:00pm in Santiago de Chile and Caracas; in Rio de Janeiro it is 2:00pm, in New York it is also noon; in Tokyo it is 3:00am.

Current and Voltage

Electrical current in Peru runs at 220 volts, 60 cycles (with the exception of Arequipa, where it runs at 50 cycles). The majority of five-star hotels have 110-volt sockets in guest rooms, although it is advisable to bring an adapter to change flat-pronged plugs to round-pronged plugs.

Telephone

- *National long-distance:* to communicate with any point in the country, dial 109 and ask the operator to connect you. In many cities of Peru there is direct-dial service as well, in which case you simply dial 0, the regional area code and the telephone number.

  The area codes of the principal cities are:

CITY	CODE	CITY	CODE
Abancay	84	La Oroya	64
Andahuaylas	84	Lambayeque	74
Arequipa	54	Lima	01
Ayacucho	64	Mala	01
Bagua	44	Mollendo	54
Cajamarca	44	Moquegua	54
Cerro de Pasco	64	Moyobamba	94
Cusco	84	Nasca	34
Chachapoyas	44	Pacasmayo	44
Chiclayo	74	Paita	74
Chimbote	44	Pisco	34
Chincha	34	Piura	74
Huacho	01	Pucallpa	64
Huancavelica	64	Puerto Maldonado	84
Huancayo	64	Puno	54
Huánuco	64	San Ramón	64
Huaraz	44	Sullana	74
Ica	34	Tacna	54
Ilo	54	Tarapoto	94
Iquitos	94	Tarma	64
Jauja	64	Tingo María	64
Juliaca	54	Trujillo	44
La Merced	64	Tumbes	74

- *International long distance:* dial 00, followed by the country code, the regional prefix code, and the telephone number. Area and country codes are generally found in telephone booths and the telephone directory (called *guía telefónica*), available in any commercial establishment. If you wish to make a collect call (*llamada a cobro revertido*) or a person-to-person call (*llamada de persona a persona*), dial 108 to contact an international operator.
- *Public telephones:* there are booths distributed throughout Lima and the provinces, from which you can access national and international direct-dial services or call through an operator. These telephones operate with coins (accepting both *nuevos soles* and *céntimos*) or telephone cards, available in kiosks and small shops.
- *Cellular phones:* these only function in Lima and other major cities. In some cases it is possible to extend the range upon client request.

  Information
  Telefónica Movistar: *Tel 981 7000, 981 8000.*
  Bellsouth: *Tel 0-800-1-5163. Cellphones dial 123.*
  TIM: *Tel 0-800-1-15151. Cellphones dial 151.*
  Central: 315 2160.
- *Telephone information:* available free of charge, 24 hours by dialing 103.

Internet

The principal Internet service providers are based in Lima:
- Terra Network Perú:
  Central: Tel 411 1260. Fax 212 5929.
  Users platform: 595 0800.
- El Comercio:
  Central: Tel 426 4676, ext. 3746.
  www.elcomercioperu.com.pe
- Red Científica Peruana: Pablo Carriquirí 410, San Isidro.
  Tel 422 4848. Fax 421 8086.

Websites with data base about Peru:
  www.promperu.gob.pe
  www.peru.org.pe
  www.enjoyperu.com

Brief History

The Origins of Peru

Man arrived in the Andes some 20 000 years ago when Europe was well into the Paleolithic era. Utensils discovered in prehistoric caves such as Pikimachay in the department of Ayacucho confirm this early occupation. A long period of hunting and gathering gradually changed around 6 000 BC into an extended period of plant and animal domestication. Among the numerous plants the ancient Peruvians domesticated were the potato, quinoa, yucca root, cotton, and corn. By 2 500 BC many people lived from agriculture, which led to the appearance of sedentary groups and the early stages of a higher culture in the Andes.

Cave paintings at Sumbay, Arequipa.

For study purposes, the successive cultures inhabiting Peru before the arrival of the Spanish have been divided into five consecutive periods: Early Horizon, Intermediate Early Horizon, Middle Horizon, Intermediate Late Horizon, and Late Horizon. The Horizons are periods in which various cultures are related by a common style of ceramics and iconography due to the influence of a predominant culture such as the Chavín, Wari, or Inca. The Intermediate Horizons, however, are characterized by a multiplicity of artistic styles as regional cultures developed.

The Early Horizon: Chavín Predominance
1200 BC – AD 200

The growth in agriculture and craftsmanship worked together in this period to spur a new social force that led to defined hierarchies with religious leaders at the top. Ceremonial centers gained in importance, particularly the one at Chavín de Huántar. The Chavín culture, with its center in the highlands of Ancash, was the first to attain significant influence throughout the mountains and coast of Peru. This influence was then projected onto two cultures that completed the Formative Period of Andean civilization: Paracas in Ica and Pucará on the Altiplano.

Mochica portrait vessel. Collection of the Museo Nacional de Arqueología, Antropología e Historia.

The Intermediate Early Horizon
200 BC – AD 600

The growing population and the development of agriculture in this period gave rise to new cultures in various parts of Peru. On the north coast, the Mochica culture flourished, a culture now famous worldwide after the discovery of its royal tombs at Sipán. On the southern coast rose the Nasca culture, equally famous for the gigantic geoglyphs they carved on the ground: the mysterious Nasca lines. Another great culture flourishing in this early regional development (which includes the Recuay, Vicús, Cajamarca, and Lima cultures) was Tiawanaco, with its center on the Altiplano, a vast, high plateau on the Peru-Bolivia border. Tiawanaco retained its importance until the Middle Horizon period.

The Middle Horizon: Wari Predominance
AD 600 – 900

In these centuries the Wari culture developed and achieved an empire-like rule that extended from the Mochica territory and Cajamarca in the north, to Cerro Baúl, Arequipa, and Sicuani in the south. Wari synthesized elements of the Ayacucho region (where it was centered) and of the Nasca and Tiawanaco cultures. Its capital at Wari (only a few kilometers from the modern-day city of Ayacucho) was one of the most populated urban centers in pre-Hispanic America. To their military conquests the Wari added the dissemination of a religious cult that many archeologists believe is a synthesis of the ancient Chavín deities, expressed in the Tiawanaco style.

The Intermediate Late Horizon
AD 900 – 1400

Chullpas of Ninamarca, Cusco.

This period, like the Intermediate Early Horizon period, was characterized by new cultures springing up throughout Andean territory. At least nine new, large cultures were formed: Chimú and Chincha on the coast; Cajamarca, Huanca, Chanca, and Inca in the sierra; Colla and Lupaca on the Altiplano; and Chachapoyas in the northern jungle.

The Chimú were one of the most powerful cultures on the coast. They were heirs of the Mochica culture and were also influenced by the Lambayeque culture. Their capital was at Chan Chan, on the outskirts of modern-day Trujillo. Another important coastal culture was the Chincha kingdom, which occupied part of the territory of the earlier Paracas and Nasca cultures. In the Titicaca basin numerous Aimara kingdoms developed, and between the Pampas and Apurímac rivers (in the area of Ayacucho, Apurímac, and Huancavelica today) arose the Chanca confederation, fierce rivals to the Incas.

The Late Horizon: Inca Predominance
AD 1400 – 1532

The Incas divided the history of their Empire or Tawantinsuyo into two dynasties: the *hurin* and the *hanan* (meaning 'lower' and 'higher' in Quechua). This division follows the principle of duality that characterized the Inca world view.

Inca citadel of Machu Picchu.

Inca trapezoidal window, Machu Picchu.

The first dynasty consists of the rulers of an early period lost in legend: Manco Cápac (c. AD 1200), Sinchi Roca, Lloque Yupanqui, Mayta Cápac, and Cápac Yupanqui, who all ruled a small territory around Cusco. The second dynasty begins with Inca Roca and continues with Yahuar Huaca, Wiracocha, Pachacútec, Túpac Yupanqui (who ruled from 1471–1493), Huayna Cápac (from 1493–1527), Huáscar and Atahualpa.

Pachacútec is attributed with having completely reorganized Inca society and beginning the swift expansion of the empire. This sovereign conquered the Collao plateau as far as Arequipa and subdued the inhabitants of the Mantaro Valley and of Chincha and Pachacámac on the coast. He added the Cajamarca region to the new empire, and succeeded in bringing the Chimú under his rule. His son and successor, Túpac Inca Yupanqui, subjugated the kingdom of Quito (in present-day Ecuador), conquered southern peoples as far as the Maule River in Chile, and even ventured into the jungle. His successor, Huayna Cápac, extended the empire as far as modern-day Colombia. He was the first Inca to receive news of the Spaniards' arrival in Peru. On his death, his son Huáscar inherited the throne, who then fought his brother Atahualpa in a bloody civil war which facilitated the Spanish conquest. Atahualpa managed to defeat his brother, Huáscar, and ordered his execution as he was being brought to Cajamarca. In this same city Atahualpa was taken prisoner by Francisco Pizarro and garroted in 1533.

The Inca Empire achieved all of this impressive growth in less than a century. At the head of the empire sat the Inca, considered divine, in his capital at Cusco. Under him were the *panacas* or Inca royal families, followed by the greater and lesser lords of Cusco and of the conquered provinces. Special privileges were also accorded to a priest class, with the highest post in the religious hierarchy being reserved for royalty. Coming last were the populace, or *hatun runa*, the social base for this theocratic society.

Each community had to meet production quotas mandated

by the State and its *curacas,* or local chieftains (representatives) by a turn of work known as the *mita.* They were also required to perform community work known as the *minka.* Because it was so large, the empire was divided into four *suyos,* or large provinces, each named for its geographical relationship to Cusco: Chinchaysuyo to the N, Collasuyo to the S, Antisuyo to the E, and Contisuyo to the W. Together they became the Tawantinsuyo, as *tawa* means 'four' in Quechua. The Sun was the principal god, but the Incas tolerated secondary cults to Wiracocha, Pachacámac and other regional deities and incorporated these gods into their imperial pantheon.

The Spanish Conquest

The autonomous development of Andean cultures changed abruptly in the fifteenth century with the Spanish conquest of Peru. In 1532, on his third voyage into the southern Pacific, Francisco Pizarro disembarked at Tumbes with some 200 men, horses and weapons. That same year he founded San Miguel de Piura, the first Spanish city in Peru, and several months later he began his campaign into the interior, which led to the capture, ransom and execution of the Inca Atahualpa at Cajamarca, leading directly to the fall of the Tawantinsuyo. In January 1535, Pizarro founded Lima as the capital of his *gobernación,* calling it the *Ciudad de los Reyes* or the City of the Magi.

The Viceroyalty

Corregidor, watercolor by Martínez Compañón.

In 1542, the Spanish emperor Charles I set up a viceroy to govern Peru in his name. In the sixteenth and seventeenth centuries the Spanish empire had two viceroyalties in America: Mexico and Peru. The Viceroyalty of Peru had jurisdiction over all of South America except for Venezuela and Brazil. In the eighteenth century the viceroyalties of New Granada and Buenos Aires were created.

Highly hierarchical and racist, Colonial society distinguished between native-born Spaniards and

Soldier, watercolor
by Martínez Compañón.

Nun, watercolor
by Martínez Compañón.

American-born Spaniards of pure Spanish blood, called *criollos*, giving greater preference to the former. Below noble *criollos* and higher functionaries were the middle-class *criollos*, minor functionaries, and finally the poorer Spanish population. Then came the *mestizos* (of mixed Spanish and native blood), who were excluded from positions of power, and then the natives, who made up the majority of the population. At the bottom of the scale were the Negro slaves, also in varying racial mixtures with the natives and Spaniards.

Allowed to trade only with Spain, Peru interacted with the world economy under a distinct disadvantage. Enormous quantities of precious metals, particularly silver, were extracted and transported to the mother country. The mines at Potosí, in what is now Bolivia, yielded an exceptional amount of silver. Mining work was entirely done by natives under the *mita* system, in which native communities throughout Peru were required to provide workers for a stint in the mines. Agriculture and livestock were broadened by new European products, but at the same time suffered from a counterproductive substitution of crops. All commerce had to go through Lima and Seville until the Bourbon-era reforms of the eighteenth century, when Buenos Aires began to compete for the Charcas markets in Upper Peru. In its evangelization of these new lands, the Roman Catholic church played a fundamental role in the conquest and colonization of Peru. The rise in mysticism in the late sixteenth century and early seventeenth century formed four Peruvian saints, Toribio de Mogrovejo, Francisco Solano, Rosa de Lima, and Martín de Porras, who were later canonized.

In the second half of the eighteenth century, native resistance to Spanish rule reached its height. The rebellion led by Juan Santos Atahualpa (1742–1752) was followed by a larger rebellion (1780–1781) led by Túpac Amaru, chieftain of Tungasuca in the Cusco region, the most significant anti-Colonial uprising of the period. Influenced by the Age of Reason, the independence of the North

American colonies and the French Revolution, a group of *criollo* intellectuals began drafting reformist projects. In the early nineteenth century, the Spanish monarchy and its Colonial empire experienced its worst crisis. The Viceroyalty of Peru survived, however, under the iron administration of Viceroy Fernando de Abascal (1806–1816) and became the bastion of Spanish power in South America.

Independence

On November 8, 1820, General José de San Martín sailed from Chile and landed his army in the Paracas Bay in the department of Ica, marched north of the capital, ordered military actions in the central Andes and authorized an expedition to the south. By early 1821, all of northern Peru had declared its allegiance to the cause of independence, and on July 28, San Martín proclaimed it in Lima.

Sworn to fight for independence until the liberation of the central and southern territories, San Martín presided over a temporary government under the title of Protector. After two military expeditions to the south led by San Martín failed, a group of the military set up José Mariano de la Riva Agüero as first president of the Republic (1823). That same year, amid the political chaos, Simón Bolívar arrived in Lima and was given absolute powers with

Surrender at Ayacucho, oil painting by Daniel Hernández.
Museo del Banco Central de Reserva del Perú.

the title of Dictator. On August 6, 1824, Bolívar defeated the royal Spanish army on the fields of Junín, and on December 9 of the same year General Antonio José de Sucre again defeated the Spanish at Quinua in Ayacucho, capturing Viceroy José de la Serna and forcing the spanish commanders to sign the surrender at Ayacucho which sealed the independence of Peru and South America.

The Early Republic

The newly independent nation plunged into political anarchy. Military leaders, former fighters in the war for independence, fought among themselves for control for 50 years, as there was no civilian group cohesive enough to assume the government. The only break in these long struggles was the government of Marshall Ramón Castilla, one of the most significant of the nineteenth century. During his administration Peru began to sell the guano (bird droppings on its offshore rocks, which made for extremely good fertilizer) and its enormous profit produced the first income for the State. Tribute was no longer required of the natives and slavery was abolished. The infighting ended in 1872 when Peru elected its first civilian president, Manuel Pardo, head of the first political party in Peru. His Civilian Party was antimilitarist and moderately anticlerical, and identified itself with the modernization of the country. In 1879, committed to a military alliance with Bolivia, Peru was forced into the War of the Pacific (1879–1883). After defeats in Tacna and Arica, Chilean forces occupied Lima for three years and left the country in ruins.

1900–1980

After its failed experimetn with civilian government and its defeat to Chile, Peru developed what it called the «Aristocratic Republic» (1895–1920), which laid the foundations for the country to enter the world economy. During those years the political and economic management of the country was in the hands of a landowner class engaged in farm exports (sugar and cotton).

Beginning in 1920, Peruvian politics changed dramatically, as the low and middle classes made their presence felt. Augusto B. Leguía began his second term in office (1919–1930) with the backing of these sectors.

In time, however, Leguía perpetuated his stay in power in a markedly personal and dictatorial manner, spurring the formation of the first parties of popular ideology. On January 22th. 1927, from the exile in France, Victor Raúl Haya de la Torre (1895–1979) founded the first cell of the American Popular Revolutionary Alliance (APRA) and, on October 7th. 1928, José Carlos Mariátegui (1894–1930) founded the Socialist Party that later became the Communist Party.

1956: Manuel Prado being carried in honor (photo: *Caretas*).

In 1930, the Great Depression was felt throughout the country at a time when antidictatorial feelings were widespread and social theory was on the rise. Leguía was defeated by Commander Luis M. Sánchez Cerro. This was the beginning of a period that lasted into the 1940s, in which economically powerful groups turned to the military for support because they had no backing of their own.

In the elections of 1945, the National Democratic Front (in coalition with a majority of the APRA, and with the support of numerous individuals not engaged in the existing political parties) put José Luis Bustamante y Rivero into office. The climate of democratic fervor in which this leadership began did not last long. In 1948, General Manuel Odría led a coup d'etat and began a repressive and authoritative regime that lasted until 1956, when Manuel Pardo took office for a second time.

At the beginning of the 1960s, the political panorama of the country again underwent significant changes. The APRA's activities were joined by the reformist enthusiasm of the Christian Democrats and the Popular Action party (a moderate, progressive party founded by Fernando Belaúnde), along with an lively radicalism from the universities. Lima began to receive increasing migration from rural areas.

In 1963, Belaúnde won the elections, but was toppled five years later by a military junta led by General Juan Velasco Alvarado,

Government Palace.
Military coup of 1968
(photo: *Caretas*).

Lima today

who then set up a nationalistic, reformist government. In 1975 Velasco was replaced by General Francisco Morales Bermúdez. In 1980, after twelve years of military dictatorship, Peru returned to democracy.

The Recent Years

The economic crisis and the rise of terrorist groups were the principal problems that Belaúnde faced in his second term in office (1980–1985). The APRA government of Alan García Pérez, who was elected in 1985, faced the same problems without success and led the country, in the late 80's to an unprecedented economical crisis characterized by rampant inflation. His controversial attempt to nationalize the banks and financial system placed opposition candidate, renowned writer Mario Vargas Llosa, at the front as the preferred candidate in the 1990 presidential race. The elections surprisingly went to Alberto Fujimori, who led a mixed group called Cambio '90 (Change 1990), for the 1990–1995 term. In 1992, Fujimori assumed extraordinary powers with the backing of the military and dissolved Congress. One year later, a referendum approved a new Constitution and a resumption of the electoral process. In 1995 Fujimori gained reelection for a second period by defeating former UN Secretary General Javier Perez de Cuellar. After his controversial second period in office, Fujimori accomplished for a third election for the period 2000-2005. His new re-election was largely considered ilegal. On November 2000, when opposition to his corrupt government had grown strong, he flew away towards Japan abandoning office. President of Congress Valentín Paniagua was raised as Provisory President up to July 2001. Economist Alejandro Toledo was elected as President of the country for the period 2001-2006.

The Royal Tombs at Sipán

WALTER ALVA

In the late nineteenth century, German archeologist Max Uhle identified a pre-Hispanic culture in the Mochica Valley of northern Peru, which he named the Mochica and which was quite different from the Chimú and Inca cultures. Since then, knowledge of this ancient people has notably increased the world's appreciation of the different cultures that preceded the Incas in the Andes.

The Mochica on the northern coast, the Cajamarca and the Recuay in the northern Andes, the Lima on the central coast, and the Nasca on the southern coast are only some of the many cultures that reached a high level of social complexity in Peru long before the arrival of the Incas.

Since the late 1980s, more and more of the Mochica culture's achievements have been revealed to the world thanks to the extraordinary archeological discoveries taking place on the northern coast of Peru. In this region, in 1987, for the first time in the history of Peruvian archeology, a ruler of ancient Peru revealed his splendid magnificence, a reaffirmation that Peru's rich, pre-Hispanic cultural heritage is the product of thousands of years.

An Intact Burial Chamber

At the end of February 1987, a veritable «gold fever» struck the quiet town of Sipán, a small rural village surrounded by sugar cane fields in the warm Lambayeque Valley of northwestern Peru. Dozens of residents from nearby villages dug frantically in search of fragments of metal on the slopes of an ancient adobe platform, where only a few days earlier a daring group of grave

WALTER ALVA is an archeologist whose specialty is the Mochica culture. He directs the excavations of the royal tombs of Sipán and is Director of the Brüning Museum in Lambayeque.

Panoramic view of the archeological complex at Sipán.

robbers, known as *huaqueros*, had opened and looted a rich tomb of some important member of the Mochica culture that had developed in this region between the first and sixth centuries AD.

Known locally as Huaca Rajada, the archeological complex at Sipán consists of two large, eroded, adobe pyramids which today look like dirt hills rising out of the sugar cane fields. These massive structures dominate the countryside. They are aligned from east to west and preceded by a low platform of three recognizable levels and a small, top platform. The two main constructions are only separated by some 60m (197ft) of space in the manner of a patio or plaza.

After great efforts to overcome the local peoples' initial resistance, in early April of the same year, the members of an archeological team, whom I was privileged to lead, set up a simple canvas tent at the site. Our work focused on the smaller platform.

Months later, our investigation led us to one of the most important finds in New World archeology: the intact burial chamber of a Mochica ruler, with all its priceless information on his society, religion, art, and way of life.

The Lord of Sipán

Our first hunch that we were looking at the grave of a high ranking Mochica was confirmed when we opened the burial chamber. Eight skeletons of servants, concubines and warriors encircled a wooden coffin containing the remains of the tomb's principal occupant and his treasure of ornaments, headdresses, emblems and jewelry of gold, gilded copper, and semi-precious stones. These objects were the symbols of power for a dignitary who died some 1 700 years ago and whom we began to call the Lord of Sipán. Never before in Peru had this form of burial been documented, nor had ornaments or decorations of such fine artistic quality been found.

One of the most frequent characters depicted in Mochica art (which is essentially religious and figurative in nature) is a personage who receives offerings, honors, and deference to his high rank, and who presides over or conducts all important events and ceremonies. Surprisingly, many of the attributes, emblems, and insignias with which Mochica artists decorate this personage were exactly the same as those discovered in the tomb at Sipán. This proved that Mochica iconography had not simply been portraying a mythical character, and that these drawings represented the man whose tomb we had discovered. His burial goods, which included

Reconstruction of the tomb of the Lord of Sipán, Museo de la Nación.

items of command as well as those of rank and power reveal that he had a three-fold authority: military, religious, and civic. To his people in his own place and time, the Lord of Sipán must have had the same authority and semi-divine status as the Inca ruler had over the Inca Empire. Positioned at the top of the regional power structure, he exercised these powers in keeping with local custom and tradition. We had discovered the lord of the ethnic group of the Lambayeque Valley, who had administered the fate of this region between the second and third centuries AD. Once we had completely recovered and made a preliminary evalua-

Depiction of a feline deity, Sipán.

tion of the site, we were certain we stood before one of the most important individuals of his society and time.

The Other Royal Tombs

Detail of a shell breastpiece, Sipán.

At the same time as we discovered the tomb of the Lord of Sipán, our team was also completing an excavation at the far southeast end of the platform, where we had found another intact burial chamber. Even though the ornaments, vestments and accompanying objects were from about the same period in time, perhaps even contemporary, their quantity and quality were much lesser and quite different.

Near the right hand of the tomb's main occupant rested a metallic cup 10cm in diameter with a circular, disk-like lid. The object immediately brought to mind the offering cups frequently portrayed in Mochica art, in scenes of sacrifice or ritual libations between the Lord and a secondary individual. We decided the secondary personage was the one in this grave, and we named him the Priest. His burial goods, although not sumptuous, helped us reconstruct the hierarchy of the privileged Mochica classes. Surprisingly enough, here there were absolutely no weapons. We are convinced that this personage was exclusively a religious authority and would have performed only religious, rather than military or political functions.

When we had finished excavating the Priest's tomb, we decided to continue our work on the platform. Another careful cleaning disclosed the sight of a bulky bundle. This burial was quite different from those of the Lord and the Priest. It was small and simple and lacked a coffin. It turned out to a much older burial.

On the right side of the main individual lay a spherical, gold capsule forming the tip of a knife-like scepter, most certainly a symbol of command. This was only one of the many objects making up an impressive array of emblems, ornaments, and metal jewelry. Although it was a simpler burial, we were sure it was the tomb of a man whose status was similar or equal to that of the Lord of Sipán. As a result, we decided to call him the Old Lord of Sipán based on his greater antiquity.

Keys to Understanding the Mochica World

The archeological work at Sipán has provided new information about the society, religion, art and technology of the Mochica people, with a few reassessments and new perspectives for their interpretation. The complex at Sipán can be considered one of the important centers of ceremony and power of the period. The information obtained from the archeological complex housing these burials proposes the first set of hypotheses on the hierarchy of the buried dignitaries, beginning with the Lord and his three-fold authority and following with the warrior chiefs and their burial offerings, and then the priest caste who would have held a secondary position in the social structure of this ancient people. In addition, the various stages that we iden-tified in this sacred construction, linked to both change in ritual and in functional requirements, date the events that culminate in the construction of the tomb of the Lord of Sipán, whose characteristics and con-tent summarize the level of regional development. The Lord of Sipán must have stood at the peak of local Mochica society, which was probably orga-nized as a kingdom.

Gold earplug
with spangles, Sipán.

The similarity between the ornaments, emblems, and other objects found in the tombs at Sipán and known depictions in Mochica art allow us to corroborate the real existence of the individuals portrayed, who had earlier been considered only mythical characters. Thus was recognized their special, semi-divine status and political and re-ligious authority, leading us to theorize a similar social structure for all the Mochica territory, which, from the Piura region in the north to the Huarmey Valley in the south, must have main-

Necklace of gold peanuts,
Sipán.

tained a similar system based on marked social classes and closed successive dynasties in a series of more or less independent kingdoms. These kingdoms shared religion and customs, as revealed in certain formal patterns in images worshipped, insignias, and emblems of rank, while the manufacturing of local crafts (such as ceramics) could exhibit normal differences. Lastly, the findings at Sipán belie the marginal position that the region of Lambayeque held until recently in the context of Mochica culture. Our excavations suggest that this ancient people ruled practically all of the Lambayeque Valley. The data obtained at Sipán reveals how, when scientifically excavated, a tomb can yield more information than the thousands of archeological pieces taken by grave robbers to be sold and displayed out of context in the private collections and museums of the world. Peru is a country of enormous archeological wealth. It is up to us whether this privilege will lead us to an understanding of a period of our history still shrouded in mystery: the era of the pre-Hispanic peoples.

Protected Natural Areas of Peru

WALTER H. WUST

Peru has been privileged with spectacular geography and a variety of climates unparalleled on Earth. This is why Peru has 84 of the planet's 104 recognized ecosystems. Considered one of the 12 countries that possess true megadiversity (along with Brazil, Indonesia, and Zaire), Peru contains more than 20% of the known plant and animal species in the world. It has more than 25 000 species of flora, 1 715 bird species, 461 varieties of mammals, 692 species of amphibians and reptiles and more than 2 000 varieties of fish, to name only a few of the most important groups. Insects are a special case: more species of ants have been documented in a single tree of the Peruvian Amazon than in all of the British Isles.

There are 53 natural protected areas in Peru, totalling more than 127 000km² (15,3% of the country's area). Of these, only 55 000km² (equivalent to the area of Costa Rica) are actually managed effectively by the State.

NATURAL AREA CATEGORIES

Strict protection (intangible) zones (national parks, national sanctuaries, and historical sanctuaries): areas in which all direct use of resources is prohibited and where only scientific research and managed tourism are permitted. *Controlled use zones* (national reserves, indigenous reservations, hunting reserves): areas in which wildlife can be utilized in a controlled manner, under the supervision of the State. *Reserve zones:* areas temporarily protected until their appropriate category can be defined.

To Help Conserve Wildlife

- Respect established paths and trails.
- Avoid building campfires in areas not designated by the local administration.
- Avoid making excessive noise, especially close to wildlife.

WALTER H. Wust is a forestry engineer, a photographer, a writer and a consultant in environmental issues. He has worked on numerous wildlife investigations in Peru.

Principal Protected Natural Areas

Parques Nacionales
1. Cutervo
2. Tingo María
3. Manu
4. Huascarán
5. Cerros de Amotape
6. Río Abiseo
7. Yanachaga-Chemillén
8. Bahuaja-Sonene

Reservas Nacionales
9. Pampas Galeras-Bárbara d'Achille
10. Junín
11. Paracas
12. Lachay
13. Pacaya-Samiria
14. Salinas y Aguada Blanca
15. Calipuy
16. Titicaca

Santuarios Nacionales
17. Huayllay
18. Calipuy
19. Lagunas de Mejía
20. Ampay
21. Manglares de Tumbes
22. Tabaconas Namballe

Santuarios Históricos
23. Chacramarca
24. Pampas de Ayacucho
25. Machu Picchu

Zonas Reservadas
26. Manu
27. Laquipampa
28. Apurímac
29. Pantanos de Villa
30. Tambopata-Candamo
31. Batán Grande
32. Tumbes
33. Algarrobal El Moro
34. Chancaybaños
35. Aymara-Lupaca

Cotos de Caza
36. Sunchubamba
37. El Angolo

Reservas Comunales
38. Yanesha

Escala gráfica

100   0   100   200 km

- Take garbage bags along when camping and bring your waste back to town.
- Respect hunting and fishing seasons. Catching shrimp is prohibited year round except January through March. There are occasional closed seasons for sea turtles and there is a minimum catch size.
- Do not purchase or transport wild orchids.
- The following are completely prohibited:
  - Gathering natural flora and fauna in protected areas.
  - Hunting, trapping, possessing, buying or selling Amazon wildlife or products made from them, with the exception of certain species that are traditionally consumed.
  - Consuming, buying or selling dolphins, porpoises, and other cetaceans.
  - Buying or selling vicuña wool or any of its derivatives. Vicuñandes is the only agency authorized by the government to do so.
- Possession of any of the aforementioned products will be penalized by confiscation, fines, and, possibly, a jail sentence.

Otorongo or jaguar
(*Panthera onca*).

Cactus.

Scarlet macaw
(*Ara macao*).

Entry Permits

To enter most protected natural areas in the country (especially national parks) you must send a letter of request to the director of the Instituto Nacional de Recursos Naturales (INRENA, Diecisiete 355, Urb. El Palomar, San Isidro, Lima. Tel 224 3298 / 224 2858. Fax 224 3218) explaining the reason for your visit and paying the entry fee, if any. The procedure is simple. Be sure to complete it and you will avoid problems.

THE PRINCIPAL PROTECTED

	NAME	DEPTS.	ACCES FROM
N O R T H E R N P E R U	S.N. MANGLARES DE TUMBES	Tumbes	Tumbes
	Z.R. TUMBES	Tumbes	Tumbes
	P.N. CERROS DE AMOTAPE	Tumbes and Piura	Tumbes and Piura
	R.N. PACAYA-SAMIRIA	Loreto	Iquitos
	Z.R. BATÁN GRANDE	Lambayeque	Chiclayo
	P.N. RÍO ABISEO	San Martín	Trujillo
	P.N. HUASCARÁN	Ancash	Huaraz
C E N T R A L	R.N. LOMAS DE LACHAY	Lima	Lima
	Z.R. PANTANOS DE VILLA	Lima	Lima
	R.N. JUNÍN	Junín and Pasco	Lima and Tarma
	S.N. HUAYLLAY	Pasco	Lima and Tarma

ABBREVIATIONS: P.N. = National Park   R.N. = National Reserve

NATURAL AREAS IN PERU

CHARACTERISTICS

The largest mangrove forest in Peru. It has abundant wildlife that is important to the area's economy (crayfish, a sort of scallop called *concha negra*, several hundred species of fish, and other crustaceans and mollusks), over 200 species of birds, and species that are rare or in danger of extinction, such as the American crocodile and the mangrove bear.

Dry equatorial forest and tropical Pacific forest. Abundant wild flora and fauna, including many endangered native species such as the black howler monkey, the American crocodile, the northwest Peruvian otter and over 200 species of birds.

Dry equatorial forest and tropical Pacific coast forest. Unique flora and fauna, some in danger of extinction: hardwood trees, American crocodile, black howler monkey, white-throated squirrel, and white-tailed deer.

The largest protected area in the country. Lakes, swamps, and tropical jungle; extraordinary biodiversity. Fresh-water dolphin, *charapa* turtles, monkeys, *paiche* fish and hundreds of other varieties of fish.

The largest stands of carob trees (*algarrobo*) on the coast and many archeological remains (pyramids) of the Lambayeque, or Sicán culture.

High Andean desert, stands of dwarf trees, high cloud forest. Habitat of the yellow-tailed wooly monkey (a native species in danger of extinction), varied endemic flora and fauna, and many archeological sites (including Gran Pajatén). This area has been declared a Natural and Cultural World Heritage.

Mountains, glaciers, lakes, and valleys of the Cordillera Blanca, the highest tropical mountain range in the world. Stands of *puya* Raimondi and *queñual* trees, as well as abundant wildlife. A Natural World Heritage.

Coastal hills, a unique habitat. Endemic flora and fauna in danger of extinction. Best visited between August and November.

Coastal wetlands on the edge of Lima. *Totora* reed groves, lagoons, and over 150 species of resident and migratory birds (mostly waterfowl).

The only habitat of the Junín lake grebe (an endemic species in danger of extinction). *Totora* reed groves and a great variety of high Andean waterfowl, large frogs and fish.

High Andean grassland called *puna*. Unique geological formations («stone forests») produced by erosion, hot springs, stands of *queñual* trees, and high Andean fauna.

S.N. = National Sanctuary   S.H. = Historical Sanctuary   Z.R. = Reserve Zone

THE PRINCIPAL PROTECTED

	NAME	DEPTS.	ACCES FROM
S O U T H E R N P E R U	R.N. PARACAS	Ica	Pisco and Ica
	R.N. PAMPA GALERAS-BÁRBARA D'ACHILLE	Ayacucho	Nasca
	S.H. MACHU PICCHU	Cusco	Cusco
	P.N. MANU	Cusco and Madre de Dios	Cusco and Puerto Maldonado
	Z.R. MANU	Madre de Dios	Cusco and Puerto Maldonado
	P.N. BAHUAJA-SONENE	Puno and Madre de Dios	Puerto Maldonado
	Z.R. TAMBOPATA-CANDAMO	Puno and Madre de Dios	Puerto Maldonado
	R.N. SALINAS Y AGUADA BLANCA	Arequipa and Moquegua	Arequipa
	R.N. TITICACA	Puno	Puno

BBREVIATIONS: P.N. = National Park   R.N. = National Reserve

NATURAL AREAS IN PERU

Coastal desert and cold-water ocean. Abundant marine life: sea lions and seals, dolphins and porpoises, turtles, rare sea otter or *chungungo*, and over 200 species of birds (including pink flamingoes and Andean condor). Archeological remains of the Paracas culture.

High Andean *puna*. The largest vicuña population in the country; also a habitat for *taruca* deer, puma, fox, and Andean condor.

Tropical cloud forests and mountains. Archeological remains of the Inca citadel at Machu Picchu and some 34 other sites located along the Inca Trail; interesting geological formations (the Urubamba canyon) and abundant flora and fauna (orchids, tree ferns, Andean cock-of-the-rock, Andean bear, dwarf deer, wooly monkey and others).

High Andean plateau (*puna*), dwarf tree forest, high cloud forest and tropical jungle. Extraordinary biodiversity: black lizards, river otter, jaguars, monkeys, and over 800 bird species. Ethnic groups with little contact with the Western world (Nahuas, Kugapakoris, Mashcos). A Natural World Heritage.

Next to the National Park. Tropical forest with great biodiversity.

High rainforest, tropical jungle, and palm tree savanna (unique in the country). Great biodiversity: stands of chestnut trees, valuable hardwoods, macaw gathering sites, other unique species in danger of extinction. Ancestral territory of the Ese'eja ethnicity.

Cloud forests and tropical jungle. Extraordinary biodiversity. World record in number of bird and butterfly species. Flocks of macaws and intact forests, ancestral territory of the Ese'eja ethnic group.

High Andean plateau (*puna*), lakes, and salt flats. Vicuñas, dwarf *taruca* deer, three species of flamingoes, stands of *queñual* trees, and fields of *yareta* plants. Unique geological formations.

Totora reed groves on the shores of the highest navigable lake in the world, home to the Uros-Chulluni Native Community. Waterfowl, large frogs, wild guinea pig, Andean ocelot, and over 15 species of native fish.

S.N. = National Sanctuary   S.H. = Historical Sanctuary   Z.R. = Reserve Zone

The Great Cuisine of Peru

RODOLFO HINOSTROZA

Peruvian cuisine begins with the fortunate encounter of two great culinary schools of the sixteenth century: the Spanish and the Andean. Despite the ocean separating them, or perhaps because of it, the two complemented each other cheerfully and peacefully while the Inca empire fell apart in a chaotic fog of war. It was on gastronomic terrain where native and invader best understood each other, surely because it is the most permeable sphere in any culture, the one closest to pleasure, necessity, and hunger. On this ground was born the first blending of cultures, with no women raped or cannons fired, when the dreaded Spaniards, ravenous and perplexed, first tasted corn, tomatoes, potatoes, avocados, yucca root, peanuts, red alpaca meat and vengeful *ají* peppers, and added their own touch of olive oil, lime, and garlic.

Purple corn.

That was at the very beginning, when the conquistadors were low on supplies and ate anything the natives offered them; they dispatched entire herds of alpaca on their military expeditions and substituted corn bread for their regular wheat bread. But as soon as they could, they produced the foods of the Iberian Peninsula: rice, wheat, pork, lamb, beef, sugar, and olives, to eat as they had in Spain. These foods from the conquistador's table soon mixed with natives' tribute: potatoes and dried fish, sweet potatoes and tomatoes. They also spread among the indigenous population as it was forced to raise sheep instead of alpaca, to cultivate wheat in place of corn.

Poet, author, and playwright, RODOLFO HINOSTROZA is an expert on gastronomy as well. He regularly contributes features on Peruvian cuisine to several newspapers and magazines.

In this manner, a culinary blending began to gradually take place, here and there, in the Spaniards' palaces and convents as well as in native villages. A third element well worth taking into account was the Moorish hand of the Arab cooks the conquistadors had brought as slaves; they are credited with the variety of fillings and minced vegetables that abound in Peruvian cuisine. A fourth contribution came from the domestic Negro servants whose presence grew in the centuries after they arrived as slave labor for the coastal haciendas. One of the most archaic *mestizo,* or racially blended, dishes is ***carapulcra criolla,*** an indigenous stew based on dehydrated potatoes, to which the Spaniards added pork, onion, and garlic, Negro slaves added peanuts, and later included *ají,* the omnipresent condiment throughout Peru.

Anticuchos, or marinated beef heart brochettes, grilled and served with *ají panca,* also seem to be a contribution from the Afro-Peruvian population. Natives discovered the savory virtues of oil and fat; they kneaded their corn dough with pork fat, filled it with pieces of chicken or pork, *ají mirasol* and olives, then wrapped it all in *achira* leaves to make ***tamales serranos,*** which rapidly spread throughout Peru in many forms.

Nor would we be wrong in supposing that ***cebiche*** comes from this bold era. It was originally a north-coast fish eaten raw

The *pachamanca,* meaning 'earth oven' in Quechua, is pre-Hispanic in origin.

Black oysters cebiche.

or seasoned with the acidic juice of the *tumbo* and *ají*, but it has since reached a happy perfection with the biting Spanish lime, the *ceutí* lime from northwest Africa that was used to prevent scurvy and which perfectly rounds off the national dish that identifies Peru whenever it is served on any table around the world. It was in this exemplary manner that the two cuisines merged, each with its own principles and cortege of ingredients. The indigenous cuisine used none of the spices that sent Columbus off to the Indies, no pepper, cloves, cumin or cinnamon —which the Spaniards used in abundance— but only seasoned their dishes with a wide variety of aromatic or curative herbs and dozens of species of the spicy *ají*. Like most ancient cuisines of the world, Peru's native cooking had both a nutritive and a curative function, which it still retains today in some Andean broths and infusions. Spanish cuisine, on the other hand, did not wander into ideology or shamanism.

For example, neither milk nor eggs were used as food among the natives, out of respect for the natural cycles of lactation and incubation, while the Spanish bypassed the ecological debate and liberally applied milk and eggs to the indigenous soups called *chupis*. One of the results was Peru's *criollo* concept of thick *chupes*, including a marvelous shrimp chowder called **chupe de camarones**, often with roe, and some oregano. Despite its original transgression, it has become one of the highest points of *mestizo* cuisine.

This culinary blending, or *mestizaje*, developed relatively slowly, as the natives lived apart from the Spanish community and only integrated over many centuries. Another barrier was the lack of roads into the interior, which prevented formal Peruvian society from reaching the farthest corners of the country.

This is certainly the reason why some isolated regions still have completely native dishes that use no foreign ingredients, such as many powerful and quite aromatic Andean soups and stews based on *chuño* (dehydrated potato), quinoa, barley, and llama jerky, or an inexplicable pudding of rotten potato known as **tokosh**, which smells like the most offensive French cheese.

The late, great Spanish gourmet, Xavier Domingo, proposed

that Peru should not be said to have a single cuisine, but rather many, diverse cuisines, because they have developed on the basis of local tradition or provincial cultures with little or sometimes no ties at all with each other apart from their shared relationship with European cuisine.

In general, we can speak of a coastal cuisine, heavily based on fish and seafood, as well as yucca, rice, bananas, lime, onion, chicken, pork and duck; of an Andean cuisine, with ingredients typical of the region, such as lamb, pork, jerky, tubers such as potatoes, *chuño*, *olluco*, and *oca*, grains such as corn, wheat, *tarwi*, quinoa, *kiwicha*, and some freshwater trout and shrimp; and lastly, the cuisine of the Amazon jungle, based on river fish such as *dorado* and *paiche*, turtle and other wild meats, vegetables such as heart of palm, rice and a profusion of tropical fruits.

Pastries and sweets.

Other Sauces

We have discussed the contribution of the Negro slaves on the coast to the birth of Peruvian cuisine, especially in terms of the culinary use of tripe and other animal viscera, as they had little access to finer cuts of meat. But theirs is not the last link in the chain of contributions that made the richness and variety of our cuisine possible. A significant Chinese component was added to the primitive blend of native, Spanish and Negro; followed by Italian and then Japanese elements. These were the result of mass migrations in the nineteenth and early twentieth centuries, creating powerful colonies that each contributed their gastronomical quota to the cultural melting pot of Peru. Minor influences followed, from countries with strong cultures but fewer immigrants, such as France, Argentina, the United States, and Palestine.

The Chinese arrived in Peru in the second half of the nineteenth century to work on the haciendas in place of the Blacks who had been freed from slavery by President Ramón Castilla.

They came primarily from the Canton region, as coolies. Little by little, they shook off their semi-slavery and became integrated as farmers and merchants in an independent Peru. They brought the custom of eating rice, which had been used as a garnish in Peruvian cuisine since the Conquest, but went on to make a substantial place for itself and is now a part of the daily meal among all social classes. And they brought their cuisine, known in Peru as *chifas*. Peru now has five or six thousand Cantonese restaurants called *chifas*, for a population of almost half a million descendants of Chinese and twenty-two million Peruvians.

Chinese food has become popular among Peruvians. Many of its dishes have taken on a Peruvian flavor, becoming ***tallarín saltado*** or ***arroz chaufa***. Others (***kam lu wantán*** and ***lomo saltado***) were created here and became everyday dishes. In any city or provincial market, one can buy bokchoy, green onions, ginger, Chinese cabbage and other Chinese vegetables, as well as noodles and *wantans,* and soy sauce, oyster sauce and sweet and sour sauce.

Japanese dish. Shrimp tempura.

Italian immigrants reached Peru in the mid-nineteenth century, many of them from the Genovese provinces. They also brought their foods and it became common for Peruvian families to serve a Sunday meal of noodles in tomato or pesto sauce. There were also many pastas and pizzas and the Peruvian version of minestrone, with beans and corn. Trattorias and pastificios are much fewer in number than *chifas* in Peru, but the Italians have had a strong influence on the food industry, producing the pastas, breads and panetone, that have been popular with Peruvians ever since.

The last, great gastronomic influence on Peruvian cooking came from the Japanese, brought by the children of the Empire of the Rising Sun, who came to Peru almost a century ago. Almost all of the Japanese immigrants were farmers from the province of Okinawa seeking better horizons in this country also on the Pacific rim.

Even though today the Japanese colony has only some one hundred thousand descendants, it has a strong social and gas-

Japanese restaurant.

tronomic influence, due to it members' vital, creative integration into Peruvian society. Adapted to the Peruvian palate, this is Japanese cuisine of fish and seafood mixed with hot *rocoto* pepper, as in the fabulous, steamed *chita* fish dishes, ***aji verde*** stuffed with **kamaboto**, or the marvelous **chita a la sal**.

They also reformulated and exalted Peru's national dish, ***cebiche***, by reducing the time it is marinated in lime and serving the fish almost raw, then created ***tiraditos*** and other imaginative variations on the dish, further enriching our national gastronomic panorama.

Eating in Peru

Specialists on the subject of food consider Lima the gastronomic capital of America as much as for the richness of its national cuisine as for the incomparable variety and quality of its offerings, two factors which no other country in America can equal. In Lima, hundreds of restaurants of all categories offer coastal cuisine along with Andean or French cuisine as readily as Spanish or Italian. The city is an incomparable showcase for fish and other seafood as well as Chinese, Japanese, and other oriental dishes.

Ocopa arequipeña.

Outside of Lima, however, the visitor finds another situation, sometimes radically different. One can generally find good restaurants on the north coast (Trujillo, Chiclayo, Piura) and on the south coast (Ica, Arequipa), in some parts of the Callejón de Huaylas, and in the central Andes (Tarma and Huancayo). Where local food is least attractive is in Cusco, the nation's tourist capital, and in provinces deep in the Andes, such as Puno, Apurímac, and Huancavelica. The Amazon, apart from a few luxurious lodges serving typical Peruvian and international cuisine, rarely has restaurants suitable for tourists, save for the La Merced region. We have here a paradox; the varied and often magnificent culinary offerings do not always run parallel with tourist and vacation attractions, both of which still have a ways to go to match the heights of Peruvian gastronomy. *Bon appétit!*

The Realm of the Raw

ANTONIO CISNEROS

In this great nation of foods, we honor the gastronomy of the uncooked more than is done in many other latitudes. The high and noble tradition of food freed from the flame. Witness the exclusive qualities of beef *au tartare. Carpacci,* whose thin slices of beef or fish taste only of oil and capers. Or duck *en magrette.* Some raw hams. The delicate simmering touch on a beef *fondue,* or a Mongolian hot pot, scalding a few fibers without affecting the raw flesh.

Pesce marinato.

That the Japanese *sashimi,* like all these other dishes, is at home among Peruvians is further evidence of the triumph of the uncooked. It is offered as transparent slices of tuna, sole, octopus or squid,

Beef carpaccio.

ANTONIO CISNEROS is a poet, a journalist and a translator. He directs a radio program in Peru and contributes personal opinion articles to newspapers and magazines.

with no seasoning at all. The seasoning for this dish is not incorporated into the food, but rather consists, aside from the pickled radish, of a sweet soy sauce and a strong mustard called *wasabi,* which somehow takes the place of a marinade.

Cebiche.

With one of the richest seas on the planet, Peru has His Majesty, the *cebiche,* as the king of the uncooked foods. Although the dish is the heritage of the entire nation, *cebiche,* with all the works, comes from the north coast. A very fresh fish with firm, white meat, a thin bed of lime zest, a sigh of garlic, salt, deveined *ají limo* (its yellow, purple and reddish skins), a few slivers of onion. Sweet potato (or yucca), corn and lettuce make up the garnish.

True, in varying forms, fish and other seafood marinated in vinegar, mustard and lime have for centuries been common foods among many peoples inhabiting the Pacific coast. Chile, Ecuador, Nicaragua, Mexico, Costa Rica and El Salvador are some in the Americas.

But, in speaking of *cebiches,* courtesy is not a sign of weakness. As opposed to the Peruvian preparation in which the fish, right out of the sea, fresh as a fruit, does not usually rest in the lime for more than ten minutes, our neighbors have the custom of leaving it to soak long hours in its citrus bath and, to make matters worse, they top it with tomato or mayonnaise.

The trouble with these less fortunate versions lies in the fear of the uncooked. A sea bass brutalized by lime and heaped with tomato is only a shameful stew. Concealing the radiant nature of the animal.

In Peru, there is, furthermore, a variant of *cebiche* called *tiradito.* In this case, the fish, the moment it touches its lime bed, is covered lightly with olive oil, but no onion. As for the rest, a cebiche (aside from the classic fish *cebiche,* made from an endless variety of fish), can be made from octopus, squid, *chanque,* shrimp, prawns, sea urchins, scallops, clams and snails. The splendor of the uncooked is, to a great extent due to the triumph of the Pacific, once called the South Sea.

The Tradicional Feast

LUIS MILLONES

Contemporary Andean festivals have their historical roots in the great pre-Columbian ceremonies that partially survived Spanish colonization. The Colonial religious authorities adapted these ceremonies to Baroque culture brought from Spain in the early seventeenth century. The common thread between the two cultural expressions was the goal of expressing authority through a show or performance, and to use the show as an instrument of education and power.

It is impossible to list the number of festivals taking place in Peru every year. Each day sees no less than ten patron saint feasts in different parts of the country. The ideal of creating a permanent calendar is also made difficult by the constant variation in dates and holy images, illustrating the astonishing vitality of Andean religion.

La Virgen de la Candelaria, Puno.

LUIS MILLONES is an ethnohistorian specializing in Andean studies. He works as a professor at the Universidad Nacional San Cristóbal de Huamanga in Ayacucho.

La Virgen del Carmen, Paucartambo (Cusco).

A superficial observation of Andean town life reveals a ceremonial calendar that runs parallel to the civic rituals dictated by the capital city of Lima. Marches and parades in honor of the country or on days celebrating parents, teachers or the like, are entries on the official calendar. Patron saint celebrations, or a town's anniversary, and other festivals that are religious and thus universal in nature, have a depth of meaning distinct from patriotic ephemera. For example, the Feast of the Crosses, celebrated throughout the country, is the occasion for each town to retrieve the cross that crowns its nearest mountain and take it to church so that the priest's blessing can renew the energy of the sacred wood and reaffirm its mission of protecting its community. The same could be said of Carnival, yet its universal nature does not impede the peculiar manner in which it is celebrated in the Andes, quite different than in Brazil or the Caribbean. Carnival takes place as the planted crops begin to sprout, encouraged by the rains that begin in December. It is a time of celebration and change from the weary pace of an agricultural society; it turns February into an explosion of sound and color that stirs Andean communities.

Organizing a festival is a serious affair which involves specific actions and duties. The individuals chosen for the job assume their responsibilities at the moment the current festivities end. In doing so, they assume diverse titles that differ with each region: majordomo, members of the feast commission, standard-bearers, etc. Their tasks are generally related to those of the brotherhoods committed to protect the patron saints' holy images in each town.

Those who fill these posts will be responsible for the processions, dance troupes, choreographies, musical groups, and fireworks that will make for an unforgettable show. At the same time, food and drink must flow in generous proportions, always competing with the previous year's celebrations. The community will be highly attuned to the success or failure of the festival commission as compared to the previous year's event. So there is some competitive anxiety and a real fear of carrying the burden of failure.

Devotees of the Señor de Qoyllur Ritt'i.

It must not be said that one regional festival is more important than another. However, the upsurge in popularity of one (such as the Feast of Qoyllur Ritt'i, near Cusco) can somewhat cloud the importance of others that are no less spectacular but draw fewer tourists, such as the Feast of the Captive Lord of Ayabaca or of the Virgin of the Door in Otuzco. The celebrations born in Colonial Lima have not only attained great importance; they also continue to expand the worship of their holy images throughout the nation.

Pilgrimage to the Qoyllur Ritt'i sanctuary, Cusco.

Procession of La Virgen del Carmen, Paucartambo (Cusco).

This is the case of the *Señor de los Milagros*, or the Lord of Miracles, a crucifixion scene painted on a wall in the seventeenth century by a Negro slave and venerated today throughout Peru. In October, this image in procession not only packs the streets of Lima, but also rouses sufficient fervor in the provinces that other processions are held with reproductions of the image. «The Purple Christ,» so named for the color of its robes, parades in the company of the Virgin of the Cloud, whose veneration dates from 1696, when her miraculous intervention restored the health of the bishop of Quito, Sancho de Andrade y Figueroa. She is patroness of Cuenca, Ecuador, where other acts of her divine intervention are also quite notable.

The Lord of Miracles procession draws over two million people, who flock to see him from every corner of the country. In the last few years, on some days, the litters carrying the images have also been transported by car to the outlying districts of the capital city. The festival has become a national event from which no political figure can be absent; the president of Peru and the mayor of Lima often accompany the archbishop in official celebrations.

Something quite similar can be said of the Feast of Santa Rosa of Lima, celebrated on August 30. This saint's original name was Isabel Flores de Oliva and she was canonized in the seventeenth century after a short life of 31 years full of miracles and sacrifices.

Her festival is solemnly celebrated in the basilica dedicated to her, near the center of Lima, part of it built over what was her parents' home. There are also other celebrations in her honor throughout the country. One of the most famous takes place at Quives, in the Chillón River valley, only a few kilometers from Lima. Rosa spent several years of her childhood there and was confirmed by Lima's archbishop Toribio de Mogrovejo, who was later canonized as well. The church and chapel where Santa Rosa worshipped have been rebuilt in an imaginative manner. They have become a highly important pilgrimage site and are the scene of a large festival every August 30 and 31. The celebrations are repeated in various parts of the country and in the central Andes are notable for their elaborately costumed dancers and the accompanying, dramatic reenactments of the capture and murder of the Inca Atahualpa.

It is difficult to find one model of festival that is repeated throughout Peru. The most notable similarities occur in rural areas and are generally related to the veneration of the Earth (Pachamama) or to agricultural and livestock celebrations. Festivals devoted to fertility and the hope of rain can also have similar characteristics in different parts of Peru, even though they might be devoted to different saints, or to Christ or the Virgin Mary. These festivals have a long history, with many contributions and imprints from the Christian faith, but at their heart they reveal the undeniable relationship of the Andean people with the natural surroundings that give them life and hope.

JANUARY	
6	Los Reyes Magos, in the Colca Canyon.
1, 6 y 18	Danza de los negritos, in Huánuco.
LAST TWO WEEKS	National marinera dance contest, in Trujillo.
16	San Sebastián, in Huancavelica.
20	Virgen de Chiquinquirá, in Caraz (*see* Callejón de Huaylas).
FEBRUARY	
2–11	Virgen de la Candelaria, in Puno and the Colca Canyon.
15–17	Festival de la Tuna y la Cochinilla, in Ayacucho.
DATE VARIES	Carnival, the most recommended celebrations are in Ayacucho, Cajamarca, and the Colca Canyon.
MARCH	
FIRST TWO WEEKS	International Grape Harvest Festival, in Ica.
19	Afro-Peruvian art festival, in San José de Chincha (Lima).
DATE VARIES	Holy Week, the most recommended celebrations are in Ayacucho, the Colca Canyon, Tarma and Porcón (Cajamarca).
APRIL	
DATE VARIES	Official National Peruvian Paso Horse Competition, in Mamacona (Lima).
MAY	
2–4	Alacitas Las Cruces, in Puno.
3	Las Cruces, in Porcón (Cajamarca). Señor de Muruhuay, in Tarma.
14	Exaltación de la Cruz, in Huaraz (*see* Callejón de Huaylas).
15	San Isidro, in the Colca Canyon.
DATE VARIES	Señor de Qoyllur Ritt'i, in Ocongate (Cusco).
JUNE	
FIRST SUNDAY	Corpus Christi, in Cusco.
SECOND WEEK	Mountaineering Week in Huaraz (*see* Callejón de Huaylas).
THIRD WEEK	Tourism Week and Music Festival, in Cusco.
24	Inti Raymi, in Cusco. San Juan, celebrated in a special manner in the Amazon.
26	Día del Colono, in Pozuzo (*see* Chanchamayo).
29	San Pedro y San Pablo, celebrated in all fishing villages and ports on the coast.

OF FESTIVALS

JULY

16	La Virgen del Carmen, in Paucartambo (Cusco).
8–18	Tourism Week at Tarapoto.
25	Santiago Apóstol Celebration at the Taquile Island (Puno) and at the Mantaro Valley (*see* Huancayo).
28–29	Independence Holidays.
	Yawar Fiesta, in Pacucha (*see* Andahuaylas).
25–7	La Cruz de Chalpón, in Motupe (*see* Chiclayo).
26–29	Beach festival, in Huanchaco (*see* Trujillo).
DATE VARIES	Amancaes Peruvian Paso Horse competition, in Mamacona (Lima).

AUGUST

15	Anniversary of Arequipa.
28	La Virgen de la Asunción, in the Colca Canyon.
LAST WEEK	Anniversary of the reincorporation of Tacna into Peru. Tourism Week and the Festival of Afro-Peruvian Art and Music, in Cañete (Lima).
30	Santa Rosa de Lima, nation-wide holiday. Anniversary and Tourism Week, in Oxapampa (*see* Chanchamayo Valley) and Lamas (*see Tarapoto*).

SEPTEMBER

8	La Virgen de Cocharcas, in Cocharcas (*see* Andahuaylas).
14	El Señor Cautivo de Monsefú (*see* Chiclayo).
22–30	Internacional Spring Festival, in Trujillo.

OCTOBER

8	Yawar Fiesta, in Abancay.
4–13	El Señor Cautivo, in Ayabaca (Piura).
13–21	El Señor de Luren, in Ica.
18 and 28	El Señor de los Milagros, in Lima.
LAST TWO WEEKS	The Señor de los Milagros bullfights in Lima.
31	Día de la Canción Criolla, in Lima.

NOVEMBER

1	Todos los Santos, celebrated nationwide.
3–9	Fiesta Jubilar, in Puno.

DECEMBER

8	Andean Christmas, the most recommended
25	celebrations are in Abancay, Ayacucho, and Cusco.

¡COMPARE!
CALIDAD COLEMAN®

Sistema de control de presión de
propano "Perfect Flow" que regula
la consistencia de iluminación a
pesar de las condiciones del tiempo

Cilindro de propano de
Coleman®
que dura hasta 14 horas

Coleman®
Propane Fuel

⚠ **DANGER**
• FLAMMABLE GAS
• FIRE/EXPLOSION HAZARD
• CONTENTS UNDER PRESSURE
NET WEIGHT 16.4 OZ/465 g (1.02 lbs.)

Coleman®

LAMPARA DE PROP

Coleman ®

Fáciles de usar, transportar, de paso ligero y seguras

Ventiladores de
porcelana inoxidables

Intensidad de luz
completamente
ajustable

e ancha para mayor
estabilidad

This is work
Photographer
"Being in an office would drive me insane."

Work boot

2

USEFUL FACTS FOR THE TRAVELER

Concerning what is ex~
pedient to know so as to fare well
on one's journeys through this land

Tourism Services in Peru

Hotels

During the last few years, hotel services in Peru have improved notably. They are not yet optimal in every part of the country and vary considerably based on their distance from major cities and points of greatest tourist traffic.

Lima, Cusco, Puno, Arequipa, and Cajamarca have five-star hotels with rates ranging from US$ 80 to US$ 250 per night. In the principal cities there are usually clean, secure hotels with rates from US$ 45 to US$ 65. There are also hostels with dining rooms, laundries, and cable television whose price (often including breakfast) is US$ 30 to US$ 55, and finally *pensiones* (usually private homes) offering room and board for US$ 5 to US$ 20.

The quality of hotels and hostels towards the interior of the country is irregular and depends more on the experience and capacity of the owners than simply the number of stars appearing over the door of the establishment. We recommend always asking what services a hostel offers before taking a room. Smaller towns of the interior may even lack accommodations for travelers.

We recommend making reservations before traveling and, if possible, requesting that your reservation be confirmed via fax. Please take into account that during local and national holidays or long weekends the demand for rooms rises with an according rise in rates.

See the calendar of festivals for the dates of special events in the area you plan to visit.

Restaurants

The primary cities of Peru possess a great variety of restaurants, from elegant top-notch ones to modest eateries heavily frequented for the quality of their food. The average price per person of a meal at a top-quality restaurant is US$ 30 to US$ 50; at more modest restaurants it ranges from US$ 15 to US$ 30. Restaurants serving *comida criolla*, or typical Peruvian food, also abound. Some are of very good quality (and price) and at many you can eat very well at surprisingly low prices, although you must be prepared for some lack of hygiene.

Five-star restaurant.

Dining in the provinces is, for the most part, very economical. Despite a locale's appearance (plastic tablecloths, dirt floors, and loud music), excellent food might be served at great prices (less than US$ 10 per person).

Lastly, almost every restaurant in Peru offers a daily *menú* (a combination of appetizer, main dish, and dessert). The *menú* is usually in great demand as it is much less expensive (averaging US$ 2 to US$ 5) than ordering *à la carte*.

A Lima eatery.

Traveler's Complaints: 24-hour Service
TEL 574 8000

This is a telephone service that functions in Lima day and night, with bilingual operators (Spanish and English). Call in the following situations:

- Breach of contract on the part of travel agencies, airlines, and tourist establishments such as hotels and restaurants.
- Unjustifiably excessive charges.

- Irregular situations with police, customs, or the Immigrations department.
- Help in the event of lost or stolen personal property or documents.

Tourism Police

In the event of emergency (theft, fraud, or loss of documents), contact the Tourism' Police (Jr. Moore 268, Magdalena; Tel 460 0844) or with the emergency telephone code (105).

In the provinces, contact local police.

Urban Transport

Taxis

In Peru, the value of a taxi ride is always arranged on the spot between driver and client, before the service is rendered. Generally, a taxi driver will ask for more money than what the ride is worth, so you should always bargain. The rate in larger cities should never exceed US$ 5, while in smaller cities it should never go over US$ 2. For safety's sake, never ask a taxi driver for a hotel recommendation. In larger cities there are also radio taxi services that will pick you up on phone call demand; they have slightly higher rates but offer much more security.

Microbuses

These are available in Lima and other principal cities of Peru and have a capacity of 20 to 40 passengers. They do not have fixed bus stops, so if you wish to disembark you must shout *¡Baja en la esquina!* (Getting off at the next corner!).

Colectivos or *Combis*

These are vans with a capacity of some 10 passengers but are often filled with as many as 15. Their low cost and speed has made them one of the most popular methods of city transport. Nonetheless, they have a reputation for driving dangerously and we do not recommend using them.

Other

Another system of unconventional public transport popular in warmer cities is the *motocar,* a motorcycle adapted to transport up to 3 passengers. They are inexpensive, but their drivers can be speed enthusiasts; we recommend telling the driver that you wish to reach your destination in one piece. A similarly unorthodox service is the *taxi cholo,* a kind of three-wheeled, roofed motorcycle with a capacity for two passengers. These are not unreasonably dangerous but can be somewhat slow.

Peru by Road

Roads

The Peruvian transportation network is made up of more than 70 000km of roads divided into three categories based on their quality and the type of vehicle recommended: highways (*autopistas*), paved roads (*carreteras*) and packed dirt roads (*caminos*

PRIMARY PAVED ROADS*	
RUTAS	**KM**
Lima–Aguas Verdes *Ecuadorian border)*	1 295
Lima–Paso de la Concordia *(Chilean border)*	1 340
Lima–La Oroya–Huancayo	305
La Oroya–Cerro de Pasco–Huánuco–Tingo María–Pucallpa	627
La Oroya–Tarma–San Ramón–La Merced	135
Lima–Huaraz *(Callejón de Huaylas)*	404
Lima–Cajamarca	862
Nasca–Abancay–Cusco–Puno	664
Pisco–Ayacucho	310
Chiclayo–Bagua–Moyobamba–Tarapoto	554
Ilo–Moquegua–Desaguadero *(Bolivian border)*	398

*INCLUDING HIGHWAYS

afirmados). Some 16 000km of this network are national highways: the Panamericana highway, some highways leading into the Andes, and the Marginal highway in the jungle. Lastly, although they are not part of the transportation network, horse trails (*caminos de herradura*) also deserve mention.

Highways (*autopistas*)

Autopistas have two primary lanes plus a shoulder in each direction of traffic and are separated by a divider. They are not generally lighted, but are well provided with signs and permit fluid movement for any type of vehicle. There are approximately 300km of *autopista* in Peru, mainly consisting of the northern and southern entries into Lima on the Panamericana highway. To drive on the *autopista,* you must pay a toll of about US$ 1.

Paved Roads (*carreteras asfaltadas*)

These have one primary lane plus a shoulder in each direction of traffic, separated by a painted line. They are not lighted but are adequate for any type of vehicle. Signs and basic services (gas stations, restaurants, auto repair) can vary enormously based on the proximity to large cities. To drive on *carreteras asfaltadas,* you must pay a toll of about US$ 1.

Choice of roads at Palpa, Ica.

REMEMBER...

- The Panamericana highway is called Panamericana Norte north of Lima and Panamericana Sur south of Lima.
- On the coast, truck transport on paved roads is heavy at night. In the Andes, on the other hand, it is heavier in the early morning.
- Beware of very strong winds and sand dunes forming in the afternoons in the following places: near Sechura, on the Panamericana Norte, and near Tanaka on the Panamericana Sur.
- Some roads can be blocked by rain and landslides in the Andes and jungle from January to March.

Packed Dirt Roads (*caminos afirmados*)

The majority of roads in Peru are dirt roads built with earth and gravel. There are three types of packed dirt roads: those belonging to the national network, secondary local roads, and lastly, jeep trails (*trochas carrozables*).

- Packed dirt roads on the national network link important cities of the sierra or jungle. They are usually very busy with heavy passenger or cargo vehicles. They allow for traffic in both directions but certain sections may be deteriorated. Any vehicle should be able to travel on this type of road.

Packed dirt road
to Puerto Maldonado.

- Packed dirt roads of secondary, or local type link nearby towns and a few remote cities. On certain sections they may only allow one vehicle to pass at a time, in one direction. They are generally used by heavy transport and all-terrain vehicles, with urban vehicles not recommended.

- Jeep trails (*trochas carrozables*) connect small towns, mines, archeological sites or lakes, and are suitable only for trucks and all-terrain vehicles. When using these, always ask the locals about road conditions and be prepared to encounter difficulties. In compensation, these roads can lead through some of the most beautiful countryside in Peru.

The road to Oxapampa.

The road to Túcume.

REMEMBER...

- Traffic on packed dirt roads can be slow (at an average of 35km/h) as the numerous blind curves prevent you from passing vehicles.
- Your windshield can be cracked or broken by stones thrown from the tires of vehicles passing you.
- Dirt roads are generally dusty, and muddy in the rainy season.
- On some packed dirt roads traffic is allowed in one direction on one day and in the other direction on the next. Ask at local towns.
- Between January and March the majority of dirt roads deteriorate due to rain and mud, and can be blocked for weeks.

Camino de herradura
a la cordillera Huayhuash.

Horse Trails (*caminos de herradura*)

These are pack trails that are heavily used by the countryfolk and pack animals. Many were built in pre-Hispanic times and have only recently been «discovered» by hikers and mountain bikers. They lack any sort of services.

Vehicles for Land Travel

Renting a Vehicle

The average price of a car rental in Peru is US$ 60 per day, with all-terrain vehicles costing US$ 100 to US$ 120 per day. The three largest car rental companies in Peru are: Avis Rent-a-Car (with agencies in Lima and Arequipa); Budget, Inka's and Hertz (with agencies in Lima only); and National Car Rental (with agencies in Lima and Talara). In the rest of the country, some small agencies are beginning to offer these services in such cities as Cusco, Arequipa, Tacna, Juliaca, Trujillo, Sullana, Chiclayo, Talara, and Piura.

REMEMBER......

- Vehicle rental includes comprehensive insurance, covering towing service and mechanical assistance.
- Some agencies charge by the kilometer.
- Most agencies require a heavy cash deposit and/or up to two signed credit-card vouchers as a guarantee.
- All-terrain vehicles are the most often requested; reserve them in advance.
- It is customary to return the vehicle with a full tank of gas.

Interprovincial Buses

There are two types of interprovincial transport in Peru: buses that stop at every town, and *directos*, slightly more expensive buses but definitely faster. The buses with large reclining seats (*bus-cama*), air conditioning, television, restroom and bar travel only on the Panamericana highway and some routes into the Andes (Arequipa, Huaraz, Huancayo). Most routes into the Andes and jungle are operated by companies with older vehicles. If you travel with one of these, be prepared for unplanned delays, stops at any point, overcrowding, and intense heat or cold as these buses are not equipped with heating or air conditioning.

Buses making trips longer than eight hours will stop at least three times on the route for restroom and dining purposes. The duration of the stop varies and often depends on the appetite of the driver. It is often the copilot who announces the re-departure with a shout; be alert as passengers are not counted or waited for.

REMEMBER...

Ticket prices rise for days before local and national holidays or long weekends and seats are often sold out.
- Bus terminals are usually in the same location as the ticket office of the bus company.
- Before traveling, call to confirm the departure time, which often varies.
- Stay near the bus to be sure your luggage is loaded, as theft is frequent.
- Don't trust strangers who offer to «help» you with your luggage and always demand a ticket for the luggage you hand over.
- Keep your valuables in sight.
- Try to travel by day.
- Take warm clothing, a flashlight, and toilet paper.

Interprovincial *Colectivos*

These are automobiles connecting Lima with provincial cities, and provincial cities with each other. They are faster and safer than buses, although somewhat uncomfortable (some five passengers travel per car) and a little more expensive. They usually make stops near the interprovincial bus stops. They have to fill up with passengers before leaving, although it is quite possible to purchase all of the seats and travel *expreso*.

Trucks

In some parts of the country where passenger transport is in-

PRINCIPAL COMPANIES

N.⁰	COMPANY	ADDRESS IN LIMA*	PHONE
1	Civa	Av. 28 de Julio, esq. Paseo de la República	332 5236
2	Cruz del Sur	Jr. Quilca 531, Lima	424 1005
3	León de Huánuco	Av. 28 de Julio 1520, La Victoria	424 3893
4	Mariscal Cáceres	Av. 28 de Julio 2195, La Victoria	474 7850
5	Oltursa y Transolano	Bustamante y Mesa 644, Lima	475 8559
6	Ormeño	Javier Prado Este 1059, La Victoria	472 1710
7	Rodríguez	Av. Roosevelt 393, Lima	428 0506
8	Tepsa	Jr. Lampa 1237-1241, Lima	427 5642
9	Expreso Huamanga	Av. Luna Pizarro 453, La Victoria	330 2206
10	Expreso Libertadores	Av. Grau 491, Lima	426 8067
11	Expreso Lobato	Av. 28 de Julio 2101, La Victoria	474 9488
12	Expreso Molina	Jr. Ayacucho 1141, Lima	428 0617
13	Transmar	Av. 28 de Julio 1511, La Victoria	433 7440
14	Turismo Doce	Jr. Montevideo 736, Lima	427 3327
15	Flores	Paseo de la República 627	424 3278
16	Soyus y Perú Bus	Carlos Zavala y Loayza 217-221	428 6252
17	Expreso Cial	Jr. Cotabambas 299, Lima	428 5218

*DIRECCIONES EN LIMA

frequent, cargo trucks act as passenger vehicles as well. Some have boards over the cargo area; on others you must accommodate yourself between the gas tank and the cargo. The price is negotiated directly with the driver and is never excessive.

Road Infrastructure

Service Stations (*grifos*)

Large cities have service stations offering diesel (D-2) and 84-, 90-, 95-, and 97-octane gasoline. These usually have clean restrooms, a stock of auto parts and fluids, fast food, minimarkets, car washes, and tire repair services. In the provinces, you can

AND THEIR DESTINATIONS

DESTINATION	COMPANY N.⁰
Abancay	9
Andahuaylas	12
Arequipa	1, 2, 5, 6, 8, 15, 17
Ayacucho	9, 12, 10
Bagua	1
Cajamarca	1, 15, 17,6
Cusco	1, 2
Chachapoyas	1
Chanchamayo Valley (San Ramón and La Merced)	11
Chiclayo	1, 2, 5, 6, 8, 15, 17
Chimbote	1, 2, 5, 7
Chincha	2, 6, 15, 16
Huancavelica	18, 10
Huánuco	3, 10
Callejón de Huaylas (Huaraz)	2, 6, 7, 13, 15, 17
Ica	2, 6, 8, 14, 15, 16
Mantaro Valley (Huancayo)	2, 4, 12, 6
Moquegua	1, 2, 6, 8, 15
Nasca	1, 2, 6, 8, 14, 15
Pisco y Paracas	6, 16
Piura	1, 2, 5, 6, 8, 15, 17
Pucallpa	3, 13
Puno	1, 2, 15
Tacna	1, 2, 6, 8, 15
Tarma	11
Tingo María	3, 13
Trujillo	1, 2, 5, 6, 8, 15, 17
Tumbes	1, 2, 5, 6, 8, 15, 17

find these services from Lima to Piura on the Panamericana Norte, and from Lima to Nasca on the Panamericana Sur. Farther than this, and on all roads going into the Andes or jungle, gas stations become rarer and services diminish. In the Andes and jungle there is often only 84-octane gasoline or diesel fuel available, and in remote towns (especially in the jungle) it is common to only find fuel only in large drums (*a granel*) and in limited quantities. For this reason we recommend taking a stock of gasoline with you on any long trip.

RECUERDE...

- In the provinces, gas stations rarely accept credit cards.
- The price of fuel rises in relation to the distance from the source of supply (Lima, Talara, and Ilo) and a gas station's distance from others on the route.
- Low octane fuels will generally not cause engine problems when you are driving at over 1 500m (5 000ft) but may cause problems at lower altitudes.
- If you plan on a trip of several days through the Andes, advance the spark on your engine to improve its performance at altitude.
- Fuel from drums should always be filtered through a cloth to avoid damaging the engine with any impurities.

Auto Repair Workshops (*talleres mecánicos*)

Only a few cities have workshops specializing in specific brands of automobiles. In the rest of the country, services are independent and do not offer guarantees (especially for newer vehicles).

For this reason you should verify that your vehicle is in good condition before traveling. You will always find tire repair workshops (*vulcanizadoras*) no matter how far you go. These are recognized by the stack of tires in front of their doors.

Towing Services

For the most part, towing services are rare and expensive. There are companies offering towing insurance and roadside service (such as AAA or the Touring y Automóvil Club) with national coverage at a reasonable cost. Always take along with you several meters of towing cord or cable just in case.

> *AAA:* Av. La Encalada 305, Surco, Lima.
> Tel 344 2405 / 344 2409 / 344 2443. Fax 344 2366.
> *Touring Automóvil Club:* César Vallejo 699, Lince, Lima.
> Tel 221 2432.

Where to Eat on the Road

Routes covered by public transport companies always have restaurants. The dishes offered are usually simple, of good proportions, and quickly prepared. The best way to know if one of these locales is good is by observing the quantity of buses and trucks stopping. Take a moment to ask about road conditions. If you are traveling on a little-frequented route, chances are you will not find restaurants, but should take food and drink along with you instead.

Recommendations for the Driver

- Always take along your personal documents
  (passport or identity card), driver's license,
  and car ownership documents.
- If you are not a Peruvian citizen,
  please keep in mind that your driver's license
  is only valid for the first thirty days of your visit.
  To obtain an international driver's license, contact
  the offices of the Touring y Automóvil Club in Lima
  (Tel 221 2432).
- Never agree to carry packages from strangers
  in your vehicle.
- In Peru, very few drivers respect traffic signals
  and speed limits. Avoid driving too fast and
  keep your seat belt on!
- Don't trust another car's turn signals or brake lights,
  as they are often wrong or simply not working correctly.
- Passenger buses and cargo vehicles often consider themselves
  first priority. Redouble your caution around them.
- Avoid driving at night as vehicles may drive
  without their headlights on, or with their high beams on.
  Roadside hold-ups are also more frequent at night.

- There are often rocks or other objects on the shoulder of the road. Many are left by drivers attempting repairs who forget them upon leaving. Stay alert.

Peru by Plane

Airports

Jorge Chávez International Airport, Lima.

Peru has 19 commercial airports, and 22 airports used sporadically for charter planes or armed forces flights. To obtain information on special flights, call the Air Force at Dirección de Comercialización del Grupo Aéreo Número 8 (Av. Faucett n/n, Callao, Tel 574 2259 / 574 1010) or any other air taxi agency (see p. 85).

CITIES WITH COMMERCIAL AIRPORTS	
CITY	**DEPARTMENT**
Arequipa	Arequipa
Ayacucho	Ayacucho
Cajamarca	Cajamarca
Chiclayo	Lambayeque
Cusco	Cusco
Ilo	Moquegua
Iquitos	Loreto
Juliaca	Puno
Lima	Lima
Piura	Piura
Pucallpa	Ucayali
Puerto Maldonado	Madre de Dios
Rioja	San Martín
Tacna	Tacna
Talara	Piura
Tarapoto	San Martín
Trujillo	La Libertad
Tumbes	Tumbes
Yurimaguas	Loreto

Air Transport

Airlines

The principal national airlines operating in Peru are Aero Perú, Aero Continente and Aero Cóndor. Flights within the country are not cheap. However, the airlines often have bargains to offer. Consult at travel agencies.

REMEMBER...

- Flights on days before local and national holidays or long weekends are usually sold out.
- Morning flights are usually more punctual than evening flights, as the latter are held up by earlier flight delays.
- Confirm your reservation twice and, upon arrival, confirm your return flight. You may be removed from the passenger list if you fail or are late in confirming.
- Arrive at the airport at least one-and-a-half hours before your flight leaves.
- For any national flight there is an airport tax of approximately US$ 3.
- All airlines permit a maximum of 25kg of personal luggage.
- Do not accept packages from any strangers for any reason.
- Close your luggage well and, if possible, ask for the *enzunchado* service (plastic band seals). It is not expensive and will help protect your luggage.

Aerotaxis

Several *aerotaxi* companies link Lima to cities of the interior and the latter to each other. Prices are somewhat high but allow for quick access to remote areas without intermediate travel.

In Nasca there are several services offering flights over the famous Nasca lines for around US$ 40 per person. This service can be contracted in Lima or directly in Paracas, Ica, or Nasca.

In Iquitos you can hire Peruvian Air Force float planes (Grupo Aéreo Número 42), which are either Twin Otters or Pilatus Porters *(see Useful Facts in the pertinent section)*.

Information
Aero Cóndor
    Juan de Arona 781, San Isidro, Lima
    Tel 441 1354 / 222 4130
    Aeropuerto, Av Faucett s/n, Callao.
    Tel 575 1528

Aero Ica
> Diez Canseco 480-B, Miraflores, Lima.
> Tel 445 0859 / 446 3026 / 242 9164.
> Telefax 444 2140.

Helicopters

Helicóptero MI-8
en trabajos de apoyo social,
Amazonas.

In Peru there are several private companies with offices in Lima, Cusco, and Iquitos offering helicopters for hire. In Lima it is also possible to hire Air Force helicopters (Grupo Aéreo Número 3) or Infantry helicopters (Aviación del Ejército). These services are expensive. The most accessible service is Heli Cusco, a company making flights to Machu Picchu from the Cusco airport at an approximate cost of US$ 90 per person, one-way.

Information

Helisur
> Carlos Concha 267, Lima. Tel 264 1770
> Abelardo Quiñones 60, Iquitos. Tel 26 4085

Grupo Aéreo N.° 3
> Av. Faucett s/n, Callao.
> (beside the Lima International Airport)
> Tel 574 1010

Aviación del Ejército
> Av. Faucett s/n, Callao.
> (beside the Lima International Airport)
> Tel 574 1656

Heli Cusco
> Arias Araguéz 369, Miraflores, Lima.
> Tel 445 6126 / 444 8702

Grupo Aéreo N.° 8

This is a branch of the Peruvian Air Force that makes periodic supply flights to almost all larger cities of the interior, especially to locations in the jungle not receiving routine commercial flights. They use Antonov, Hercules, and DC-8 transport planes. This service is open to the public, but prior confirmation is necessary as seat availability depends on the cargo. Itinerary and date of departure can vary without notice. These flights are much cheaper than commercial ones.

Information

Dirección de Comercialización del Grupo Aéreo N.° 8

Av Faucett s/n, Callao.

(beside the Lima International Airport)

Tel 574 1010, anexo 2107

Peru by Train

Railways

The primary rail line in Peru (and the most frequented by tourists) connects Arequipa with Juliaca, Puno, and Cusco. To travel direct from Arequipa to Cusco, without stopping in Puno, you must change trains at Juliaca. The trip from Arequipa to Juliaca lasts all night; from Puno to Cusco it lasts all day (12 hours).

Ferrocarril
en Desamparados, Lima.

Cusco is the point of departure for a rail route leading to Machu Picchu and then down to Quillabamba in the jungle. This last section is temporarily out of service.

Another rail line connects Lima to Huancayo and Huancavelica. The first part is out of service (although on Sundays the train reaches Tornamesa, at km 76 on the Central highway). The section between Huancayo and Huancavelica is recommended, although not generally frequented by tourists.

Categories of Service

The *autovagón* traveling the Cusco–Machu Picchu route is the best service available. In descending order, the next category is Pullman (or *buffet*), then first class, executive tourist, and second class. Traveling first class is cheaper and more comfortable

RAIL LINES
ROUTE DISTANCE DURATION

ROUTE	KM	DURATION
Arequipa-Juliaca-Puno	350	12 h
Puno-Cusco	350	8 h
Cusco-Machu Picchu	104	3 h 20 min
Lima-Tornamesa*	62	2 h 15 min
Huancayo-Huancavelica*	100	2 h 30 min

* At the present time out of service.

than the average bus ride, although somewhat slower. Second class, generally 25% cheaper than first class, is always full of passengers and cargo; the difference in price is not usually worth the discomfort.

Information
Train Transport PERÚRAIL

Av. Armendáriz 397, Miraflores Lima.

Tel 444 5025. Fax 447 5926

www. perurail.com

reservas@perurail.com

REMEMBER...

- Buy your tickets beforehand. If possible, do so through a travel agency. These will charge a small commission but you will avoid long lines and ensure the reservation of a comfortable space.
- The theft of personal items and luggage is common, especially on the nightly Arequipa–Juliaca–Puno route, and is even more so in second class. It is best to travel in groups and to stay alert.
- In general, all types of food are available on board.
- Some routes traveled can cause difficulties due to the altitude. Take appropriate precautions and bring a coat.

Peru by Boat

Maritime Transport

In Peru there are no tourist maritime agencies. There are, however, small boats offering one- or two-day trips to a few points on the coast (such as from Ancón to the Palomino islands or from Paracas to the Ballestas islands), and fishing boats that can be hired in any coastal fishing port or village.

River Transport

The rivers of the Amazon are known as the «highways of the jungle» as many towns lack access roads or airports. The primary river ports in the Peruvian Amazon are Iquitos and Yurimaguas (in the department of Loreto), Pucallpa (in the department of Ucayali) and Puerto Maldonado (department of Madre de Dios). Fares for river trips are sold directly at the ports, where destination and itinerary information is also available. Time of departure often depends on the speed with which passengers buy tickets and cargo is loaded. The principal boats running the rivers of the Amazon are:

Peque-peques

Canoes with stationary engines that have become the most common method of passenger and cargo transport in the Amazon. They have a capacity of some 30 people and, although slow and noisy, are cheap and can be found at any river port. Ideal for short trips.

Peque-peque on the Candamo River, Puno

Canoes with Outboard Engines

These boats are similar to *peque-peques* but are equipped with outboard engines. They are faster but more expensive than the former. Ideal for short or long trips.

Heavy Cargo Boats

Cargo boats and barges travel the larger rivers, often carrying up to 300 passengers. They usually have two decks, with the lower one reserved for merchandise and the upper one for passengers. Although bunks are available they are not recommendable because of the heat and abundance of mosquitoes. We recommend sleeping in the hammocks abovedecks where the river breeze is refreshing. Food is offered on board, but for hygienic reasons it is better to take along your own supplies. Don't forget to bring along clean drinking water and toilet paper.

Barges on the Madre de Dios River.

Because of their low cost, these boats are ideal for longer trips.

Speedboats

These are aluminum boats with outboard engines for passenger use only. They have a maximum capacity of 12 and are rapid and secure, although more expensive than canoes with outboard motors. Ideal for short trips.

Lake Transport

Lake transport in Peru mainly occurs on Lake Titicaca. Vessels leave the port of Puno daily for the principal cities and islands of the lake: the Uros-Chulluni native community, Taquile island, and Amantani island. There are also some boats that travel from Puno to Copacabana (in Bolivia) upon client request.

General Recommendations

When to Go • What to Take

To the Coast

The summer months (December to April) are ideal for traveling the coast, as the sun shines brightly, nights are fresh and the ocean waters warmer. During the rest of the year, with the exception of far north (Piura and Tumbes) and central south (Ica), the coast stays cloudy and humid.

Remember that Peru is close to the equator and the sun has a stronger effect than in temperate zones. Don't overexpose yourself without sunblock and be sure to drink plenty of water.

Mosquitoes abound on many parts of the coast; take along a good repellent.

In winter, the coastal desert nights can be surprisingly cold. Take warm clothing.

To the Andes

If you are going to the Andes, the ideal time is during the dry season (May to October). Remember that in regions higher than 3 000m (10 000ft), extreme cold and intense solar radiation accentuate the risks of sunburn. Take along abundant warm clothing and sunblock, and take special care to protect your lips.

Traveling the Bayóvar coast, Piura.

To fight altitude sickness called *soroche*, drink large quantities of water, avoid rapid movements, eat simple foods, avoid alcohol and give your body time to adapt. Coca leaf tea (*mate de coca*) is a strong ally for getting acclimatized.

Cajamarca countryside.

To the Jungle

The dry season (May to October) is the best for a visit to the Amazon. Take into account that the humidity of the region makes for an abundance of mosquitoes and biting flies, carriers of tropical disease.

Crossing the Aguaytía River, Ucayali.

Some diseases (yellow fever, tetanus, hepatitis A and B, influenza, and typhoid fever) can be prevented by early vaccination while others (malaria) require taking preventive medication.

We recommend seeking medical advice before traveling. To avoid insect bites, eat a lot of garlic, take vitamin B complex, or brewer's yeast capsules one week before traveling.

Take along a raincoat, long pants, light long-sleeved shirts, and always sleep under a mosquito net. Use insect repellent and sunblock during the day.

Food and Water

Unfortunately, diseases such as cholera and typhoid fever are common in Peru. To avoid them, never drink untreated tap water, but take along clean drinking water or drink only boiled water. Avoid eating on the street at kiosks.

Fish and seafood are excellent on the coast, but make sure they are fresh beforehand and try to eat them well-cooked. Peel fruit before eating it.

In provincial restaurants, what the menu indicates may be quite different from what is actually served; ask beforehand to confirm the ingredients.

Photo and Video

Photographic equipment is expensive and difficult to obtain in Peru. There is a good variety of photo and video film available (VHS and Video 8) in Lima and the principal cities, but not in the rest of the country.

Film development quality is acceptable although somewhat expensive (about US$ 0,30 per picture). Only Lima offers slide development services.

In some places, being photographed or filmed can be considered annoying or offensive. Avoid taking snapshots if you note that the subject is uncomfortable, or simply ask permission beforehand (good manners are often rewarded). Do not be surprised if you are asked for a tip afterwards.

The following areas are forbidden for filming or photography: military centers or garrisons, oil drills or refineries, naval bases and airports, railway stations, airbases, mines, police stations, bridges, power plants or water treatment plants. If you are in doubt, ask permission before taking photographs. One final, good piece of advice: have your camera out of its bag only during the actual time you are taking the picture.

Customs

It is absolutely prohibited to take objects of historical or archeological value out of the country. If you are unsure of an object's value, ask at the main office of the National Cultural Institute (INC, Av. Javier Prado Este 2465, San Borja, Lima. Tel 224 3724).

To export wildlife (flora or fauna) you must obtain a permit from the National Natural Resource Institute (INRENA, calle 17, 355, urbanización El Palomar, San Isidro, Lima. Tel 224 3037) and the National Agricultural Health Service (SENASA, Pasaje Zela n/n, tenth floor, Jesús María, Lima. Tel 332 5990). Species in danger of extinction can only be exported with a CITES permit granted by INRENA.

It is absolutely prohibited to possess, consume, or carry any narcotics (including marijuana and cocaine).

DESTINATIONS

Concerning the many townes and innes that will make yours a pleasant journey through this vast territory

2 378 M / 7 802FT
47 000 POP.
897 KM
SE OF LIMA

Abancay

P. 78

ROUTE MAP

7

The city of Abancay, capital of the department of Apurímac, is located in the Mariño River valley, at the foot of the imposing, snow-capped Mount Ampay (5 240m, or 17 192ft), guardian of the city. Abancay is one of the most beautiful and least known cities of the southern Andes. According to the chronicler Antonio Vásquez de Espinosa [1629], its name comes from the Quechua *amancay*, a yellow flower that grows throughout the Peruvian highlands.

The Abancay region was the ancestral territory of diverse eth-

Suspension bridge over the Pachachaca River.

nic groups originating from Quechua stock. Skilled farmers, the ancient inhabitants were distinguished by their hostile, war-like spirit. They considered themselves descendants of the puma, and chroniclers described them as extremely insolent.

With a distinctive Colonial style, Abancay is characterized by its steep and narrow streets, its tile roofs (now mostly replaced by corrugated steel), and its large, older homes with their abundant arches and wide entryways. Meeting its inhabitants is one of the principal attractions for the tourist, for the *Abancaíno* is

> *Dry climate, warm during the day and cold at night, with a yearly mean temperature of 16°C (60°F). Rainy season from December to March.*

among the most hospitable of Andean peoples, a fact particularly evident during the local festivals. The region concentrates the greatest percentage of Quechua speakers in the nation today; for this reason it is very common to hear a curious mix of Spanish and Quechua spoken in the city.

Among the principal products of the Mariño Valley are corn (the department of Apurímac is the country's second-largest producer of this crop), potatoes, wheat, beans, and barley. Its fruits (strawberries, peaches, quince, and apples) deserve special mention; for both taste and size they are considered among the best in the country. The upper reaches of the valley, for the most part pastoral lands, are used for important livestock production.

Local Dishes

Entrées
- Trigo atamalado: wheat cooked with crayfish, cheese, hard-boiled eggs, potatoes, and olives.
- Uchullachua: potatoes served with a sauce of spicy *ají* pepper and *huacatay*, an aromatic herb.

Main Dishes
- Huatia: various meats and potatoes, cooked between hot stones with aromatic herbs.

SACRIFICE OF THE CONDOR

The Yawar Fiesta begins with the rite of capturing a live condor. To catch this gigantic bird, men hide in a hole covered with dry branches and a freshly killed animal on top. After circling for a long while, a condor will fall for the trap and descend to feed. Having caught the condor, the men bind its feet and carry it to town, where they adorn it with colorful ribbons and parade it around the main square, accompanied by the leading authorities. They then tie it to the back of a bull. Blood runs from the wounds of both animals until the bull is finally killed in a symbolic victory, to the rejoicing of the participants. Some consider this a brutal spectacle, but it is, nonetheless, one of the most traditional festivals in the Peruvian Andes.

Festivals

One of the festivals celebrated in this region is the notable Yawar Fiesta (meaning 'festival of blood' in Quechua) in Antabamba, in honor of the Virgen del Rosario on October 8. This festival is an Andean version of the Spanish bullfight, a rite representing the confrontation between the Andean and Spanish worlds. Its main event is a «bullfight» in which a live condor (captured especially for the occasion) is tied to the back of a bull.

Christmas in Abancay is the ideal time to enjoy *la danza de los negritos* (the dance of the black men), a colorful, acrobatic dance that expresses the impact of the African population on the Apurímac highlands. You can also hear the *waylías*, single women who dance and sing in honor of the Christ child and the Virgin Mary.

Other important festivals in Abancay are: Carnival, during which the young men called *secollo* fight each other with whips; the dance of the *yunsa*, or *cortamonte*, in which a gift-laden tree is chopped down (February); Corpus Christi (June, date varies); the feasts of San Salvador (August 6) and of Nuestra Señora de la Merced (September 24) in Antabamba; the feast of the Virgen del Rosario in Abancay (October 10); and the day of Abancay (November 3).

Points of Interest in the City

Traditional Locales

- *Plaza de Armas:* with its classic African palms, the plaza frames the austere Cathedral whose façade curiously faces a side street and not the plaza itself. The Cathedral's single tower, with its clock keeping perfect time, rises above the surrounding roofs and dominates the city.

Churches

- *El Señor de la Caída*, Plazoleta La Victoria: one of the oldest churches in Abancay. This church, modest in appearance but with a solemn beauty, contains exquisite paintings of the Cusco school and an altarpiece of finely carved Central American mahogany. At the foot of the main altar, worshippers place hundreds of candles, giving the interior of the church a very special atmosphere.

The Cathedral.

Excursions

Saywite

2 400 MSNM

An archeological site located in an older *hacienda* or country estate in the upper Curahuasi valley, 47km (1 hour) NE of Abancay, on the packed dirt road to Cusco. This place, origi-

The Saywite Stone.

nally an Inca town, is the site of the famous Saywite stone, a semispherical monolith weighing several tons and carved with a hundreds of men, animals, plants and buildings of the Andean world. It is thought to have been carved for use in rituals involving worship of water and mountains.

Curahuasi Valley

2 400M / 7 874FT ON AVERAGE   )

A temperate valley, famous for its anise liqueur, 72km (2 hours) NE of Abancay on the packed dirt road to Cusco. Upon leaving Abancay and crossing the pass in this direction, there is a natural lookout point from which you can see numerous plots and fields as a patchwork of color covering the surrounding mountain slopes. At 15km from the small town of Curahuasi, by a dirt road in good condition are the hot springs of Jónoc. To visit them, find a guide in Abancay. There are no lodgings in this valley, but there are some simple restaurants.

The Curahuasi Valley.

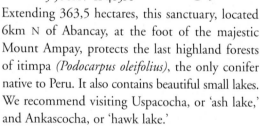

Ampay National Sanctuary.

Chakpá flower
(*Embotrium grandiflora*).

Ampay National Sanctuary

3 500M / 11 483FT   ◯ ▶

Extending 363,5 hectares, this sanctuary, located 6km N of Abancay, at the foot of the majestic Mount Ampay, protects the last highland forests of itimpa *(Podocarpus oleifolius)*, the only conifer native to Peru. It also contains beautiful small lakes. We recommend visiting Uspacocha, or 'ash lake,' and Ankascocha, or 'hawk lake.'

There are numerous species of fauna and flora in danger of extinction, such as the *ucumari*, or Andean bear (*Tremarctos ornatus*), the *sachacabra*, or dwarf deer (*Pudu mephistopheles*), and the *cantuta* flower (*Fuchsia spp.*). To reach the lake region, you must first go to Arcopunco, 1,8km from Abancay on the packed dirt road to Cusco. From here, it is 4km on a very rough road to the Sahuannay reservoir, where a zigzagging descent through forest leads to the slopes of Ampay. Camping allowed.

Valley and Canyon of the Apurímac River

2 500M / 8 202FT ON AVERAGE

Apurímac River.

Beautiful, natural scenery 90km (2 hours) NE of Abancay, on the packed dirt road to Cusco. The impressive Apurímac Canyon (in Quechua, 'he who speaks like a lord') is considered one of the deepest and most beautiful in the world. Its enormous stone walls and the lush vegetation surrounding it has made it a favorite destination among avid trekkers and rafters. The agencies that organize expeditions to the canyon are based in Cusco.

Hotels

Hotel de Turismo Abancay ★★
 Av. Díaz Bárcenas 500. Telefax 32 1017. US$ 35
Hostal Saywite ★
 Av. Núñez 212. Tel 32 1692. US$ 10
Hostal Leonidas ★
 Av. Arenas 131. Tel 32 1199. US$ 10
Hostal Residencial Victoria
 Av. Arequipa 305. Tel 32 1301.
Hostal y Restaurant Turístico El Dorado
 Av. Arenas 131-C. Tel 32 2107.
Hospedaje Samaywasi
 Av. Arequipa 309, Las Américas. Tel 32 3316.

RATES ARE APPROXIMATE AND, UNLESS OTHERWISE NOTED, ARE FOR DOUBLE OCCUPANCY.

Restaurants

✔ Restaurant at the Hotel de Turismo
Av. Díaz Bárcenas 500.

✔ Alicia
Av. Díaz Bárcenas 509.

✔ Restaurante Turístico El Dorado
Av. Arenas 131-C.

✔ Las Canastas
Av. Arenas 173, 2nd. floor.

✔ Don Geraldo
Av. Arequipa 210.

✔ Lafayette
Av. Arenas 156.

✔ Cebichería Viri
Av. Arenas 143.

✔ Chifa Fay Chi
Av. Arenas 154.

Useful Facts

AREA CODE **84**

☎

Basic information

Hotels and Tours at Abancay:
Av. Díaz Bárcenas 500.   32 1628

Instituto Nacional de Cultura:
Av. Prado 310.   32 4116

Farmacia Luren:
Av. Díaz Bárcenas 519.   32 1101

Hospital de Apoyo IPSS:
Venezuela s/n.   32 1165

Post Office:
Av. Arequipa 213.   32 1088

IPERÚ:
Information and Assistance for Tourists
01-574-8000 Lima.

Andahuaylas

2 899 M / 9 511FT
40 000 POP.
1 046 KM
SE OF LIMA

P. 82

P. 78

ROUTE MAP

7

The city of Andahuaylas is located in the department of Apurímac, on the banks of the torrential Chumbao River, at the foot of Mount Campanayoc. Its name means 'meadow of the beautiful skies' in Quechua. A typical Andean city, with narrow streets, tile roofs, and some Colonial architecture, Andahuaylas conserves the solemn atmosphere that characterized it in the past.

The site of this city and its environs was the dominion, between the twelfth and fifteenth centuries, of the fearsome Chanca

Carnival in Huancabamba.

people, historical rivals of the Incas. The chroniclers relate that in the time of the Inca Wiracocha panic seized Cusco when the Chanca sent a large and well-provisioned army to conquer the imperial city. Nonetheless, thanks to the help of his son Yupanqui, Wiracocha was able to defeat and subjugate the Chanca. This victory was so important in Inca history that the young Yupanqui was named Inca ruler and he changed his name to Pachacútec, meaning 'he who moves the world'. In recognition of their courage, Pachacútec made large concessions to the Chanca.

A dry climate with very cold nights and a yearly mean temperature of 14°C (57°F). Rainy season from December to March.

The region was once again in upheaval in 1536, when the people of Andahuaylas joined the rebellion of Manco Inca, who fought against the conquistadors from his jungle refuge at Vilcabamba. Once the region was pacified, Andahuaylas was divided into six territorial divisions called *corregimientos*, each of which had to provide *mitayos,* or Indian laborers, for the mercury mines at Huancavelica.

Today, Andahuaylas is the most industrious city in the department of Apurímac. It is located in a heavily cultivated region,

A downtown street.

planted mostly to wheat, potatoes, corn and barley. Livestock-raising (cattle and camelids) also plays an important role in the local economy. Although Andahuaylas lacks developed infrastructure for tourism, it does have small restaurants and hotels.

Local Dishes

- Cuy relleno: guinea pig stuffed with minced meat, herbs, and nuts.

Festivals

One of the festivals celebrated in this region is the notable Yawar Fiesta (meaning 'festival of blood' in Quechua) held in Pacucha on July 28. This festival is an Andean version of the Spanish bullfight, a rite representing the confrontation between the Andean and Spanish worlds. Its main event is a «bullfight» in which a live condor (captured especially for the occasion) is tied to the back of a bull. Also in July (date varies) is the feast of Santiago Apóstol, with traditional branding of livestock.

Other important festivals are: El Niño Jesús de Praga in Andahuaylas (January 25); the feast of the Virgen de la Candelaria in San Jerónimo (February 2), and the feast of Nuestra Señora de Cocharcas in Cocharcas (September 8).

Points of Interest in the City

Traditional Locales

- *Plaza de Armas:* bordered by the Cathedral and handsome Colonial homes, its centerpieces are an ancient fountain carved from a single piece of stone and an enormous bronze bell.

Churches

The Cathedral.

- *The Cathedral*, Plaza de Armas: this imposing church is a singular example of seventeen-century religious architecture. Especially notable are its walls of huge granite blocks and its sober facade, with an inclined roof crowned with clay tiles. It is best to visit during Mass, when which the worshippers' devotion, the candlelight and the sound of the canticles add much to its interior beauty.

Excursions

San Jerónimo

2 800M / 9 186FT   )

A district located 4km NW of the city, via packed dirt road. Famous for its green countryside, it is reached by a long, tranquil eucalyptus-lined avenue. In its Plaza de Armas is a monument to the Chanca leader Ancohuallo. It has a beautiful church and restaurants serving typical dishes.

Rooftop crosses protect the home.

Pacucha
3 091M / 10 141FT)

A beautiful, small lake, about 20km (30 minutes) NE of Andahuaylas on the packed dirt road to Abancay. It is famous for the spectacular sunsets reflected on its still waters. Nearby is the town of Aguaitando, where there are some simple restaurants. The archeological site of Sóndor, a Chanca town, is a twenty-minute walk away.

Sóndor.

Waywaka
3 350M / 10 991FT)

An archeological site located on the hills overlooking the city of Andahuaylas from the north. It is accessed by 9km of packed road that starts at the city limits. This is the site where the oldest example of Peruvian goldwork (fragments of hammered gold sheets) was found.

Lake Pacucha.

Cocharcas
3 068M / 10 066FT ○

A traditional town 121km NW of Andahuaylas on a packed dirt road, with a monumental Colonial-era church dedicated to Our Lady of Cocharcas. Legend has it that a devout Indian promoted the raising of this church, whose main altar is made of wood decorated in a flower motif.

A field of tarwi in Pacucha.

Hotels

Hotel Turístico Andahuaylas ★★
   Lázaro Carrillo 620. Tel 72 1229. US$ 20
Hostal Residencial Las Américas ★
   Francisco Ramos 410. Tel 72 1646. US$ 10
Hostal San Agustín ★
   Ramón Castilla 264. Tel 72 1383. US$ 10

Hostal Delicias
  Juan Francisco Ramos 525. Tel 72 1104.
Hostal Residencial Cristal Place
  Pedro Casafranca 595. Tel 72 1462.
Hostal Cusco
  Pedro Casafranca 520. Tel 72 2148.

> RATES ARE APPROXIMATE AND, UNLESS OTHERWISE NOTED,
> ARE FOR DOUBLE OCCUPANCY.

Restaurants

✔ Restaurant at the Hotel Turístico de Andahuaylas
  Lázaro Carrillo 620.
✔ Chifa Chun Yion
  Constitución 309.
  Restaurante Venecia
  Guillermo Cáceres Tresierra 353.
  Pollería La Casona
  Av. Perú 260.

Useful Facts

AREA CODE **84**

☎

Basic information

Hospital General de Andahuaylas:
  H. Pesce 180.   72 1090
Farmacia Santa Rosa:
  Santa Rosa 169.   72 1279
Post Office:
  Av. Perú 234.   72 1062
IPERÚ:
  Information and Assistance for Tourists
  01-574-8000 Lima.

Arequipa

2 335 M / 7 661FT
619 200 POP.
I 003 KM
S OF LIMA

P. 82   P. 85

P. 78

The city of Arequipa (capital of the department of the same name) is located in the Chili River valley, flanked by three snow-capped volcanoes: Misti (5 821m, or 19 098ft), Chachani (6 075m, or 19 931ft), and Pichu Pichu (5 425m, or 17 799ft). Some say its name originates from the Quechua phrase *ari-que pay*, meaning 'yes, stay here,' words pronounced by the Inca Mayta Cápac upon seeing an auspicious place for his armies to camp; another version holds that the name originates from the Aymara phrase *ari-queppan*, or 'resounding trumpet.' Known as

ROUTE MAP

8

The Cathedral and Misti at dusk.

the 'white city,' Arequipa definitely does justice to its nickname, as its buildings are of *sillar*, a white volcanic rock that abounds in the area. The stone embellishes the façades of the city's homes and churches.

The Arequipa region has been heavily populated since pre-Hispanic times, as evidenced by the spectacular terracing in the Colca and Churajón valleys.

The Incas conquered the region in the fourteenth century and built many shrines on Pichu Pichu, Chachani, and many

Dry, temperate climate with sunny days and cold nights most of the year and a yearly mean temperature of 18° C (64° F). Rainy season from December to March. It is best to visit between June and September.

other peaks. People climbed to these summits with their offerings. In 1995, Arequipa captured world attention when a group of archeologists found, on the summit of the Ampato volcano (6 310m, or 20702ft), the intact mummy of a young Inca woman, sacrificed some 500 years ago as an offering to the imposing, snow-capped peak. The Maiden of Ampato, as she has been called, or more affectionately, «Juanita,» can be visited in the city *(see Museums, p. 117).*

Arequipa was founded on August 15, 1540 by Captain Garci Manuel de Carbajal under the name of Villa de la Asunción de Nuestra Señora del Valle Hermoso de Arequipa.

SMOLDERING COLOSSI

Arequipa is a land of volcanoes. Close to a hundred smoldering colossi dot the landscape of this southern department. This is why *sillar* —a white volcanic rock whose porous composition makes it easy to work— is the most common construction material used in Arequipa. *Sillar* continues to be extracted from quarries at Añashuayco, NE of the city.

The site was chosen for its proximity to the coast, to enable the settlers to trade the products of Cusco and the southern Altiplano, especially the products of the mines at Villa Imperial de Potosí, in Upper Peru (now Bolivia).

Arequipa soon became the center of all commerce between Lima and these regions. The discovery and exploitation of the Caylloma silver deposits in the early seventeenth century and cultivation of wheat, corn, and grapes all contributed to the region's economic growth.

The city retains the Colonial style of its founding, which gives it a very special charm. Its first

View of Misti from Sabandía.

buildings were the Cathedral, the town hall, the old Bolognesi bridge, the prison, a chapel, the hospital, the slaughterhouse, several businesses, and the convent of Santa Catalina. After Peru gained its independence in 1824, many British concerns set up shop in Arequipa to market the lamb, alpaca and vicuña wool transported by llama from the interior.

From then on, the city became the principal center for gathering and shipping wool to England via the Port of Mollendo. Some local families, primarily Britishers whose second generations adopted Peruvian citizenship, amassed enormous fortunes. From this period survive numerous British surnames and stately mansions.

Arequipa continues to be the world center of the alpaca wool textile industry. It is the second most important city in Peru, after Lima, and the primary commercial, industrial, and cultural center for the southern part of the country. It has absorbed many immigrants from Puno and Ayacucho, regions desolated by drought and violence during the 1980s.

Regionalists to a fault, its inhabitants (known as *Characatos*) are so independent from the rest of Peru that they offer visitors passports to the «Independent Republic of Arequipa»... With its eternally blue sky, delightful sunshine, and green countryside, Arequipa is without a doubt one of Peru's most beautiful cities. It also has an extraordinary gastronomic heritage; do not fail to try some of its exquisite dishes in traditional restaurants called *picanterías*.

Local Dishes

DE CHUPES Y CAMARONES

«It is as if a painter created it for the delight other painters.» With these words, Adán Felipe Mejía —a renowned Peruvian journalist at the turn of the century— praised *chupe de camarones*, one of Arequipa's most representative dishes. «It is finely, moderately, affectionately rose in color,» continued Mejía, in a verse devoted exclusively to the virtues of this regional dish. The people of Arequipa are ardent fans of the *camarones* or crayfish that abound in their rivers (especially the Ocoña and the Majes) and prepare it in thousands of ways: grilled, steamed, braised in *ocopa*, in *cauchi*, and other delectable dishes. It is no surprise that experts rate the cuisine of Arequipa as the best mix of the Spanish and the local, indigenous, culinary traditions.

Entrées
- Cuy chactado: flattened, panfried guinea pig.
- Escribano: salad of potatoes, rocoto, vinegar, oil, tomato, and parsley.
- Ocopa a la arequipeña: boiled potatoes in a cheese, peanut, and *huacatay* herb sauce.
- Rocoto relleno: hot *rocoto* pepper stuffed with chopped beef, cheese and milk, served with potatoes.
- Solterito: salad of fresh cheese, broad beans, onions, olives and hot rocoto pepper.
- Zarza de patas: sliced onions, pigs' feet, and the same ingredients as *zarza de tolina*.
- Zarza de tolina or chanque: sliced onions with broad beans, rocoto, tomato, corn, cilantro, parsley, oregano, and *tolina* or *chanque* (similar to abalone).

Soups
- Chupe de camarones: crayfish chowder.
- Pebre: soup of lamb, beef, dried mutton, *chuño* (freeze-dried potato), potatoes, garbanzo beans, and rice.

Main Dishes
- Adobe arequipeño: pork stewed with *chicha* (fermented corn punch) and spices in a clay pot.

Desserts
- Queso helado: ice milk with cinnamon and vanilla.
- Sweets, jellies, and juices made from the Arequipa papaya.

Festivals

The main festival in Arequipa is the anniversary of its founding, celebrated on the 15th of August. Celebrations last an entire week and include cultural events, serenades, fireworks, and float parades. The week of Arequipa is brought to a close with traditional bullfights.

A bullfight at Huasacache.

Other festivals celebrated in Arequipa and its surroundings are: the feast of the Virgen de la Candelaria in the district of Cayma (February 2); the feast and pilgrimage of the Virgen de Chapi (May 1); the festival of the Characato, with bull runs and cockfights (June 24); the feasts of the Virgen de Carmen (July 14-17); of the Virgen de la Merced (September 8); and of the Virgen del Rosario, celebrated in the district of Yanahuara on October 8.

Folkcrafts

Among Arequipa's handicrafts are the lovely textiles of alpaca wool, considered one of the world's finest wools. Sweaters, shawls, and scarves can all be obtained in Arequipa. You can also find attractive objects in wrought iron, hammered copper, and silver or silverplate. *Sillar* is also worked, as is embossed leather. For antique lovers, Arequipa contains numerous antique shops.

Points of Interest in the City

Traditional Locales

- *Yanahuara:* a picturesque district perched on a hill overlooking the city. Its name means 'black trousers' in Quechua. It resembles Seville, with its narrow streets, Colonial façades and workshops. We recommend a stroll through this district to the small plaza or *plazuela* of Yanahuara, with its arches of sillar framing one of the best views of the city. Also worth visiting is the church of San Juan Bautista which dates from

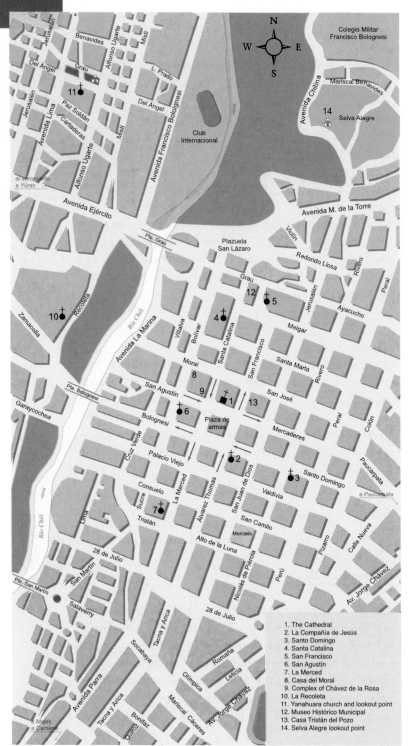

1. The Cathedral
2. La Compañía de Jesús
3. Santo Domingo
4. Santa Catalina
5. San Francisco
6. San Agustín
7. La Merced
8. Casa del Moral
9. Complex of Chávez de la Rosa
10. La Recoleta
11. Yanahuara church and lookout point
12. Museo Histórico Municipal
13. Casa Tristán del Pozo
14. Selva Alegre lookout point

AREQUIPA CITY MAP

1750. The façade of this church is one of the most beautiful examples of the *mestizo* style of decoration, for the profusion and quality of its relief work, which shows carved figures in profile and cherubim wearing crowns of feathers, a distinctly pre-Hispanic motif.

- *Cayma:* an historical district of Arequipa, accessed through Yanahuara. It has a beautiful church, San Miguel Arcángel, which dates from 1739. The doorway to this church, lavishly decorated, incorporates singular imagery; such as women carrying baskets of fruit on their heads, which recall the indigenous women who brought

Church of San Juan Bautista, Yanahuara.

their offerings to the church. Interesting paintings decorate its interior, such as those by Jacinto de Carbajal (1780), narrating the miracles of the Virgin during earthquakes, and the eighteenth-century sculpture of the Virgen de la Candelaria, patron of the district. To one side of the church sits the parsonage, where Simón Bolívar (1783–1830) stayed when he passed through Arequipa.

Churches

- *The Cathedral*, Plaza de Armas: the construction of this church began in 1544. In the mid-seventeenth century, a second building was raised, after the first was destroyed in a series of earthquakes. In 1844 the second building was destroyed by fire, and the current one was built. It is the prime example of nineteenth-century religious architecture in Peru. The Cathedral is predominantly in the Neoclassic style, with three naves, enormous columns, a great Belgian organ and a French neo-Gothic pulpit. It possesses splendid treasures of gold and silverwork, such as two monstrances of gold and precious stones.
    Visits during Mass..
- *Santa Catalina*, Santa Catalina 501: one of the most beautiful convents in Peru, founded in 1580 to shelter a select group of the religious order. It is a veritable Colonial small town made up of houses for the nuns and their servants, cloisters, plazas and narrow streets, kitchens, refectory and laundry, as well as

The Santa Catalina convent.

Church of La Compañía.

Arches of *sillar* in the cloisters of La Compañía.

the church with its single nave, cupola, and square tower. It houses a collection of paintings of the Cusco school and of the Zurbaranesque style. Its architecture has perfectly preserved the Colonial atmosphere.

Visiting hours: daily, 9am to 4pm.

• *La Compañía de Jesús*, General Morán 118, Plaza de Armas: a magnificent church that has been rebuilt several times, although its principal construction dates from the seventeenth century. With its three naves and cupola, the central attraction is the extraordinary work of the main façade, considered the best example of the *mestizo* style in Arequipa. Its lateral façade was carved by the Spaniard Simón de Barrientos in 1654 and its tympanum, with its image of Santiago Matamoros, or St. James the Moorslayer, was carved by a native artist. It has the best Baroque altarpieces of Arequipa, a beautiful pulpit, four paintings by the great Mannerist painter Bernardo Bitti (c.1550–1610), others from the seventeenth century attributed to Diego de la Puente, and many from the Cusco school. Outstanding sculptures include a sixteenth-century San Sebastián by Diego Rodríguez, a crucifixion attributed to the seventeenth-century Sevillan Gaspar de la Cueva, and effigies of Jesuit saints. The ancient vestry is particularly beautiful, with its cupola and walls covered in murals that recall the jungle of Paraguay. The ancient Jesuit seminary is famous for its principal cloister with its arches richly carved in the *mestizo* style.

Visiting hours: daily, 9 to 11:30am, and 3 to 5:30pm.

• *San Francisco*, Plaza San Francisco: located in an attractive plazuela, the church and convent of San Francisco constitute one of the most beautiful architectural complexes in the city. It was designed by Gaspar Báez in 1569; the lateral naves were added in the seventeenth century. Built in the shape of the Latin cross, it has a classic brick entryway; a quadrangular tower and a cupola. The sillar reliefwork of the arch in the choirloft is lovely, as is the splendid pulpit. The convent has a large central patio bordered by pillared arches. Next door to San Francisco is the church of the Tercera Orden Franciscana, or Third Franciscan Order, raised in 1777. It possesses a magnificent façade with bas-reliefs of Santa Clara and San Francisco de Asís, grapevines, wolves and rosettes and other decorative elements.

Visiting hours: daily, 9am to noon, and 3 to 6pm.

- *Santo Domingo,* corner of Santo Domingo and Piérola: built at the end of the seventeenth century, the church and convent of Santo Domingo are fine examples of Baroque architecture in the *mestizo* style. The façade dedicated to San Pablo is the oldest *mestizo*-style façade in the city, from about 1677–1680. The church contains excellent sculpture, such as a crucifix dating from the seventeenth century, carved from wood. A highlight in the convent are the principal cloisters, dating from 1734, as well as notable paintings and polychrome reliefwork.

Santo Domingo Church.

Visits during Mass.

- *La Merced*, La Merced, block three: rebuilt several times after various earthquakes, this church of three naves and cupola possesses an extraordinary wood sculpture of Nuestra Señora del Consuelo (Our Lady of Solace) by the sixteenth-century Sevillan Gaspar del Águila and two beautiful statues of Christ crucified from the eighteenth century. The convent contains stately arched cloisters, beautiful paintings, a valuable library, and in its main hall, a unique, Gothic, vaulted and ribbed ceiling.

Visits during Mass.

- *San Agustín*, corner of San Agustín and Sucre: the building of this church was begun in 1576. Its façade, completed in the first half of the eighteenth century, and that of La Compañía de Jesús are some of the most splendid examples of *mestizo* expression. Preserved in the sacristy is a cupola carved with Baroque and Moorish bas-reliefs.

Visits during Mass.

- *La Recoleta*, Recoleta 117: Franciscan convent built in 1648. It possesses beautiful cloisters, a library of more than 18 000 books

MESTIZO ARCHITECTURE

In the late 17th century, a style of architectural decoration was born in Arequipa and its influence spread as far as Lake Titicaca and even into Upper Peru (now Bolivia). This style, known as *mestizo*, freely mixed papayas, parrots and other indigenous designs with the Western motifs of shells and mermaids Its building material was predominantly *sillar*. The *mestizo* style was one of the most original contributions to architecture from the American Colonies. The profuse decorations on many church façades in Arequipa are manifestations of this style.

(among them American incunabula), wood and ivory sculptures, paintings of the Cusco school, and a collection of jungle objects acquired by missionaries.

Visiting hours: Mon-Sat, 9am to noon, and 3 to 5pm.

Historical Homes and Buildings

- *Casa del Moral*, Moral 318: one of the most enchanting examples of the eighteenth-century *mestizo* style. It has a splendid façade with a richly decorated tympanum, barred windows, and an ample patio with an ancient mulberry tree, which gave the house and the street their name.
- *Casa Iriberry, or Arróspide*, Santa Catalina: this *sillar* manor house is nicknamed «Arequipa's talking house» for the numerous messages over its doorways. One of them reads, in old Spanish, «This house was made in the year 1743. I ask God that he who would live in it, recite an Our Father.»
- *Casa Goyeneche*, La Merced 301: This house in the Neoclassic style possesses a sober façade noteworthy for the size of the ecclesiastical coat-of-arms of Arequipa's bishop José Sebastián Goyeneche (1784–1872). It contains a large patio with large, attractive windows, a seventeenth-century sculpture of *Ecce Homo* linked to the Andalusian school of that century, and a good collection of oil paintings in the Cusco style. It is currently a branch of the Banco Central de Reserva.

  Visiting hours: Mon-Fri, 9:15am to 3pm.
- *Casa Bustamante*, La Merced, block one: notable showpiece of Arequipa architecture of the second half of the seventeenth century. Enlarged in 1760 and again in 1797, it possesses a simple façade which turns into a wide entryway, an attractive patio with sillar doorways, and large windows barred in wrought iron.
- *Casa Tristán del Pozo*, San Francisco 108: this large mansion,

finished in 1738, has been a seminary, the archbishop's palace, a school, and finally a commercial establishment. It is distinguished by its imposing façade, with its tympanum in the shape of a candelabra of cantuta flowers and monograms of the Holy Family. Currently a branch of the Banco Continental.

Visits during office hours.

Museums

- *Museo Histórico Municipal,* Plaza San Francisco: contains paintings by Arequipa artist Jorge Vinatea Reinoso (1900–1931), an interesting collection of photographs, ancient plans of the city, and an area dedicated to archeology.

  Visiting hours: Mon-Fri, 8am to 5pm.
- *Museo Santuarios Andinos Universidad Católica Santa María-CERVESUR,* Santa Catalina n/n: collection of Stone Age pieces, ceramics, and mummified remains. A refrigerated display case displays the remains of «Juanita,» Maiden of Ampato, the perfectly preserved mummy of a 14-year-old Inca girl discovered in 1995 on the summit of Mount Ampato.

  Visiting hours: Mon-Fri, 9am to 1pm, and 3 to 7pm.

«Juanita», Maiden of Ampato.

Excursions

Sabandía

2 250M / 7 382FT

District 8km SE of the city center, in the Arequipa countryside, where a flour mill built in 1621 can be seen (today it is a museum). The mill is powered by the neighboring waterfall and is surrounded by bucolic countryside, making this excursion very pleasant.

Two kilometers beyond the mill is Paucarpata, an area of extensive terracing, from which you can

Tinajones in Sabandía.

The Sabandía mill.

get a very good view of the Misti volcano. Highly recommended.

Visits to the mill: daily, 9am to 5pm.

Mansión del Fundador (Huasacache)

2 250M / 7 382FT   )

The Mansión del Fundador.

Ancient hacienda 6,5km from Arequipa, which belonged to the city's founder, Garci Manuel de Carbajal. At the end of the sixteenth century it was sold to the Jesuits, who used it as a retreat center, and in the eighteenth century it passed to the Goyeneche family, who kept it until 1947. This manor house possesses a beautiful church and is fully restored. Do not fail to visit.

Visiting hours: daily, 9am to 5pm.

Baños Termomedicinales de Jesús

2 250M / 7 546FT   )

6km E of Arequipa. From these hot spring baths, with rustic facilities, you can obtain a panoramic view of the city and surrounding countryside. Nearby are the baths at Yura hot springs (30km on the paved highway to the Colca Canyon), and at the Socosani hot springs (7km from Yura).

Churajón

2 900M / 9 514FT)

One of the largest areas of pre-Inca agricultural terracing in the region; drive 50km N of Arequipa on the La Pulpera packed dirt road, then hike 2h. This place also contains burial constructions called chullpas and the remains of a small town. Hire a guide in Arequipa for this excursion.

Reserva Nacional de Salinas y Aguada Blanca

3 700M / 12 139FT ON AVERAGE ◯

A protected cultural area 35km NW of the city on packed dirt road. With an area of 366 936 hectares located in the departments of both Arequipa and Moquegua, this reserve contains the beautiful bosque de piedras (stone forest) of Sumbay and Lake Salinas (70km and 80km from Arequipa, respectively). This is a land of volcanoes, deep canyons and hot springs, inhabited by the condor *(Vultur gryphus)*, the vicuña *(Vicugna vicugna)* and the flamingo, or parihuan *(Phoenicopterus spp.)*. It was created with the aim of conserving flora and fauna, along with the beautiful high Andean landscapes, in particular their singular geological formations, and to foment the rational use of their renewable resources, including the South American camelids. Access to the reserve is easy by following any of the routes which lead to the Colca Canyon (via Charcani, Yura, or Chiguata). There is no lodging in this area, but camping is allowed. If you decide to camp, bring proper equipment, as the nights are very cold. Restaurants along the way are simple.

The stone forest
at Sumbay..

Vicuñas in Salinas
y Aguada Blanca.

El Misti

5 821M / 19 098FT ◯ ▶

Guardian of the city and, without a doubt, the symbol of the people of Arequipa. This volcano is relatively easy to climb although the sand and ash of its slopes make walking an effort. The climb takes some ten hours and is done in two stages, the

The Arequipa countryside.

first to the base camp at Nido de las Águilas (eagles' nest), where there is a rustic cabin in which to spend the night. It is best to make the climb between May and November. Take lots of warm clothing, food, and plenty of water.

Information: Club de Montañismo (Romaña 206), or contac guides Max Arce (Tel 23 3697) or Guillermo Portocarrero (Tel 23 4966).

Valle de los Volcanes
5 821M / 19 098FT

377km (10 or 12 hours) NE of Arequipa via a packed dirt road in fair condition. This place is known as «Vulcan's Playground» for its many (about 80) volcanic cones. For some 80km, the Andagua River flows through this valley, located on the slopes of the Coropuna volcano (Peru's highest, at 6 425m, or 21 080ft). Downstream, on the outskirts of the town of Andagua (3 600m, or 11 812 ft), the river disappears for 17km, flowing underground between lakes Chachas and Mamachocho, before joining the Colca River. In Andagua there are hostels and simple restaurants.

Cotahuasi Canyon and Valley
2 645M / 8 678FT

A church in Cotahuasi.

375km NW of Arequipa via packed dirt road, passing through the towns of Sihuas, Corire, Aplao and Chuquibamba at the foot of the imposing Coropuna volcano (6 425m, or 21 080ft), to the town of Cotahuasi (2 683m, or 8 803ft). The canyon, formed by the erosive action of the Cotahuasi River as it passes through the Solimana range, is the deepest in the world (3 354m, or 11 004ft), even deeper than the Colca Canyon. Among the attractions of this valley are the Sipia waterfalls (a two-hour walk from the town of Alca); the canyon of Las Maravillas (the marvels), nestled between the snow-capped peaks of Solimana (6 117m, or 20 070ft) and Sarasara (6 000m, or 19 686ft); the hot springs at Lucho,

Lucha, and Antabamba; Lake Huanzococha, the Inca terracing at Huaynacotas and Pampamarca, and the ruins at Marpa. There are also professionals in Arequipa who organize and guide rafting expeditions on the river *(see Useful Facts, p. 127)*. Tourist services are scarce in the valley.

This and the difficulty of access makes this an excursion for adventurers only.

Toro Muerto

1 200M / 3 937 FT

In the Majes River valley, 165km W of Arequipa by packed dirt road. This is a large, desert plain with over 500 pre-Hispanic rock carvings depict-

The Cotahuasi Valley.

ing warriors, dancers, and stylized animals (llamas, condors, alpacas, and pumas). This excursion can be done on the return trip from the Colca Canyon to Arequipa (via Cabanaconde, Huambo, and Majes). There are hostels and simple restaurants in Corire, the town closest to the petroglyphs. Don't forget to try the prawns!

Colca Valley

See p. 155.

Hotels

Hotel Libertador *(ex Hotel de Turistas)* ★★★★★
Plaza Bolívar n/n, Selva Alegre. Tel 21 5110. US$ 100
hotel@libertador.com.pe

Hotel Lago Resort ★★★★
Road towards the Molino n/n, Sabandía. Tel 44 8383.
ellago@terra.com.pe

Portal Hotel ★★★★
Portal de Flores 116, plaza de armas, Cercado. US$ 80
Tel 21 5530. Fax 23 4374.
Reserva@portalhotel.com.pe

La Posada del Puente ★★★
Nearby Grau bridge and Av. Bolognesi 101,

Yanahuara. Tel 25 3132. Fax 25 3576. US$ 70

hotel@posadadelpuente.com

★★★ Maison d'Elise

Av. Bolognesi 104, Yanahuara. Tel 25 6185. Fax 27 1935.

mdelisehotel@mail.interplace.com.pe

★★★ El Conquistador

Mercaderes 409, Cercado. Tel 21 2916. Fax 21 8987.

★★★ La Plazuela

Plaza Juan Manuel Polar 105, Vallecito. Tel 22 2624.
Fax 23 4626

casagrande@viabcp.com.pe

★★★ Hostal Casa Grande

Luna Pizarro 202, Vallecito. Telefax 21 4000. US$ 55

casagrande@viabcp.com.pe

★★★ Arequipa Suites

Urb. Magisterial N.º 2, Mz. A-0, Umacollo. US$ 60
Tel 25 2623. Fax 25 2820.

aqpparthotel@mismail.com

★★★ Hotel La Posada del Monasterio

Santa Catalina 300, Cercado. Telefax 28 3076. US$ 60

★★★ Hotel A'Grada SRL

Portal San Agustín 113-A, Cercado. US$ 50
Tel 21 9859. Fax 23 7334.

★★★ Hostal La Plazuela

Plaza Juan Manuel Polar 103, Vallecito. Tel 22 2624.
Fax 23 4626. US$ 50

★★★ La Fontana Hotel

Jerusalén 202, Cercado. Tel 23 4161. Fax 23 4171. US$ 45

lafontana@terra.com.pe

★★★ Hotel Jerusalén

Jerusalén 601, Cercado. Tel 24 4441/81. Fax 28 7420.

jerusalem@terra.com.pe

★★★ Hostal Arequipa Inn

Rivero 412, Cercado. Tel 24 1711. Fax 22 9188. US$ 35

★★★ Hostal Residencial Las Mercedes

Corner Av. La Marina and Consuelo, Cercado. US$ 35
Tel 21 3601.

★★★ La Casa de mi Abuela

Jerusalén 606, Cercado. Tel 24 1206. Fax 24 2761.

Hostal Casa Kolping Yanahuara ★★★
León Velarde 406, Yanahuara. Tel 25 3748.
Reservations Lima Tel 461 6184. US$ 30
Hostal Fernández ★★★
Quezada 106, Yanahuara. Tel 25 4152. Fax 27 2932.

RATES ARE APPROXIMATE AND, UNLESS OTHERWISE NOTED,
ARE FOR DOUBLE OCCUPANCY.

Restaurants

Local and International Cuisine

La Posada del Puente ✔
Av. Bolognesi 101, Yanahuara.
La Chopería ✔
San José 103, Cerro Colorado.
El Cerrojo ✔
Portal de San Agustín 111-A, plaza de armas, Cercado.
Las Quenas ✔
Santa Catalina 215, Cercado.
El Dólar ✔
San Juan de Dios 106.
André de París (El Emperador) ✔
Santa Catalina 207, Cercado.
Harumi ✔
San José 216.
La Bóveda ✔
Portal de San Agustín 129, Cercado.

Pizzas • Pasta

Pizzería San Antonio ✔
Jesrusalén 222, Cercado.
Pizzería Los Leños ✔
Jerusalén 407, Cercado.
Trattoria Gianni's ✔
San Francisco 304, Cercado.
Pizza Presto ✔
Gral. Morán 108, Cercado.

Grills

✔ Mediterráneo Chicken

    Av. El Ejército s/n, C. C. Cayma.

✔ El Pollo Real

    Av. El Ejército 705, Yanahuara.

✔ Shuler Pollería

    Av. España 225, Selva Alegre.

Vegetarian Food

✔ Govinda

    Jerusalén 500-A, Cercado.

Picanterías *(serving typical Arequipa food)*

✔ Sol de Mayo

    Jerusalén 207, Yanahuara.

✔ La Fonda del Sol

    Av. Aviación 602.

✔ Los Guisos Turísticos

    Av. Pizarro 111, Lambramani, Paucarpata.

✔ La Cantarilla

    Calle Tahuaycani 106-108, Sachaca.

✔ La Cau Cau II

    Tronchadero 404, Yanahuara.

✔ Tradición Arequipeña

    Av. Dolores 111, Paucarpata.

✔ Mi Ranchito

    Paucarpata.

◆ Pubs • Cafes

Café Bóveda

◆   Portal San Agustín 129. Cercado.

La Empanadita

    Gral. Morán 121, Cercado.

Useful Facts

☎

Basic information

IPERÚ:
Information and Assistance for Tourists.
   Portal de la Municipalidad 110, plaza de armas.   22 1228
   Open: Mon-Fri 8:30 to 19:30 h.
   iperuarequipa@promperu.gob.pe

Rodríguez Ballón Airport
   Lobby.   44 4564
   Open: Mon-Fri 8:30 to 18:30 h.
   iperuarequipaapto@promperu.gob.pe

Tourism Police Aid   20 1258

Instituto Nacional de Cultura
   Alameda San Lázazro 120, Cercado.   21 3171
   Open: Mon-Fri 8:30 to 18:30 h.

Railway Station PERÚRAIL:
   Av. Tacna y Arica 206.   21 5350
                       Fax 22 2032

Travel Agencies

Cusipata: Jerusalén 408-A, Cercado.   20 3966
gvellutino@terra.com.pe

Handicraft Shops

Alpaca 21: Jerusalén 115, Cercado.   21 3425
El Tumi: Zela 214, Cercado.   23 4532
La Uruguaya: Mercaderes 133, Cercado.   21 5861
Artesanías del Perú: Gral. Morán 120.   21 2066
L. Paulet-Joyas Peruanas:
   Cloisters at La Compañía, Cercado.

Post Office: Moral 118, Cercado.   21 5245
Clínica Arequipa S.A.:
   Nearby Grau bridge and Av. Bolognesi, Yanahuara.   25 3424

CONTINUE ➡

AREA CODE 54

☎

Botica Cosmo: Puente Bolognesi 113, Cercado.	21 1581
Farmacia Americana: Portal de San Agustín 103, plaza de armas, Cercado.	21 1071
InkaFarma: Mercaderes 214.	20 4685

Taxi Service

Taxi Seguro	45 0250
Fono Tour	46 3346

Car Rental

Localiza Rent a Car: Villa Hermoza 803, Cerro Colorado	25 2499
Avis G&B Rent a Car: Palacio Viejo 214.	28 2519
Fax	21 2123

Ayacucho

2 746 M / 9 009FT
105 900 POP.
VIA PISCO 545 KM
VIA HUANCAYO 560 KM
S OF LIMA

The city of Ayacucho (in Quechua, 'corner of the dead') is located in south-central Peru, in the Huatata River valley, a tributary of the Mantaro River. Capital of the department of the same name, Ayacucho is known as «the city of churches». This is due to its thirty-three stone churches which, with their Renaissance, Mannerist, and Baroque façades, compete in beauty and give the city a very special feel. The population is primarily *mestizo*, or mixed race, and more than half speak Quechua, in a very soft and expressive dialect. Ayacucho is located in a pre-

P. 82

P. 78

ROUTE MAP

Huanta villagers celebrate.

dominantly agricultural department, even though irrigation is highly dependent on the rains.

The region of Ayacucho was populated early on by the first hunters and gatherers who reached the Andes from the north. Remains of Stone Age tools, humans and the animals they hunted, found in some of the region's caves (such as at Pikimachay) are evidence of this occupation. In the early centuries of our era the Warpa culture flourished and built many terraces and settlements in the area. Nonetheless, it was the Wari culture that achieved the greatest development in the region. At its

Pleasant climate, sunny most of the year, with cold nights (especially from May to August) and a yearly mean temperature of 17°C (63°F). Rainy season from December to March.

height (around AD 600), the Wari influence was felt from Piura and Cajamarca in the north to Cusco and Tacna in the south. The capital of this powerful state, the ancient city of Wari, is just a few kilometers from Ayacucho.

Around AD 800, the Wari culture declined and the local peoples again broke up into small feudal states. At the beginning of the fifteenth century one of these peoples, the Chanca, became part of the legend of the founding of the Inca empire. According to the best-known story, the Tawantinsuyo (the Inca's name for their empire) was formed after the Chanca chiefs were defeated by the Inca Pachacútec, who then established his local political and administrative center at Vilcashuamán, on the banks of the Pampas River (some four hours from Ayacucho). Because of their traditional enmity with the Incas, the Chancas allied with the Spanish in their conquest of Peru.

A downtown street.

In 1539, Francisco Pizarro founded the city of Ayacucho under the name of San Juan de la Frontera de Huamanga. This was a strategic move, as this area bordered the territories controlled beginning in 1536 by the rebel Incas at Vilcabamba (NW of Cusco). In 1542, a plain outside the city limits was the site of the famous battle of Chupas.

It was here that the first governor of Peru, Cristóbal Vaca de Castro, seeking to put an end to the in-fighting between the conquistadors following the death of Francisco Pizarro, defeated Diego de Almagro the Younger.

Once the rebels at Vilcabamba were defeated, Ayacucho gained enormous economic and cultural importance. On the one hand, it was located at the midpoint along the highland route that connected Lima, Jauja, Cusco, and Potosí (today in Bolivia). On the other, it was located close to the mines of Santa Bárbara, and became the resi-

The feast of *Señalacuy*.

dence of the affluent families who exploited the mercury mines there. In the seventeenth century, Ayacucho possessed an important textile industry, was the site of a bishopric, had painting studios —on a par with those in Lima and Cusco— that supplied works to both religious orders and secular patrons, and had a university (San Cristóbal de Huamanga). All of this made it one of the most important cities in the Peruvian Viceroyalty.

Nonetheless, Ayacucho played a key part in Peruvian independence. On the outskirts of this city patriots fought royal troops in the celebrated battle of Ayacucho in 1824, sealing the independence of South America. In this glorious confrontation, the patriots under the command of General Antonio José de Sucre defeated the royalists commanded by the viceroy himself, José de la Serna.

After long years of crisis which culminated in the instability and violence of the 1980s, Ayacucho once again became a land of peace and hope. With its perpetually blue sky, this city continually surprises the visitor with its Colonial flavor. Ayacucho is known as the Peruvian capital of handicrafts: small towns, such as Sarhua, have seen their art travel the world over. It is also the land of distinguished guitarists.

We highly recommend a visit here. The best time to go is

THE SCISSORS DANCE

One of the most characteristic dances of the southern Andes is the *danza de las tijeras*, performed to the music of a violin, a harp and curious metal instruments resembling scissors, that the dancers themselves «play.» The ritual performance is a lengthy competition in which the dancer with the most skill and endurance wins. The winner is then believed to be under the protection of the *wamani* (or *apu*), an Andean deity or spirit of the mountain.

during Holy Week, with one caveat for this period: lodging is scarce, so make reservations ahead of time.

Local Dishes

Entrées
- Hapchi: salad of tender potatoes with fresh *cachipa* cheese, yellow *ají* pepper, oil, and minced onion.
- Tecte or picante: broad beans stewed with peas, *ají*, garlic, fresh cheese, eggs, and milk.

Soups
- Mondongo: soup of entrails, beef, corn, and the savory *huacatay* herb.
- Patachi: wheat soup with legumes, bacon, and beef.
- Pushla: soup of ground barley, herbs, eggs, and milk.

Main Dishes
- Adobo ayacuchano: beef stewed with *ají* and spices.
- Cuy: guinea pig, spicy or flattened and pan-fried.
- Puca picante: pork cracklings in peanut sauce with *ají colorado*, beets, and ground *achiote,* or annato.

Desserts
- Llipta: sweet corn pudding with milk.

Celebrating Holy Week.

Festivals

Of all the festivals celebrated in Ayacucho, Holy Week (March or April) is undoubtedly the most spectacular and receptive. During an entire week, all regular activity in the city comes to a standstill. Ayacucho becomes a city of flower-carpeted streets, solemn masses, processions and fireworks. Images depicting various scenes of the Passion of Christ emerge from the principal churches of the city. The famous livestock and trade fair of Acuchimay is held on Easter Saturday, and on the morning of Easter Sunday the holy procession issues

from the Cathedral, circles the Plaza de Armas once amid total silence, and reenters the church, marking the end of the festivities. We recommend watching the festivities from the Plaza de Armas and, if possible, view them from one of the balconies.

A Holy Week musical group.

Other important festivals in the Ayacucho region: Carnival (February); the Festival de la Tuna y la Cochinilla, or Prickly Pear and Cochineal, from which carmine dye is extracted (February 15-17); the Señalacuy, or branding of livestock, celebrated throughout the region with joyful dance and song (July 26); the water festival, with dancing to harps and violins (August or September); the feast of El Señor de Maynay in Huanta (September 18); and the Andean Christmas in Ayacucho, an excellent ooportunity to contemplate the allegorical works that artisans create for the churches of their districts.

Folkcrafts

Ayacucho is a land of renowned artisans. The famous *retablos*, or holy scenes originated from the double-doored, portable altars first made from the alabaster of Huamanga. Later they were made of plaster, and today they are fashioned from a mix of plaster and potato flour.

An Ayacucho *retablo*.

Handmade candles.

Retablos traditionally have two sections: the upper level with sacred images and the lower with scenes from daily life. They are painted in bright colors, then varnished. You can find them in all sizes and prices.

Other important crafts of Ayacucho are the famous carvings in Huamanga stone; the ceramic churches, which are typically made in Quinua and which local folk place on their roofs for good luck or spiritual protection; and miniature ceramic bulls. Also well-known are the works in embossed leather, the tin candelabra and decorated crosses, the carved gourds, the horns engraved with country scenes, and the rugs and weavings in alpaca wool dyed with natural colorings such as *añil*, *ayrampo*, *chilco*, and *aliso*.

Especially noteworthy are the famous painted beams of Sarhua, named after the town where the tradition of adorning the houses of newlyweds with these decorated boards originated. These smoothly finished wooden beams are painted with traditional motifs and daily scenes.

A good place to acquire these handicrafts and view their making is in the city district of Santa Ana. Outside of the city, try the town of Quinua.

Points of Interest in the City

Traditional Locales

Plaza de Armas and Cathedral.

- *Plaza de Armas*: also known as Plaza Sucre to the locals, this plaza is one of the largest and most beautiful in the country. Four streets lead into it and its stately stone arches flank the cathedral, the town hall, the prefecture, the main offices of the University of Huamanga, and other Colonial buildings.
- *Barrio Santa Ana*: known as the district of weavers, this *barrio* is located in the upper part of the city. It is famous for its beautifully colored shawls, ponchos, and rugs and for its Huamanga stone carvings. A highlight is the Baroque church of Santa Ana de los Indios with its handsome altar of embossed silver.

Churches

- *The Cathedral*, Portal Municipal, Plaza de Armas: built between 1615 and 1672, this church's façade is of a style midway between Renaissance and Baroque. Inside are sixteen high vaults and a proportionate cupola.

  Its main altar is a rare piece of work, complete with paintings from the late Renaissance, a splendid altar hanging, gradins

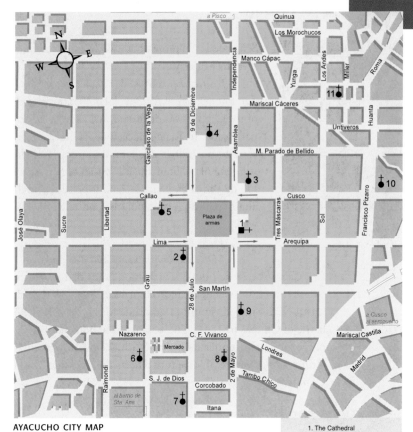

AYACUCHO CITY MAP

1. The Cathedral
2. La Compañía de Jesús
3. San Agustín
4. Santo Domingo
5. San Francisco de Paula
6. Santa Clara
7. San Juan de Dios
8. San Francisco de Asís
9. La Merced
10. La Amargura
11. La Magdalena

or shelves for candlesticks, and a silver tabernacle. The Baroque side altars rival the main altar in elegance and wealth with their magnificent carvings covered in gold leaf; the pulpit, Baroque as well, is one of the most notable in the city. Beautiful paintings and statues complete the decoration of this church.

Visiting hours: Mon-Sat, 5:30 to 7pm; Sunday mornings.

• *La Compañía de Jesús*, 28 de Julio, block one: built in the seventeenth century, its austere façade of brick and red stone contrasts with the decor of its eighteenth-century towers, with their nine rows of cut stone depicting four stylized leaves. To one side is the notable Renaissance doorway, in red stone, of the old Jesuit seminary, with its plateresque decoration that includes lion and gryphon heads. The church holds a painting by the master Diego de la Puente and a sculpture of El

Church of La Compañía.

Señor de la Columna, both works from the mid-seventeenth century.

Visiting hours: Mon-Sat, 9am to noon.

- *San Francisco de Asís*, 28 de Julio 305: this church of three naves was dedicated in 1723. Its principal façade, in Renaissance style, is quite attractive, with carvings depicting the miracle of the stigmata of St. Francis, and statues of San Antonio de Padua and Santa Clara. It possesses lovely altars, paintings and polychrome reliefwork as well.

Visits by appointment only,
Mon-Sat, 9am to noon, and 3 to 5pm.

- *San Cristóbal*, 28 de Julio 651: tradition holds that this is the oldest church in Ayacucho and that it was Cristóbal Vaca de Castro who ordered it built in gratitude for his victory at the battle of Chupas in 1542. Combatants from both sides of the battle are buried under its floors. With a single tower, small atrium and one nave, its austerity reflects the war times of the Conquest.

Visits by appointment only.

Church of Santo Domingo.

- *Santo Domingo*, 9 de Diciembre: this seventeenth-century church is unusual because it has a construction or narthex projecting from the main façade. The one-nave church, designed in the shape of the Latin cross, possesses a magnificent cupola, handsome Baroque altars and a beautiful pulpit. The tympanum of the convent's portal is carved in Spanish and native motifs.

Visiting hours: Mon-Sat, 5:30 to 7pm.

- *Santa Clara*, Grau, block three, central market: begun at the end of the sixteenth century, this church has two notable Renaissance-style entryways and a single tower of two belfries. Worth noting are its main altar, the sculpture of Nuestro Señor de la Caída, the carved wooden gate of the choirloft and the exceptional Moorish craftsmanship of the painted wood presbytery, one of the few remaining examples in America. It has a notable 1752 painting of Jesus before the Sanhedrin, by the Cusco master Basílico Pacheco, and a Renaissance pulpit of carved cedar. Next door is the convent of the order of St. Clair, which dates from 1568 and is the second oldest in Peru.

Visiting hours: Mon-Sat, 6 to 7pm, by appointment only.

- *San Francisco de Paula*, corner of Callao and Garcilaso de la Vega: this one-nave church, shaped like a Latin cross, was finished in 1710. With its two towers and austere façade, its highlights are the Baroque altars, oil paintings of the life of the Virgin, a painted organ, and the splendid gold and silver monstrance and another one studded with diamonds.

  Visiting hours: Mon-Sat, 9am to noon, and 3 to 6pm;
  Sun, 8 to 10am.

- *Others:* Santa Teresa, which contains one of the most extraordinary Baroque altars in Peru; La Merced; San Juan de Dios, with notable oil paintings inspired by the work of the Flemish artist Peter Paul Rubens; San Agustín; San Juan Bautista; Pampa San Agustín; and La Magdalena.

Historical Homes and Buildings

- *Casa de la Viuda de Alcalá*, Portal Independencia, Plaza de Armas: handsome example of Colonial architecture. This historic home was the lodging of General Antonio José de Sucre after his victory at the battle of Ayacucho in 1824.

Overlooking the city.

- *Casona de la Universidad Nacional San Cristóbal de Huamanga*, Portal Independencia, Plaza de Armas: owned by Bishop Don Cristóbal de Castilla y Zamora, who founded the university there in 1667. Its wide patios and passageways, salons and arched portals, stone staircases and gallery overlooking the Plaza de Armas, all make it a beautiful example of Ayacucho architecture.

    Visiting hours: Mon-Fri, 7am to 8pm.

- *Casa del Marqués de la Totora*, Portal Unión, Plaza de Armas: possesses a stately stone doorway, lovely arches, stone walls made in the Inca style and raised in the sixteenth century, a patio with thick columns capped with carvings of zoomorphic figures, long staircases, and a large garden with an ancient fountain. Currently the Guamán Poma de Ayala school of fine arts.

    Visiting hours: Mon-Sat, 9am to 5pm.

- *Others:* the Casa del Municipio or town hall; the Casa del Canónigo, the former home of clergyman Manuel Frías; the Prefecture; the Casa del Marqués de Valdelirios; the Casa-Quinta La Tinajera, a country estate; and the Palacio del Marqués de Mozobamba are other buildings that give an aged appearance to this city of great architecture character.

Museums

- *Museo Andrés Avelino Cáceres, or Casona Vivanco*, 28 de Julio 508: a sober Colonial edifice administered by the military. It offers an interesting collection of paintings and testimony of the life of General Andrés Avelino Cáceres, who led the resistance during the War of the Pacific (1879–1883). The museum also contains a representative collection of Colonial paintings, presumably from the eighteenth century, most of them painted by indigenous or mestizo artists, and a magnificent grave stone carved in the shape of an armored, recumbent sixteenth-century warrior and originally found in La Dolorosa altar of the La Merced church.

    Visiting hours: Mon-Sat, 9am to noon, and 2 to 5pm.

THE LAST BATTLE

On December 9, 1824, the battle that sealed the independence of Peru and South America was fought on the Pampa de la Quinua. It began at nine in the morning when the royalists charged down Mount Condorcunca to engage the patriots camped at La Quinua. The combat lasted until one in the afternoon. That night, José de Canterac, acting for the injured Viceroy José de la Serna, signed the Surrender at Ayacucho, the document that ended Spain's rule in Peru and its other American colonies. In honor of this event, Simón Bolívar decreed that the department and the city of Huamanga were to be known as Ayacucho.

Excursions

Quinua

2 600M / 8 531FT)

A picturesque town of potters 32km (1 hour) E of Ayacucho via paved highway. Close by is the Pampa de Quinua, site of the glorious Battle of Ayacucho in 1824. A monument on the site commemorates the battle. Quinua has some simple restaurants but no lodgings.

Huanta

2 628M / 8 622FT)

Town 50km (1,5 hours) N of Ayacucho via paved highway. Huanta has always been a favorite spot for rest and recreation among the people of Aya-cucho and Huancavelica. Surrounded by moun-tain highlands and high rainforests, the city is tucked in a warm, fertile valley containing avo-cado, willow, and elderberry trees, and lovely manor houses. In comparison to Ayacucho, this area is

Huanta's Plaza de Armas.

very green, earning it the name «Garden of the Andes». Typical restaurants abound and there is some simple lodging. Ideal for a day trip.

Wari

2 850M / 9 351FT)

An archeological site 25km (1 hour) NE of Ayacucho via packed dirt road. This was the capital of the Wari state and one of the largest pre-Hispanic American cities. The characteristic aspects of this urban and ceremonial center are its trapezoidal, rectan-gular, and square enclosures, sometimes extending three stories underground, and its laboriously built, stone walls, some ex-tending over 100m. There are indications that the city was di-vided into districts housing specialized artisans. A visit here can be combined with the excursion to Huanta.

Church and Inca walls at Vilcashuamán.

Vilcashuamán

3 470 M / 11 385FT3 470 M / 11 385FT ○

A town and archeological site 110km (3 to 4 hours) SE of Aya-cucho via the packed dirt road to Andahuaylas. Its name in Quechua means 'sacred falcon.' Access here is via a dirt road (in poor condition) that climbs to Toccto and then descends to Condorcocha and the pampas of Sachabamba, ending in the Pampas River valley. Vilcashuamán was a Chanca administrative and religious center that studies suggest housed some 20 000 people. The town was captured by the Incas, and it was the Inca Pachacútec who had the largest buildings constructed. In the central plaza of the archeological site, also the center of town today, you can see that the church has an obvious Inca foundation. Across from the church is the ushno, or Inca ceremonial platform, with its stone seat for the governor. Services are basic in Vilcashuamán.

A stand of *puyas* in Titancayoc.

Titancayoc

3 500 M / 11 484FT ○ ◗

Enclave of the Raimondi cactus (*Puya raimondii*), the plant with the tallest flower stalk in the world, 94km (6 hours) S of Ayacucho. Its name derives from the enormous *puyas*, or titanccas, that grow in the area. To reach this spectacular place you must first travel to the town of Vischongo, and then follow a horsepath for two to three hours. Find a guide in Ayacucho who can help you hire pack animals. Ideal for the adventure lover.

Hotels

Ayacucho

Ayacucho Hotel Plaza *(ex Hotel de Turistas)* ★★★
9 de Diciembre 184, plaza de armas, Cercado.
Tel 81 4467. Fax 81 2314. US$ 60
Reservations Lima, Tel 261 0240.
hplaza@derramajae.org.pe

Hostal Marqués de Valdelirios ★★★
Alameda Bolognesi 720. Tel 81 4014.

Hostería Santa Rosa ★★
Lima 166.
Tel 81 2083. US$ 25

Hotel Yáñez ★★
Av. Mariscal Andrés A. Cáceres 1210.
Tel 81 4918. Fax 81 2464. US$ 20

Hostal Florida ★★
Cusco 310. Tel 81 2565. US$ 15
hostalflorida@terra.com.pe

Hostal Samary ★★
Callao 335. Tel 91 2442. US$ 10

Ciudadela Warpa Picchu
A 5 km. Carretera al Cusco.
verbist@terra.com.pe

Huanta

Hostal La Posada del Marqués ★
Av. Sáenz Peña 160. Tel 81 1022. US$ 25

Hostal Ambassador ★
Av. Mariscal Castilla 615. Tel 83 2294. US$ 15

RATES ARE APPROXIMATE AND, UNLESS OTHERWISE NOTED, ARE FOR DOUBLE OCCUPANCY.

Restaurants

- ✔ El Nino
  Jr. Salvador Cavero 124.
- ✔ La Casona
  Jr. Bellido 463.
- ✔ La Pileta (Hotel Santa Rosa)
  Lima 166.
- ✔ Tradición
  San Martín 406.
- ✔ El Retablo
  San Martín 446.
- ✔ Urpicha
  Jr. Londres 272.
- ✔ Morochucos
  Jr. 9 de Diciembre 265.

Useful Facts

AREA CODE **64**

☎

Tourist Information

IPERÚ:

Information and Assistance for Tourists.

Portal de la Municipalidad 48, plaza de armas.   81 8305
Open: Mon-Fri 8:30 to 19:30 h.
iperuayacucho@promperu.gob.pe

Tourism Police Aid: 81 9466

Instituto Nacional de Cultura:

Av. Independencia s/n, Huamanga.   81 2056

Travel Agencies

Central Tours: Portal Constitución 17.   81 1546

Post Office: Asamblea 293.   81 2224

Hospital de Apoyo Huamanga:

Av. Independencia 355.   81 2181

Farmacia Del Pino: 28 de Julio 123.   81 2080

Farmacia Huamanga: 28 de julio 183.   81 2500

Cajamarca

2 720 M / 9 023FT
92 400POP.
862KM
NE OF LIMA

P. 82

P. 78

ROUTE MAP
3

The city of Cajamarca, capital of the department of the same name, is located in the Mashcón River valley on the western slope of the northern Andes. Its name, in Quechua, means 'cold land.' It is impossible to speak of Cajamarca without mentioning its rich history, splendid architecture, and picturesque country-side, the inspiration for its famous local painters. In addition, the people of Cajamarca are some of the most cheerful and hos-pitable of Andean peoples. If you want to see for yourself, you have only to visit the city in February, during Carnival celebra-

Detail of the Cathedral façade.

tions. The oldest human remains in this region date from about 3 000 years ago, when the region experienced a strong influence first from the Cupisnique culture, and later from the Chavín culture. From very early on, Cajamarca established close ties with the cultures of the northern coast. In the sixth and seventh centuries AD, it was influenced by the Wari culture of Ayacucho, and in the thirteenth century it was the center of a confederation of independent kingdoms that extended to the Upper Marañón River. Around 1450, and after strong resistance, the

Dry and temperate climate, with a yearly mean temperature of 14 C (57° F). Warm during the day but the temperature can drop sharply at night. Rainy season from December to March.

region was integrated into the Inca empire. Cajamarca became an important administrative center and a place of rest for the Cusco royalty.

In 1532, the present-day Plaza de Armas was the site where Francisco Pizarro captured the Inca Atahualpa, who had refused to submit to the Spanish crown and the Christian faith. In exchange for his freedom, the Inca offered to fill a room once with gold and another, twice with silver. It is said that the volume of the ransom was so great that the melting of the precious metals took more than thirty days. In spite of the ransom, the conquistadors condemned the Inca to death by garrotte nine months after his capture. From this point on, the Spanish took control of the city and changed its Inca design to their rectangular, or checkerboard layout. Little remains of the original Inca city of Cajamarca.

A downtown street.

During Colonial times, the economy of Cajamarca was based on agriculture, the raising of livestock, and the making of textiles (for example, the sailcloth for the ships that navigated the South Pacific was manufactured here). The city reached its height in the seventeenth century with the discovery and exploitation of the silver mines at Hualgayoc. Cajamarca has numerous Colonial buildings, which give it a very special atmosphere. The city was declared a Historical and Cultural Heritage of the Americas by the Organization of American States.

Today Cajamarca is the most important city of the northern Peruvian sierra. It is currently experiencing a period of economic growth through the development of gold mining, its traditional dairy industry (famous for its cheeses and condensed milk products), dry-land farming (corn being the principal crop), and, more recently, tourism. Surrounded by beautiful countryside, this city is an excellent tourist destination. Don't miss it.

Typical Dishes

Entrées
- Chicharrón colorado: pork cracklings with *ají* pepper, garlic, and parsley.
- Choclo con queso: tender corn served with cheese.

Soups
- Chupe de papa seca: chowder of dried potato, cheese, milk, eggs, and *ají* pepper.
- Chupe verde: potato soup based on beef stock, mint, and fresh cheese.

Other
- Jamón del norte: pork loin, salted and dried.
- Cheeses, butter and *manjarblanco*.

Festivals

Cajamarca's most famous festival is the Carnival, called Carnavalón (February or March), one of the most modern in Peru, with colorful dances and mask parades.

Other festivals celebrated in this city and its environs are: Semana Santa (Holy Week), with a famous pilgrimage on Palm Sunday (March or April) and the Feast of the Crosses (May 3), both in Porcón; Corpus Christi in Cajamarca (May or June); the Livestock, Handicraft, Agro-industrial, and Tourist Fair in Cajamarca (July 22-29); Tourism Week in Cajamarca (August); the Huanchaco festival in the Baños del Inca district of Cajamarca

COWS, CHEESE, AND MILK

Green grass, Holsteins and aluminum kettles brimming with fresh milk are the unmistakable features of the Cajamarca countryside. It is no surprise that Cajamarca is Peru's primary milk producer and its livestock, perfectly adapted to the Andean climate, is of the best quality. Many farms of Cajamarca are engaged exclusively in the production of milk and dairy products such as *manjarblanco* (a sweet milk paste), butter and cheeses. The bulls of one farm, San Roque, have won many awards.

Straw hats of Cajamarca.

(September 8); All Souls' Day in Porcón (November 2); and the Cajamarca Song and Dance festival (December 24 to January 4).

Folkcrafts

Cajamarca is famous for its crochet work, pottery, basket weaving, fine straw hats and other weavings, such as saddlebags. It is also known for the granite carving done in Porcón, work in embossed leather, carved animal horns, and replicas of pre-Hispanic ceramics.

 ## Points of Interest in the City

Traditional Locales

- *Plaza de Armas:* one of the largest in Peru, this plaza is the site the Inca Atahualpa's execution. A highlight is its lovely octagonal fountain dating from 1699. Some Colonial constructions surround the plaza and it is flanked by the Cathedral and the church of San Francisco.
- *Santa Apolonia:* a hill some 100m S of the Plaza de Armas.

Church of San Francisco and Plaza de Armas.

CAJAMARCA CITY MAP

1 The Cathedral
2 Church of San Francisco
3 Ransom Room
4 Conjunto Monumental Belén
5 Church of La Recoleta
6 Santa Apolonia hill

Here there is an Inca shrine known as the Seat of the Inca and carved stone on even older foundations. This is a terrific lookout point over the entire city. The spot can be reached on foot (using the stairs) or by taxi.

Churches

- *The Cathedral*, Plaza de Armas: in a Baroque and Plateresque style, this church was raised during the seventeenth and eighteenth centuries on a foundation of stones taken from an Inca building. It was originally the parish church of Santa Catalina and was known as the «Spaniards' church,» as native worshippers were not allowed to enter. It possesses an extraordinary Baroque façade of volcanic stone with Salomonic columns, pilasters, and carved reliefs. It contains a large monstrance

The Cathedral.

(La Preciosa) worked in gold and silver, a lavishly adorned pulpit, and an extensive collection of Colonial oil paintings. Next door is a chapel built in 1686. Curiously, like most of the churches in the city, it has no towers. Popular belief holds that upon finishing the church, too many taxes would have been due the Crown if towers were built.

Visiting hours: daily, 8 to 11am, and 6 to 9pm.

- *San Francisco*, Plaza de Armas: this monumental church of enormous columns and stone arches was built in the eighteenth century, although its towers were added in 1951. It was known as the «Indians' church,» as only the native population attended Mass there. It contains some religious imagery and paintings (celebrated works of San Crispín and San Cipriano). Behind the main building is the chapel of La Virgen de los Dolores, patron saint of Cajamarca. There is also a small museum of Colonial-era religious art located in one of the cloisters of what was the convent adjoining the church. It contains handsome works of religious imagery, ceremonial furniture and ornaments, as well as valuable works of the Cusco and Quito schools of art.

Visiting hours: Mon-Fri, 9am to noon, and 4 to 6pm.

- *La Recoleta*, Av. El Maestro n/n: built in the seventeenth and eighteenth centuries, this beautiful church has a sober façade in carved stone and svelte, triple-arched steeples.

Historical Homes and Buildings

- *Cuarto del Rescate* (the Ransom Room), Amalia Puga 750: a reconstruction of the rooms that the Inca Atahualpa had filled with gold and silver to pay his ransom to the conquistadors. The entryway exhibits paintings by famous local artists such as Camilo Blas (1903–1985) and Andrés Zevallos.

ATAHUALPA'S RANSOM

«The Governor asked him how much gold and silver he would give. Atahualpa said that he would fill the room where the Governor was, and the large shed where the Spaniards were gathered he would fill twice over with silver as his ransom. When he had said this, Governor Francisco Pizarro, on his own and his captains' advice, had a secretary summoned to record the Indian's offer as a formal pledge [...]. Once this was done, Atahualpa dispatched his captains to gather this great treasure and have it brought.»

Pedro Pizarro, *Relación del Descubrimiento y Conquista del Perú* [1571].

Visiting hours: Mon-Fri (except Tue),
8:30am to 12:30pm, and 2:15 to 5pm;
weekends and holidays 8:30am to noon.

- *Conjunto Monumental Belén*, Belén n/n, one block from Plaza de Armas (facing the *plazuela* of the same name): this handsome architectural monument (today occupied by the National Institute of Culture of Cajamarca) was built by Bethlemites between the seventeenth and eighteenth centuries. It is a prime example of the Latin American Baroque style and includes a hospital for men, one for women, and a church. The church, completed in 1744 (except for the tower), boasts an original Baroque façade, while its interior is a mix of Gothic and Renaissance styles. It possesses a beautiful polychrome cupola supported by eight angels carved in stone. To one side of the church is the former men's hospital of Nuestra Señora de la Piedad, today a medical museum, while the women's hospital, today an archeological museum, is separated from these buildings by Junín street. This complex also possesses an art gallery with works by José Sabogal (1888–

Church of Belén.

1956) and other established local artists, and an ethnographic museum that exhibits a sampling of the typical dress, musical instruments, and tools of the region.

To one side of the Belén church is the entrance to the Belén School.

Visiting hours for all museums:
Mon-Fri (except Tue), 8:30am to noon,
and 4 to 6pm; weekends and holidays,
8:30am to noon.

Colonial doorway in the city.

- *Casa del Conde de Uceda*, corner of Apurímac and El Comercio: This mansion has one of the most elaborately carved stone doorways in the country. Its interior, Moorish in style, is also notable. Currently houses a branch of the Banco de Crédito.

Visits during office hours.

- *Colonial façades:* Cajamarca possesses more Colonial façades than any other Peruvian city.

There are over a hundred carved stone doorways, mostly with Baroque-*mestizo* motifs, while others are in the Neoclassical style.

Museums

• *Casa Museo Mario Urteaga*, Dos de Mayo 777: contains valuable paintings and personal items belonging to the famous Cajamarca painter Mario Urteaga (1875–1957). Also presents temporary exhibits.

Visiting hours: Mon-Fri, 4 to 7pm.

Excursions

Baños del Inca

2 667M / 8 750FT)

Hot springs 6km E of the city via paved road with some baths dating from Inca times. Tradition has it that the Inca Atahualpa and his retinue were here when the conquistadors arrived. It offers individual or group baths, sauna, and bungalows for lodging.

Bathing hours:
Daily, 6am to 6:30pm (morning hours
are best for avoiding the crowds).
Hours for sauna:
Daily, 5 to 7am for men; 7 to 9am for women;
and continuing alternately until 8pm.

Otuzco.

Outskirts of Llacanora.

Ventanillas de Otuzco

2 850 MSNM)

An archeological site 8km NE of the city via paved road for 3,5km, then following a dirt road that is sometimes in poor condition. The *ventanillas*, or windows, named for their window-like appearance, are carved into a wall of volcanic stone. This type of construction, very common in the area, was a necropolis, or burial ground. From here you

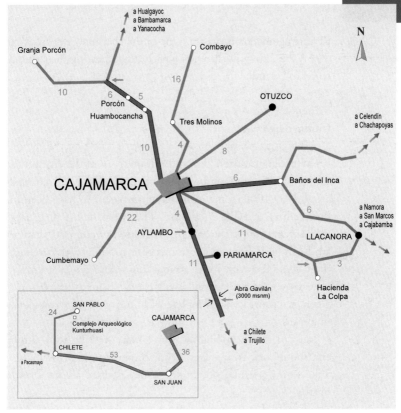

CAJAMARCA EXCURSION MAP

can get a good view of the green Cajamarca countryside, and visit el Jardín de las Hortensias (the Garden of the Hydrangeas).

Visiting hours: daily, 8am to 6pm.

Llacanora • La Colpa

2 606M / 8 550FT

A picturesque town 13km (30 minutes) s of the city via the packed dirt road to San Marcos. Llacanora is famous for its *clarines*, or reed trumpets, up to several meters long. Two waterfalls are a twenty-minute walk away: the first is small; the second, five minutes from the first, is much higher and more beautiful. The water has carved out pools, in which you can take a refreshing dip. Also very close to Llacanora is the former hacienda of La Colpa. This hacienda was owned by the Castro Mendívil family and is currently a cattle ranch owned by the El

Rescate agrarian cooperative. One of the charming aspects of the area is the calling of the cows, which, upon hearing their names, come to be milked.

Cumbemayo

3 500M / 11 484FT   )

An archeological site 22km (40 minutes) SW of the city, on the slopes of Mount Cumbe. It is believed to have been built around AD 1000; some of its structures seem to have been influenced by the Chavín culture. The site contains three large monument groups: the Sanctuary (grotto carved in the shape of a human head from an enormous cliff, contains rock carvings); the Caves (also with rock carvings); and the Aqueduct (an impressive complex of open canals carved from volcanic rock). There is a tourist stop complete with restrooms and a small site museum.

You can take a fascinating, three-hour walking tour among enormous rock formations, cacti, bromelia, moss and lichen. Take warm clothing, food, and water, as there are no services nearby.

You should leave Cajamarca very early and return at midday, although you can also continue on to Frailones to complete the day. If you enjoy long walks, this excursion can be done on foot

The stone forest of Cumbemayo.

from Cajamarca. Guides to this area can be found in the environs.

Visiting hours: daily, 8am to 6pm.

Frailones

3 500M / 11 484FT

A complex of imposing megalithic formations on the outskirts of Cumbemayo, some 25km (45 minutes) SW of the city via dirt road, also known as the Bosque de Piedras de los Frailes (Stone Forest of the Monks) because these large, eroded rocks resemble a group of hooded monks. Arrive early to enjoy the spectacular morning light. Take warm clothing to protect yourself from the penetrating cold wind which blows constantly.

The *frailones*, or hooded monks.

Huambocancha • Porcón Bajo

3 200M / 10 500FT

Picturesque hamlets located 15km and 20km (10 and 20 minutes), respectively, N of Cajamarca via partially paved road. Both are famous for their stone handicrafts: fountains, flowerpots, benches and statues. They are also ideal spots for enjoying the legendary hospitality and beautiful countryside of Cajamarca.

Cajamarca countryside.

Granja Porcón

3 200M / 10 500FT

Previously an hacienda and now the Atahualpa-Jerusalén cooperative, 31km (50 minutes) N of the city via partially paved road. To get to Gran Porcón, pass through Huambocancha and Porcón Bajo, then turn off at the 20km mark for a descent of 10km on a packed dirt road in good condition.

Here are 10 000 hectares of pine forest, the result of recent reforestation, potato plants, and over 600 head of cattle. It also has a small zoo containing vicuña, deer, lynx, monkeys, eagles, and other species. Spectacular countryside, ideal for enjoying a day outdoors. You can fish for trout and purchase dairy products.

Ventanillas de Combayo
3 000M / 9 843FT)

An archeological site 20km (45 minutes) NE of Cajamarca on a dirt road often in bad condition. This is a large, pre-Inca necropolis with tombs in niches carved from the rock, more numerous and better preserved than those of Otuzco. Afternoons can be chilly.

Yumagual
2 200M / 7 218FT)

A former hacienda with hot springs by the river. Take the road W towards San Juan to the turnoff one hour from Cajamarca (ask the locals). Park and walk 30 minutes on the trail leading to the baths. These waters mix with the river water, allowing you to choose your preferred water temperature for bathing.

Hotels

★★★★★ Hotel Laguna Seca
Manco Cápac 1098, Baños del Inca. Tel 82 3149.
Fax 82 3915. Reservations Lima Tel 212 2037. US$ 85

★★★ El Ingenio
Av. Vía de Evitamiento 1611-1709.Telefax 82 7121.
ingeniocaj@terra.com.pe

★★★ Hotel Hacienda San Vicente
Dos de Mayo 311 (information). Tel 82 2644. US$ 55
hacienda-san-vicente@yahoo.com

★★★ Hotel Sierra Galana
Jr. del Comercio 773, Cercado.
Tel 82 2472. Fax 82 2470.
gallardo@protelsa.com.pe

★★★ Hotel Cajamarca
Dos de Mayo 311. Tel 82 2532. Fax 82 1432. US$ 50
hotelcaj@caxanet.com.pe

Hotel Continental ★★★
   Jr. Amazonas 760. Tel 82 2758. Fax 82 3024. US$ 60

Hotel Fundo Campero San Antonio ★★★
   Road towards Baños del Inca km 6. Tel 82 1237. US$ 40
   hsanantonio@terra.com.pe

Hostal Los Pinos Inn ★★★
   La Mar 521. Tel 82 5992. US$ 30

Hostal El Portal del Marqués ★★★
   Jr. del Comercio 644. Telefax 82 8464. US$ 20
   portaldelmarques@terra.com.pe

Albergue Turístico Baños del Inca
   Manco Cápac s/n, Baños del Inca. Tel 82 7385. US$ 25

Posada del Puruay
   Carretera Porcon km 4,5. Tel 82 7928. Fax 82 7028.
   Reservations Lima Tel 336 7835.

RATES ARE APPROXIMATE AND, UNLESS OTHERWISE NOTED,
ARE FOR DOUBLE OCCUPANCY.

Restaurants

El Cajamarqués ✔
   Amazonas 770.

La Vaca Loca ✔
   San Martín 330.

Restaurant at the Hotel Sierra Galena ✔
   Jr. del Comercio 773, plaza de armas.

Salas ✔
   Amalia Puga 637.

El Batán ✔
   El Batán 369.

Los Faroles ✔
   Jr. Dos de Mayo 311.

Cascanuez Café-Bar ✔
   Amalia Puga 554.

El Zarco ✔
   Jr. del Batán 170.

El Fogón ✔
   Manco Cápac 1058.

Useful Facts

AREA CODE 44

☎

Basic information
IPERÚ:
Information and Assistance for Tourists.
Tel 01-574-8000, Lima.
Tourism Police Aid: 105
Instituto Nacional de Cultura:
Conjunto Monumental Belén Cdra. 6.   82 2601

Travel Agencies
Cajamarca Tours: Dos de Mayo 323.   Telefax 82 2823

Handicraft Shops
Artesanía Kuntur Wasi: Amalia Puga 673.
Mercado Central: Amazonas 515.
Artesanía Laysón: El Batán 181.

Cheese Sale
Planta Quesera Chugur: Amalia Puga 937.
Fábrica de Productos Lácteos La Pauca:
Amazonas 713.
Fábrica de Productos Lácteos Rosell:
Dos de Mayo 600.

Post Office: Amazonas 433.   82 2206

Hospital Regional Cajamarca:
Mario Urteaga 500.   82 2523
Clínica San Francisco: Grau 851.   82 2050
Farmacia Continental: Mario Urteaga 445.   82 1555
Botica Uceda: Jr. del Batán 162.   82 3440

Car Rental:
Prolongación Angamos E-19.
Taxi Seguro: Bolívar 382.   82 5103

The Colca Canyon 3500 M / 11483FT

The fabulous Colca Canyon is reached via three packed dirt roads. All leave from the city of Arequipa and lead to the town of Chivay (the starting point for a visit to the canyon), crossing the Salinas and Aguada Blanca national reserves.

The shortest road (148km, or 4 hours), which is recommended since it is in good condition, goes NW from Arequipa towards Yura and then climbs to the *puna,* or high plateau, and desolate plains of Pampas de Cañahuas and Tocra. There you can see herds of vicuña, the Puruña stone forest, and the Sumbay caves with

P. 78

ROUTE MAPS

Women at Cabanaconde festival.

rock carvings. After about three hours, you reach a pass known as the Mirador de los Cóndores at 4 700m (15 420ft) not to be confused with the Cruz del Cóndor, near Cabanaconde. From this pass, where you can contemplate the snowy summits of the Ampato (6 310m, or 20 703ft) and Sabancaya (5 976m, or

Dry and temperate climate, with sunny days and cold nights, with a yearly mean temperature of 19° C (66° F). Rainy season from December to March. The best season for visiting is when the canyon is at its greenest, from April to June.

19 607ft) volcanoes, you finally descend to Chivay.

A second route (160km, or 5 hours), also in generally good condition, goes N from Arequipa (via Charcani), ascends to the arid Pampa de los Arrieros, passing the foot of the Chachani volcano (6 075m, or 19 932ft), and joins the first route near the village of Patahuasi. From there, continue to Chivay.

A third route goes east from Arequipa to Chiguata and Laguna de Salinas, climbs to the arid *puna* at Pampa del Confital, and passes through the village of Imata to finally join the previous routes near Tocra and continue to Chivay. This route is longer (251km, or 7 hours) and is not always in good condition, but passes through fantastic scenery and interesting geological formations, such as the Bosque de Piedras (stone forest) of Maucarquipa and the Laguna del Indio. This route is only recommended if you have time and an all-terrain vehicle.

The stone forest of Maucarquipa.

Vicuñas in the Colca Valley.

Indio Lake.

Geography

The Colca Canyon is an impressive geological formation carved out by the river as it has descended between the mountains (made of largely volcanic materials) over millions of years. The area of greatest interest to tourists begins at the town of Chivay and continues NW for more than 60km until reaching the lookout known as the Cruz del Cóndor near the town of Cabanaconde. From here the valley narrows significantly, giving origin to the fame of the Colca Canyon as one of the deepest in the world. The deepest part of the Colca has been calculated at 3 680m, or 12 074ft (almost twice as deep as Colorado's Grand Canyon) from the highest points at Mount Yajirhua (5 212m, or 17 100ft) and Mount Lucerna (4 245m, or 13 928ft) to the river bed. Its steep walls begin on the heights of the Chila range, on the right bank of the Colca River, and continue almost vertical for 40km to the confluence with the Andamayo River (900m, or 2 953ft), where the Colca Canyon becomes the Majes River valley. Note that Colca, Majes, and Camaná are the names given to different parts of the same river.

Callalli, on the way to Cusco.

Colonial bridge on the outskirts of Chivay.

Attractions

Near Chivay.

Perhaps one of the major attractions of the area, which led writer Mario Vargas Llosa to call it the «Valley of Wonders», is its spectacular terracing, considered among the most extensive in southern Peru. These works, which allow cultivation and meticulously controlled irrigation of the steep slopes of the canyon, were built by the Collagua and Cabana ethnic groups between the ninth and fourteenth centuries AD. The Collaguas occupied the eastern and central parts of the valley and had their largest centers at Yanque and Lari. They apparently spoke Aymara and believed themselves to be descendants of the Collaguata volcano. The Ca-

banas, who apparently spoke Quechua and thought of themselves as descendants of Mount Hualca-Hualca, settled in the lower part of the Colca, with their center at Cabanaconde. Towards the middle of the fifteenth century the Colca was conquered by the Incas, who took advantage of and even expanded the terracing. According the chronicler Garcilaso de la Vega [1609], the Inca Mayta Cápac formalized the conquest of the Colca by marrying Mama Tancaray Yacchi, daughter of the Collagua chieftain at Coporaque, and built a small palace of copper for her near the town of Sibayo. Today the inhabitants of the Colca still use some of the terraces for cultivation of corn, potatoes, broad beans, alfalfa, quinoa, barley and wheat.

MASTER ENGINEERING

The terraces built on the steep slopes of the Colca Valley were not the only spectacular work of the valley's ancient inhabitants. The people also ingeniously resolved the dilemma of how to bring water to the fields, since the Colca River ran in a deep gorge, far below their lands. Since pre-Hispanic times, the local people have resolved this problem by building canals to divert water from the melt-off of neighboring peaks. Even today, with few exceptions, the towns of the Colca receive their water from mountain peaks. The primary source of water for the town of Yanque, for example, comes from snows of mounts Mismi and Chucura.

Another attraction of the Colca is its unique towns. Founded under orders of Viceroy Francisco de Toledo in 1570 as *reducciones*, or settlements of native inhabitants, each one has managed to maintain its original appearance despite the passing of years. During the Colonial period these centers were used to manage the primary economic activities of the region: agriculture, livestock breeding, textiles, and the silver mines at Caylloma, discovered in 1626. Evidence of the cultural height reached during the viceroyalty are the imposing churches in Renaissance and Baroque-*mestizo* style raised in each town. Many preserve valuable examples of carved, Colonial-era altarpieces, silverwork, decorated pulpits, paintings, and sculpture.

The long history of the Colca is not solely reflected in its ancient constructions but also, and most notably for the visitor, in the traditions zealously kept by its amicable inhabitants. The traditional clothing, still worn by the majority of women, the legends recounted by its inhabitants, and the festivals by which agricultural cycles are marked with song and dance, all reveal the history of the Colca Valley.

Lastly, the possibility of observing the flight of

the condor in its native habitat, and the impressive scenery of one of the most beautiful spots on Earth add to the attractions already mentioned, making the Colca Canyon one of the most important travel destinations in the southern Andes.

Calendar of Festivals

Andean condor
(*Vultur gryphus*).

January
2	Anniversary of Cabanaconde.
6	Los Reyes Magos, in Achoma.
12	Los Reyes Magos, in Lari

February
2	La Virgen de la Candelaria, in Chivay, Achoma, Ichupampa, and Madrigal. Wititi, in Maca. La Virgen de Chapi, in Chivay, Lari and Maca.
DATE VARIES	Carnival throughout the valley.

March
19	San José, in Chivay, Lari, and Madrigal.

April
DATE VARIES	Holy Week, celebrated in all towns.

May
1	La Virgen de Chapi, in Yanque.
3	The Feast of the Cross, in Yanque.
13	La Calera, on the outskirts of Chivay.
15	San Isidro, in Coporaque, Achoma, Ichupampa, Maca, and Yanque.

June
13	San Antonio, in Coporaque, Chivay, and Yanque.
24	Sagrado Corazón de Jesús, in Coporaque, Chivay and Madrigal San Juan Bautista, in Ichupampa.

A young Collagua celebrates.

Carnival in the valley.

July

16	La Virgen del Carmen, in Cabanaconde, Chivay, Achoma, and Madrigal.
25	Santiago Apóstol, in Coporaque and Madrigal.
29	San Antonio, in Maca.

August

PRIMERA SEMANA	The cleaning of irrigation channels, in Yanque.
10	San Lorenzo, in Huambo.
15	La Virgen de la Asunción, in Chivay, Coporaque, Maca, and Yanque.
30	Santa Rosa in Chivay, Ichupampa, Achoma, Madrigal, and Yanque.

September

14	Señor de la Exaltación, in Yanque.
23	Fiesta de la Primavera (the Spring Festival), in Yanque.
29	San Miguel, in Coporaque.

October

7	La Virgen del Rosario, in Chivay, Achoma, Ichupampa, Maca, and Yanque.
18	San Lucas, in Coporaque.

November

1	Todos los Santos (All Saints' Day), celebrated in all towns.

2	Los Fieles Difuntos (All Souls' Day), celebrated in all towns.
3	San Martín de Porras, in Coporaque and Chivay.
29	Señor de los Milagros, in Chivay.
30	San Andrés, in Chivay.

December

8	La Virgen Inmaculada, in Chivay, Ichupampa, Lari, Madrigal, and Yanque.
	Wititi, in Chivay.
25	Wititi, in Yanque.

Folkcrafts

The Colca Valley is noted for its textiles: beautifully designed rugs and brocade work (women's vests, dresses, and blouses), trimmed with embossed tin details. Also worth seeing are the images of San Isidro Labrador (St. Isidore the Laborer) with a pair of yoked oxen, the hachones, or large, fat candles, and works in carved wood, as well as the *keros* (carved goblets) and the ceramics that are part of the popular tradition of the Colca. Several towns in the Colca (Chivay, Yanque) have handicraft shops.

Artisan of Yanque.

Visiting the Colca

Two packed dirt roads out of Chivay (one on each side of the valley) lead to the picturesque towns of the region. The first crosses the river and runs along the right side of the valley, to five towns (Chivay, Coporaque, Ichupampa, Lari, and Madrigal) in a fascinating excursion of approximately one and a half hours. This road runs approximately 50km and ends in Madrigal (it is necessary to go back to Chivay to return to Arequipa). The second road runs along the left side of the valley to the towns of Yanque, Achoma, Maca, Pinchollo, and Cabanaconde for a distance of about 60km. This is the most-traveled road and, if taken downriver from Cabanaconde, leads back to Arequipa through the towns of Tapay (a region known for its excellent fruit, and for the Collagua archeological complex at Ccacca-tapay), Huambo, and the Majes Valley (an agricultural zone). The most popular return to Arequipa from Cabanaconde is

by retracing the path to Chivay and, from there, the original road back to town. This route is less risky as the road through the Majes Valley is not always in good condition. Nonetheless, if an all-terrain vehicle is available, we recommend descending to the Majes Valley and following the course of the river, after asking locals about the state of the road.

Terraces in use near Yanque.

Arequipa has various tourist agencies which offer one-day excursions to the Colca. This option is not recommended as the time is insufficient and the danger of altitude sickness (*soroche*) is high. For this reason we recommend excursions of two to three days, using one of the towns of the Colca as a point of departure, and if possible returning to Arequipa via the road through Huambo and the Majes Valley. You won't regret it.

Excursions

The Left Side of the Valley

Chivay

3 650M / 11 976FT

160km (4 hours) N of Arequipa. This is the principal town of the region and the departure point for visiting the Colca. Its church, Nuestra Señora de la Asunción (Our Lady of the Assumption), was once decorated with beautiful polychrome motifs but was later covered in white plaster. It contains a splendid eighteenth-century Baroque altarpiece and seven other Neoclassic *retablos* (holy scenes), as well as a sixteenth-century baptistery with a golden ciborium and wall paintings from the seventeenth and eighteenth centuries depicting the baptism of Christ and the Apostles. Don't fail to visit the hot springs at La Calera (on the outskirts of town) and taste the delicious prickly pears (*tunas*), the excellent cheese and the fresh trout available there. This town has a variety of hotels and restaurants.

Yanque

3 580M / 11 746FT)

10km (15 minutes) W of Chivay. This was the headquarters of the Franciscan missionaries in the Colca. Its church, Inmaculada Concepción, which burnt down in the late seventeenth century and was rebuilt in 1702, is the most important Baroque-*mestizo* building of the Colca. Its main façade, richly carved with saints (including Santa Rosa de Lima) and foliage, and the lateral façade with a Renaissance base and a Baroque upper level, are the most notable in the valley. Inside are a series of polychrome retablos and a sixteenth-century silver processional cross. Its main altar has a ciborium, stepped shelves for candles, and a pedestal all plated with embossed silver and a ciborium of gilded wood in the Renaissance style. On the outskirts of town (at the Choquitico lookout point) you can see spectacular terracing at a place known as Llactacucho, or 'amphitheater.' An even better view can be had from the other side of the river.

Achoma

3 680M / 12 074FT)

18km (30 minutes) W of Chivay. This town has a handsome church raised at the end of the eighteenth century, with Rococo decorations on the capitals of its columns. Its interior is adorned with wall paintings, a Neoclassic altarpiece of stone and stucco,

Church of La Inmaculada Concepción, Yanque.

a pulpit from the eighteenth century and numerous images from the seventeenth and eighteenth centuries. A beautiful view of the valley can be had from this town, and it is also possible to descend to the river to enjoy a good dip. Try the local cheeses.

Maca

3 400M / 11 155FT)

A town located 23km (45 minutes) W of Chivay, at the foot of the imposing Sabancaya (5 976m, or 19 607ft) and Hualca-Hualca (6 075m, or 19 932ft) volcanoes. An earth-

quake almost entirely destroyed the town several years ago. Its effects are evident in the town's beautiful church of Santa Ana, which was seriously damaged, but still stands today. This church, built in 1812, is considered one of the most original in the region.

Its façade contains a curious «open chapel» in the form of an arched balcony, used to present sacred images to the native population. It has gilded Baroque altars, as well as a ciborium and a statue of Christ crucified dating from the sixteenth century. Its beautiful main altar has embossed silver candle shelves and a rich Baroque altar decoration in the same metal. On the way out of town, you can see a stone at the side of the road, carved in a scale model of the surrounding terraces.

Detail on Church of Santa Ana in Maca.

Pinchollo

3 390M / 11 123FT)

A small town 27km (55 minutes) W of Chivay, famous for its miniature carved handicrafts depicting the valley's traditions. A highlight is its church to San Sebastián, with its unique doorway to the baptistery painted with large *chinchircuma* flowers (*Mutisia sp.*), giving the visitor the distinct impression that the entire baptistery is a huge Ayacucho-style *retablo*. The church holds interesting Renaissance and Baroque altarpieces and a statue of Christ crucified dating from the early seventeenth century.

La Cruz del Cóndor

3 320M / 10 893FT)

60km (1 hour, 30 minutes) from Chivay and 220km from Arequipa. Natural observatory from which you can see the deepest part of the Colca Canyon and, quite frequently, the flight of the imposing Andean condor. The best times to catch it in flight are the morning and the late afternoon. You can camp in the area, although there are hostels and restaurants in the nearby town of Cabanaconde (one hour by foot).

Cruz del Cóndor observatory.

Cabanaconde

3 200M / 10 499FT)

A picturesque town surrounded by terraces, 65km (1 hour, 45 minutes) W of Chivay. Marks the beginning of the territory of the Cabana ethnic group, which lived in the lower Colca. Its church, San Pedro Alcántara, rebuilt after the earthquake of 1784, is an imposing stone building of two towers carved with reliefs of sun, moon, and stars. Its Neoclassic doorways are noteworthy, as are the walls of its atrium, inspired by Inca stonework. It possesses an important series of images of Christ crucified and a crowned Virgin dating from the mid-eighteenth century. From Cabanaconde a trail zigzags down to the Colca River, where the climate is ideal for a good swim. The walk (with guides) is well worth the effort; take mosquito repellent. Crossing the river, you come to the town of Tapay and an area rich in fruit production.

Others

Other towns of interest on this side of the valley, both with handsome Colonial-era churches, are Canocota, Tisco and Callalli.

THE ANDEAN CONDOR

The Andean condor (*Vultur gryphus*) is the largest flying bird in the world; its wingspan can exceed 3m and it weighs up to 10kg. It inhabits the Andean Cordillera from Mérida, Venezuela, to Tierra del Fuego in Chile and Argentina, but is especially abundant in Peru, Chile and Bolivia. It's extraordinary eyesight and a great sense of smell, allow it to scrutinize every corner of its enormous, diverse domain in search of carrion, its only source of food. One of this bird's most amazing characteristics is its ability to soar on currents of air for hours on end, without ever flapping its wings.

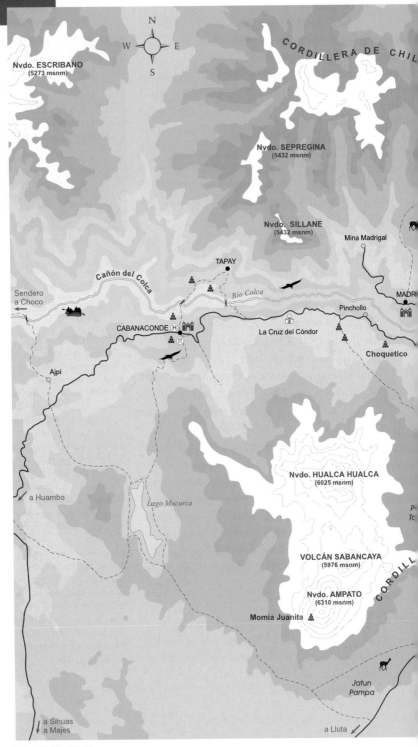

THE COLCA VALLEY

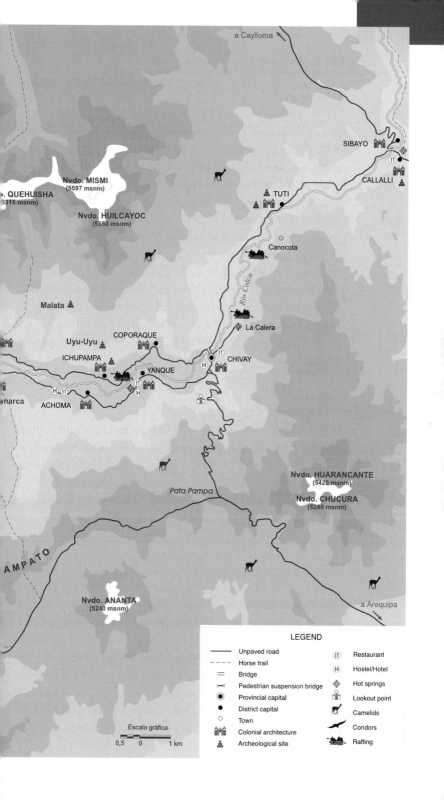

a Caylloma

SIBAYO

CALLALLI

TUTI

Nvdo. MISMI
(5597 msnm)

. QUEHUISHA
5315 msnm)

Nvdo. HUILCAYOC
(5350 msnm)

Canocota

Río Colca

Malata

La Calera

COPORAQUE

Uyu-Uyu

ICHUPAMPA

CHIVAY

YANQUE

marca

ACHOMA

Nvdo. HUARANCANTE
(5420 msnm)

Nvdo. CHUCURA
(5280 msnm)

Pata Pampa

AMPATO

Nvdo. ANANTA
(5240 msnm)

a Arequipa

LEGEND

——	Unpaved road		Restaurant
---	Horse trail	(H)	Hostel/Hotel
=	Bridge		Hot springs
	Pedestrian suspension bridge		Lookout point
◉	Provincial capital		Camelids
●	District capital		Condors
○	Town		Rafting
	Colonial architecture		
	Archeological site		

Escala gráfica

0,5   0   1 km

The Right Side of the Valley

Coporaque
3 700M / 12 140FT)

8km (15 minutes) W of Chivay, this is the first town you come to on the right bank of the Colca River. Its church, Santiago Apóstol, is the oldest in the valley and boasts an impressive façade of sixteenth-century Italian Renaissance design. It holds very old works in silver, chasubles, vestments, remains of the primitive Renaissance-style main altar, and an important polychrome triangular relief of effigies depicting the coronation of the Virgin, from the sixteenth century. Statues from the same era depict Nuestra Señora de la Candelaria, Santa Úrsula, La Dolorosa, and San Antonio Abad. Facing one of its lateral doors, and almost hidden by a small bullring of recent construction, is the Renaissance-style façade of the chapel of San Sebastián which was built in 1565 and is the oldest of its genre remaining in Peru.

Ichupampa
3 710M / 12 173FT)

A town 19km (30 minutes) W of Chivay. Its church dates from the end of the eighteenth century and possesses a graceful honey-colored columned façade. In its interior stand Neoclassic altars of stone and stucco. Seventeenth-century statues of San Francisco and two gilded angels can be seen, as well as a splendid statue of Santa Rosa de Lima from the eighteenth century.

Lari
3 390M / 11 123FT)

A town 27km (45 minutes) W of Chivay. Its church, Purísima Concepción, is the largest of the valley and one of the most important of the department of Arequipa. It is a massive, but harmonious building dating from the mid-eighteenth century, with tall square towers, thick buttresses, a large narthex and the only cupola in the Colca. It has a splendid group of polychrome altars in a style between Baroque and Neoclassic, a magnificent pulpit, a statue of the Inmaculada Concepción from the seventeenth century paired with works by the great Andalusian sculp-

Church of La Purísima Concepción, Lari.

tor Juan Martínez Montañés (1568–1649), and a lovely eighteenth-century statue of Santa Rosa de Lima.

Madrigal

3 200M / 1 088FT)

A town 50km W of Chivay. Its church of Santiago de Madrigal is one of the oldest in the valley, built in the late sixteenth and early seventeenth centuries. It possesses a Renaissance doorway with a relief of St. James the Moorslayer (very similar to the one on La Compañía in Arequipa) and a magnificent gilded main altar with sculptures and mirrors. The baseboards of its entryway boast a seventeenth-century mural.

Others

Other towns of interest on this side of the river, with lovely Colonial-era churches, are Tuti and Sibayo.

The Cross of Sibayo.

Archeological Sites

In addition to the terraces, there are many archeological remains in the area, such as the shelter of such as the shelter of Ccollpa, the refuge of the valley's first inhabitants, the rock carvings at Mo-

The *colcas* of Choquetico.

llepunku, the mysterious citadels of Juscallacta and Uyu-Uyu, the caves of Pumunuta, the stone and *colcas*, or grainaries, of Choquetico, the *colcas*, of Chininia and some curious stone constructions near the village of Yanque. There are also remains of palaces of ancient chieftains in Yanque and Lari. For more information on these excursions, access routes and road conditions, consult the local guides or tourist companies (based in Chivay, Yanque, and Achoma).

Hot Springs

There are several different hot springs (*aguas termales*) along the Colca Canyon. Some are found at Sibayo (35km N of Chivay), at La Calera on the outskirts of Chivay, and near Yanque. Ask at each town.

Climbing • Trekking

For those who enjoy the heights, the region offers a wide variety of challenges. The best are the Coropuna (6 425m, or 21 080ft) and Ampato (6 310m, or 20 703ft) volcanoes, and the summits of the Chila range, including Mount Mismi (5 597m, or 18 364ft), considered by some scientists as the source of the Amazon River. There are many other trekking options.

Rafting the Colca River.

Rafting

The Colca River came to world attention when a Polish expedition ran it in 1981. There are now tours guided by professionals who organize river expeditions that are safe for visitors. The expedition packages last nine days and include rafts and camping equipment, all food, experienced guides and a number of stops at valley attractions. The expeditions generally set out from Chivay by road to the town of Huambo. A two-hour walk from there leads to Cancos, where the expedition takes to the water. Other packages offer seven days and set out from Arequipa for the Majes Valley and enter the river at the town of Ayo.

> *Further information can be obtained from*
> Apumayo: *Bellavista 518, Miraflores, Lima.*
> *Tel 444 2320;*
> *or Garcilaso 265, of. 3, Cusco. Tel 24 6018.*

Chivay   Hotels

Hotel Rumi Llacta
   Huaynacápac s/n. Tel 52 1098.
   Reservations Arequipa Tel 20 0294.   ★★★
   rumillacta@terra.com.pe

Hostal Wasi Kolping
   Av. Siglo XX. Nearby the market place. Tel 53 1076. US$ 30

Colca Inn Hotel   ★★★
   Salaverry 307. Tel 53 1088. Fax 53 1111. US$ 20

Posada Chivay   ★★★
   Salaverry 325. Tel 52 1032. Fax 53 1108. US$ 20

Hotel Wasi   ★★★
   Av. Siglo XX. Tel 20 0294.

                                                             ★★

Yanque

Mirador de los Collaguas
   Yanque. Reservations Arequipa Tel 44 8383. US$ 35

Parador del Colca   ★★★
   Puente Bolognesi 132, Yanque km 12,5.
   Reservations Arequipa Tel 28 8440. US$ 60   ★★★

Colca Lodge
   Only a few meters from the Colca River. US$ 60
   Reservations Arequipa Tel 21 2813. Fax 22 0147.   ★★★

Aldea Turística de Colca
   30 min distance from Chivay, towards Cabanoconde.
   Reservations Arequipa Tel 22 5382.

RATES ARE APPROXIMATE AND, UNLESS OTHERWISE NOTED, ARE FOR DOUBLE OCCUPANCY.

3 399 M / 11 152 FT
255 600 POP.
1 089 KM
SOUTH OF LIMA

Cusco

P. 82   P. 85

P. 78

ROUTE MAP

11

The city of Cusco, capital of the department of the same name, lies in the Huatanay River valley in the southern highlands of Peru. Cusco, in Quechua means 'navel of the world,' for this city, capital of the Inca empire, or Tawantinsuyo, was the hub of a network extending to each of the four *suyus,* or regions, that formed the «four parts of the world» according to the Incas' world view. The Incas believed Cusco to be a dwelling place of the gods and it is certainly one of the most fascinating cities in the Peruvian Andes. Its unique architecture of Euro-

Full moon over the city.

pean styles set against with the solid grandeur of Inca foundations highlights the beauty of a city with a dazzling past and despite strong Spanish influence the city maintains an unmistakably Andean air. It is called the archeological capital of South America, as its proximity to the Inca citadel of Machu Picchu makes it one of the world's principal travel destinations.

Contrary to common belief, the region of Cusco was inhabited long before the Incas occupied it. Some 3 000 years ago,

Temperate climate, with a yearly mean temperature of 15° C (59° F), warm days and cold nights, and a heavy rainy season from December to March.

the Marcavalle culture had developed a notable civilization in this territory; around 2 000 years ago the Chanapatas had settled here, and in the sixth and seventh centuries AD the Wari culture from Ayacucho wielded a strong influence on the region. Beginning in the fourteenth century and in less than 100 years, the Incas transformed the little kingdom they had founded some two centuries before at Cusco into an empire extending from the south of present-day Colombia to the central valleys of Chile, including the Bolivian Altiplano and the northwest of Argentina.

The Inca founding of Cusco is lost in legend. According to chronicler Garcilaso de la Vega [1609], it was Manco Cápac and his sister-wife Mama Ocllo who emerged from Lake Titicaca and received the command from their father the Sun to civilize the lands of Cusco. Another legend tells of four mythical brothers and their sister-brides, who emerged from a cave in Pacaritambu (in the province of Paruro, S of Cusco) and underwent a number of perils along the way until only two were left, the founders of the city: Ayar Manco and Mama Ocllo.

It is thought that the city of Cusco was first laid out in the shape of a puma. The city was originally divided into two sectors: a higher one, or *hanan*, and a lower one, or *hurin*. According to most chron-

CUSCO OF THE INCAS

«One of the principal idols of the Inca Kings and their vassals was the imperial city of Cusco, which they worshipped as if it were holy [...]. Such was their veneration that they exhibited it even in commonplace ways, so that if two natives of equal status were to meet on a road, one coming from Cusco and the other going there, the one entering would respect and defer to the one coming away, as an inferior would a superior, solely because he had been in the city...»

Garcilaso de la Vega, *Comentarios Reales de los Incas* [1609].

iclers, the lower sector was home to the rulers who had preceded the Inca Roca, the sixth Inca, and their family groups called *panacas*. In the upper sector lived the rulers who succeeded the Inca Roca, also with their family groups. The Inca Pachacútec (1438–1471) is attributed with having built the

Women of Ocongate
with Ausangate as backdrop.

principal buildings in Cusco, channeling the rivers that flow through the city and building the spectacular agricultural terracing in the surrounding countryside.

With the arrival of the conquistadors in 1533 and the fall of the Tawantinsuyo, the Spanish founded their own city on the site of Cusco on March 23, 1534, and destroyed the majority of the Inca constructions in the city.

Some were conserved and their stone foundations used for European-style buildings. Cusco soon became one of the most important cities in the Viceroyalty of Peru and one of the highest expressions of *mestizaje*, or hybridism, in America. For several centuries the surviving Inca royalty, the Spanish, the native commoners, *criollos*, and *mestizos* built a life together here.

La Merced Tower
seen from the Plaza de Armas.

A wall of worked stone
in the city.

In colonial times, Cusco was a very prosperous city thanks to agriculture, livestock breeding, the textile industry, mining, and commerce, as it became a stopping point on the road between Lima and the famous silver mines at Potosí (today in Bolivia). It was the site of the first bishopric in South America. The wealth of the Church and the founding of many different religious orders soon spurred intense cultural and artistic activity in the city.

An important step was the founding of the Universidad San Antonio Abad in 1669 and the formation of a Cusco school of painting with its own unique characteristics. The native Peruvian artists of Cusco added their own perception of religious ideas to styles imported from Spain. The local flavor they added is visible in their choice of colors and their addition of local motifs taken from the region's flora and fauna.

After the Peru gained its independence in 1824, Cusco lost the spotlight to the economic boom in Arequipa based on the wool business, which spurred heavy emigration to the cities on the coast. In 1911 Cusco gained international attention when North American explorer Hiram Bingham discovered the nearby citadel of Machu Picchu, an event which was followed by a strong, local, cultural movement. In the 1920s renowned intellectuals lived in Cusco, such as ethnohistorian Luis E. Valcárcel, photographer Martín Chambi, considered the most «universal *cusqueño* of the twentieth century,» and José Sabogal, founder of the indigenous school of painting. Today Cusco lives mostly from agriculture and tourism, and is the seventh largest city in Peru.

Local Dishes

Entrées
- Chicharrón: deep-fried pork accompanied by potatoes, kerneled corn, onion and *hierbabuena* (mint).
- Kapchi: broad bean or mushroom stew, or soup, with potatoes, milk, eggs, and cheese.
- Pastel de choclo: pastry made with fresh corn, either savory with a layer of stewed pork, or sweet with raisins.
- Choclo con queso: boiled corn with fresh cheese.
- Humita: similar to the *tamal*, but sweet, with cinnamon and raisins and wrapped in a corn leaf and steamed.
- Tamal: soft corn dough with meat filling, wrapped in a banana leaf and steamed.

Soups
- Chuño cola: beef soup with rice, garbanzo beans, and ground, freeze-dried potato called *chuño*.
- Lawa: corn soup with broad beans, dried yellow *ají* pepper, and *huacatay* herbs.

THE CUSCO SCHOOL

In the second half of the seventeenth century, one of the most important schools of Colonial American art was created at Cusco. To the art of Spanish origin, the artists of Cusco, mainly natives and *mestizos,* added their own perceptions of religious ideas, using different colors and inserting their own cultural motifs such as local flora, fauna and clothing styles. They also gilded their paintings, a very original technique. Some of the most characteristic themes of this school are: angels with flintlock arquebuses (some specialists believe these have no precedent in Europe), virgins with triangular dresses, a form the natives could associate with their *apu* or mountain spirit, and St. James the Moorslayer, the patron saint of the conquistadors, who in America took the name of St. James the Indianslayer.

Main dishes
- Adobo de chancho: pork stewed with *chicha de jora* (corn beer) and condiments.
- Lechón asado: tender young pork condimented with *ají* pepper, garlic, pepper, and pisco.
- Locro de carne: beef stew with potatoes and red *ají* pepper.
- Olluquito con charqui: a stew of *olluco* (a tuber similar to the potato) with llama jerky.
- Timpo: a stew of various meats with cabbage, potatoes, *moralla* (preserved potatoes), garbanzo beans, and rice.

Drinks
- Frutillada: *chicha de jora*, strawberries, and aromatic herbs.
- Tecte: a fermented drink based on peanuts, white corn, quinoa, *chicha de jora* (corn beer), and aromatic herbs.

Festivals

Some of Cusco's most important festivals take place in the months of May and June. Shortly before the Feast of Corpus Christi, many make the pilgrimage to the sanctuary of Qoyllur

The traditional procession of Corpus Christi.

Ritt'i in the Sinakara valley (province of Quispicanchis) at 4 800m (15 749ft). With a mix of pre-Hispanic and Christian tradition, three days of dancing and offerings honor the mountain spirit or *apu* of Ausangate and the Lord of Qoyllur Ritt'i. This pilgrimage draws over 20 000 worshippers, many of them dancers and masked characters, and is considered one of the most important in the Americas.

Pilgrimage to the Qoyllur Ritt'i sanctuary.

During Corpus Christi (one of the city's most striking festivals), each city district carries its saint in procession to the tolling of the bells of the city's principal churches. The religious images are treated as living individuals as it is widely believed that they have taken the place of the mummified bodies of Inca ancestors, or even the pre-Hispanic gods. After the processions, the people eat, drink, and dance in the Plaza de Armas.

Andean villagers celebrate.

The feast of the Virgen del Carmen (June 15-17) is the most important in Paucartambo and one of the best opportunities to enjoy the festive ambiance of Cusco. In this festival multitudes come out to see the procession of the Virgen, accompanied by many musical ensembles and masked dancers. For this occasion many communities at higher altitudes, under the leadership of their *varayoc* or mayors, descend to Paucartambo to honor the Virgin. The 24th of June is the festival of Inti Raymi, a reenactment of the Day of the Sun which symbolically united the nations of the Tawantinsuyo. Last but not least, a week-long festival of music and tourism, that is sponsored by a local brewery and draws crowds of young people, begins in June as well (date varies).

Other important festivals are: Holy Week, with a famous procession of the Señor de los Temblores (the Lord of Earthquakes), patron of Cusco, celebrated since 1650 (March or April); the Feast of the Cross, or Cruz-Velacuy (May 3); the patron saint's festival of Calca (August 15-17); la Virgen de la Natividad in Chinchero (September 8-9); the feast of the Señor de los Temblores (October, date varies); and Santuranticuy in Cusco, a long Christmas season fair in which artisans from the entire region proffer their works (December 24).

Folkcrafts

A Cusco craftsman in San Blas.

Cusco offers an wide range of handicrafts which can be purchased at almost any spot in the city center, although we do recommend going to the city district of San Blas. Some of the best are the clothing in alpaca, llama, and lamb's wool, as well as hats made of felt. Fine silverwork with Inca and Colonial motifs, gourds carved with country scenes, varied ceramics, musical instruments (*quenas, zamponas, charangos*), mirrors with plaster frames painted in gold, and paintings of regional motifs can all be found.

Cusco is especially known for its sculptures of saints, virgins, and archangels with elongated necks, made by the Mendívil family from a paste of wheat and rice flour and plaster. These are true collection pieces.

 ## Points of Interest in the City

Traditional Locales

Plaza de Armas.

Archades in the city.

- *Plaza de Armas:* The Incas called this plaza *Aucaypata* or 'Warrior's Plaza,' and it is said to have been designed by the Inca Manco Cápac. It is flanked by old and stately, Colonial stone arches two stories high, the great Cathedral and the beautiful church of La Compañía.
- *San Blas:* this, Cusco's most picturesque city district, is known as the district of craftsmen, for here live the city's most famous artists. Its steep, narrow streets are lined with charming Colonial buildings that have been recently restored.

  Don't fail to visit its small streets and plazas, as well as its handicraft stores. Its church, San Blas, has a spectacular pulpit (see Churches, p. 184).

- *Plazuela Las Nazarenas:* legend has it that this peaceful *plazuela* or little plaza, now encircled by Colonial buildings on Inca foundations, was the site of the *Yachayhuasi*, or 'House of Knowledge,' during the Inca reign. Its buildings include the novitiate and the former quarters of the University of San Antonio Abad, now the Hotel Monasterio, and the church of San Antonio Abad built in the seventeenth century. Also worth seeing are the Las Nazarenas church and quarters for the lay sisters. To one side of the plaza is the street of Siete Culebras (seven snakes), the site of the home of conquistador Mancio Sierra, who is said to have gambled away the golden disc taken from the Koricancha temple, his portion of the booty from the capture of Cusco.

- *Calle Hatun Rumiyoc:* this street is two blocks from the Plaza de Armas via Triunfo street on the way to the San Blas district. Its stone walls, part of the palace of the Inca Roca, hold the famous twelve-angled stone.

The twelve-angled stone.

Churches

- *The Cathedral*, Plaza de Armas: its construction was begun in 1560 and it was consecrated in 1669. Like the Cathedral in Lima, it has had Gothic, Mannerist-Renaissance and Baroque influence. Flanked by two solid towers, its side doorways are Mannerist in style, and the central one is discreetly Baroque. Its altars are splendid, in the Renaissance, Baroque, and Neoclassic styles. Its seventeenth-century pulpit of carved wood is magnificent, as are the choir stalls. It also holds a good collection of paintings from the Cusco school, with works by Diego Quispe Tito, Basilio

Side view of the Cathedral.

Santa Cruz Pumacallao, Marcos Zapata, and Basilio Pacheco. Its gold and silverwork are some of the richest treasures known in Colonial art and include an immense monstrance of gold and precious stones, a solid silver shrine for the Corpus Christi procession, a silver bier for the Señor de los Temblores (the Lord of Earthquakes) and La Linda images, lecterns, candelabra, lovely altarpieces. This church has its own

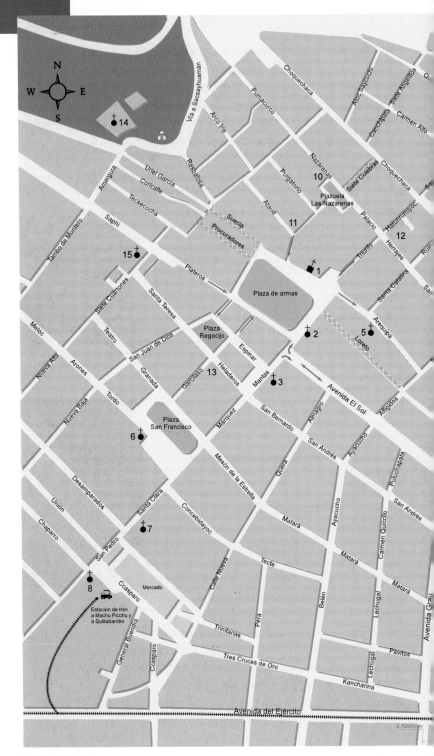

CUSCO CITY MAP

Colonial stone arcade.

Narrow street at San Blas.

1 The Cathedral
2 Church of La Compañía de Jes
3 Church of La Merced
4 Convent of Santo Domingo
5 Convent of Santa Catalina
6 Church of San Francisco
7 Church of Santa Clara
8 Church of San Pedro
9 Church of San Blas
10 Casa Cabrera
   (Museo de Arte Colonial)
11 Palacio del Almirante
   (Museo Inka)
12 Archbishop's Palace
   (Museo de Arte Religioso)
13 Casa Garcilaso de la Vega
   (Museo Histórico Regional)
14 Church of San Cristóbal
15 Church of Santa Teresa

chapel to the Señor de los Temblores, patron of Cusco. The renowned María Angola bell hangs in the Evangelio tower. Next to the Cathedral is the church of El Triunfo, built in 1733 over a small church raised in the seventeenth century to commemorate the Spanish victory over native leader Manco Inca. On the other side of the Cathedral is the church of Jesús, María y José, built in the eighteenth century. It contains beautiful altars, statues, and a frontispiece of silver. The three buildings were built on top of the palace of the Inca Wiracocha, called Quishuarcancha.

Visit during Mass: Mon-Sat, 10 to 11:30am, and 2 to 5:30pm.

- *La Compañía de Jesús*, Plaza de Armas: this is one of the most notable buildings in the Andean Baroque style and was built over the palace of the Inca Huayna Cápac, called Amarucancha. In 1650, an earthquake destroyed the earlier, Renaissance-style church and the present one was finished in 1668. Its has a splendid set of golden Baroque altars, a seventeenth-century painting of the Ascension of Christ by Diego de la Puente, magnificent sculptures of Jesuit saints and the seventeenth-century painting portraying the wedding of Beatriz Clara Coya, an Inca princess, to Spanish captain Martín García de Loyola, the grandnephew of San Ignacio de Loyola.

Towers of La Compañía.

Church of La Compañia, and the San Antonio Abad university.

Visit during Mass.

- *La Merced*, Calle Mantas n/n, near the Plaza de Armas: this building was almost completely rebuilt after the earthquake of 1650. Its doorways are still in the Mannerist style and contrast with the exuberant Baroque work of the belfry. It has important, Plateresque choir stalls and religious paintings, such as the seventeenth-century painting of San Laureano by Basilio Santa Cruz Pumacallao. Here are buried the two Diego de Almagro, the Elder, who died in 1538, and the Younger, who died in 1542. Its cloisters are considered among the finest in South America. It possesses oil paintings from the sixteenth century by Bernardo Bitti and from the seventeenth century by Ignacio Chacón, magnificent carvings, and a splendid monstrance of gold, silver and precious stones, which includes a famous pearl in the shape of a mermaid.

> *Visits to the church: daily during Mass,*
> *7 to 9am, and 5 to 7pm.*
> *Visits to the convent: Mon-Sat, 8am*
> *to noon, and 2 to 5pm.*

- *Santo Domingo / Koricancha*, Av. El Sol n/n, Plazoleta de Santo Domingo: this Dominican church and convent was built on the foundations of the Koricancha, or 'place of gold,' the Incas' principal religious building, dedicated to the worship of the sun. According to the chroniclers, its interior walls were covered in plates of gold. Visitors can easily see how the construction of the church utilized the fine stonework of the Inca sanctuary. Its doorway is a splendid example of Renaissance style, while its tower, similar to that of the La Merced church, is Baroque. It possesses a fine series of paintings on the life of Santo Domingo de Guzmán.

Patio of the San Antonio de Abad university and towers of La Compañía.

Walls of Koricancha and the church and convent of Santo Domingo.

> *Visiting hours: Mon-Sat, 8am to 5:30pm.*

- *Santa Catalina*, Santa Catalina Angosta n/n: this church and convent were founded in 1605, but had to be rebuilt after the earthquake of 1650. The church has fine Baroque altars and a large pulpit. The altars were the seventeenth-century works of masters Pedro de Oquendo and Diego Martínez de Oviedo. Its oil paintings are some of the most remarkable in Cusco, signed by Juan Espinoza de los Monteros and Lorenzo Sánchez de Medina and dating from the mid-seventeenth century. There are also a number of anonymous, Zurbaranesque paintings from the same period variously depicting martyrs and Latin saints. The convent was built on the foundation of the Acllahuasi, or 'House of the Chosen Virgins of the Sun,' with some of the most brilliant and best-conserved pre-Hispanic construction in Cusco. It contains admirable works in precious metals, a great museum, and the nuns prepare delicious sweets as well.

> *Visit during Mass.*

- *San Francisco*, Plaza San Francisco n/n: Viceroy Francisco de

Church of San Pedro de Andahuaylillas.

Toledo strongly supported the building of this church in 1572 and it was restored after the earthquake of 1650. Its base is in the shape of the Latin cross, it has three naves and a tall square tower. The façade towards the plaza is in the Renaissance style. Its choir stalls are among the most celebrated in Hispanic America because of their magnificent relief work. The convent survived the earthquake of 1650, remaining a singular example of sixteenth-century, Plateresque architecture, detailed with *azulejo* tiles from Seville. It contains paintings by the most important painters of the seventeenth century: Diego Quispe Tito, Marcos Zapata, Basilio Santa Cruz, Juan Espinoza de los Monteros and Antonio Sinchi Roca.

Visits during Mass.

• *San Pedro*, facing the central market: when the older church raised by Sebastián Garcilaso de la Vega, father of the famous Cusco-born chronicler, was destroyed in 1650, this one was built on the site in the late seventeenth century. It was designed by the indigenous architect and sculptor Juan Tomás Tuyru Túpac, and has two towers and a Renaissance façade, and its base is in the form of the Latin cross. Its nave has high vaults and there are six side chapels. Its main altar has a Baroque frontispiece, gradins or candle shelves and a tabernacle in silver, and it has a beautiful pulpit. It possesses a good collection of paintings.

• *San Blas*, Plazoleta San Blas: the principal wealth of this church, built in 1563, consists of its important collection of paintings, its splendid Baroque altar and, in particular, its famous Baroque pulpit, carved from a single piece of cedar and considered the finest example of Colonial carving in America. This major monument of the Cusco school dates from the late seventeenth century and is attributed to Juan Tomás Tuyru Túpac.

Visiting hours: Mon-Sat, 2 to 5:30pm.

- *Others:* Belén de los Reyes, San Cristóbal, Santa Teresa, and Santa Clara.

Museums

- *Archbishop's Palace or Museo de Arte Religioso*, corner of Hatun Rumiyoc and Herrajes: this mansion, which was built over the palace of the Inca Roca, belonged to the line of the Marquis of San Juan de Buenavista. In its interior are handsome salons and a magnificent chapel with a gilded Baroque altarpiece, and a significant display of sixteenth- to eighteenth-century paintings from the Cusco school. Its main wall (Hatun Rumiyoc street) holds the famous Inca, twelve-angled stone.

Balcony of the Archbishop's palace.

Visiting hours: Mon-Sat, 8 to 11:30am, and 3 to 5:30pm.
- *Casa Garcilaso de la Vega or Museo Histórico Regional*, corner of Heladeros and Garcilaso: this manor house belonged to Captain Sebastián Garcilaso de la Vega, father of the chronicler Garcilaso Inca de la Vega, who described his childhood here in his *Royal Commentaries of the Incas* [1609]. It has a large, informative collection of pre-Hispanic and Colonial art.

Visiting hours: Mon-Sat, 7am to 6:30pm.
- *Museo de Santa Catalina*, Santa Catalina Angosta n/n: contains a splendid collection of Baroque *retablos* and paintings from the Cusco school, including works by Diego Quispe Tito, Juan Espinoza de los Monteros, and Lorenzo Sánchez Medina, and also houses Colonial-era rugs and gold and silverwork.

Visiting hours: Mon-Thu and Sat, 9am to 5:30pm; Fri, 9am to 3pm.

- *Casa Cabrera or Museo de Arte Colonial*, Plaza de la Nazarenas 231: this ancient house, today a branch of the Banco Continental, has on display a beautiful collection of photographs by the talented Cusco photographer Martín Chambi (1891–1973) as well as different temporary displays.

    Visiting hours: Mon-Fri, 8am to 5:30pm;
    Sat, 10am to noon, and 3 to 5pm.

- *Palacio del Almirante or Museo Inka*, Cuesta del Almirante 153: raised on Inca foundations by Admiral Aldrete Maldonado in the early seventeenth century, this home has a magnificent Baroque doorway emblazoned with the admiral's coat-of-arms, a large arched patio and salons with coffered ceilings. It exhibits *keros* (carved ceremonial goblets), weavings, mummies and silver and gold figurines, as well as Inca weapons, tools and ceramics.

    Visiting hours: Mon-Fri, 8am to 5pm;
    Sat, 8:30am to 12:30pm.

 Excursions

Sacsayhuamán

3 600M / 11 812FT)

An impressive example of Inca military architecture, 2km (10 minutes) from the center of the city via paved road. Strategically placed on a hill overlooking Cusco, this spectacular fortress guarded the capital of the empire. It name means 'satisfied falcon' in Quechua. It is renowned for its enormous carved stones joined with astounding precision to form the outer walls. Some of these stones stand over 9m (30ft) tall, and weigh over 350 tons. It is said that its construction, begun by the Inca Túpac Yupanqui, took more than seventy years and required the labor of over twenty thousand men.

The Incas laid out the city of Cusco in the shape of a puma, with Sacsayhuamán as the head. The site has three levels, each with a zigzagging wall ('the teeth of the puma'), the Rodadero (a

Wall of worked stone, Sacsayhuamán.

Trapezoidal doorway.

natural rock outcropping) and the Throne of the Inca, worked from a single large stone. Sacsay-huamán looks very different today than it did when the conquistadors arrived, because the Spaniards used the fortress as a quarry for building Colonial Cusco.

Walls of Sacsayhuamán.

Qenko • Puca Pucara
)

3 680M / 12 074FT

Archeological sites 4km and 6km (15 minutes), respectively, NE of Cusco via paved highway. Qenko is a limestone formation which has been intricately carved with depictions of mythical beings, as well as winding underground passageways and a semicircular amphitheater. It is believed to have been used in worshipping the earth. Puca Pucara, whose name means 'red fortress' in Quechua (for the color of its walls at dusk) is a military construction comprised of layered terraces, high walls and stairways. Along with Sacsay-huamán, it was part of Cusco's defense system.

Qenko.

Tambomachay.

Tampumachay (Baños del Inca)
)

3 700M / 12 140FT

An archeological site 7km (15 minutes) NE of Cusco via paved highway. This complex is called the «Inca Baths,» and is comprised of fine stonework, aqueducts, and waterfalls fed by neighboring cold and hot springs. The site is thought to have been built for the worship of water, one of the pillars of the Inca world view. From a nearby tower you can see the site of Puca Pucara.

Urubamba Valley
)

2 850M / 9 351FT ON AVERAGE

27km (1 hour) NE of Cusco via paved highway in

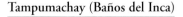

The people of the
Urubamba have
many reasons
to be proud. One is
their corn. The soil
and climate conditions
of the Urubamba Valley
are ideal for a variety
of corn with exceptionally
large, savory kernels.
Corn from the
Urubamba is known
worldwide and exported
to Japan, Spain,
Canada and the
United States.

good condition. The Urubamba Valley, also known
as the Sacred Valley, follows the length of the Vilcanota River (which later changes name to Willcamayu, or simply Urubamba) and consists of the
area between the towns of Písac and Ollantaytambo. Access is possible via two paved roads: the most
traveled road leaves Cusco and goes NW via Chinchero (28km), to the town of Urubamba (57km).
The second goes NE from Cusco towards Písac
(32km), then follows the course of the Vilcanota
River to the town of Calca (51km) in the heart of
the Valley. This road is less traveled than the first
as it deteriorates frequently. A succession of picturesque towns (some with splendid Colonial churches), agricultural terraces, and many archeological
sites, as well as the world's most famous corn, com-
bine with an exceptional climate to make this an
obligatory destination for all visitors to Cusco.

The most interesting activities here are: mountain climbing, on the snowy slopes of Chicón, Wakay Willca (also known as Puma Sillo or Verónica),
Pitusiray, Sawasiray, Terijway, and Suchubamba (all
summits in the Vilcanota Range are over 5 000m
(16 405ft), trekking, river rafting (on sections be-

The Urubamba Valley as seen from Písac.

tween Písac–Calca–Huarán–Ollantaytambo), horse-riding, and mountain biking. The towns in the valley have a good number of hotels and restaurants serving typical dishes. We recommend staying here if possible.

Písac

2 950M / 9 679FT)

A picturesque town and important archeological site 32km (1 hour) NE of Cusco via paved highway.

Gateway to the Sacred Valley, Písac has an «old town» (considered one of the most beautiful Inca complexes) and a «new town» from the Colonial era.

To reach the archeological site (one of the most important fortresses built to guard the capital of the empire) requires an uphill walk past some of the most spectacular terracing in the region. At the top are splendid walls, a few towers, the sundial or *intihuatana* (Quechua for 'hitching post of the sun') and various enclosures and storage places built of fine

Panoramic view of Písac.

stonework. The «new town» has a Colonial-era church where Mass is still said in Quechua, and there is a colorful fair every Sunday which we recommend visiting (there are also minor fairs on Tuesdays and Thursdays).

Ollantaytambo

2 750M / 9 023FT)

A typical town of Inca origin at the far W end of the Sacred Valley, at 93km (1 hour, 30 minutes) NE of Cusco via paved highway. Its design and the foundations of the majority of its buildings date from the Inca era, when it was a strategic military, religious, and agricultural center. Above it stands a fortress

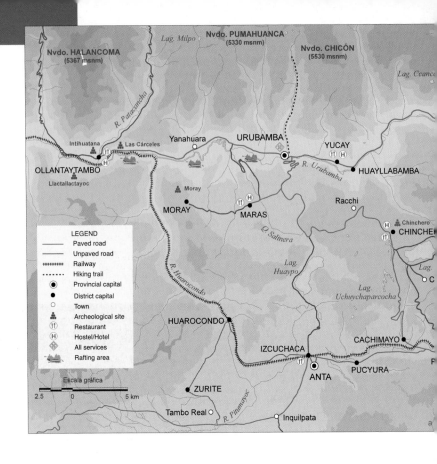

LEGEND

———	Paved road
———	Unpaved road
++++++++	Railway
········	Hiking trail
◉	Provincial capital
●	District capital
○	Town
⛏	Archeological site
🍴	Restaurant
Ⓗ	Hostel/Hotel
✳	All services
🚣	Rafting area

Escala gráfica

2.5   0   5 km

which guarded the entry to this part of the valley and protected it from possible invasion from the lower jungles. The fortress consists of a series of superimposed terraces of carved stones accessed by long staircases. The upper terrace contains large, admirably worked stone. It was here that Manco Inca fought the troops of Hernando Pizarro in 1537, leading a fierce resistance against the Spanish which continued for many years from Inca hideouts in the jungles of Vilcabamba.

Ollantaytambo has several hotels and restaurants and is a good base from which to visit the valley. The train to Machu Picchu stops here and many tourists prefer getting off here to continue the return to Cusco by bus (a faster option).

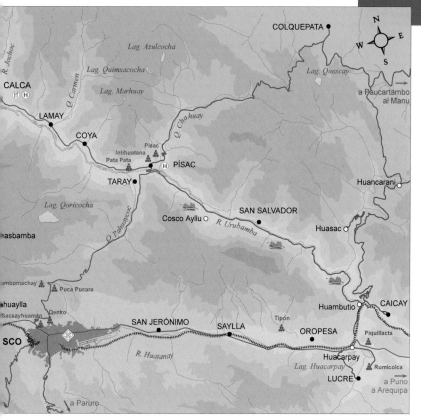

THE URUBAMBA VALLEY

Chinchero

3 160M / 10 368FT

A town of Inca origin 28km (45 minutes) N of Cusco via a paved highway that climbs to 3 762m (12 343ft). The town is guarded by the snowy peak of Chicón and its name comes from the Quechua word *sinchi*, or 'courageous man.' Its Plaza de Armas has an enormous Inca wall with ten large trapezoidal niches in perfect condition, and one of the most important Colonial-era churches of Cusco with Baroque altars and walls with richly painted scenes.

Also on the plaza is the former home of Mateo García Pumacahua, who led a rebellion against Spanish rule in 1814. It is impossible to speak of Chinchero without mentioning its colorful, well-attended Sunday fair, that draws countryfolk once a week from all corners and heights of the valley to exchange their products. From this town you can visit lakes Guaypó and Piuray.

Maras

3 028M / 9 935FT   )

A picturesque town 67km (1 hour) N of Cusco (9km from Urubamba) via paved highway. This was a very prosperous community in Colonial times and still has a lovely church and various manor houses sporting the coats-of-arms of native nobility. Close to Maras are salt mines from the Inca era that are still worked today. Highly recommended for photography buffs.

Salt mine nearby Maras.

Moray

3 176M / 10 420FT   )

An archeological site 7km from Maras via packed dirt road. Composed of a series of concentric agricultural terraces, some as deep as 150m. This is thought to have been a large agricultural laboratory where the Incas were able to create different microclimates to grow a large variety of crops. This is a highly recommended excursion for both its archeological value and the beauty of the countryside.

Calca

2 930M / 9 613FT   )

A picturesque town of Inca origin, at the foot of the two snow-capped peaks, Pitusiray and Sawasiray, 50km (1 hour) NE of Cusco via paved highway, in the Sacred Valley. The market here is the largest in the Sacred Valley because its strategic location links it to the tropical Lares valley. It possesses a handsome colonial church and Inca foundations are common among its buildings. Nearby are the archeological complex of Huchuy Qosqo, the medicinal sulphur hot springs of Machacancha and the cold, carbonated mineral springs of Minasmoqo.

Urubamba
2 871M / 9 419FT)
A town of Inca origin 76km (1 hour, 15 minutes) NE of Cusco via Písac, and 57km (45 minutes) via Chinchero.

Located at the heart of the Sacred Valley, Urubamba is surrounded by beautiful countryside and guarded by Mount Chicón. It was one of the principal agricultural centers of the Inca empire. In its plaza stands a Colonial-era church, it has several hotels and well-patronized country restaurants and *picanterías* serving typical dishes.

Boulevard of *pisonayes*, Urubamba.

Yucay
2 890M / 9 482FT)
A town of Inca origin 78km (1 hour 15 minutes) NE of Cusco (28km N of Calca) via paved highway, in the center of the Sacred Valley. Here are the remains of the palace of Inca Sayri Túpac, one of the rebel Incas who hid out in Vilcabamba, a splendid Colonial church and a small site museum. The town has good hotels.

Piquillacta • Lake Lucre
3 150M / 10 335FT)
An archeological area with beautiful landscapes, 22km (45 minutes) S of Cusco along the paved highway to Puno. Piquillacta, whose name means 'city of fleas,' was one the most spectacular centers of the Wari culture. It has more than 700 structures and walls standing almost 12m (39ft) high.

Nearby is the beautiful Lake Lucre (or Huacarpay), home to many species of local fauna. There is a small hostel and restaurant on the lake. The town of Lucre has the second oldest textile factory in Peru, built in 1861.

Remains of a wall in Piquillacta.

Andahuaylillas
3 198M / 10 493FT)
A pretty town 35km (1 hour) S of Cusco along the paved highway to Puno. Its unique church, San Pedro de Andahuaylillas,

is the biggest attraction for the visitor. Built at the beginning of the seventeenth century, the interior of this church is decorated with murals from the same era attributed to Luis de Riaño and depicting the road to heaven and the road to hell. His work is also seen in the paintings which decorate the baseboards and an oil painting of the Archangel Michael. This church also houses a majestic organ, numerous paintings of the Cusco school, silverwork and Baroque altars. The Plaza de Armas of Andahuaylillas, with its leafy *pisonay* trees is one of the most beautiful in the region.

A few kilometers away is the town of Huaro, where it is said that sorcerers lived in the times of the Incas. In Huaro there is a magnificent Colonial church whose murals are by Tadeo Escalante (1803), one of the last masters of the Cusco school.

Church of San Pedro, Andahuaylillas.

Plaza de Armas in Andahuaylillas.

A church in Urcos.

Tipón.

Urcos

150M / 10 335FT)

A town 48km (1 hour, 15 minutes) S of Cusco, along the paved highway to Puno. At the entrance to town there is a small, beautiful lake into which, according to legend, the Inca Huascar threw a gold necklace to keep it from the Spaniards. Urcos has a lovely Plaza de Armas with a stone church decorated with a mural of the baptism of Christ, by the native Renaissance-style painter Cusi Huamán. The plaza also has an impressive iron statue portraying the natives' resistance to the Spaniards.

Nearby are the ruins of Tipón (23km S of Cusco on the road to Urcos).

Paucartambo

3 020M / 9 908FT ○

A typical Colonial town some 100km (4 hours) E of Cusco. You must first take the paved highway to Puno. Beyond Huacarpay, take a packed dirt road

NE to Písac that climbs to the towns of Huanca-rani and Huambutío to finally descend to the fertile valley of Paucartambo. With its beautiful church, its Colonial-era bridge, narrow cobblestone streets, small plazas, and homes adorned with balconies and wide entryways, Paucartambo still retains its strong Colonial air. It is also the town that contributes the most dance troupes to perform in the feast of Corpus Christi and the pilgrimage to Qoyllur Ritt'i.

Countryfolk on the Colonial bridge of Paucartambo.

From this town the road climbs to Acjanaco and Tres Cruces (at the south end of Manu National Park), from where you can see the loveliest sunrise in the world. From Acjanaco you can continue down the Kos-ñipata Valley to the towns of Atalaya and Shintuya, on the banks of the Madre de Dios River. The hotels and restaurants in Paucartambo are simple. Take warm clothing.

Machu Picchu

See p. 340.

Hotels

Cusco

Hotel Libertador ★★★★★
Plazoleta Sto. Domingo 259. Tel 23 1961.
Fax 23 3152. Reservations Lima Tel 441 6345. US$ 185
hotel@libertador.com.pe

Hotel Monasterio ★★★★★
Palacio 136, plaza Nazarenas s/n. Tel 24 0696.
Fax 23 7111. US$ 185
reservas@peruorientexpress.com.pe

Hotel Savoy ★★★★
Av. El Sol 954. Tel 24 0247. Fax 22 1097. US$ 125
savoycusco@telser.com.pe

Hotel Posada del Inca ★★★★
Portal Espinar 142. Tel 22 7061. Fax 24 8090.

Reservations Lima Tel 422 4777. US$ 100
posada@el-olivar.com.pe

★★★★ San Agustín Internacional
Maruri 390. Tel 22 1169. Fax 22 1174. US$ 100
inter@terra.com.pe

★★★★ Hotel Don Carlos (Holyday Inn)
Av. El Sol 602. Tel 22 4457. Fax 24 1375.
Reservations Lima Tel 225 8633 / 225 8634. US$ 90
dcarloslima@terra.com.pe

★★★★ Hotel Royal Inka II
Santa Teresa 335. Tel 24 1397. Fax 23 4221. US$ 90
royalin@terra.com.pe

★★★★ San Isidro Labrador
Saphy 400. Tel 23 1001. Fax 22 1591. US$ 80
hisidrolabrador@latinmail.com

★★★ Hotel San Agustín Plaza
Av. El Sol 596. Tel 23 8121. US$ 105
Fax 23 7375.

★★★ Hotel El Dorado Inn
Av. El Sol 395. Tel 23 3112. Fax 24 0993. US$ 95
Reservations Lima Tel 472 1415.
doratour@telser.com.pe

★★★ Hotel Royal Inka I
Plaza Regocijo 299. Tel 23 1232. Fax 22 3876. US$ 90
royalin@terra.com.pe

★★★ Inca Tambo Hacienda
2 km ahead the road to Sacsayhuamán. US$ 90
Tel 22 2045 / 22 2126.
Reservations Lima Tel 446 2062.

★★★ Hotel Los Andes de América
Garcilaso 236. Tel 24 0275. Fax 22 3058. US$ 90
losandes@telser.com.pe

★★★ Hotel Ruinas
Ruinas 472. Tel 26 0644. Fax 23 6391. US$ 80
ruinas@terra.com.pe

★★★ El Balcón
Tambo de Montero 222. Tel 23 6331. US$ 60
Fax 22 5352.
balcon1@terra.com.pe

Hostal Centenario ★★★
   Av. Centenario 689. Tel 22 4235 / 23 1681. US$ 60

Hostal Monarca
   Esq. Recoleta y Pumapaccha 290. Tel 22 9934. US$ 50 ★★★
   hostalmonarca@terra.com.pe

Hostal Los Portales ★★
   Matará 332. Tel 22 3500. Fax 22 2391. US$ 45

Conquistador
   Santa Catalina Angosta 149. Tel 23 3661. US$ 40
   Fax 23 6314. ★★
   Orientours@telser.com.pe

Hostal Incawasi
   Portal de Panes 147, Cercado. Tel 24 7139. US$ 25 ★★
   Incawasi@telser.com.pe

Hostal Raymi ★★
   Av. Pardo 950. Tel 22 5241.

Sacred Valley

Hotel Posada del Inca ★★★
   Plaza Manco II 123, Yucay. Telefax 20 1107. US$ 110
   Reservations Lima Tel 221 2120.

Hotel San Agustín Urubamba ★★★
   Av. Ferrocarril s/n. Tel 20 1025. Fax 20 1443. US$ 75
   inter@terra.com.pe

Hotel San Agustín Monasterio de la Recoleta ★★★
   Recoleta 260. Tel 20 1025. Fax 20 1420.
   riviera@terra.com.pe

Hotel Royal Inka Písac ★★★
   Písac-Ruinas road. Tel 20 3046. US$ 50
   Fax 20 1443.

Hotel Valle Sagrado ★★★
   Av. Ferrocarril s/n. Tel 20 1117. US$ 35
   Reservations Lima Tel 445 8248.

Hotel Incaland ★★★
   Av. Ferrocarril s/n. Tel 20 1126 / 20 1127.
   Fax 20 1071.
   incaland@terra.com.pe

RATES ARE APPROXIMATE AND, UNLESS OTHERWISE NOTED,
ARE FOR DOUBLE OCCUPANCY.

Restaurants

- ✔ Inka Grill
  Portal de Panes 115, Cercado.
- ✔ Tunupa
  Portal de Confituras 233, 2nd. floor.
- ✔ La Yunta
  Portal de Carnes 214, Cercado.
- ✔ La Taberna del Truco
  Plaza Regocijo 261.
- ✔ Mesón de los Espaderos
  Espaderos and plaza de armas.
- ✔ Tratoría Adriano
  Esq. Av. El Sol y Mantas.
  Tel 23 3965.
- ✔ Tai Won
  Av. El Sol 210.
- ✔ Pucara
  Plateros 309.
- ✔ Chez Maggy
  Plateros 339.
- ✔ La Barceloneta
  Procuradores 347.
- ✔ La Retama
  Portal de Panes 123, 2nd. floor, Cercado.
- ✔ Macondo
  Cuesta de San Blas 571.
- ✔ El Patio
  Portal de Carnes 236, plaza de armas.
- ✔ Paititi
  Portal Carrizos 270, Cercado.
- ✔ Los Portales
  Portal de Panes 163, Cercado.
- ✔ La Estancia Imperial
  Portal de Panes 137, 2nd. floor, Cercado.
- ✔ Govinda (vegetarian)
  Espaderos 128, Cercado.
- ✔ El Grano (Assian)
  Santa Catalina 398.

El Buen Pastor (Pies and Dessert)   ✔
 Cuesta San Blas 579.
Víctor Victoria (Israeli)   ✔
 Tigre 130.
El Cuate (Mexican)   ✔
 Procuradores 386.
Kin Taro (Japanese)   ✔
 Heladeros 149. Tel 22 6181.

Sacred Valley
Hirano's   ✔
 Mariscal Castilla, Urubamba.
Luna Nueva   ✔
 Grau y Manrique, Urubamba.
Quinta Los Geráneos   ✔
 Grau y Manrique, Urubamba.
New World Café   ✔
 Jr. Comercio y Mariscal Castilla, Urubamba.
Huayoccari Hacienda Restaurante   ✔
 Km 64, Cusco-Urubamba road. Tel 26 2224.

Cafes, Pubs • Discoteques
Trotamundos   ◆
 Portal de Comercio 177, Cercado.
El Ayllu   ◆
 Portal de Carnes 208, Cercado.
Café Bagdad   ◆
 Portal de Carnes 126, Cercado.
Cross Keys Pub   ◆
 Portal de Carnes 233,
 plaza de armas.
Plus Café   ◆
 Portal de Panes 151, 2nd. floor, Cercado.
Varayoc Café Literario   ◆
 Calle Espaderos 142.
Café Kusikuy   ◆
 Garcilazo 210.
La Oveja Negra (trova music, cultural bar)   ◆
 Arco Iris 511, San Cristóbal.

◆ Paddy O'Flaherty's (irland pub)
Triunfo 124, 2nd. floor. Tel 24 6903.

◆ Norton's Rat Tavern (bar, pool, sandwichs)
Loreto 115, 2nd. floor.

◆ Discoteca Kamikase I
Plaza Regocijo 274.

◆ Ukuku's Pub II
Plateros 316.

◆ Discoteca Up Town
Calle Suecia 302.

◆ Discoteca El Muki
Santa Catalina 114.

◆ Las Quenas Club
Av. El Sol 954 (basement of the Hotel Savoy).

◆ Discoteca Mama África
Espaderos 135, 2nd. floor.

• **Folk** *Peñas*

◆ Centro Qosqo
Av. El Sol 604.

◆ Inti Raymi
Saphy 605.

◆ Inka's
Portal de Panes 105, plaza de armas.

◆ Teatro Municipal
Mesón de la Estrella 149. Tel 22 7321.

Useful Facts

AREA CODE **84**

Basic information

IPERÚ

Information and Assistance for Tourists

Velasco Astete Airport (lobby).   Telefax 23 7364
Open: Mon-Fri, 6am to 1pm.
iperucuscoapto@promperu.gob.pe

CONTINUE ⟩

Portal de Carrizos 250, plaza de armas.	Telefax 25 2974
Open: Mon-Fri, 8am to 7:30pm.	23 4498
iperucusco@promperu.gob.pe	
Tourism Police Aid:	24 9654
Open daily, 24 hours..	24 9652
Ecology Police:	27 5051
Instituto Nacional de Cultura:	
Calle San Bernardo s/n.	23 6061
Inmigration Office:	22 2741
Av. El Sol (next to the post office)	
Open: Mon-Fri, 8 am to 4pm,	
and Sat, 8am to noon.	
Main Office of the Manu National Park	23 4179
and Reserve Zone:	
Micaela Bastidas 310, Wanchaq	

Railway Stations (PERÚRAIL)

Reservations:	23 8722
Trains to Puno and Arequipa:	
Estación Mario Jara Schenone	23 3592
(ex Wanchaq): Av. San Martín s/n.	22 1931
Trains to Machu Picchu and Quillabamba:	
Estación San Pedro: Ccascaparo s/n.	22 1313

Travel Agencies

Explorandes: Av. Garcilazo 316-A.	23 8380
fnegri@explorandes.com.pe	24 5700
Lima Tours:	22 1266
Portal de Harinas 177, plaza de armas	22 8481
Cóndor Travel: Saphy 848.	24 8181
condorcusco@condortravel.com.pe	24 8282

Car Rental

Explorandes: Av. Garcilazo 316-A.	23 8380
Transportes Explorer's: Plateros 305.	23 3498
Turismo Orellana: Garcilazo 206.	62 1758
Touring y Automóvil Club del Perú	
Av. Sol 457 (305).	
Osdi Rent a Car	
Urb. Mateo Pumacahua 3-10, Wanqaq.	

CONTINUE ⮕

AREA CODE **84**

Craftsmen Workshops

Hilario Mendívil
  Plazoleta San Blas 634.
Edilberto Mérida
  Carmen Alto 133.
Antonio Olave Palomino
  Siete Angelitos 752.
Víctor Vivero
  Tandapata 172.
Luis Aguayo Revollar
  Cuesta del Almirante 211-156.

Handicraft Stores

Mercado Artesanal: Av. Sol, 4th. block .
La Mamita: Portal de Carnes 244, plaza de armas.
Galería Latina: San Agustín 427.   24 6588
Galería de Arte Aguayo: Av. Sol 616.   23 7992
La Paloma: Cuesta San Blas 552,
  plazuela Santa Catalina 211.
Maranganito: Portal Mantas 158.
Coordinadora Sur Andina: Calle del Medio 130,
  plaza de armas.

Camp Equipment

Soqllaq'asa Camping Service: Plateros 354.   25 2560
Camping & Deportes: Av. Sol 346, stand 118.

Post Office: Av. Sol 800.   22 5232
24 hours Medical Emergencies :   24 9494
  Av. Infancia 508.   65 1888
Clínica Pardo: Av. De la Cultura 710.   62 4186
Clínica Paredes: Lechugal 405.   22 5265
Mastercard: Almagro 125.
Visa card Banco de Crédito: Av. Sol 189.
Western union: Av. Sol 627.
Internet service: Calle del Medio 117.

Chachapoyas

2 334 M / 7 658 FT
15 800 POP.
1 225 KM
NW OF LIMA

P. 82

P. 78

ROUTE MAPS

3   9

Situated on the eastern slope of the northern Andes, the city of Chachapoyas is the capital of the department of Amazonas. «Chacha,» as it is affectionately known to its inhabitants, is located on the top of a hill, surrounded by eucalyptus forests and imposing mountains. It is an Andean city, even though it lies within the cloud forest, one of the habitats richest in species and also one of the most threatened.

The spot on which the city stands was once part of the extensive territory of the Chachapoyas, a culture that headed a con-

Street in the hillside city district.

federation of small kingdoms scattered over the northeastern Andes and reached its height around AD 1000. The Chachapoyas fiercely resisted the attempts of the Incas to dominate them, but were finally conquered by the Inca Túpac Yupanqui in the second half of the fifteenth century. Nonetheless, they rebelled during the reign of Inca Huayna Cápac, who punished them with a series of repressive measures. Legend has it that, having learned their lesson, they sent an older concubine of

Temperate climate, typical of the transition zone between the Andean heights and the high rainforest. Yearly mean temperature of 22°C (72°F) with heavy rain, especially December to March. Cool nights.

Túpac Yupanqui's (whose sons were soldiers in the Inca army) as a emissary for peace, a gesture which so moved the Inca that he agreed to a solid, lasting truce for the region. All historical data seems to contradict this story, however, and indicates rather that the population here maintained a constant state of rebellion against the government in Cusco.

In what is today the district of Levanto, Major General Alonso de Alvarado founded the city of Chachapoyas on September 15, 1538, naming it San Juan de la Frontera. A few months later

Cloud forest in the Utcubamba Valley.

the city was moved to its present location due to the inconvenient terrain of the first. Spanish presence has left a considerable architectural imprint on the city, as reflected in its Plaza de Armas, which still has some Colonial-era buildings, and in the design of its steep and narrow cobblestone streets.

Today Chachapoyas is a city with a population mostly of immigrants from the nearby highlands and valleys. It has some hotels and simple restaurants, and is the departure point for exploring an archeological region —with remains as important as those of Kuélap— that is beginning to attract enormous interest.

On the outskirts of Chachapoyas.

Local dishes

Entrées
• Inchik uchu: yucca simmered in peanut sauce, *ají* pepper, and cilantro.

Soups
• Cazuela chachapoyana: the soup that «raises the dead,» made of chicken, beef, and lamb.
• Zarapatera: turtle soup, with banana and *fariña* (yucca flour), cooked in the turtle's shell.

Festivals

Some of Chachapoyas' best festivals are its carnival season and the felling of the *humishas* (gift-laden trees) in Luya (second week of February); the patron saints' days of Luya and Jalca Grande (June 24); of San Pedro in Jalca Grande (June 29); of la Virgen de Asunta in Chachapoyas (August 1-15); the anniversary of Chachapoyas (September 5); and the patron saint's day of Lamud (second week of September).

THE CLOUD FOREST

Running in a narrow fringe along the eastern slopes of the Andes, at an altitude of 1 800m to 2 500m (5 900ft to 8 200ft), cloud forests are so named for their intense humidity. The unique, warm and rainy climate, and the steep, complex topography produce a lush and diverse flora, characterized by ferns, orchids and bromeliads (*Tillandsia sp.*). Its fauna includes the Andean bear (*Tremarctos ornatus*), the Andean cock-of-the-rock (*Rupicola peruviana*) and the rare *huácharo* or oilbird (*Steatornis caripensis*), the only nocturnal bird that feeds on fruit. The large number of archeological remains in these forests indicate that they were densely populated in pre-Hispanic times.

Points of Interest in the City

Museums

- *Museo del Instituto Nacional de Cultura*, Junín 817: exhibits interesting pre-Hispanic remains that were found in the city's environs.

  It is best to call before a visit. Tel 75 7047

Excursions

Kuélap

3 000M / 9 843FT

A pre-Hispanic citadel 74km (5 hours) SW of Chachapoyas. This is the most important archeological attraction in northeastern Peru. It is located in the district of Tingo, on a crest of

Citadel of Kuélap.

Bromeliad and detail in worked stone, Kuélap.

rock overlooking the valley of the Utcubamba River, a tributary of the Marañón River. It was discovered in 1843 and the majority of its construction has been dated to around AD 800.

Kuélap is built in a north-south orientation. It consists of two large platforms on which a considerable city of circular buildings were built. The most impressive aspect of this place are its enormous ramparts, 25m high at some points and 600m long. The citadel has three entrances, two to the east and one to the west, designed as large passageways that funnel into narrow apertures allowing only one person to pass through at a time, thus aiding the defenders of the citadel. At the south end rises a circular construction some six meters high, in the shape of a truncated, inverted cone; it seems to have served a ceremonial function.

To reach Kuélap, take the packed dirt road from Chachapoyas to Tingo (2 hours, 30 minutes), where there is lodging and some simple restaurants, and from there continue 26km on the same type of road. Vehicles are left in a designated parking and

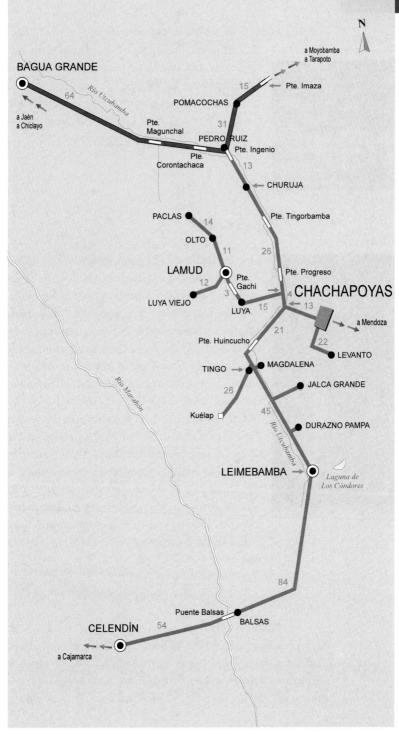

CHACHAPOYAS. EXCURSION MAP

camping zone, from which a marked trail leads to the citadel (15 minutes). It is possible to visit Kuélap in a single day, but you should leave quite early from Chachapoyas. Nonetheless, if you have enough time, camping in the area will give you the opportunity to enjoy a spectacular view of the great wall at dawn. Take warm clothing and rain gear.

Stone frieze, Kuélap.

Jalca Grande

2 890M / 9 482FT

One of the most picturesque towns in the region, 85km (4 hours) S of Chachapoyas. Known as the «folklore capital of Chachapoyas,» it is unique for its adobe houses with their cone-shaped straw roofs, and for its church, built in the sixteenth century. It has a small museum housing a collection of objects from the Chachapoyas culture, as well as the curious vestments of missionaries who frequented the town. Very close by is the archeological site of Ollape. To reach Jalca Grande, take the road to Tingo, pass the turnoff to Kuélap, and continue several kilometers further along the Utcubamba Valley. The road then begins a weaving ascent to the upper part of the mountains and enters Jalca Grande from the west. This town has simple restaurants, lodging can be requested, and camping in the outskirts is allowed. Take warm clothing and rain gear.

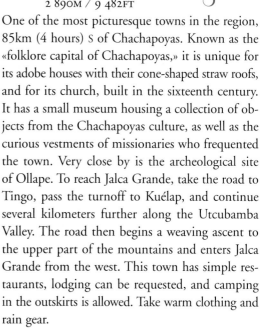
Tingo waterfall.

Chipuric

2 515M / 8 252FT

An archeological site 35km (1 hour) NO of Chachapoyas (and 3km from the town of Luya) via packed dirt road. Consists of numerous circular stacked-slate constructions fenced in by a stone wall, making them each individual forts. A necropolis in a nearby cliff of the same name has clay sarcophagi that stand 1,5m tall facing the Marañón River.

Sarcophagi of Karajía
2 760M / 9 056FT

An archeological site 48km (5 hours, 30 minutes) NW of Chachapoyas. Yet another extraordinary excursion which can be made from this city. Facing the deep valley of Juscubamba, these fired-clay sarcophagi stand two meters high; their wide, flat fronts are painted in geometric motifs and they are strategically placed on the heights of a limestone cliff. Access to this site is via a dirt road leading to the towns of Luya and Lamud, 40km (approx. 1 hour, 30 minutes) from Chachapoyas. Hiring a guide and pack animals here is recommended. From Lamud, continue some three hours on foot or by burro, crossing the settlements of Corazón de Jesús and Huaychopampa, to reach the picturesque town of Shipata on the edge of the Juscubamba gorge. Shipata (which has simple restaurants and some lodging) is the ideal place from which to view the sarcophagi. In the interest of protecting these archeological treasures, you should not attempt to climb to them. From Lamud it is also possible to reach the sarcophagi via a dirt road to the settlement of Trita (1 hour, 30 minutes) and continuing on some fifteen minutes on foot.

Rural family in Luya.

Levanto
2 050M / 6 726FT

The original site of the city of Chachapoyas, approximately 22km (1 hour) S of the present-day city. Contains an enormous concentration of archeological attractions and beautiful landscapes. One highlight is the site of Yálape, with its geometric friezes; the circular building (Chachapoya-Inca era) of Colla-Cruz, accessed by packed dirt road; the pre-Hispanic canal of Aishpachaca and the Colonial-era water works of Molino-Huayco (1 hour 30 minutes from town). There are no tourist services in Levanto.

Hotels

★★ Hotel Amazonas
Grau 565, plaza de armas. Tel 77 7199. US$ 25

★★ Gran Hotel Vilaya
Ayacucho 755. Tel 77 7664. Fax 77 8154. US$ 25
vilaya@wayna.rcp.net.pe

★★ El Gran Kuélap Hotel
Amazonas 1057. Tel 77 7136. US$ 20

★ Hotel Revash
Jr. Grau 517, plaza de armas. Tel 77 7391.
Fax 77 7356.
revash@tsi.com.pe

★ Hostal Yohumanji
Ayacucho 711. Tel 77 7279. Fax 77 7819. US$ 10
olvacha@ddm.com.pe

★ Casa Vieja
Jr. Chincha Alta 569. Tel 77 7353. US$ 5

★ Choctamal Lodge
Road to Kuélap. Reservations Tel 77 8078.

★ Chillo Hacienda
A 5 km de Tingo. Reservations Lima Tel 440 2022
postmaster@incanatura.com.pe

★ Casona Monsante
Amazonas 746. Tel 77 7702.

★ El Tejado
Grau 543, plaza de armas.

RATES ARE APPROXIMATE AND, UNLESS OTHERWISE NOTED,
ARE FOR DOUBLE OCCUPANCY.

Restaurants

✔ El Chacha
Grau 565, plaza de armas.

El Portoncito ✔
  Ortiz Arrieta 262.
Las Rocas ✔
  Ayacucho 932.
Las Vegas ✔
  Corner of Amazonas and Chincha Alta.
Chifa El Turista ✔
  Amazonas 575.
Picantería la Olla de Barro ✔
  Parque Santa Ana 150.
Matalache ✔
  Ayacucho 616.
El Carbón, Kuélap, La Estancia, El Tejado. ✔

Useful Facts

AREA CODE **44**

☎

Basic information

Vilaya Tours:
  Jr. Grau 624. 77 7506
Servicios Turísticos Revash:
  Grau 517. 77 7391
• Tourism Police Aid:
  Bagua Grande 77 4450
  Bagua Chica 77 1751
Botica Perpetuo Zocorro:
  Grau 533. 75 7121
Hospital de Apoyo IPSS:
  Ayacucho 436. 77 7986
Instituto Nacional de Cultura:
  Jr. Ayacucho 1200. 77 7045
Post Office:
  Grau 561. 77 7019
IPERÚ:
  Information and Assitance for Tourists
  01-574-8000 Lima.

The Chanchamayo Valley

SAN RAMÓN	775M
LA MERCED	751M
310 KM	
E OF LIMA	

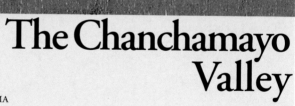

P. 78

ROUTE MAPS
5 10

Full of tropical exuberance, San Ramón and La Merced are two of the most popular destinations for the resident of Lima in search of relaxation and contact with nature, due to their proximity to the capital (5 hours away). These «*mestizo* cities» lie on the banks of the Chanchamayo River (Quechua for 'torrential river'), which shares its name with this wide, generous valley located in the lower jungle on the eastern flank of the Andes.

It is impossible to think of these cities separately, as they are

Rainbow and storm clouds in the valley.

united by both history and modern commercial activity. Both are important marketing centers for tropical products such as coffee (the region ranks first place in national production), cocoa, rice and wood; the cities' fruit and ornamental plants are also famous. This is the area where German naturalist Arthur

Typical tropical climate, with hot, humid days year round and annual mean temperature of 25° C (77° F). A heavy rainy season from December to March, altghough rain showers are not uncommon at other times of the year. The ideal time to visit is from May to October.

Brell (1907–1978), who discovered the curative properties of the now-famous *uña de gato* (*Uncaria tomentosa*), lived in the 1950s.

The Chanchamayo Valley and its surroundings were the ancestral territory of the Asháninka and Yánesha ethnic groups. Franciscan monks entered the area at the beginning of the seventeenth century and founded numerous missions. Contact led to a series of epidemics which devastated the region and depleted the native population. This sparked a rebellion led by Juan Santos Atahualpa (1742–1752), which impeded colonization here for more than eighty years.

In 1847, President Ramón Castilla resolved to recover the region and founded a fort at San Ramón to defend the region from attacks by the natives. On another site, at what had been the Franciscan mission at Quimiri, the city of La Merced was founded in 1855. The almost 10km of paved highway linking these two are a veritable delight for the traveler; on either side of the highway rise gentle hills covered in orange and tangerine plantations, with the high jungle vegetation and the waterfalls contributing to the beauty of this fantastic countryside.

UÑA DE GATO

In the 1950's, Arthur Brell completed the first scientific studies on *uña de gato*, or cat's claw, a plant collected from the Chanchamayo Valley. *Uña de gato* is a climbing vine that grows up to 15m in length on the eastern slopes of the Andes at an altitude of 200m to 800m (650ft to 2 600ft). It was traditionally used as a contraceptive and anti-inflammatory by tribes of the central jungle, but it is now revolutionizing the world of medicine today as laboratory tests show that it combats inflammation and regulates the immune system. It is also believed to inhibit the growth of cancer cells.

Torneo de cinta in Oxapampa.

Festivals

Highlights among the festivals celebrated in this area are the Día del Colono (Day of the Settler) in Pozuzo (July 26-30), in which the arrival of settlers to this area is commemorated with cockfighting championships and *torneos de cinta* (where young men joust at rings that hold embroidery local women have made during the year); the festival at Oxapampa (August 30), with rodeos, dances, and abundant beer; the anniversary of La Merced (September 24); the anniversary of San Ramón (November 14); and the anniversary of the province of Chanchamayo (December 31).

Excursions

Cascada El Tirol

800M / 2 625FT   )

Recently discovered as a tourist attraction, this 35m waterfall is located only a few kilometers E of San Ramón. To reach it, take the road to the right of the Puntuyacu bridge for some 15 minutes, park the car after passing the town of Playa Hermosa, and follow a wagon road for some 30 minutes. The crystalline waters are ideal for bathing. By asking the locals, it's easy to find.

Orchid
(*Bletia catenulata*).

Jardín Botánico El Perezoso   )

840M / 2 756FT

17km (20 minutes) NW of La Merced via the packed dirt road to Oxapampa. Interesting display of wildflowers native to the region, ideal for photography.

Destilería Colombo   )

780M / 2 559FT

27km (1 hour) NE of La Merced via the packed dirt road which runs through the Los Italianos *quebrada* (canyon). Here there is an ancient sugar cane mill called a *trapiche*, and a distillery of *aguardiente*

THE CHANCHAMAYO VALLEY. EXCURSION MAP

(cane liquor), famous for medicinal plant extracts. An all-terrain vehicle is recommended for this excursion

Pampa Hermosa
890M / 2 920FT ◯

An indigenous reservation 24km (2 hours) E of La Merced (or, from San Ramón, leaving from the Victoria bridge), accessed by a dirt road only passable during the dry season, with an all-terrain vehicle. This is a handsome forest with ancient cedars (*Cedrela sp.*), walnut trees (*Alnus sp.*) and lush vegetation, ideal for bird watchers and orchid lovers. It has an ideal spot for observing the *gallito de las rocas* (Andean cock-of-the-rock, *Rupicola peruviana*).

San Isidro Farm, Oxapampa.

Oxapampa

1 814M / 5 955FT

72m (2 hours, 30 minutes) NE of La Merced via packed dirt road. Founded in 1891 by European immigrants coming from the Pozuzo colony, its name, meaning 'hay meadow' in the native tongue, alludes to the extensive natural pastures which used to exist in the valley. Oxapampa is famous for European-style wooden homes, cattle raising, sawmills, honey, and its fields of hot *rocoto* peppers. Highly recommended for its pleasant climate, it is also the point of departure for trips to the Yanachaga–Chermillén National Park.

Villa Rica

1 350M / 4 429FT

54km (2 hours) E of La Merced via packed dirt road, this picturesque, high jungle town is engaged primarily in cultivating tropical food products, such as coffee, avocado, and *rocoto*. It was founded in 1928 by European colonists seeking lands free of the malaria and yellow fever epidemics that afflicted their countrymen in other parts of the jungle. This is the point of departure for visiting the waterfalls at Yesu (3km from town) and the Casa Comunal Yánesha (36km, on the way to Puerto Bermúdez), and ideal place for handicrafts.

Panoramic view of Pozuzo.

Pozuzo

908M / 2 979FT

163km (6 hours) N of La Merced by packed dirt road, this town was founded by Austrian and German immigrants in 1857. Invited by the Peruvian government to populate the region, the colonists were left to their fate, surviving solely on their wits and their desire to get ahead. Its name comes from the Yánesha language and means 'salty water,' alluding to a course of brackish water that rises near town and flows to the Huancabamba River. Its two sections are named for the homelands of the first German and Austrian settlers: Prussia and Tyrol. Its festivals are well-known, with rodeos and *torneos de cinta*, as are its woodwork and its beautiful women who have European features and speak with a marked jungle accent. The road from Oxapampa (81km, or around 4 hours) is, quite simply, spectacular. However, it is presently in poor condition and several stream crossings are necessary, for which we recommend an all-terrain vehicle.

Day of the Settler in Pozuzo.

A typical home of Pozuzo.

Hotels

San Ramón

El Refugio ★★★
   Av. Ejército 490. Tel 33 1082.
   Fax 33 1002. US$ 35
   hotelrefugio@infotex.com.pe

Hotel Conquistador ★★★
   Progreso 298. Tel 33 1157. US$ 30

Hostal Venus ★★
   Paucartambo 247. Tel 33 1004. US$ 20

Hotel Chanchamayo ★
   Progreso 288. Tel 33 1008. US$ 15

La Merced

★★★ Golden Gate

Just before the Herrería bridge (before entering La Merced). Tel 53 1483. Fax 43 2572. US$ 35

★★★ Gad Gakun

1 km away from Herrería bridge.

★★ Hostal El Edén

Áncash 347. Tel 53 1183. Fax 53 2340. US$ 30

★★ Hostal Mercedes

Tarma 576. Tel 53 1304. US$ 20

★★ Gran Hotel Romero

Palca 419. Tel 53 1106. US$ 20

★★ Hostal Residencial Rey

Prolong. Junín 103. Tel 53 1185. US$ 15

Oxapampa

★★ Hospedaje Loechle-Sinty

Av. San Martín 12th block. Tel 76 2180. loechlesinty@yahoo.com

★★ Hospedaje Curly Hassinger

Fundo San Francisco s/n

★★ Hostal Arias

Bolognesi 238. Tel 76 2312. US$ 20

★★ Hotel Isolina

Bolognesi 172. Tel 76 2305. Fax 76 2036. US$ 15

Family Lodgings of Miller, Travis, Verde, Robertson and others.

Pozuzo

★★ Frau María Egg

Av. Los Colonos s/n.

★★ Gastelhaus Schmidt

Av. Cristóbal Johan s/n, Prusia.

★★ Camping Toropampa

Crossing the Vogt bridge. Reservations Tel 70 7005. fns@ec-red.com

RATES ARE APPROXIMATE AND, UNLESS OTHERWISE NOTED, ARE FOR DOUBLE OCCUPANCY.

Restaurants

San Ramón ✔

Parrilladas El Parral
  Uriarte 361. ✔

Hotel Conquistador Restaurant
  Progreso 298. ✔

Chifa Felipe Siu
  Progreso 440. ✔

Hotel El Refugio Restaurant
  Av. Ejercito 440.

La Merced ✔

El Campa
  Plaza de armas.

Pizzería La Romana ✔
  Arica 309.

Oxapampa

Oasis ✔
  Bolognesi 363, plaza de armas.

La Llegada ✔
  Bolognesi 154, plaza de armas.

La Cabaña ✔
  Bolognesi 186, plaza de armas.

Pozuzo

El Pozuzino, El Bambú y El Horizonte. ✔

Useful Facts

☎

Basic information

Centro de Salud San Ramón:
 Jr. Chanchamayo 291.   33 1728
Clínica Elena:
 Calle Tarma 194.   33 1454
Botica Mi Salud:
 Progreso 107.   33 1094
Botica Santo Domingo:
 Progreso 497.   33 1890
Instituto Nacional de Cultura:
 Jr. Arequipa 599.
 Huancayo.   23 3233
Tourism Police Aid:
 Huancayo   81 9466
IPERÚ:
 Information and Assistence for Tourists
 01-574-8000 Lima.

☎

Hospital de Apoyo La Merced: Tarma 140.   53 1002
Botica La Merced: Tarma 355.   53 1026
Botica San Francisco: Tarma 268.   53 2479
Instituto Nacional de Cultura:
 Jr. Arequipa 599.
 Huancayo.   23 3233
Tourism Police Aid:
 Huancayo   81 9466
Post Office:
 2 de Mayo n/n.   53 1174
IPERÚ:
 Information and Assistence for Tourists
 01-574-8000 Lima.

Chiclayo

29 M / 7 658FT
411 500 POP.
765 KM
NW OF LIMA

P. 82

P. 78

The city of Chiclayo, capital of the department of Lambayeque, is flanked by the fertile Zaña and Lambayeque valleys, famous for their sugar cane, cotton, and rice plantations. Due to its proximity to the sea, Chiclayo is a typically coastal town, always closely linked to the sea.

The region in which the city is located has been home to successive pre-Hispanic cultures whose remains are only now being revealed to the world. In 1987, a group of archeologists discovered the royal tombs of Sipán, in which were buried important

ROUTE MAP
2

Boats at the port of Pimentel.

dignitaries of the Mochica culture, the dominant culture in this region from the first to the seventh centuries AD. Towards the end of the sixth century, this area was heavily influenced by the central coast cultures who in turn were trading with the Wari culture of the southern sierra. The fusion of these cultures with the Mochica yielded the Sicán, or Lambayeque culture (AD

Warm and sunny climate year round, with a yearly mean temperature of 24° C (75° F) and a light rainy season from December to March that becomes heavier with the El Niño.

SIPÁN AND SICÁN

The names sound almost alike, but are not the same. Sipán is a town in the Lambayeque Valley where archaeologists found the royal tombs of the Mochicas. Sicán, on the other hand, is the name some archeologists give to a culture that flourished between AD 800 and 1100 (after the Mochica culture) and which had its capital at Batán Grande in the La Leche Valley. This ancient people repeatedly depicted a mythological being (the «Sicán god») in their art. They believed this god had the power to provide water. Curiously, Batán Grande burned down around the year AD 1050. There is evidence of a long period of drought followed by heavy flooding prior to this event. In Muchik (one of the many languages existing in Peru at the time of the Conquest), Sicán meant 'temple of the moon.'

600–900) and the legend of their origin, in which a mythical character named Naymlap populated the central coast with his progeny. The region was later ruled by the Chimú from the city of Chan Chan (in Trujillo) and afterwards conquered by the Incas.

It is said that Chiclayo was once the site of a modest settlement when founded in the seventeenth century. As a consequence of intense commerce with towns in the sierra, the settlement grew and two centuries later was a vigorous city, engaged in commerce with Lima and Panama through the port of Pimentel. The city was home to several social groups then known as *criollos* (first-generation Peruvian-born Spaniards), *mestizos* (of mixed-race birth), and natives, along with a considerable population of Negro slaves who worked on the large haciendas of the region. At the end of the nineteenth century, Chinese laborers, or coolies, arrived to replace the Negro labor force lost after slavery was abolished.

Today Chiclayo is the largest commercial center in the northern Peru, a point of confluence for the towns of the coast, sierra, and northern jungle. Because of its festive character, it is said to be the city where «work can wait, but never a party!» In contrast to other coastal cities, Chiclayo is a modern town containing relatively few attractions, with the

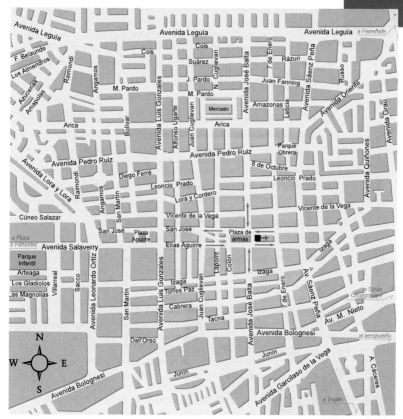

CHICLAYO CITY MAP

exception of its Cathedral, built at the end of the nineteenth century on a foundation designed by French engineer Gustaf Eiffel, and its public market, with its colorful stands of fruits and vegetables, as well as a most surprising array of products for the traditional healing practices known as *curandería*. For its friendly people, its exquisite cuisine, and the many attractions of its surroundings (archeological sites and handicraft centers), Chiclayo is an ideal destination at any time of the year.

A shaman's stall at the local market.

Local Dishes

Entrées
• Chifles con cecina: banana chips and bacon.

- Chiringuito: a *cebiche* of dried guitar fish.
- Mala rabia: a purée of banana cooked in milk, with cheese and *ají* pepper.

Main Dishes

- Arroz con pato a la chiclayana: rice and duck cooked with beer, *hierbabuena*, and cilantro.
- Cabrito a la chiclayana: tender goat kid stewed after marinating in *chicha* and vinegar.
- Tortilla de raya: egg omelet with reconstituted, dried rayfish.

Desserts

- King kong: layered cookie of *manjarblanco*, pineapple preserves and peanuts.

A Peruvian Paso horse.

Festivals

A highlight among the festivals celebrated in Chiclayo and its environs is the procession of the Señor Cautivo de Monsefú (Our Captive Lord of Monsefú), an effigy of Christ which, according to tradition, floated ashore at Lambayeque in a casket. Local lore has it that the image has a tendency to escape, leaving its church to perform miracles in other towns, which is why they keep the image in chains. This festival is celebrated with fireworks, dances, and musical ensembles. It begins August 31 and lasts until September 30, with the principal day being September 14.

Other important festivals are: the Purísima Concepción in Túcume (February, date varies); the Señor de la Justicia in Ferreñafe (April, date varies); the anniversary of the creation of the province (April 18); the festival of the Niño del Milagro in Eten (July 15); the handicraft fairs of Monsefú (last week of July); the feast of the Cruz de Chalpón in Motupe, a pilgrimage to the cross on Mount Chalpón and an agricultural and handicraft fair (July 25 to August 7); and Chiclayo Tourism Week (second week of December).

The city of Chiclayo is also quite famous for its Paso horses. It hosts several important competitions, such as the Armando Baca Rossi Departamental Paso Horse Competition every November (exact date varies).

Folkcrafts

Among the handicrafts of the region are the famous hats and centerpieces in woven straw, the fine embroidery of Monsefú, and the silverwork of Motupe, as well as the engraved gourds of Eten and Monsefú. In Chiclayo you can also find handsome work in carved wood, ceramic, and embossed leather.

Excursions

Sipán
80M / 262FT)

An archeological site 29km (40 minutes) SE of Chiclayo by paved highway. This site of the famous royal tombs is named for a small, nearby town. The complex consists of two adobe pyramids. Here, in 1987, the Peruvian archeologist Walter Alva and his team uncovered the richest pre-Hispanic burial yet discovered in the Americas, belonging to a young Mochica dignitary of the fourth century AD, which they called the Lord of Sipán. After this discovery, two more tombs were found, one of a priest and another of an older dignitary, designated the Old Lord of Sipán *(for more information see p. 37)*. There are numerous agencies in Chiclayo that can organize a visit here.

Panoramic view of Sipán.

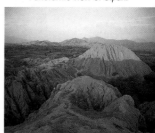

Lambayeque • Museo Brüning
57M / 187FT)

10km (15 minutes) N of Chiclayo by paved highway. Small northern city which reached its height

Travelling by burro.

at the beginning of the eighteenth century when the rich families of Zaña, affected by flooding, took up residence here. It contains interesting examples of colonial architecture including the large homes in the city center, the Cathedral and the churches of Santa Catalina, San Francisco, San Roque and Santa Lucía. It is also the site of the Brüning Museum (Av. Huamachuco n/n. Tel 28 2110), which contains a spectacular archeological collection gathered by the German Enrique Brüning at the end of the nineteenth century and acquired by the Peruvian government in 1921. This collection is enriched by pieces recovered from the trade in contraband, donations, and new finds, the latest being the royal tombs at Sipán. The museum, directed by archeologist Walter Alva, occupies a modern, functional building

CHICLAYO. EXCURSION MAP

whose design is inspired by the architectural works of Le Corbusier.

Visiting hours for the museum:
Mon-Fri, 8am to 4:30pm; Sat-Sun, 9am to 1pm.

Túcume or The Valley of the Pyramids

45M / 148FT   )

An archeological site 33km (40 minutes) N of Chiclayo via paved highway, in the La Leche River valley. This place, an important settlement of the Lambayeque, or Sicán culture, consists of some twenty adobe pyramids almost 40m (131ft) high and other lesser buildings, all built around Mount Purgatorio (also called Mount La Raya). Occupied and redesigned by the Chimú and then by the Incas, it was abandoned after the conquest by the Spanish, who founded a settlement quite close by, of which a few walls of the original church are all that remain. The modern town of Túcume, famous for its master *curanderos* (traditional healers) is about 2km from the pyramids. The archeological site has an educational site museum.

The valley of the pyramids.

An adobe pyramid
in Túcume.

National Reserve Batán Grande

49M / 161FT   )

A national archeological and ecological reserve 50km (45 minutes) N of Chiclayo by packed dirt road, in the La Leche valley. This is a fascinating spot in the middle of the Poma woods, the largest carob tree forest in Peru, the site of some twenty truncated pyramids of the Sicán or Lambayeque culture. In recent decades, a group of researchers led by Japanese archeologist Izumi Shimada began exploring this site and found several tombs of high-ranking individuals which compete in wealth with those of Sipán and reveal that Batán Grande was one of the most important metallurgical centers in Peru.

An ancient carob tree
in the Poma woods.

Monsefú

15M / 49FT)

8km (10 minutes) SW of Chiclayo via paved highway. Famous for its musicians and weavers, this is a town where you can acquire fine straw hats and baskets, woven textiles, and objects of skillfullly carved *zapote* and *guayacán* wood. A highlight is its singular church dedicated to Jesus of Nazareth.

Pimentel

)

A port and beach resort 10km (20 minutes) W of Chiclayo via paved highway. Originally a small fishing port, today it also includes a handsome beach resort next to the port where traditional reed fishing craft still compete with surfers on the waves. With its restaurants and several hostels, it is the fashionable summer spot among residents of Chiclayo. South of Pimentel is the Las Rocas beach, less frequented but equally pleasant.

The old iron pier in Pimentel.

Santa Rosa

)

A picturesque fishing port 16km (20 minutes) SW of Chiclayo and 6km S of Pimentel, by paved highway. Santa Rosa is famous for its *cebiches*, *chiringuitos*, and *tortillas de raya*. Fishing boats can be rented.

Ruins of the church of La Merced, Zaña.

Zaña

32M / 105FT)

A traditional town 51km (35 minutes) S of Chiclayo. To reach Zaña, turn off the Panamericana Norte highway at kilometer 733 and continue 10km on paved road. Zaña was founded in 1563 by the wealthy families of the region, and 157 years later was destroyed when the river flooded. A legend from the time of slavery recounts that this catastrophe was divine punishment for the wantonness and wastefulness of its inhabitants. Today, its mansions, churches and convents lie in ruins as testimony to the tragic event. However, the remains of the church of San Agustín and its cloisters, as well as the façades and walls of the buildings of other religious orders are still impressive. To visit the ruins of the old town, hire a guide from Chiclayo. The new town of Zaña is the land of shamans and of those who venerate the Cross of Chalpón.

Ruins of the church
of San Francisco, Zaña.

Salas

460M / 1 509FT)

Town known for its traditional healers 70km (1 hour, 30 minutes) NE of Chiclayo via partially paved road. The shamans of Salas do their healing with medicinal plants. The most famous shamans live in the Tempón, Lalita, Lilasca, Naranjo, and Humedades hills, on the outskirts of town. You can reach Salas via the highway to Olmos, taking a side road to the right at 43km from Lambayeque. From there, 17km of packed dirt road lead to town. There are some hotels and simple restaurants. An enjoyable excursion which can be combined with a visit to Túcume and Motupe.

Hotels

Gran Hotel Chiclayo ★★★★
Av. F. Villareal 115. Tel 23 4911. Fax 22 3961. US$ 55
granhotel@lima.business.com.pe.

Garza Hotel ★★★★
Av. Bolognesi 756. Tel 22 8172. Fax 22 8171. US$ 55

Hotel Sipán ★★★★
V. Dall' Orso 150. Tel 24 2564. US$ 45

Hostal Costa del Sol ★★★
Av. Balta 399. Tel 22 7272. Fax 20 9342. US$ 35
costasol@efe.com.pe.

Inca Hotel ★★★
Luis Gonzales 622. Tel 23 5931. Fax 22 7651. US$ 30
incahotel@cpi.eduep.com.pe.

★★★ Hostal Aristi
Francisco Cabrera 102. Tel 23 1074.
Fax 22 8673. US$ 25

★★★ Hostal Eras
Vicente de la Vega 851. Tel 23 6333.
negotour@chiclayo.net

★★★ Hostal Tambo Real
Av. Luis Gonzales 532. Tel 20 5067.
negotour@chiclayo.net

★★★ Hostal Fortuna
Alfredo Lapoint 1270. Tel 23 8080.

★★★ Hostal Silvana
Alfredo Lapoint 1058. Tel 22 4170. US$ 20

★★★ Hostal Santa Victoria
La Florida 586. Telefax 22 5074. US$ 15

RATES ARE APPROXIMATE AND, UNLESS OTHERWISE NOTED,
ARE FOR DOUBLE OCCUPANCY.

Restaurants

✔ Pueblo Viejo
M. María Ízaga 900.

✔ Fiesta
Av. Salaverry 180.

✔ El Rancho de los Mellizos
José Balta 1115.

✔ La Parra
M. María Ízaga 752.

✔ El Blasón
Av. F. Villareal (2nd block).

✔ Chifa Men Wha
Pedro Ruiz Galoo 1059.

✔ Las Terrazas
Elías Aguirre 631 (4th floor).

✔ La Cabaña
Los Laureles 235, Urb. Bancarios.

✔ Las Tinajas I
Elías Aguirre 957, Parque Central.

La Casa del Cebiche   ✔
   Av. Grau 350.

Huariques

Huariques are restaurants specializing in the typical dishes of Chiclayo. The majority are located on La Unión, Grau, and Bolognesi avenues. The following good locales include: La Bartola, Garza Real, and La Colmena

Useful Facts

AREA CODE 74

☎

Travel Agencies
Tumi Tours: Av. Elías Aguirre 576.   22 5371
Costa Mar Tours: Av. San José 777.   27 4149

Car Rental
Chiclayo Rent a Car: Federico Villareal 115.   24 4291

Tourism Police Aid: 23 6192
                                                      23 5181
Clínica Lambayeque: Vicente de la Vega 415.   23 7961
Farmacia Arcángel: Luis Gonzales 682.   22 2921
Inka Farma: Av. Luis Gonzales 684.   20 8648
Instituto Nacional de Cultura:
   Av. Luis Gonzales 345.   23 7261
Post Office:
   Av. Elías Aguirre 140.   23 7031
Airport   23 3192
IPERÚ:
   Information y Assistence for Tourists
   01-574-8000 Lima.

3 675 M / 12 057FT

31 100 POP.

360 KM VIA HUANCAYO

520 KM VIA PISCO AND CASTROVIRREYNA

SE OF LIMA

Huancavelica

P. 85

P. 78

ROUTE MAP

6

Located in the heart of the Andes, Huancavelica, capital of the department of the same name, is a small, welcoming city of Colonial origins. Its name may derive from the Quechua words *huanca* and *huillka*, meaning mean 'stone idol.'

Huancavelica was founded in 1571 by Francisco de Angulo, a mine operator, when the Santa Bárbara mercury mine was discovered in 1563.

The story goes that a Spanish landowner, Amador de Cabrera, located the deposit on a tip from a native chieftain. This discov-

Threshing barley on the outskirts of town.

ery dramatically improved the processing of silver mined in Peru, as mercury, or quicksilver, is essential to extracting silver from the ore and obtaining a much higher purity. Santa Bárbara (along with Potosí, in Bolivia) became one of the most important mines in the Viceroyalty of Peru, and because of its importance a city was founded nearby and named Villa Rica de Oropesa in honor of Viceroy Francisco de Toledo, a native of Oropesa, Spain.

Dry, temperate climate, with a yearly mean temperature of 18°C (64°F). In winter nightly temperatures can dip below freezing. Rainy season from December to March.

From its beginning, Huancavelica was home to miners, muleteers and merchants. The Spanish came hoping to obtain a concession to dig for mercury, but forced much of the native population in the region to do the actual mining.

Furthermore, Huancavelica's strategic location made it an important regional market linked to markets as distant as Quito and Cusco. All of these factors helped Huancavelica residents to amass large fortunes.

Nonetheless, the Santa Bárbara mine declined in the second half of the seventeenth century, and in 1840 a report prepared by the prefect of the department referred to Huancavelica as a ghost town.

In the twentieth century, Huancavelica suffered an acute social crisis, aggravated by a series of intense droughts and floods. In the 1980s, terrorist violence further lashed the region, causing more poverty and precipitating a massive migration of its population to the coast. Today, this city of miners and farmers is working to restore its past prosperity.

THE MERCURY ROUTE

In Colonial times, Huancavelica was the starting point of the renowned «Mercury Route.» Caravans of llamas and mules carried the precious, liquid metal in leather bags to the port of Tambo de Mora (in the department of Ica). From there, it was shipped to Arica (now in Chile) and on to the silver mines at Potosí (now in Bolivia).

Colonial doorway in the Santo Domingo district.

Panoramic view of the city.

Local Dishes

Soups

• Caldo de mondongo: tripe with corn, *hierbabuena*, and other meat trimmings.

Main Dishes

• Ropa vieja: beef with beans, potatoes, rice, and cabbage.

Festivals

The most colorful festivals celebrated in Huancavelica are the Feast of the Magi (January 6) and the Feast of San Sebastián (January 16).

Folkcrafts

You can find work in embossed leather, products of woven alpaca wool, carving in hardwoods (*queñual* and *chachacomo*), and utilitarian ceramics.

Points of Interest in the City

Traditional Locales

• *Plaza de Armas:* bordered with stately arches and flanked by the Cathedral, the town hall, and some Colonial homes. At its center stands a fountain built in 1862, made entirely of granite.

Churches

- *The Cathedral*, Plaza de Armas: its two sturdy white towers contrast with its red stone entry with a broken pediment and profusely decorated Salomonic columns. Its interior holds a good collection of paintings attributed to native artists, luxurious holy scenes, and a Baroque pulpit richly worked and gold-painted.
- *San Sebastián*, Plaza San Sebastián y San Francisco: the popular image of the Christ child of Lachoc is venerated in this church, built in 1662. According to legend, the image alerted Peruvian troops to the arrival of Chilean forces during the War of the Pacific (1879–1883).

Church of San Sebastián.

- *San Francisco*, Plaza San Sebastián y San Francisco: the building of this Baroque style church began in 1774. It possesses an eighteenth-century doorway whose upper section contains ingenious reliefs of angels and lions, and it holds an interesting collection of paintings of the Holy Family and the twelve Apostles.
- *Others:* Santa Ana, the first church built in the city, Santo Domingo, San Cristóbal, Santísima Trinidad de Conayca, Santa Bárbara, and La Ascensión.

Church of Santo Domingo.

Excursions

Aguas termales de San Cristóbal

3 600M / 11 812FT)

4,5km (15 minutes) NW of the city, these hot springs, which emerge at 28°C (82°F), have a great reputation for curing skin diseases. Ask at the hotels for information about access and visiting hours.

Bosques de piedras

3 750M / 12 304FT ON AVERAGE ○

Shepherd's hut in Choclococha.

These unique rock formations, called «forests of stone,» are produced by the combined erosive effects of wind and water. One of these formations, ideal for walks and picture-taking, is located on the road to Huancayo (20km, or 45 minutes N of Huancavelica), another is near Toccyac (29km, or 45 minutes E of Huancavelica via packed dirt road). There are other nearby stone forests at Sachapite, Huayanay, and Paucará. These are best visited with a guide from the city.

Hotels

★★★ Hotel Presidente
    Plaza de armas n/n. Tel 75 2760. US$ 35
★★ Hotel Camacho
    Carabaya 481. Tel 75 3298. US$ 15
★★ Hotel Tahuantinsuyo
    Corner of Carabaya and M. Muñoz Tel 75 2622. US$ 10

RATES ARE APPROXIMATE AND, UNLESS OTHERWISE NOTED, ARE FOR DOUBLE OCCUPANCY.

Restaurants

✔ Joy
    Corner of Toledo and Arequipa.
✔ Los Portales
    Plaza de armas.
✔ La Casona
    Virrey Toledo 103.
✔ Paquirri
    Arequipa 137.
✔ La Olla de Barro
    Gamarra 305.

Useful Facts

☎

Basic information

ESSALUD:

Av. Escalonada 145.   75 1147

Farmacia Jesús de Nazareth:

Virrey de Toledo 472.   75 1253

Farmacia La Salud:

Arequipa 1st. block.   75 2970

Instituto Nacional de Cultura:

Plazoleta San Juan de Dios n/n.   75 3420

Post Office:

Ferrua 107.   55 2750

IPERÚ:

Information and Assistance for Tourists

01-574-8000 Lima.

RAIL SERVICE TO HUANCAYO

From Huancavelica you can reach Huancayo most easily by train, as the access road is in a constant state of disrepair. Nevertheless, by the time this edition was been closed, the so called «*tren macho*» that used to make daily trips between Huancavelica and Huancayo was set out of service.

3 249 M / 10 659FT
258 200 POP.
305 KM
E OF LIMA

Huancayo

P. 82   P. 85

P. 78

ROUTE MAPS
⑤ ⑥

Huancayo is located on the left bank of the Mantaro River at the southern end of the valley of the same name. It is the capital of the department of Junín and the most important city of the central sierra of Peru. Its name comes from the Quechua word *huanca-yoc*, meaning 'place of the large stone,' in allusion to a stone which once stood in what is now the Plaza Huamanmarca. In addition to stands of eucalyptus and flowering yellow broom sage called *retama*, the Mantaro, an agricultural valley par excellence, has fields of corn, potatoes,

Carnival dancers in Jauja.

barley, wheat, and artichokes. Livestock breeding is also wide-spread.

This was once the territory of the Huanca culture (c. AD 900 to 1400), and its hardy inhabitants and able merchants were conquered by the Inca Wiracocha in the fifteenth century. According to chroniclers' reports, the Inca used «cunning rather than strength of arms» to overcome local resistance. Under Inca rule, the Huanca helped build the road that crossed the Mantaro Valley and went on to link Quito to Cusco. But the people

A temperate to warm climate, with a yearly mean temperature of 25° C (77° F). Temperature rarely drops below freezing, but nights are cold. Rainy season from December to March.

were unhappy with their Cusco lords and lent their aid to the Spanish during the Conquest. In return, the Spanish did not lay waste to the region, thus distinguishing it from other parts of the central sierra.

Impressed by the beauty of the valley and its benign weather, Francisco Pizarro chose it as the site of the first capital of Peru, the city of Jauja, founded April 25, 1534. The city of Huancayo was founded some time afterwards, on the June 1, 1572.

During the war for independence, when Huancayo was still a small city, the royal troops took refuge here and stayed in the valley for three years. It wasn't until 1824, after winning the battle of Junín, that Simón Bolívar was able to dislodge the royalists. In 1839, the city housed the Congress of the Republic that dissolved the Peru-Bolivia Confederation. Here in Huancayo, in 1854, President Ramón Castilla signed the decree abolishing slavery in Peru. Some years later, the Mantaro Valley was the site of the bloody battles in which the Peruvian army under General Andrés Avelino Cáceres (the «Wizard of the Andes») fought Chilean troops during the War of the Pacific (1879–1883).

The history of this valley is kept alive in the col-

THE MANTARO RIVER

The Mantaro River begins in Lake Yanacocha, in Junín, and is augmented by numerous tributaries until it becomes the large waterway that produces one of the most beautiful and productive valleys in the country. Crossing the Andes at about 3 250m (10 663ft) above sea level, it flows through the departments of Junín, Huancavelica, and Ayacucho and finally enters the jungle to merge with the Ene River, a tributary to the Amazon. Huancayo is the largest city it passes on its way.

The Mantaro Valley.

San Pedro de Cajas.

orful dances that characterize its patron saint feasts. While the *auquis* (dancers wearing masks made of hide) represent the mountain spirits venerated in pre-Hispanic times, the *avelinos*, dressed in rags, commemorate the local people who disguised themselves as beggars in order to infiltrate the Chilean troops.

Huancayo today is a populous, growing city, mostly engaged in commerce, a tradition inherited from its ancestors the Huanca. It is an important economic hub that links the productive regions of the high rain forest and the central sierra to the coast and it has the best hotels and restaurants in the region. The city itself has no major attraction. Nonetheless, it is an important departure point for visiting the Mantaro Valley with its picturesque towns of craftsmen (the area is one of Peru's largest handicrafts centers) and its rich folklore.

Local Dishes

Entrées
- Papa a la huancaína: potatoes served with a renowned sauce of fresh cheese and *ají* pepper.

Papa a la huancaína.

Soups
- Human caldo: broth of mutton head with mint and *ají* pepper.
- Mondongo: soup of tripe and meats accompanied with *mote* (kerneled corn).
- Yacuchupe: soup of potato, cheese, and aromatic herbs.
- Wallpa chupe: chicken broth with vegetables and noodles.

Main Dishes
- Cordero al palo: whole lamb cooked over coals.

- Pachamanca: diverse meats, potatoes, and corn cooked underground with hot stones and aromatic herbs, in the pre-Hispanic style.
- Picante de cuy: a guinea pig stew in a sauce of ground peanuts and *ají* pepper.

Others

- Cheese, butter, and *manjarblanco* (sweet milk paste).

Festivals

One of the most significant festivals celebrated in the Mantaro Valley, is the Feast of Apóstol Santiago, or St. James, whom the locals affectionately call Taita Shanty. He is the patron saint of livestock breeders and his day is July 25th. During this celebration, the people of every town brand their livestock with a very festive ambiance in which all participants celebrate with drinks and typical dances of the region. This festival mixes Christian tradition with pre-Hispanic rituals that invoke the protection of Andean deities.

Other important festivals are: Carnival (in February), celebrated with the *huaylía* and *huaylarsh* dances and the *yunsa*, or *cortamonte*, a very traditional dance in which couples circle a gift-laden tree, striking it with hatchets until it falls; Jala Pato in Jauja (January 20); the Feast of the Crosses, during which irrigation canals are cleaned throughout the valley (May 3); San Juan (June 24); Tourism Week in Huancayo (June, date varies); the Hualhuas handicraft fair (last week of August); the Virgen de Cocharcas in Sapallanga (September 8); and Todos los Santos or All Saints' Day (November 1).

Engraved gourd from Cochas.

Folkcrafts

The towns of the Mantaro Valley are known throughout Peru for their handicrafts. The fine weavings in lamb and alpaca wool made in Hualhuas and San Pedro de Cajas are famous; as are the hats also made in San Pedro; the embroidery of Sapallanga; the ceramics of Acos; the carved gourds of Cochas; the silver filigree work of San Jerónimo de Tunán; the diverse types of masks used in the traditional dances (such as the *chon-*

guinada and the *huaconada*), and the musical instruments (*zamponas*, *quenas*, and *charangos*).

All of these handicrafts can be obtained at the Sunday fair in Huancayo, although at somewhat higher prices than in their towns of origin. Other handicraft fairs are: Monday, in Huayucachi; Tuesday, in Pucará; Wednesday, in San Jerónimo de Tunán; Saturday, in Chupaca; and Sunday in Concepción and Jauja.

 ## Points of Interest in the City

- *Sunday fair*, Huancavelica and adjacent streets, in the center of town: this, Huancayo's traditional fair, accurately reflects the swift pace of local commercial activity. You can find everything from handicrafts of great beauty and workmanship, to televisions and foodstuffs. It is best to go in the morning. Be on guard against pickpockets and purse snatchers.

 ## Excursions

Hualhuas

3 290M / 10 795FT)

A picturesque town of weavers 14km (20 minutes) N of Huancayo via paved highway. Among the items made by the craftsmen are rugs, ponchos, and shawls of finely woven alpaca wool dyed with natural substances following ancient customs. You can visit the artisans in their own homes and workshops and enjoy their hospitality.

San Jerónimo de Tunán

3 260M / 10 696FT)

A town of consummate silversmiths, 13km (25 minutes) N of Huancayo via paved highway. The filigree work here is famous. The town has a small church built in the seventeenth century and declared a National Historical Monument because of the extraordinary beauty of its Renaissance and Baroque wooden altars. It is said that the cheiftain's daugther, Catalina Huanca,

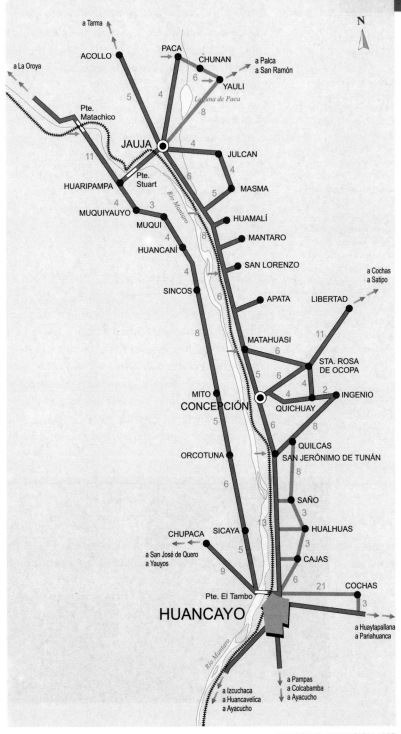

HUANCAYO EXCURSION MAP

lies buried below its foundation and that she was the last to know the secret location where the treasures from the sanctuary of Pachacámac (Lima) were buried..

Cochas
3 280M / 10 762FT)

21km (35 minutes) N of Huancayo via packed dirt road are the «twin towns» of Cochas Chico and Cochas Grande. These towns are both famous for their extraordinary, carved gourds known worldwide, and called *mates burilados*.

Santa Rosa de Ocopa
3 290M / 10 795FT)

25km (35 minutes) NW of Huancayo via paved highway. Located near the town of Concepción, this Franciscan monastery was founded in 1725 by Father Francisco de San José on a spot where there had once been a small chapel dedicated to Santa Rosa of Lima. This was the departure point for the Franciscan missionaries who made dauntless attempts to proselytize the natives of the east-

Old cloisters of the Santa Rosa de Ocopa convent.

ern jungles of Peru. It has an exceptional library of some 20 000 volumes (among them numerous incunabula and several bibliographical jewels), paintings and reliefwork in alabaster and stone of Huamanga, a small museum of natural history, and a collection of Colonial-era images.

> *Visiting hours: daily (except Tue),*
> *9am to noon, and 3 to 6pm.*

Boulevard leading into Santa Rosa de Ocopa.

Ingenio
3 300M / 10 827FT)

A town located between two watercourses which empty into the Mantaro River, 23km (35 minutes) NW of Huancayo via paved highway. This is the trout enclave of Peru. There are numerous trout farms and country restaurants that prepare both rainbow and white-meat trout in a variety of ways.

Jauja and Laguna Paca
3 390M / 11 122FT)

48km (45 minutes) NW of Huancayo via paved highway. The town of Jauja was originally Tunanmarca, the main center of the Huanca culture. Pizarro chose it to be the first capital of the Viceroyalty of Peru. Quiet and peaceful (unlike Huancayo), it has some Colonial buildings, as well as various manor houses of adobe and a mud-and-rush construction called *quincha*. It is famous for its agreeable climate highly sought out in the nineteenth century for the healing of pulmonary ailments. This is the departure point for a visit to the beautiful Lake Paca (6km to the N), surrounded with stands of *totora* reeds that are home to many waterfowl. On the shores are restaurants, hostels, boat rentals, and even an astronomical observatory. From Jauja you can visit the archeological sites at Hurin Jauja, Hanan Jauja, Kancha Huanca, and Sucsunya.

Outskirts of Jauja.

Lake Paca.

cJauja itself has hotels and rustic restaurants. We recommend a visit to its colorful Sunday fair, where numerous artisans and farmers of the valley gather.

Torre Torre

3 300M / 10 827FT)

A curious geological formation 4km (15 minutes) NE of the city.

Here wind erosion has carved sandstone sculptures that are predominantly long and cylindrical in shape and ideal for photography. On the way here, you can visit Mount Libertad, which affords a splendid view of the city of Huancayo and the surrounding Mantaro Valley.

Torre Torre.

Huari Huillca

3 290M / 10 794FT)

An archeological site 6km (15 minutes) S of Huancayo. Its name means 'ancient place of worship' in Quechua and perfectly describes the sacred character of this ancient ceremonial center. According to the legend recorded by the chronicler Pedro Cieza de León in 1550, this was the place of origin of the Huanca people. The ruins extend over a small mesa on the bank of the Mantaro River and include high walls and underground enclosures. The ceramics found in this area also link it to the Wari culture.

Cordillera de Huaytapallana

4 500 MSNM PROM. ○

A 48 km (1 h) al E de la ciudad, tomando el camino afirmado a Satipo. Esta imponente cadena montañosa, ideal para la práctica del andinismo y el *trekking*, separa las tierras altas de la puna de las de la ceja de selva. Posee nevados de gran belleza, entre los que destacan sus mayores cumbres: Lasuntay (5 780 msnm) y Chuspi (5 400 msnm). No existen servicios en la zona. No olvide llevar abrigo.

Summits of the Huaytapallana range.

Hotels

Huancayo

Hotel Presidente ★★★
  Av. Real 1138. Tel 23 1275. Fax 23 1736. US$ 65

Huancayo Plaza *(ex Hotel de Turistas)* ★★★
  Áncash 729. Tel 23 1072. US$ 45

Hotel Kiya ★★★
  Av. Giráldez 107. Tel 21 4955. Fax 21 4953. US$ 35

Hostal Santa Felícita ★★
  Av. Giráldez 145. Tel 23 5285. Fax 23 5476. US$ 30

Hostal El Dorado ★★
  Piura 428. Tel 22 3947. US$ 15

Alpaca ★★
  Av. Giráldez 494. Tel 23 3136.

Perú Andino ★★
  Psje. San Antonio 113. Tel 22 3956.

Fundo El Porvenir (bungallows)
  Carretera Central km 4,5. Tel 22 3956.

Concepción (*on the way to Santa Rosa de Ocopa*)

Hotel Huaychulo
  Av. Oriente km 2.
  Telefax 58 1001. US$ 25

Hotel Loma Verde
  Tambo Alapa. Telefax 58 1569.
  Reservations Lima Tel 241 7599 / 447 5697.

RATES ARE APPROXIMATE AND, UNLESS OTHERWISE NOTED,
ARE FOR DOUBLE OCCUPANCY

Restaurants

El Olímpico ✔
  Av. Giráldez 199.

El Leopardo ✔
  Corner of Huánuco and Libertad 706.

El Padrino ✔
  Huancavelica 481.

✔ Lalo's
　　Av. Giráldez 365.
✔ El Inca
　　Puno 530.
✔ La Cabaña
　　Av. Giráldez 652.

Useful Facts

AREA CODE **64**

☎

Basic information

Hospital Daniel Alcides Carrión:	
Av. Daniel A. Carrión 1552.	23 2222
Clínica Ortega:	
Av. Daniel A. Carrión 1124.	23 5430
Farmacia Socorro:	
Real 970.	25 3150
Inkafarma:	
Real 537.	21 9977
Tourism Police Aid:	21 9851
Instituto Nacional de Cultura:	
Jr. Arequipa 599.	23 3233
Post Office:	
Centro Cívico, Foco N° 1.	21 8762
IPERÚ:	
Information and Assistance for Tourists	
01-574-8000 Lima.	

Huánuco

1 894 M / 6 214FT
118 800 POP.
405 KM

P. 82

P. 78

Situated in the transition zone between the Andes and the high rain forest, Huánuco lies on the left bank of the Pillco River (which joins the Huallaga several kilometers downstream), in a wide valley encircled by mountains dominated by Mount Pilcomoso.

Capital of the department of the same name, Huánuco is famous for its clear blue sky. It is very close to the town of Cerro de Pasco, which lies at the uncomfortable altitude of 4 338m (14 232ft), so travelers heading east to Huánuco find it truly a

ROUTE MAPS

④ ⑩

View of Alameda de la República.

blessing to make the swift descent and find relief here from altitude sickness.

The region of Huánuco was the once the territory of the Yaro (or Yarowilca), a culture of proud warriors and farmers. After a long war with the Incas, the Yaro sided with them and helped them in their northward incursions. This coalition was so suc-

Warm climate with many days of sunshine throughout the year, although quite windy in the afternoons. The yearly mean temperature is 20° C (68° F) and the rainy season is from December to March.

cessful that during the reign of the Inca Huayna Cápac large constructions were built in the region, such as «were built only in distinguished, highly favored provinces» (Garcilaso de la Vega, 1609). One of these was Huánuco Pampa, the largest Inca administrative center in the region.

Captain Gómez de Alvarado founded the first city of Huánuco on the site of Huánuco Pampa on August 15, 1539 and named it León de los Caballeros de Huánuco. A few months later, the city was moved to its present location due to the hostility of the natives and the old site was called Huánuco Viejo, or Old Huánuco. The new city was known as a «gateway to the land of savages» as its proximity to the Amazon made it a principal entry point for the Franciscan missionaries sent to evangelize the region.

In the early twentieth century, Huánuco reached its height with the cultivation of sugar cane and the harvesting of the eucalyptus forests to provide wood for the silver mines at Cerro de Pasco.

Today, Huánuco is a small city engaged in commerce and agriculture. It retains some fine Colonial buildings and is popular for its climate.

AN ILLUSTRIOUS CITIZEN OF HUÁNUCO

One of the most illustrious citizens of Huánuco is unquestionably Daniel Alomía Robles, author of one of the best-known musical compositions in the world: *El Cóndor Pasa*. Born in 1871, Alomía Robles studied medicine and traveled Peru to classify herbs. Only then did he discover the music of his country and begin to meticulously compile a collection of Andean melodies. He composed *El Cóndor Pasa* in 1913, using words written by Lima journalist and writer Julio Baudouin de La Paz (1886–1925). This *zarzuela* of eight parts (only one of which is still played) had a message very much in the vanguard for its day. It told the story of an indigenous revolt in a mining region of Peru, in which a condor in flight symbolized liberty.

Local Dishes
Main Dishes
- Chivo perseguido: goat barbecued with garlic and cane liquor called *aguardiente*.
- Locro: chicken stewed with onion, potatoes, and *ají* pepper.
- Pato enterrado: fried duck in hot *rocoto* pepper sauce.

Desserts
- Mazamorra de pituca: sweet pudding of the *pituca* root, a tuber somewhat like a sweet potato.

Festivals
On January 1, 6, and 18, Huánuco is the scene of one of the most colorful dances in Peruvian folklore: *la danza de los negritos*, or «the dance of the black men.» It dates from the days when Negro slaves worked the sugar cane fields of Huánuco, and among all of the *negritos* dances presented in Peru, Huánuco's is the most acclaimed. Other important festivals are: Carnival and the Feast of Don Calixto (January-February); the Feast of the Virgen de la Asunción, patroness of Huánuco, which coincides with the city's anniversary and Tourism Week (August 15); and the festival of the Señor de Burgos, patron of Huánuco (October 27 to 29).

Folkcrafts
Huánuco's best handicrafts are its silverwork, straw baskets and wicker furniture, tablecloths embroidered in local motifs, ceramics, and carved steer horns.

Handmade mask.

Points of Interest in the City

Traditional Locales

- *Plaza de Armas:* adorned with leafy jacaranda and rubber trees, the plaza has a fountain built in 1845 over a single, solid piece of granite. Huánuco's heroes of the 1812 rebellion

Plaza de armas.

Calicanto Bridge.

were executed here, and Peru's independence was declared here on December 15, 1820. The plaza has monuments to José de San Martín, known as The Liberator, and Huánuco's own Mariano Ignacio Prado, President of Peru, who signed the declaration of war against Chile in 1879.

- *Puente Calicanto*, Jr. General Prado, block one: this bridge over the Huallaga River was built in 1884 with stones joined with a mix of sand, lime and, according to tradition, egg whites.

Churches

- *The Cathedral*, Plaza de Armas: this modern building holds the fine image of the Lord of Burgos, the city's patron saint. It also contains important relics, including chasubles that belonged to the second archbishop of Lima, St. Toribio de Mogrovejo (1538–1606), and the crosier of Monsignor Manuel Teodoro del Valle (1813–1888), religious administrator of the city. It also contains a collection of paintings from the Cusco school.
- *Nuestra Señora de las Mercedes*, corner of Huánuco and Hermilio Valdizán: built in 1556 by Fray Diego de Porras, this church has been declared a National Historical Monument. It possesses one of the oldest Renaissance altars in Peru, dating from 1594, and paintings by the great Italian master Mateo Pérez de Alesio and his assistant Pedro Pablo Morón. It also conserves the birth certificates of illustrious citizens born in Huánuco: Coronel Leoncio Prado, hero of the battle of Huamachuco (1883), and composer Daniel Alomía Robles, composer of the famous song *El Cóndor Pasa* (1913).
- *San Teodoro*, Jr. Aguilar, two blocks from the Plaza de Armas: this Dominican convent was the home of St. Toribio de Mogrovejo and of Fray Diego de Hojeda (1571–1615), author of *La Cristiada*, one of the most notable religious epic poems of the Colonial period. It possesses an important library with valuable books from the Colonial era.

- *San Cristóbal*, Jr. San Cristóbal: this austere building was the first church built in the Pillco Valley. It has valuable Baroque statues, including images of San Agustín, the Virgen Dolorosa, the Cristo de Malta, and the Virgen de la Asunción, patroness of Huánuco, as well as an elegant chalice that belonged to St. Toribio de Mogrovejo.
- *San Francisco*, corner of Jr. Dámaso Beraún and Jr. San Martín: the architecture of this church, once dedicated to San Bernardino, is Neoclassic in style. Its main altar and some secondary altars are in the extravagant Churrigueresque style and painted in gold. Its columns are decorated in local bird and flower motifs and it has a collection of paintings that includes the Immaculate Conception, attributed to the great Italian painter who lived in Lima, Angelino Medoro (1547–1629).

Church of San Francisco.

Excursions

Andabamba • Tomayquichua

2 200M / 7 218FT ON AVERAGE)

Picturesque towns 8km and 18km (15 minutes) S of Huánuco. Leaving Huánuco on the paved highway to Ambo, you first come to Cayhuayna, a natural lookout point from which you can see the shape of a man on Mount Marabamba, also know as Pilcomoso. Continuing south, you will come to the town of Andabamba, which has several Colonial buildings built by the Franciscans. Two kilometers beyond is the Vichaycoto hacienda, traditional producer of cane liquor.

Continuing on the road to Cerro de Pasco, on the right bank of the Huallaga River, you come to the town of Tomayquichua ('temperate valley' in Quechua), known for its green countryside. It has typical restaurants and several places of interest on its outskirts, such as the Cachigaga and Quicacán haciendas (the latter was a Mercedarian convent that has an ancient mill still used for pressing sugar cane

Tomayquichua.

and making cane liquor) and a group of five small lakes set amid beautiful natural scenery.

Kotosh
I 925M / 6 316FT

An archeological site 4km (10 minutes) E of the city via paved

road, on the right bank of the Higueras River.

Here you will find the famous church of the crossed hands, a small building of stone that was later stuccoed and which holds two ancient pairs of crossed hands modeled in clay. The original building is calculated to be some 5 000 years old, one of the most ancient in Peru.

Stone enclosures at Kotosh.

Huánuco Pampa (Huánuco Viejo)
2 250M / 7 382FT

An archeological site 141km (4 hours) N of Huánuco, at the site of the original city of Huánuco. This site, built by the Incas in the second half of the fifteenth century, was an important administrative center on the network of roads which led to Cusco. It is thought to have been a work center for *mitimaes*, the temporary laborers that each community had to provide the empire. There seem to have been districts here for each specialty: potters, metalworkers, weavers, etc. In the middle of its central plaza stands a rectangular ceremonial platform called an *ushnu*, accessed by a staircase guarded by four pumas carved from stone. Consult with local guides about road conditions and access to this site.

National Sanctuary
Bosque de Piedras de Huayllay
4 000M / 13 124FT ON AVERAGE

This «forest of stone» is a national sanctuary 185km (2 hours,

30 minutes) S of Huánuco, or 80km from the city of Junín. To reach it, take the paved highway towards Lima to the town of Vicco (120km from Huánuco). From here a packed dirt road goes W 25km to the town of Huayllay.

This 6 815-hectare sanctuary was created to protect its impressive geological formations. On one side, the imposing Huayhuash range accentuates the beauty of this place. The community of Huayllay has a simple hostel, a restaurant, and hot springs. Camping is allowed among the stone towers, where you can enjoy the company of amusing, herbivorous rodents called *vizcachas*. Take lots of warm clothing.

Lake Junín, Chinchaycocha or Los Reyes
4 080M / 13 386FT

This lake also goes by the names of Chinchaycocha and Los Reyes. It is located on the Bombón mesa, 150km (2 hours) S of Huánuco via the paved highway called the Carretera Central and is the second largest lake in Peru. It is an important refuge for the waterfowl of the high Andes (ducks, coots, flamingos, and grebes), which is why 53 000 hect-

ares of this area was declared a national reserve in 1974. This is the only home of a seriously endangered bird species: the *zambullidor del Lago Junín*, or «Lake Junín diver» (*Podiceps taczanowskii*). The picturesque towns on the lake shores raise livestock and farm (Junín is the primary producer of *maca* root in Peru), and harvest frogs for local consumption. Unfortunately, a large part of the lake is seriously contaminated by mining waste. There are several towns in the area that have simple restaurants and hostels. If you wish to camp, take warm clothing, as the nights are cold.

Junín Lake as seen from Óndores.

Emerald tucanet (*Aulacorhynchus derbianus*).

Tingo María
652M / 2 139FT

This cheerful, bustling city, is located in the high rain forest 120km (2 hours, 30 minutes) NE of Huánuco via paved highway. Its surrounding natural

The Yuracyacu River outside Tingo María.

environment is very beautiful and considered by many a paradise for adventurers and ecotourists. We recommend a visit to the Tingo María National Park, the Cueva de las Lechuzas (Owls' Cave), the Cueva de las Pavas (Turkeys' Cave), and the Velo del Ángel (Angel's Veil) waterfall, ideal for a refreshing dip. «Tingo», as the locals call it, has several good hotels and restaurants.

Hotels

★★★ Gran Hotel Huánuco *(ex Hotel de Turistas)*
Dámaso Beraún 775. Tel 51 4222.
Fax 51 2410. US$ 40

★★★ Real Hotel
Dos de Mayo 1125, plaza de armas.
Tel 51 3411. Fax 51 2765. US$ 35

★★★ Gran Hotel Cusco
Huánuco 614. Tel 51 3578. US$ 35

★★★ Hostal Astoria
Gral. Prado 984. Tel 51 2310. US$ 30

★★ Hostal Las Vegas
28 de Julio 940. Tel 51 2315. US$ 20

RATES ARE APPROXIMATE AND, UNLESS OTHERWISE NOTED,
ARE FOR DOUBLE OCCUPANCY.

Restaurants

Restaurante del Gran Hotel Huánuco ✔
   Dámaso Beraún 775.
Restaurante del Hotel Cusco ✔
   Huánuco 616.
El Edén ✔
   Huánuco–Tingo María road km 3,6.

Useful Facts

AREA CODE **64**

☎

Basic information
ESALUD:
   Constitución 601.   51 1502
Hospital Regional Hermilio Valdizán:
   Hermilio Valdizán 950.   51 2400
Botica 24 horas:
   Huánuco 613.   51 1131
Botica Valles:
   Huánuco 577.   51 3388
Instituto Nacional de Cultura:
   Jr. 2 de Mayo 668.   51 2507
Post Office:
   Jr. 2 de Mayo 1151   51 2503
IPERÚ:
   Information and Assistance for Tourists
   01-574-8000 Lima.

Callejón de Huaylas

2 800   M/9 187FT ON AVERAGE
HUARAZ   404 KM
NE OF LIMA

P. 82

P. 78

ROUTE MAP
④

Access Routes

Access to the Callejón de Huaylas is possible by various routes. The most popular, because of its good condition, is a paved road that starts on the outskirts of Pativilca (km 206 of the North Panamericana highway) and climbs, following the Fortaleza River, up to Conococha at more than 4 000m (13 000ft), within sight of Lake Conococha, the source of the Santa River. From here the road descends the Santa River valley (the Callejón)

Mountaineer on the shores of Lake Carhuacocha, Cordillera Huayhuash.

as it widens approaching Huaraz and the other valley towns. The total distance from Lima on this road is 404km and takes some 6 hours *(see Circuit 4, p. 495)*.

Another route, on a packed dirt road less traveled than the first, starts from the town of Santa at 12km N of Chimbote (km 443 of the North Panamericana) and climbs towards the E following the Santa River upstream, passing through the towns

> *Temperate climate, with sunny days, cold nights and a yearly mean temperature of 16°C (61°F). Recuay is the coldest area in the valley and Caraz is the warmest and most pleasant. Rainy season from January to March. The dry season, from May to October, is the most recommended for a visit.*

of Vinzos and Chuquicara and the spectacular Cañón del Pato, to finally reach Huallanca at the far northern, lower end of the Callejón de Huaylas. From Huallanca, the road to Huaraz (89 km) is paved. The route from Santa takes some 4 hours and despite its somewhat fair condition, is suitable for any kind of vehicle. From Lima, this route is 685km in length and takes some 9 hours.

A third route, also on a packed dirt road, leaves the city of Casma (km 375 of the North Panamericana) and enters the Callejón after passing through the villages of San Miguel, Yaután, Pariacoto, and Chacchán, offering an impressive mountain panorama as its crosses the Cordillera Negra range, especially at Punta Callán, the high point of the route at 30km from Huaraz. The road is in poor condition and is only recommended for all-terrain vehicles. From Lima, this route is 524km in length and takes some 7 hours, 30 minutes.

The Cross of Rataquenua.

Pocpa.

A final way to reach the Callejón de Huaylas is by air. There is a small airstrip at the town of Anta, 25km N of Huaraz, but commercial flights are only scheduled at irregular intervals.

For more information contact one of the air taxi

services *(see Useful Facts for the Traveler, p. 83)* or Grupo Aéreo Número 8.

Geography

Located 350km NE of Lima, the Santa River valley is known as the Callejón de Huaylas where it passes between the Cordillera Negra and the Cordillera Blanca ranges that run parallel to the coast. The Callejón is approximately 180km long (measured from Cátac at the south end to Huallanca at the north end) and is a narrow inter-Andean valley blessed with extraordinary scenery, picturesque towns, stands of eucalyptus and cultivated fields. The Cordillera Negra, or «black range,» rises on the left, or western bank of the Santa River, with summits reaching more than 5 000m (16 400ft) but lacking permanent snowpack due to the warm winds off the Pacific Ocean. On the eastern side of the valley, where conditions are diametrically opposed, close to a hundred snow-clad peaks (35 of them tower over 6 000m, or 19 600ft in height) rise majestically in the Cordillera Blanca, or «white range,» the highest tropical mountain range on the planet.

CONQUERING HUASCARÁN

The southern peak of Mount Huascarán (the highest mountain in Peru) was first climbed in 1932 by a German-Austrian expedition led by P. Borchers. The climbers took seven days to complete their objective: five days on the ascent and two on the descent. Two decades later, Peruvian climbers Apolonio Guido and Pedro Yánac reached the summit.
With ideal weather conditions, an expedition today takes about three days, round trip. The best season for an attempt is from April to November.

Local Attractions

Without a doubt, the principal attractions of the Callejón de Huaylas are the spectacular natural surroundings, especially on the east side of the valley where the Cordillera Blanca rises. Many of the summits are dramatic and overwhelmingly beautiful (Alpamayo, Huandoy, Chopicalqui, Chacraraju), but one of them especially draws the traveler's attention: Mount Huascarán. Known as «the roof of Peru,» it is the second highest peak in South America and towers 6 768m (22 206ft) over the town of Yungay. The Cordillera Blanca has some

22 hot springs and more than 600 beautiful lakes coloring the landscape like emeralds set in snow and granite. Its sheltered valleys are sanctuaries for growths of *puya* Raimondi (*Puya raimondii*) as well as some of the largest stands of *queñual* (*Polylepis spp.*) remaining in Peru, the highest altitude trees in the world. These woods are some of the last habitats for a large variety of beautiful, threatened or endangered flora and fauna, such as the Andean condor (*Vultur gryphus*), the puma (*Puma concolor*), and the *taruca* dwarf deer (*Hipocamelus antisiensis*). The Quechua word *huaylas* means 'meadows' and perfectly describes the scenery awaiting visitors to the Callejón.

Market in Yungay.

This lovely valley is also distinguished by the friendliness and hospitality of its inhabitants. On the right bank of the Santa River lie a series of welcoming towns with farm economies (flowers and fruit in the lower areas, cereals and tubers in the higher areas).

During the larger festivals (Mountain Climbing Week, the Independence Holidays, and Holy Week) there are many visitors to the Callejón. Remember to make reservations well in advance.

Old bell-tower in Llámac.

Local Dishes

Entrées
- Cebiche de pato casmeño: steamed duck marinated in orange and lime.
- Jamón del norte: ham smoked with *ají colorado* pepper.

Soups
- Llunca kashki: chicken stewed with wheat and *huacatay*, an aromatic herb.
- Patasca: soup of various meats, Andean corn, tripe, wheat, and broad beans.

- Pecan caldo: sheep's head broth with tripe and aromatic herbs.

Main Dishes
- Picante de cuy: guinea pig fried with *ají colorado* pepper, toasted peanuts and potatoes.

Desserts
- Manjarblanco: sweet milk paste.
- Alfajores and bizcochos: cookies and small cakes.

Drinks
- Chicha de maní: a fermented peanut beverage.

Festivals

TREKKING IN THE ANDES

The daily costs of hiking in the Blanca and Huayhuash cordilleras are approximately:
- Guide: US$10
- Cook: US$ 7
- Mule driver: US$ 4
- Burros: US$ 4 each

The cost of contracting the services of a guide, a cook, four mules and their driver for a five-day excursion comes to about US$185.

One of the most important festivals celebrated in Huaraz is the Feast of the Señor de la Soledad, or Our Lord of Solitude (May 3 to 14), patron saint of Huaraz, who is believed to protect the city from earthquakes. The main event of this festival comes on May 14 with the Feast of the Exaltation of the Cross.

Other festivals celebrated in the towns of the Callejón are: Christmas in Carhuaz (third Sunday in January); the Feast of the Virgin of the town of Chiquinquirá (January 20); Carnival throughout the Callejón with the traditional *yunsa* or *cortamonte* dance (February); Holy Week (March or April); Corpus Christi and Mountain Climbing Week in Huaraz (June); Tourism Week in Caraz (July 24 to 27); the Feast of Santo Domingo (August 4) and Santa Rosa (August 30), both celebrated in Yungay with processions and folk dances; the Virgen de las Mercedes in Carhuaz, with processions, music bands, and bullfights (September 24); the Feast of the Señor de Burgos in Recuay, with the famous *danza de los negritos*, or dance of the black men (September 11 to 15); the Feast of the Virgen de la Merced also in Recuay, in which bad luck is foreseen for the coming year if someone does not die accidentally during the celebrations (September 24); the Virgen del Rosario in Yungay (first week in October); the anniversary of Yungay (October 25 to 28); and finally, All Saints' Day (November 1), in which crowds of people visit the cemeteries of the Callejón accompanied by music bands.

Folkcrafts

Some of the best handicrafts typical of the Callejón de Huaylas are woolen textiles, hats, embossed leather purses and pottery. In Chavín de Huántar, there are artisans specializing in miniature stone and plaster works imitating ancient artifacts of the Chavín culture.

Along the entire Callejón, models of birds, flowers, bulls, and religious images are made of agave to adorn crosses used in holy festivals.

Seeing the Valley

Down the Santa River from its source at Lake Conococha, in order of appearance, are the towns of Cátac (km166), the turn-off to Chavín de Huántar, the town of Recuay (km168), the city of Huaraz (km203), and then, descending through stands of eucalyptus and yellow-flowered broom sage called *retama*, the towns of Carhuaz, Yungay, and Caraz. The road continues

Callejón de Huaylas with the Cordillera Negra as backdrop.

A high Andean meadow in Ancash.

along the Santa River to Huallanca (106km from Huaraz), where it turns W and enters an deep, narrow gorge (almost 25km long and over 1 000m, or 3 000ft deep) carved by the Santa River through the Cordillera Negra and named the Cañón del Pato. The builders of this road had to carve much of it out of the sheer rock cliffs, requiring 39 tunnels in all. At the mouth of the gorge, the road continues along the Santa River as it flows to the Pacific Ocean *(see Circuit 4, p. 497)*.

There are other, longer routes out of the Callejón. One packed dirt road starts at Huallanca and goes behind the Cordillera Blanca and north through the Callejón de Conchucos and the towns of Sihuas, Pomabamba, Piscobamba, San Luis, and Huari before reentering the Callejón de Huaylas at the town of Cátac. Another, also a packed dirt road, leads to Corongo (3 141m, or 10 306ft) 100km N of Caraz.

 ## Excursions

Huaraz

3 052M / 10 013FT

Located in the central section of the Callejón de Huaylas, Huaraz is the capital of the department of Ancash and the valley's main city. The earthquake of 1970 toppled the few Colonial buildings that had survived the earthquake of 1941.

Following these fatal events, Huaraz has regrown as an unorganized, concrete city of bustling commercial activity. Although the city offers few attractions to the visitor, it does have some the best restaurants and hotels in the valley. It is also the point of departure for the Cordillera Blanca. The Regional Museum of Huaraz in the Plaza de Armas (in the Instituto Nacional de Cultura building) has an interesting collection of ceramics and monolithic sculptures from the ancient cultures of the region (Chavín and Recuay).

National Park of Huascarán

3 800M / 12 467FT ON AVERAGE

This park not only includes the area around the imposing Mount Huascarán but also the entire Cordillera Blanca range over 4 000m (13 000ft) —with the exception of Mount Champará (5 743m, or 18 843ft) at the extreme N end— totaling a surface area of 340 000 hectares. Access to the park is by a number of packed dirt roads starting from the valley towns and climbing eastward. The most popular routes are from Yungay to the lakes at Llanganuco and from Pachacoto to Mount Pastoruri *(see Circuit 4, p. 497)*. The park was mainly created to preserve the flora, fauna, geological formations, archeological remains and beautiful scenery of the Cordillera, as well as to contribute to the quality of life of the surrounding inhabitants. Unesco has recognized the park as a Natural World Heritage. It has an extensive water network consisting of three river basins with 663 glaciers, 296 lakes and 41 rivers. The park contains important species of native flora and fauna including *puya* Raimondi and extensive stands of *queñual* trees. Other inhabitants are the Andean condor, vicuña, white-tailed deer, the endangered *taruca* or Andean

Guaraguan
(*Phalcobaenus albogularis*).

Andean passion flower
(*Passiflora sp.*).

Lake in Quilcayhuanca Canyon.

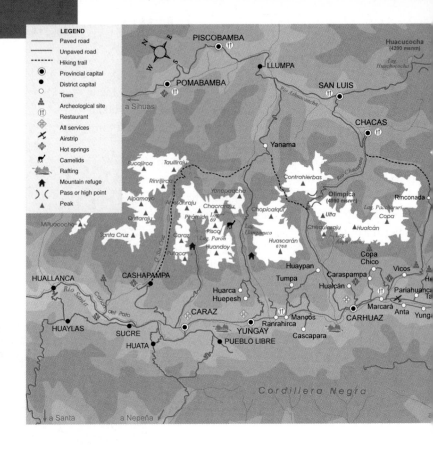

dwarf deer, puma, Andean lynx, Andean fox, *vizcacha* rodent and several dozen species of birds including *huallatas*, *yanavicos*, *lique-liques*, ducks, *gallaretas*, and *chocas*. There are two entrance gates, at Llanganuco and Carpa (on the way to Pastoruri), where visitors pay an entrance fee of approximately US$ 1. There are regulations within the National Park; respecting them will help conserve this natural paradise.

Chavín de Huántar

3 150M / IO 335FT

An archeological site 115km SE of Huaraz in the Mosna River valley (Callejón de Conchucos), a tributary of the Marañón River. Some 2 500 years ago, Chavín was a religious center that drew pilgrims from far away, bringing offerings and hoping to consult the prestigious oracle housed there. As a result, the sanctu-

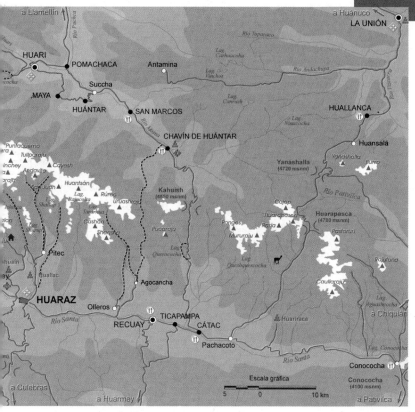

CALLEJÓN DE HUAYLAS

ary had a strong religious, cultural, and political influence in the Andes. At its height (800–500 BC), the complex consisted of a group of stone-walled buildings arranged around a great plaza and containing numerous subterranean galleries and passageways. The best known buildings are:

The Old Temple: a horseshoe-shaped structure. In a cramped room where two of its passages come together there is a stone obelisk standing almost 5m high and finely carved with anthropomorphic reliefs.

The New Temple (commonly called The Castle): is a truncated pyramid with a rectangular base and a massive doorway half of white slate and half of black slate (the Black and White Portico or the Portico of the Falcons).

Stone tenon head, Chavín de Huántar.

The New Temple or Castle, Chavín de Huántar.

Both temples are profusely decorated with bas-reliefs representing anthropomorphic beings and evil-looking animals. Originally, many stone heads projected from the walls, sculpted with a fierce mix of human and feline features. Only one can still be seen in its original setting.

Access to Chavín is via 75km of packed dirt road (2 hours, 30minutes) starting at the town of Cátac in the upper section of the Callejón de Huaylas. The road weaves its way through beautiful Andean landscapes: climbing past Lake Querococha (3 420m, or 11 221ft) and the *pampas* (or flats) of Lampas. At the top, it runs through a 578m tunnel, the longest in Peru, at the Kahuish pass (4 550m, or 14 928ft), and then descends through the narrow Mosna River valley. A day visit to Chavín requires a very early start from Huaraz (and a late return) or you can choose to spend the night at the nearby towns of Chavín or Huari, where there are simple hotels and restaurants.

Recuay
3 394M / 11 132FT

This town marks the entrance to the Callejón de Huaylas. It lies on the left bank of the Santa River 27km (30 minutes) above, or

S of, Huaraz via paved road. With a beautiful view of nearby snow-clad peaks, its narrow streets and tile roofs give it a warm and welcoming aspect. Nearby are the ruins of Pueblo Viejo (home to the ancient Recuay culture), hot springs at Burgos, a mining settlement at Ticapampa and some onyx quarries. To visit any of these, contact local guides. From Cátac, 15km from Recuay, a road leads to Chavín de Huántar and the Callejón de Conchucos. Along this road, 30km from Recuay, near the Kahuish tunnel on the way to Chavín de Huántar, is beautiful Lake Querococha.

The Callejón de Conchucos.

Glaciar Pastoruri

4 950M / 16 241FT

70km (3 hours) S of Huaraz on a 26km packed dirt road that starts at the town of Pachacoto (US$ 1 toll fee). Despite its height, Mount Pastoruri draws thousands of visitors each season in search of snow and a chance to ski (its ski slope, barely 400m, or 1 312ft long, is considered the highest in the world). We recommend caution because of the altitude (it is best to spend a few days acclimatizing in Huaraz first), as many visitors suffer from altitude sick-

Camp on the Cordillera Huayhuash.

ness (called *soroche*) when attempting the 45 minutes ascent to the glacier. There are horses and mules available for the ascent, as well as restrooms and food services. Don't forget to bring along a spare pair of shoes, as yours will get wet on the glacier, and remember to pack out all your trash. On the walk up to the glacier there is a cluster of *puya* Raimondi, the spring of Pumapashimi (an incredibly emerald-green color) and a mineral spring of carbonated water.

Hot Springs at Monterrey and Chancos

2 700M / 8 859FT MONTERREY
3 000M / 9 843FT CHANCOS

5km and 28km (30 minutes) NW of Huaraz. The Monterrey hot springs are located on the paved road to Carhuaz and have fully developed facilities. Their waters issue from the ground at

49°C (120°F) and are said to be effective in treating rheumatism. The Chancos hot springs, located in the village of Vicos at the foot of Mount Copa, issue from the ground at 70°C (158°F). They have some simple services and a place for taking steam baths. Access to Chancos is by taking a 3km packed dirt road starting at the town of Marcará (25km NW of Huaraz).

Carhuaz
2 645M / 8 676FT)

A traditional town lying 32km (30 minutes) N of Huaraz on a paved road. Its name comes from the Quechua word *ccarhuash*, meaning 'yellow,' most likely for the abundance of *retama* flow-

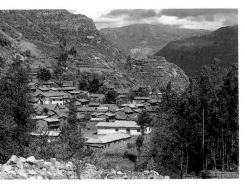

Llámac.

ers in the area. It is located on the slopes of the Mount Hualcán (6 150m, or 20 178ft) and still has a few Colonial-era homes that withstood the earthquake of 1970. This is the starting point for a visit to the Ulta Canyon, an alternative route to the Callejón de Conchucos via a packed dirt road that runs along the feet of the snow-capped peaks of Huascarán Sur, Chopicalqui, Ulta, and Contrahierbas, crosses the Punta Olímpica pass (4 990m, or 16 372ft) and comes to the towns of Pompey and Chacas (the latter is famous for its wooden handicrafts). This is a stunningly beautiful route.

Yungay
2 458M / 8 062FT)

39km (40 minutes) N of Huaraz via paved road. Its name comes from the Quechua word, *yunga*, meaning 'warm lands.' Famous for its beauty, this small city was previously considered the jewel of the Callejón de Huaylas. Located at the foot of Mount Huascarán (whose two peaks tower 6 721m, or 22 052ft and 6 768m, or 22 206ft high and only 14km from the road), the city was completely buried by a landslide when the 1970 earthquake dislodged the glacier from the north face of Huascarán. On the old site of the town, now called Campo Santo, meaning 'holy ground' or cemetery, you can still see the tops of the four palm trees of its Plaza de Armas. New Yungay has been built 1,5km from the original site. Although it has no quality services, it is a departure point for the famous Llanganuco lakes. There are a few hotels and restaurants, and a popular Sunday fair.

Llanganuco Lakes

3 800M / 12 468FT

25km (45 minutes) E of Yungay, accessed by a winding and somewhat difficult packed dirt road through tremendous scenery. These turquoise-colored lakes lie in a narrow glacial valley flanked by the snow-capped peaks of Huascarán (Quechua for 'whip') and Huandoy (6 428m, or 21 090ft).

Stands of *queñual* trees at Llanganuco.

The first lake is called Chinancocha ('female lake') and has dense stands of *queñual* trees on its shores. There is a trail that provides a one-hour, downhill walk through simply beautiful nature. The other lake is Orconcocha ('male lake') and is smaller and at the end of the valley. From here the road continues climbing to the Vaquería pass (at 4 750m, or 15 585ft) and the towns of Llumpa and San Luis in the Callejón de Conchucos. To visit Llanganuco we recommend leaving early and taking warm clothing along because there are strong, cold winds in the afternoons.

Caraz

2 256M / 7 401FT

Plaza de Armas in Mancos.

A picturesque town 67km (50 minutes) N of Huaraz, via paved road, whose name comes from the Quechua word, *ccaras*, meaning 'leather.' This town has the best weather in the Callejón. It is famous for the hospitality of its inhabitants, its sweets and its pastries. Towering over its typical, narrow streets are the snow-capped peaks of Aguja, Alpamayo

A peak on the Cordillera Huayhuash.

(6 120m, or 20 080ft), Santa Cruz, and Huandoy. Caraz is the departure point for visiting the beautiful Lake Parón (31km to the E, or 2 hours, at 4 200m, or 13 780ft), the largest lake in the range, located at the foot of mounts Pirámide Garcilaso (5 885m, or 19 309ft) and Chacraraju (6 185m, or 20 293ft). Near town is the archeological site of Tumshucayco. Mountain climbers leave from Caraz for the summits of mounts Alpamayo and Huaylas. There are several restaurants and hostels in town.

Cordillera Huayhuash

4 300M / 14 104FT ON AVERAGE   ◯ ❘

To the S of the Cordillera Blanca and bordering the department of Huánuco is some of the most spectacular scenery in the Andes. Because access to this area has been very difficult until recently, the natural scenery has remained almost intact. The area is ideal for climbing and trekking; its sharp summits are quite high and difficult, such as Mount Yerupajá (6 634m, or 21 766ft), the highest summit in the Amazon basin and the second highest in Peru. In the area are some of the prettiest lakes of the central Andes, such as Carhuacocha, Viconga, and Jahuacocha, three lakes following each other like steps. Other highlights are its sheltered valleys where agricultural terraces alternate with beautiful waterfalls. There is varied wildlife, including puma, condors, vicuñas, *vizcacha* rodents, and *taruca* deer. You can only reach the Cordillera Huayhuash on foot, starting from the town of Chiquián (3 200m, or 10 499ft) 31km from Conococha (over the pampa de Lampas). Chiquián has several restaurants and simple hotels. We recommend the San Miguel hostel (Jr. Comercio 211. Tel. 71 7001) and the Las Tejas and Yerupajá restaurants. A walk well worth the effort and considered by experts as one of the most spectacular in the world, this route leaves Chiquián towards the towns of Llamac and Pocpa, skirts Lake Jahuacocha and reaches the settlement of Janca. From here it continues S towards lakes Carhuacocha and Viconga to end at the town of Cajatambo, the exit to the coast. This circuit takes eight to fourteen days and is limited to experienced walkers as most of the circuit lies at over 4 000m (13 124ft). We guarantee some of the most spectacular scenery on this part of the planet.

Rataquenua Lookout
3 320M / 10 893FT)

2km SE of Huaraz via packed dirt road in the area known as El Pedregal. This spot offers a magnificent view of Huaraz and its surroundings, ideal for photography.

Pre-Inca ruins at Willcahuaín.

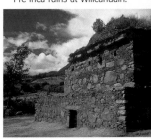

Archeological Sites

Willcahuaín, Honcopampa, Janku, Huaullac, Kekamarca, Marcún and Keyash. Ask for information at the offices of the Instituto Nacional de Cultura or at the Casa de Guías in Huaraz *(see Useful Facts, p. 276).*

Hotels

Huaraz
Andino Club Hotel   ★★★★
   Pedro Cochachín 357. Tel 72 1662.

Fax 72 2830.

reservas@hotelandino.com

★★★ Gran Hotel Huascarán
Av. Centenario 1021. Tel 72 1640. Fax 72 2821.
Reservations Lima Tel 425 1670. US$ 55

★★★ Hotel Real Huaraz
Antúnez de Mayolo (10th. bock). Tel 72 1640. US$ 40

★★★ Hostal Los Portales
Av. Raimondi 903. Tel 72 8184. Fax 72 1247. US$ 40
losportales@hotmail.com

★★★ Hostal Colomba
Francisco de Zela 278. Tel 72 1501. US$ 40

★★★ Hotel El Tumi
San Martín 1121. Tel 72 1852. US$ 35

★★★ Complejo Turístico Eccame
18km Airport Huaraz. Telefax 72 1933. US$ 25

★★ Youth Hostel Alojamiento Alpes
Plaza Ginebra 28-G. Tel 72 1811.

★★ Albergue Juvenil La Montañesa
Augusto B. Leguía 267. Tel 71 1287.

Monterrey

★★★ Hotel Real Monterrey
Av. Monterrey s/n, Parte Alta. Tel 72 1717. US$ 45

★★★ Hotel El Patio
Av. Monterrey. Tel 72 0209.
Reservations Lima Tel 437 6567. US$ 45

Carhuaz

★★ La Casa de Pocha
1km on the road to Hualcán. (a 600m from the plaza
de armas). US$ 18 (price per person).
Cel 61 3058.

★ Hostal El Abuelo
Corner of Jr. 9 de Diciembre and Tumbes. Tel 79 4149.

Caraz

★ O'Pal Inn
San Luis Farm, Pativilca–Huaraz road

km 266.6 (1km from Caraz). Tel 70 1015.
Reservations Lima Tel 476 4857. US$ 40

Hostal Chamana ★★★
  Av. Nueva Victoria 185.
  Huaraz–Huallanca road km 258. US$ 25

Albergue Turístico Los Pinos ★★
  Pque. San Martín 103, La Merced. Tel 79 1130.

Caraz Dulzura ★
  Sáenz Peña 212. Tel 79 1523.

Fundo San Luis ★
  On the road to Caraz, km 266.

RATES ARE APPROXIMATE AND, UNLESS OTHERWISE NOTED,
ARE FOR DOUBLE OCCUPANCY.

Restaurants

Huaraz

Creperie Patrick ✔
  Av. Luzuriaga 424.

Monte Rosa ✔
  J. de la Mar, (6th block).

La Familia ✔
  Av. Luzuriaga 431.

Euskalerria ✔
  Av. Luzuriaga 406.

Chez Pepe ✔
  Raimondi 642. Luzuriaga 570.

Alpes-Andes ✔
  Plaza Ginebra s/n.

Pizzas Bruno ✔
  Av. Luzuriaga 834.

Le Bistró de los Andes ✔
  J. De Morales 823.

Carhuaz

Restaurante Campestre Bertita ✔
  Huaraz-Huallanca road km 235.

Heladería El Abuelo ✔
  Plaza de armas.

✔ El Palmero
    Av. Progreso 490.

Caraz

✔ Jenny
    Plaza de armas.
✔ Palmira
    Huaraz-Huallanca road km 66,5.
✔ El Mirador
    Sucre 1202.
✔ La Olla de Barro
    Sucre 1004.
✔ Caraz Dulzura
    Plaza de armas.

Useful Facts

AREA CODE **44**

☎

Basic information

ESALUD: Campamento Vichay n/n.	72 2912
Clínica San Francisco de Asís: Av. Raimondi 751.	72 9290
Intifarma:	
Hr. Julián de Morales 661.	72 6606
Inkafarma:	
Av. Luzuriaga 435.	72 9222
Head Office of the Huascaran National Park:	
Prolongación Raimondi n/n.	71 2086
Guides' House: Plaza Ginebra n/n.	72 1333
Center for authorized climbing and trekking guides. Provides specialized information on ecotourism and adventure sports.	
Tourism Police Aid:	72 6343
Post Office:	
Av. Luzurriaga n/n.	72 1030
IPERÚ:	
Information y Assistance for Tourists 01-574-8000 Lima.	

Ica

406 M / 1 332FT
161 400 POP.
300 KM
S OF LIMA

P.78

ROUTE MAP
6

The city of Ica, capital of the department of the same name, is located in a valley which, despite its lack of water, is an ever-growing agricultural oasis. Its cotton fields are extensive (the department of Ica is the primary producer of cotton in the nation), as are its fields of lima beans, asparagus, pecans, and grapes for wine production (Ica is considered the grape and wine capital of Peru).

The territory around the city was previously inhabited by some of the most important cultures of ancient Peru: Paracas,

Outskirts of Villacurí.

Nasca, and Wari. Around AD 900, the region became part of the kingdom of Chincha, and around the fifteenth century it was conquered by the Incas. Nonetheless, the most important archeological remains in the department of Ica are not found near the capital but further south, near Nasca *(see Nasca, p. 359)*.

In 1534, the Spanish conquistadors reached the valley of Ica

Dry and sunny climate year round, with a yearly mean temperature of 22° C (72° F). As with all of the coastal desert, the temperature varies greatly during the day; it can reach as high as 32° C (90° F) during the day and fall as low as 8° C (46° F) at night. Rainfall is scarce in Ica, although the El Niño weather phenomenon can bring occasional rains.

for the first time and, in 1563, Viceroy Conde de Nieva ordered that a Spanish city be founded there. Ica was founded under the name of Villa de Valverde in June of that year, by the Sevillian Luis Jerónimo de Cabrera (who years later also founded the city of Córdoba in Argentina). Since then, the region's predominant agricultural activity has been the cultivation of grapes, which the Spanish introduced with much success; *«En Ica hincha la bota y pica»* (in Ica the wineskin swells and stimulates), was the well-known saying. Nothing much remains of the city's Colonial past; there are, however, several original buildings to admire, such as the Casa de las Cornucopias (Dos de Mayo 158), the Casa del Valle (San Martín 159), and the Edificio del Estanco (Excise-House, Lima 390).

El Carmelo.

Carob tree (*Prosopis pallida*).

Today Ica is a friendly city and the departure point for visiting some of the best beaches on the Peruvian coast, as well as the famous Nasca lines. It possesses numerous wineries where some of Peru's finest piscos and wines are produced (well worth tasting), and it is an important center for the breeding of the elegant Paso horses. Its people and its sweets (be sure to try the *tejas*) are some of the best attractions of this city. Its pleasant climate and proximity to Lima make Ica an excellent travel destination.

Local Dishes

Main Dishes
- Morusa: roast beef served with lima bean puree.
- Picante de pallares: spicy lima bean stew with milk, eggs, and fresh cheese.

Soups
- Chupe de pallares: lima bean soup with fish, corn, rice, and milk.

Desserts
- Dulce de pallares: lima beans cooked with milk, cinnamon, vanilla, and sesame seeds.
- Tejas: candied pecans, figs, or lemons with *manjarblanco* (sweet milk paste).

Drinks
- Cachina: drink based on fermented grape must.
- Piscos.
- Wines.

THE SECRETS OF PISCO

«First came out the water, then came out the liquor and then, God forgive me! I came out drunk...» This old song refers to the making of Peruvian pisco, the pure grape brandy used to prepare the national cocktail of Peru: the pisco sour. While the majority of liquors are made by distilling cold musts or prepared wines, Peruvian pisco is distilled from warm, recently fermented, musts. Another characteristic of this liquor is that water is never added to dilute its alcohol content, neither before nor after it is distilled.

Festivals

The Ica festival best known to tourists is the International Grape Harvest Festival (first two weeks of March). This is an excellent time for visiting Ica's wineries.

On Holy Thursday (March or April) and the third Monday of October the image of the Señor de Luren, patron saint of this city, is carried in procession. This beautiful, night-time candle-lit event, accompanied by musicians and thousands of the faithful, is Ica's most significant religious celebration.

June, on the other hand, is the ideal time to see the Peruvian Paso horses of this region, as the Sol de Oro horse competition is held then (exact date varies).

(Other festivals celebrated in Ica are: Carnival (February); the Feast of the Crosses (May); the anniversary of Ica (June 17); the Ica Tourism Festival (last week of September); the Feast of the Virgen de Guadalupe (December 12); and the Paseo de Negritos, or Walk of the Black Men (Christmas day), which commemorates the once strong presence of Negro slaves in the region.

Points of Interest in the City

Museums

- *Museo Regional de Ica*, Prolongación Ayabaca, 8th block, Urb. San Isidro. Tel 234 4383: one of Peru's best regional museums, with a significant collection of ceramics, funerary bundles, and utensils from the Paracas, Nasca, Wari, Chincha, and Ica cultures. Be sure to see the remains of a Chincha-area farmer more than 6 000 years old.

  Visiting hours: Mon-Sat, 9am to noon, and 2 to 6pm; Sun, 9am to noon.

- *Colección Cabrera*, Bolívar 170, Plaza de Armas: a unique collection of more than 11 000 carved, round stones which, according to Dr. Cabrera Darquea who discovered them, relate the history of a bygone civilization. Worth visiting, although of dubious archeological value.

  Visiting hours: Mon-Sat, 9am to noon, and 4 to 8pm.

Excursions

Huacachina

410M / 1 345FT   )

An oasis with a beautiful lagoon, 5 km W of the city, reached via the paved road that sets out from the circle (*óvalo*) on Av. Los Maestros next to the Hotel Real Ica. Set among enormous dunes of fine sand, from 1920 to 1950 Huacachina was an exclusive resort that drew visitors for the medicinal effects of its sulfur springs. The lagoon is surrounded by date palms and carob trees which give shade to the old residences, the handsome walkway, and the famous Hotel Mossone. Local legend has it that every year the siren who lives in the depths of the lagoon emerges to steal a young man from its shores.

Oasis of La Huacachina.

Tacama

415M / 1 362FT)

An hacienda that produces some of the best wines in the country, 11km NE of the city via a partially paved road. Its vineyards originally belonged to the Augustine order and were later ac-

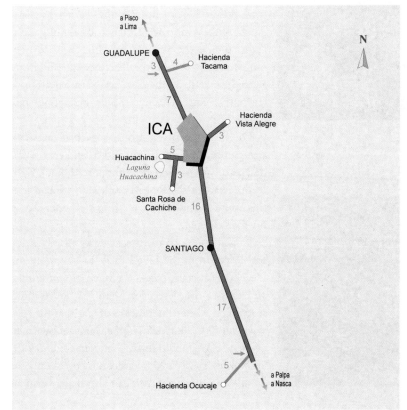

Dunes in Ocucaje.

quired by the Olaechea family. Be sure to taste the pisco called Demonio de los Andes or the excellent Blanc de Blanc wine. Tel 22 8394

Visiting hours: Mon-Sun, 8:30am to noon, and 3 to 4:30pm.

Vista Alegre

415M / 1 361FT   )

Hacienda and winery 3km SE of Ica, over the Grau bridge. This is the largest winery in the country, founded in 1857 by the Picasso brothers.

Visiting hours: Mon-Fri, 8am to noon, and 3 to 5pm.

Beaches

Laguna Grande, Paracas.

Talpo Beach, Paracas.

From the city of Ica you can reach some of the most beautiful beaches on the Peruvian coast. There are several packed dirt roads leading west, across the desert, to the ocean, but the most recommended is to take the Panamericana highway N to the coast at the Paracas National Reserve (turnoff at km 245), this should take about one hour.

For the more adventurous, a packed dirt road starts at km 251 (near Pozo Santo) and crosses the desert to Laguna Grande (45km or 2 hours), right in the heart of the Reserve, although we consider this route suitable only for those experienced in off-road driving.

A third approach to Paracas (also for adventurers) leaves from the Hotel Real Ica (formerly the Hotel de Turistas), passes the town of Comatrana and crosses the desert for 50km (2 hours) until reaching the beautiful beaches of Carhuas (or Karwas) and Cruz de Hueso, in the center of the Independencia Bay. Unfortunately, this route is unmarked and quite deteriorated and recommended only for an all-terrain vehicle. You can also reach Carhuas by following the coast from Paracas (via Yumaque, Mendieta, and Laguna Grande); this is the access route to Barlovento, El Negro, Antana, Gallinazo, and other beaches favored by the sole and *corvina* fishermen. To reach these an all-terrain vehicle and experience in off-road driving are necessary, as well as previous knowledge of the route *(for more information on the Paracas Reserve, see p. 368).*

The Nasca Lines

See Nasca, p. 361.

Hotels

Hotel Las Dunas ★★★★
Angostura 400 (Panamericana Sur km 300).
Tel 25 6224. Reservations Lima Tel 442 4180. US$ 90
reservas@onvertur.com.pe.

Ocucaje Sun & Wine Resort ★★★★
Panamericana Sur km 336, district of Ocucaje.
Telefax 40 8003. Reservations Lima Tel 444 1158. US$ 80

Hotel Real Ica *(ex Hotel de Turistas)* ★★★★
Los Maestros 422. Tel 23 3330.
Reservations Lima Tel 425 1670. US$ 65

Hotel Mossone ★★★★
Resort of Huacachina n/n. Tel 21 3630.
Fax 23 6136. Reservations Lima Tel 440 6527. US$ 65
hmossone@derramajae.org.pe

Hostal El Carmelo ★★★★
Panamericana Sur km 301. Tel 23 2191. US$ 50
el_carmelo@hotmail.com

Hostal Sol de Ica ★★★
Lima 265. Tel 23 6168. US$ 45

Hostal Siesta ★★★
Independencia 160. Tel 23 4663. US$ 20

Residencial El Carmen ★★
Angostura 1020.
(a few blocks from Hotel Las Dunas).
Tel 25 6098. US$ 20

★★ Hostal Suizo

Angostura, 8th block (a few blocks from Hotel Las Dunas). US$ 20

★★ Hostal Presidente

Amazonas 223. Tel 22 5977. US$ 15

Fundo Hotel El Arrabal

Tel 25 6249.

arrabal@huayna.rcp.net.pe

RATES ARE APPROXIMATE AND, UNLESS OTHERWISE NOTED, ARE FOR DOUBLE OCCUPANCY.

Restaurants

✔ El Catador

Fundo Tres Esquinas, Subtanjalla.

✔ San Isidro

San Martín 1149.

✔ El Fogón

Municipalidad 276.

✔ El Otro Peñoncito

Bolívar 255.

✔ El Velero Azul

Bolívar 437.

✔ Panadería Velasco

Grau 199.

✔ Evangelina Robles

Lima, cdra.4.

✔ Rosalía

Ayacucho 309.

Useful facts

AREA CODE 34

☎

Basic information
IPERÚ:
Information and Assistance for Tourists
01-574-8000 Lima.
Instituto Nacional de Cultura:
Prol. Ayabaca 8th block, Urb. San Isidro.   23 2881

Travel Agencies
Huacachina Tours: Angostura 355.   25 6582

Aerotaxis (for flights over the Lines at Nasca)
Aero Cóndor: 25 7069
Angostura 400. (Hotel Las Dunas).
Panamericana Sur, km 300   25 7210
Aero Ica: Diez Canseco 434, oficina 102,   445 0850
Miraflores, Lima.   446 3026
Office in Nasca: Panamericana Sur km 447   52 3776
Aero Paracas:
Office in Nasca: Panamericana Sur km 901.   52 2688

Post Office:
Libertad 119-A. / San Martín 398.   23 4549
ESALUD: Matías Manzanilla 652.   23 4271
Clínica Virgen del Rosario: Callao 263.   23 4083
Farmacia María del Pilar: San Martín 1449   22 2618
Taxi Ya   23 4212

106 M / 348FT
274 800 POP.
NE OF LIMA

Iquitos

P. 82

P. 87

ROUTE MAP
12

The city of Iquitos, capital of the department of Loreto, is located on the shores of the Amazon River, the longest and widest river with the greatest volume of water in the world. It is flanked on either side by the mouths of the Nanay and Itaya rivers. Even though it is the largest city in the Peruvian jungle, there are no westward roads joining it to the coast or the Andes; it can only be reached by air or by river.

In the past, this territory was populated by different ethnic groups of hunters and fishermen, including the Iquitos, Coca-

Cocama village on the bank of the Itaya River.

mas, Yaguas, Huitotos, Boras, Ticunas, and Orejones. In 1542, Francisco de Orellana and a handful of Spanish explorers navigated the river for the first time and contacted the people who lived in this area. This was the beginning of a series of expeditions that ended when the Spaniards realized that there were no large mines in the region and its inhabitants were scattered and unwilling to help. Eventually, the Colonial government del-

A classically tropical climate; warm, humid and rainy, with a yearly mean temperature of 28°C (82°F). Like all jungle towns, it has a heavy rainy season from December to March. The dry season (May to September) is best for visiting.

egated the administration of these «frontiers of civilization» to the Jesuits.

There are various stories of the founding of the city of Iquitos. One attributes it to the Jesuits, who established a frontier camp called San Pablo de los Napeanos in 1757. Over time, this name may have been shortened to Iquitos. Other sources, however, link it to a town established in 1840 by a group of settlers who arrived from the village of Borja after being expelled by the natives of the Marañón River valley. In either case, when the Italian traveler Antonio Raimondi arrived here in the mid-nineteenth century, he wrote that he had only seen a «small Indians' quarters».

It was not until the height of the rubber boom (1880–1912) that Iquitos was to claim importance. With the arrival of the rubber barons and the enormous wealth that the extraction of latex produced, Iquitos experienced a period of colossal luxury and ostentation. It was soon named the capital of the department, a privilege that had gone to Moyobamba until then. As evidence of the city's economic bonanza (it was a paradise for fortune seekers in the early twentieth century), there are several interesting examples of architec-

THE KING OF RIVERS

After descending from the Andes, the Amazon River is joined by the waters of over 1 100 tributaries until it becomes a liquid mass of unimaginable proportions. Stretching for 6 762km, it is the longest and widest river, with the greatest volume of water in the world. In Peru, it drains some 956 751km² and close to 900 species of fish have been identified in its waters.

Day's end in Santo Tomás.

River port on the Amazon.

ture: the Casa Eiffel, designed entirely of steel by the renowned French architect; luxurious hotels and homes in the Moorish style, decorated with objects brought directly from Europe by their affluent owners; the Naval Factory, and a small locomotive standing in the Plaza 28 de Julio. At the end of the First World War (1918), as a consequence of the worldwide drop in the price of rubber, Iquitos fell into decay.

Today Iquitos is a spirited, bustling city, living from the lumber industry, ecotourism, and mostly river-based commerce. Nearby are some native communities (Yaguas, Cocamas, Huitotos) that retain their original customs, but most have left them and become incorporated into the pace of modern society. Recently Iquitos' night time has turned on vigorously. Pubs and restaurants have been installed in a section of the old Malecón Tarapacá which newly designed is called now Boulevard Maldonado.

Local Dishes

Entrées
- Juane: a bundle of rice and chicken, wrapped in banana leaf and steamed.

Soups
- Inchicapi de gallina: chicken soup with peanut, cilantro, and yucca root.
- Timbuche de carachama: soup of *carachama* fish, with banana and cilantro.

Main Dishes

Amazonian fishes.

- Paiche con chonta: filet of *paiche* fish with palm salad.
- Tacacho con cecina: grilled or fried banana mashed with jerky.

Drinks
- Aguajina: delicious punch of *aguaje* fruit.
- Chapo de plátano capirona: banana punch served hot or cold.

- Chuchuhuasha: a sour, astringent root extract, said to help rheumatism, mixed with liquor or Coca-Cola.
- Masato: a drink made of mashed yucca root marinated with sweet potato or sugar.
- Beverages made of *cocona, ungurahui, camu camu*, and other delicious wild fruits.

Pijuayo fruit.
(*Bactris gasipaes*).

Festivals

The most colorful festivals celebrated in Iquitos and its environs are the city's anniversary (January 5); Carnival (February or March); the Feast of San Juan and Tourism Week in Iquitos (June 24); the Feast of San Pedro in Bellavista and Nanay (June 29); the Santo Tomás handicraft fair (August 21); the Feast of Santo Tomás (September 23-25); and the Feast of La Purísima in the Iquitos city district of Punchana (December 8).

Folkcrafts

The best handicrafts are the ceramic utensils made by Coca-ma natives, decorated with geometric motifs; Yagua textiles made of native cotton dyed with *achiote* (annato) and *huito*; bows, arrows, and blowguns; necklaces made by the natives of seeds and the feathers, scales and bones of various animals, as well as carving done in hardwoods such as *palo sangre* and *huayruro*.

Points of Interest in the City

Traditional Locales

- *Malecón Tarapacá:* a must stroll for the first-time visitor along the banks of the majestic Amazon River. The old homes and buildings display the ostentatious Art Nouveau architecture that adorned the city during the rubber boom.
- *Belén:* a city district at the junction of the Itaya River and the Amazon. Built entirely on rafts and pilings, the district floods during the rainy season and its buildings rise and fall with on

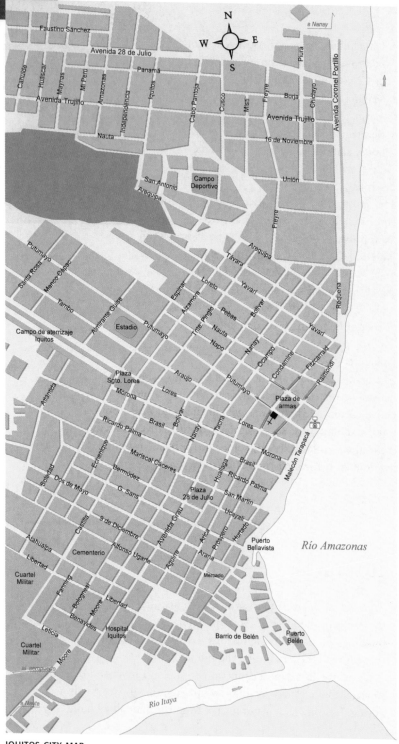

IQUITOS CITY MAP

the height of the river. At present, it is only possible to reach Belén by canoe. The district is a significant commercial center for jungle products and a supply center for the city and it is a colorful, picturesque area despite the difficult conditions faced by its inhabitants. Many consider Belén the true face of the Amazon, while others feel it is a center of misery and poverty.

Floating district of Belén.

Historical Homes and Buildings

- *Casa Eiffel or Casa de Fierro*, corner of Putumayo and Próspero, Plaza de Armas: This «house of iron» was designed by the renowned French architect Gustave Eiffel, made in Europe, shipped here, and assembled in 1889.
- *Casa de Barro*, corner of Napo and Próspero, Plaza de Armas: a two-story building with a wooden balcony. This was the rubber warehouse of Carlos Fermín Fitzcarrald, one of the most prosperous rubber barons in Peru.
    Visits during office hours.

Old manor house decorated with tiles.

- *Others:* the Pinasco, Morey, and Cohen family homes, located near the city center and ostentatious, with traces of Moorish design, are a good example of the city's wealth and splendor during the rubber boom. Especially interesting are their tiles brought from Europe, particularly those from Portugal.
    Visits by previous arrangement with their owners.

Museums

- *Biblioteca Amazónica*, Malecón Tarapacá 354: one of the most important libraries in America, especially in regional subjects.
    Visiting hours: Mon-Fri, 8am to noon, and 3 to 7pm.
- *Museo Amazónico*, Malecón Tarapacá 386: an interesting collection of statues of natives of the region's various ethnic groups, in typical dress and with various tools.
    Visiting hours: Mon-Sat, 8am to noon, and 3 to 7pm.

Excursions

Quistococha Turistical Center

110M / 361FT)

13,5km (15 minutes) W of the city on the paved road to Nauta. An interesting zoo and fish farm consisting of native species. There are rowboats, restaurants, and a small site museum. Highly recommended for a day trip.

Beaches at Nanay and Moronacocha

120M / 394FT)

The former, 12km (15 minutes) E of the city, is located on the banks of the Nanay River and is known locally as Playa Santa Clara. It is an ideal place to enjoy a swim in the river, a boat ride, or do some handicraft shopping. The latter is a beach on a lake located 3km E of the city, with boats available for visiting nearby villages and with good fishing. Both are accessed via paved road.

Cenepa River.

Santo Tomás

120M / 394FT)

A village on the shores of a lake 15km (15 minutes) NE of Iquitos via paved road. Set within lush scenery, the lake belongs to the Cocama native community and is an ideal place for water sports. The settlement is known for its carved root and ceramics handicrafts.

Canopy trail upon the jungle of Napo river.

Pacaya–Samiria National Reserve

120M / 394FT ON AVERAGE

18 hours by river, at the confluence of the Marañón and Ucayali rivers, this reserve is the largest protected area in Peru. Access is by river, navigating the Amazon to the town of Nauta and then going up either the Marañón or Ucayali River. This is the most common route, which enters the heart of the reserve through the Puinahua canal, near the

White heron (*Casmerodius albus*) in the Pacaya–Samiria National Reserve.

town of Requena. The trip takes a day and a half and hiring the services of a specialized tourist agency is recommended. It is also possible to hire a float-plane in Iquitos and then enter the reserve in a rented boat. We recommend seeking advice from a local tourist agency *(see Useful Facts, p. 298)*.

With a little over two million hectares, this reserve extends over what is considered one of the principal natural depressions of the Amazon. It contains a vast network of lakes, lagoons, canals, swamps, and wetlands, as well as the complete lengths of the Pacaya and Samiria rivers. There is an impressive variety of flora and fauna here, including several species in danger of extinction: the *charapa* turtle (*Podocnemis expansa*); the *paiche* fish (*Arapaima gigas*), largest of the Amazon; the manatee (*Trichechus inunguis*); two species of fresh-water dolphin (*Inia geoffrensis* and *Sotalia fluviatilis*); the black cayman (*Melanosuchus niger*); and the giant river otter (*Pteronura brasiliensis*). The area of Pacaya–Samiria National Reserve is considered the «larder» of the northeastern Peruvian jungle, as many of the species of fish marketed by the inhabitants of the Amazon reproduce in its tranquil waters.

CREATURES OF THE AMAZON

Paiche fish, pink fresh-water dolphin, and giant river turtles are creatures intimately linked to the northern jungles of Peru. The tasty *paiche,* weighing as much as 300kg and measuring up to 3m (10ft) long, is the largest freshwater fish in the world.

The pink fresh-water dolphin is an able fisher. The natives also believe it has supernatural powers, that it is able to impregnate women who come near the river. The *tortuga charapa* or giant river turtle, the symbol of the region, can grow to over 1m (3ft) in diameter and lays more than a hundred eggs, while most turtles lay only twenty or thirty. None of these species are found in the southern Amazon; they are kept out by rapids, waterfalls and other natural obstacles to migration.

*For more information on entry permits and regulations
in the protected area, contact Pro-Naturaleza
in Iquitos (Napo 449, Tel 23 8754),
or the office of the Reserva Nacional Pacaya–Samiria
(see Useful Facts, p. 297).*

The Peru-Colombia and Peru-Brazil Borders

The cities of Santa Rosa (Peru), Leticia (Colombia), and Tabatinga (Brazil) are very close to each other in a special «tri-national» zone and are continually linked by ferries and taxi-boats. Boats leave Iquitos three times a week for these destinations. Fares vary from US$ 20 to US$ 50, depending on the speed of the boat and the trip takes 15 hours to two and a half days. Le-

ticia is the largest town in the area and has the best services. It is linked to Tabatinga by a small bridge. One and a half hours downstream from Leticia are the ports of Islandia (Peru) and Benjamín Constant (Brazil), which lack services and are connected to Leticia via ferry, twice a day. Requirements for crossing from the tri-national zone into Colombia are generally strict, so we recommend check-

Riverside village.

ing the requirements at the immigrations (Migraciones) office in Iquitos beforehand. All boats stop at border stations for a complete document check; remember to keep yours handy. The boat captain can tell you the location of border stations because they change position with the height of the river. You can wander freely between the three border towns in the tri-national zone, with no need of border stamps, but not out of the zone. The crossing into Brazil is less complicated. There are boats linking Tabatinga to Manaos at an average fare of US$ 100 for a three-to-six-day trip.

Hotels

Hotel El Dorado ★★★
  Napo 362. Tel 22 1985. US$ 80
  dorado@mneet.com.pe

El Dorado Plaza Hotel ★★★
  Napo 258. Tel 22 2555. Fax 22 4304.
  sales@eldoradoplazahotel.com

Hotel Victoria Regia ★★★
  Ricardo Palma 252. Tel 23 1983. US$ 80
  chasa@meganet.com.pe

Real Hotel de Iquitos *(ex Hotel de Turistas)* ★★★
  Malecón Tarapacá n/n. Tel 23 1011.
  Reservations Lima Tel 425 1670. US$ 60

Copoazú Hotel ★★★
  Próspero 844. Tel 22 4372.

Hostal Acosta ★★★
  Calvo Araujo y Huallaga. Tel 23 1761. US$ 65
  chasa@meganet.com.pe

Hotel Río Grande ★★★
  Próspero 644. Tel 23 1694. Fax 22 4312. US$ 60
  contactanos@riograndehotel.com

Hotel Amazonas ★★★
  Arica 108, plaza de armas. Tel 24 2431. US$ 55

Hostal Europa ★★★
  Próspero 494. Tel 23 1123. US$ 45
  heuropa@mnet.com.pe

RATES ARE APPROXIMATE AND, UNLESS OTHERWISE NOTED,
ARE FOR DOUBLE OCCUPANCY.

Lodges in the Jungle

Explor Napo ★★★
  160km from Iquitos on the Napo River (7 hours by
  river, or 20 minutes by floatplane).

Explorama Inn ★★★
  1 hour, 30 minutes from Iquitos on the Amazon River.

Explorama Lodge ★★★
  At Llachapa. 160km from Iquitos.

★★★ Amazon Conservatory of Tropical Studies
   Nearby the suspencion bridge,
   withing the Explor Napo reserve.
   A 45 min walk distance.

★★★ Explortambo Lodge
   The most distant and rustic lodge
   withing the Explor Napo reserve.
   A 2 hours walk distance.

★★★ Ceiba Tops Lodge & Resort
   Unique lodge inside the jungle with resort type facilities.
   40km distance from Iquitos, on the Amazon river.

   All 6 lodges are run by the same company.
   Office in Iquitos: Av. La Marina 340.
   Tel 25 2526. Fax 25 2533.
   E-mail: info@explorama.com.
   Web page: http://www.explorama.com.

★★ Amazon Camp
   1 hour, 30 minutes from Iquitos by river, on the left
   bank of the Momón River.
   Office in Iquitos: Requena 336. Tel 23 1611.
   Fax 23 1265. Reservations Lima Tel 446 6354.

★ Amazonas Sinchicuy Lodge
   1 hour, 30 minutes from Iquitos on the Amazon River.
   Office in Iquitos: Pevas 246. Tel 23 1618.
   Fax 23 2324. Reservations Lima Tel 241 7614.
   Fax 446 7943. Bajada Balta 131 Of. 4, Miraflores.
   Tambo Yanayacu and Tambo Amazónico are run
   by the same company.

★ Zúngaro Cocha
   Office in Iquitos: Calle Ricardo Palma 242.
   Tel 23 1983. Reservations Lima: Av. Las Camelias
   511, Of. 402, San Isidro. Tel 442 4515. Fax 442 4338.
   ventas@heliconialodge.com.pe

★ Cumaceba Lodge
   37km distance from Iquitos, on the right bank of the
   Amazon river. *Office in Iquitos:* Putumayo 184, Casa
   de Hierro. Tel 23 229. Reservations Lima Tel 346 1834.

Amazon Rainforest Lodge ★

45km distance from Iquitos,
on the right bank of the Momón river.
Office in Iquitos: Putumayo 159. Tel 24 1628.
Reservations Lima Tel 445 5620. Fax 447 2651.
schneide@amauta.rcp.net.pe

Muyuna Amazon Lodge & Expeditions ★

120km distance from Iquitos, upstream,
and 100km far away from Pacaya-Samiria N. Reserve.
Office in Iquitos: Tel 24 2858.
Reservations Lima Tel 264 2906.
muyuna@peru.com

> **RATES ARE NOT INCLUDED,**
> **AS VISITS TO THESE LODGES ARE ORGANIZED**
> **IN PACKAGES WITH VARYING PRICES.**

Restaurants

Fitzcarraldo ✔

Corner of Calle Napo 100 and Boulevard.

La Gran Maloca ✔

Sargento Lores 170.

Useful Facts

AREA CODE **94**

☎

Basic information
IPERÚ:

Information and Assistance for Tourists
F. Secada Vignetta Airport (main lobby)   26 0251
Open: Mon-Fri from 8 to 13:30 h
and from 16:30 a 20:30 h.
iperuiquitos@promperu.gob.pe

Tourism Police Aid: Sargento Lores 834   24 2081

Instituto Nacional de Cultura:
Jr. Huallaga 274.   23 4031

Head Office of Pacaya-Samiria N. Reserve: 23 2980

CONTINUE ▬▬➡

CODE AREA **94**

☎

Brazilian Consulate: Sargento Lores 363   23 4133
  Open: Mon-Fri from 9 to 12 h and from 15 to 18 h.
Colombian Consulate: 23 1461
  Callao 200, plaza de armas.
  Open: Mon-Fri from 8:30 to 12:30 h
  and 15 to 17:30 h.

Travel Agencies

  Explorama Tours: Av. La Marina 340   25 2526
      Fax 25 2533

  Amazon Tours & Cruises Iquitos: 23 1265
     Requena 336.   23 1611
     amazon@amazoncruises.com.pe

Floatplanes (overflights on this area)

  Grupo Aéreo N.° 42: Base Aérea FAP
     Sargento Lores 127.   23 4632

Helicopters (overflights on this area)

  Helisur: Las Azucenas 319, San Juan.   26 0508

Handicraft Stores

  Amazon Arts & Crafts: Airport.   26 0900

Post Office: Arica 402.   23 1915
Hospital Regional de Loreto: Av. 28 de Julio n/n.   25 1882
Botica La Loretana: Próspero 363   23 4461
Farmacia Próspero: Ramón Castilla 288   23 1578
JB Car Rental: Yavarí 702.   24 2965
Airport   26 0147

Lima

154 M / 505FT
6 321 200 POP.

Located on the coast at the mouth of the Rímac River (which means 'talking river' in Quechua), Lima was once known as «the pearl of the Pacific».

In pre-Hispanic times, the valley was a verdant oasis and the site of fishing and farming settlements from very early on. The ancient Lima culture flourished between the first century BC and the seventh century AD, contemporary to the Mochica and Nasca cultures. Beginning in the sixth century AD, it was heavily influenced by the Wari culture from Ayacucho. In this

P. 82

P. 78

ROUTE MAP

5

Villena Rey Bridge, Miraflores.

period, the construction of the largest pre-Hispanic complex in the area began at Cajamarquilla. Much later, towards the fourteenth century AD, the Rímac and Lurín river valleys became part of the Ychma kingdom, which was in turn under the rule of the Pachacámac sanctuary located 31km S of Lima today. In

An extremely humid climate with a yearly mean temperature of 19° C (66°F). Skies are usually cloudy and gray, except in the summer months of December to March. Although it does not rain, a light drizzle, or garúa, *is common in winter. Because of the high humidity and the permanent cloud cover, it feels quite cold in winter and hot in summer despite the relatively moderate range of temperature in Lima.*

Panoramic view of San Isidro.

Balconies on Jirón Conde de Superunda.

the fifteenth century, the Inca Pachacútec annexed the region to the Inca Empire by sending an army commanded by his son and successor, Túpac Yupanqui.

The first Spanish conquistador to reach the Rímac Valley was Hernando Pizarro, sent from Cajamarca with his men in 1533. Two years later, his brother, Francisco Pizarro, decided to found his capital here, because of the fertile plains irrigated by the Rímac and the natural port at Callao.

Pizarro founded the city of Lima on January 18, 1535, the day of the Three Magi (or Kings), calling «The City of Kings.» He laid it out in a checkerboard pattern with square city blocks distributed around a central plaza, today the heart of the city's historical district. In the hope it would become «as large and prosperous as it should be,» it was designated the capital of the Viceroyalty of South America in 1542 and, three years later, it was made the seat of an archbishopric. San Marcos, the first university in America, was founded here in 1551. The city was walled towards the end of the seventeenth century.

As a consequence of its political, strategic, and economic importance (all merchandise entering or leaving the viceroyalty was required to go through the port of Callao), stately manor houses were built during the seventeenth and eighteenth centuries, with handsome balconies of carved wood. The city retained its colonial structure until the nineteenth century.

After its walls were torn down during the presidency of José Balta (1868–1872), Lima began to expand into the surrounding farm land (which became the districts of Magdalena, Barranco, Chorrillos, and Miraflores) and underwent a number of modernization projects. Larger buildings and avenues (Colón and La Colmena) were built, and in 1906 the first electric tramway was inaugurated. In the mid-twentieth century, with a surge in industry and the beginning of a great migration from the provinces Lima began to expand into adjacent rural areas. The immigrants (primarily from economically depressed areas in the Andes) settled on the sandy hills surrounding the city and founded settlements they called *pueblos jóvenes*, or «young towns.»

Traveling around modern-day Lima provides a good idea of the complexity of the country of Peru: a country of marked contrasts that is struggling to blend the traditions of a rural farming society with the realities of modern industry and market economies. The results are often incongruous and sometimes quite bizarre. Lima is an overpopulated city of six million, most of whom come from rural areas, but despite its disorder and lack of services, it is a city of friendly and cordial people that still retains a great charm. Please join us in a visit.

FROM COUNTRY TO CITY

With its 49 districts, Metropolitan Lima (Lima and Callao) is the largest city in Peru, home to almost 30% of the national population. Its 6 321 200 inhabitants (according to a 1993 census) make it almost seven times larger than Arequipa, the second largest city in Peru. One of every three inhabitants is from the provinces; most from the department of Ancash, followed by those from Junín and the department of Lima itself.

Government Palace.

Local Dishes

Cebiche.

Anticuchos.

Entrées

- Anticuchos: skewers of beef heart marinated in vinegar and *ají panca*, broiled on a grill.
- Causa rellena: mashed yellow potatoes seasoned with ground *ají* pepper and stuffed with tuna.
- Cebiche: fresh fish marinated in lime, with onion and *ají limo*.
- Choros a la chalaca: mussels seasoned with onions, a bit of *ají* pepper and lime juice.
- Escabeche: fish or chicken prepared with vinegar and onion.
- Tiradito: similar to cebiche, but with the fish cut in strips and omitting the onion.

Soups

- Parihuela: a thick soup of fish and seafood.
- Sancochado: a stew of beef with corn, sweet potatoes, carrots, cabbage, yucca, and potatoes; all with various sauces and a broth served on the side.

Main Dishes

- Ají de gallina: stewed chicken mixed with a sauce of milk, cheese, *ají* pepper, and nuts.
- Cau-cau: stew of diced viscera, potatoes, *palillo* spice, and mint.
- Lomo saltado: sliced beef sautéed with onion, tomato, *ají* pepper, and fried potatoes and served with rice.
- Pescado a la chorrillana: fish fried with onion, tomato, and white wine.
- Pescado a lo macho: fish fried in a seafood sauce with *ají amarillo*.
- Tacu-tacu con sábana: an «omelet» of beans and rice with breaded beefsteak and onion sauce.

Desserts

- Mazamorra morada: a custard made with purple corn flour and sweet potato flour, with fresh and dried fruit.

- Picarones: deep-fried «doughnuts» made of sweet potato and squash batter, garnished with cane molasses.
- Suspiro a la limeña: a rich custard topped with meringue and vanilla.

Festivals

One of the most significant festivals celebrated in Lima is the procession of the image of El Señor de los Milagros (Lord of Miracles), patron of Lima, which leaves the Las Nazarenas church during the second half of October. Over half a million people attend this procession on its main days, October 18 and 28, dressed in purple attire and intoning hymns and prayers. Typical Lima sweets and religious objects are sold in the streets, along with potions and amulets for preventing or healing a wide variety of ills. The event is well worth seeing. This religious feast is accompanied by the Señor de los Milagros bullfights (the most renowned in America) in the Plaza de Acho bullring during October and November.

Lima is also the place to enjoy some of the most famous Peruvian Paso horsemanship competitions, such as the Peruvian Paso Horse Competition in the Lurín Valley (February, exact date varies); the official National Peruvian Paso Horse Competition in Mamacona, Lurín (April, exact date varies); and the Amancaes Peruvian Paso Horse Competition, also in Mamacona (July, exact date varies).

Other festivals celebrated in Lima are the city's anniversary (January 18); the Feast of the Crosses, in which a procession ascend the San Cristóbal hill (May 3); the Feast of Santa Rosa de Lima, patron saint of America and the Philippines (August 30); and Día de la Canción Criolla, or Peruvian Music Day (October 30), an ideal day for visiting one of the many folk music clubs in the capital.

THE ORIGINS OF A FOLLOWING

The origin of the cult of the Señor de los Milagros (Lord of Miracles) dates back to the seventeenth century when a black slave painted an image of Christ on a wall that miraculously withstood the earthquake of 1655. This event attracted public attention and publicized the worship of the Black population, which had already founded a brotherhood to care for the image. The members of the brotherhood that presides over and organizes the event continue to be of African descent. A few experts believe, nonetheless, that the worship of the Señor de los Milagros is actually a continuation of the cult to Pachacámac, an Andean deity believed to control earthquakes.

◆ The Historical City Center

To truly feel the spirit of the city, you must stroll through its streets. For a complete visit to the historical center of Lima we suggest three walking circuits and one by taxi (it is longer and crosses a few zones not recommended for walking). Each circuit takes about 3 to 4 hours. It is best to go in the morning, when there are fewer pickpockets about. The walking circuits are clearly marked on the Lima map *(see p. 306-307)*. For the taxi circuit, we recommend contracting a service by an hourly rate from one of the companies operating in Lima *(see Useful Facts, p. 339)*.

Touring the Plaza Mayor
by carriage.

Walking Circuits

Circuit 1
Central Lima ~ Barrios Altos

Plaza Mayor (Main Square)
Cathedral
Church and Convent
    of San Francisco
Casa de Pilatos

Casa de las Trece Monedas
Escuela Nacional de Bellas Artes
Casa Canevaro
Buenamuerte Church
Plaza Bolívar

Neo-colonial balcony, Archbishop's Palace.

Museum of the Holy Inquisition
Plaza Italia
Church of Santa Ana
Chinese quarter,
> *an excellent spot for lunch, tea, or having
> your I' Ching read*

Balconies of Jirón Azángaro.

Circuit 2
Central Lima
Plaza Mayor (Main Square)
Cathedral
Church of San Pedro
Torre Tagle Palace
Casa Goyeneche
Central Reserve Bank Museum
Church of La Merced
Plaza San Martín
Parque Universitario
Casona de San Marcos
> *You can finish off this circuit
> with a visit to the districts
> of Miraflores or San Isidro
> for a meal and/or shopping.*

Circuit 3
Central Lima
Plaza Mayor (Main Square)
Cathedral
Church and Convent
  of Santo Domingo
Palacio Osambela
Church of San Agustín
Casa de Riva Agüero
Church of San Marcelo
Church and Convent
  of Las Nazarenas
Sanctuary of Santa Rosa de Lima
> *If it is still early, you could
> lunch in Callao and take a
> stroll along its beautiful
> seaside promenade.*

Cloisters of the Santo
Domingo Convent.

By Taxi

Barrios Altos ~ Rímac
Quinta Heeren
Cerro San Cristóbal
Plaza de Acho
Paseo de Aguas
Church and Convent of
  Los Descalzos
> *has a small restaurant
> for lunch or a snack*

LIMA CITY MAP

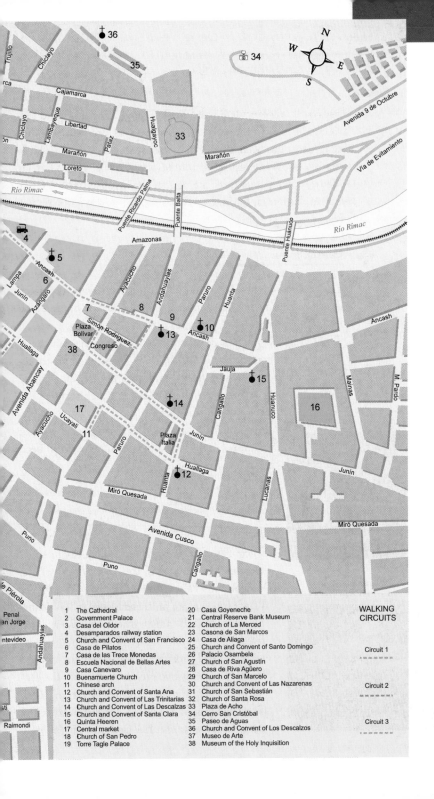

36 †

34

N
W · E
S

Trujillo

Chiclayo

Cajamarca

rca

Chiclayo

Lambayeque

Libertad

Palaz

Marañón

Loreto

Avenida 9 de Octubre

Huaylillo

35

33

Marañón

Vía de Evitamiento

Río Rímac

Puente Ricardo Palma

Puente Balta

Puente Huánuco

Río Rímac

4

Amazonas

5 †

Ancash

Lampa

Junín

Azángaro

6

Ayacucho

Andahuaylas

Paruro

Huanta

Ancash

7

8

Simón Rodríguez

Plaza
Bolívar

Congreso

38

Huallaga

9

13 †

10 †
Ancash

Jauja

15 †

Cangallo

Huánuco

16

Mainas

M. Pardo

Avenida Abancay

Ayacucho

Ucayali

17

11

Paruro

14 †

Plaza
Italia

Junín

Junín

Junín

12 †

Huallaga

Huanta

Miró Quesada

Lucanas

Miró Quesada

Avenida Cusco

Puno

Puno

Cangallo

le Piérola

Penal
an Jorge

ntevideo

Andahuaylas

sti

Raimondi

1	The Cathedral	20	Casa Goyeneche
2	Government Palace	21	Central Reserve Bank Museum
3	Casa del Oidor	22	Church of La Merced
4	Desamparados railway station	23	Casona de San Marcos
5	Church and Convent of San Francisco	24	Casa de Aliaga
6	Casa de Pilatos	25	Church and Convent of Santo Domingo
7	Casa de las Trece Monedas	26	Palacio Osambela
8	Escuela Nacional de Bellas Artes	27	Church of San Agustín
9	Casa Canevaro	28	Casa de Riva Agüero
10	Buenamuerte Church	29	Church of San Marcelo
11	Chinese arch	30	Church and Convent of Las Nazarenas
12	Church and Convent of Santa Ana	31	Church of San Sebastián
13	Church and Convent of Las Trinitarias	32	Church of Santa Rosa
14	Church and Convent of Las Descalzas	33	Plaza de Acho
15	Church and Convent of Santa Clara	34	Cerro San Cristóbal
16	Quinta Heeren	35	Paseo de Aguas
17	Central market	36	Church and Convent of Los Descalzos
18	Church of San Pedro	37	Museo de Arte
19	Torre Tagle Palace	38	Museum of the Holy Inquisition

WALKING
CIRCUITS

Circuit 1

Circuit 2

Circuit 3

The Thrice-crowned Villa

Because Lima is so large and has so many attractions and services, the information in this chapter —as opposed to other chapters— has been organized by district. The districts in Lima that are most interesting to tourists are: Central Lima, Barrios Altos, Rímac (these three are part of the historical city center), Callao, La Punta, Barranco, Chorrillos, San Isidro and Miraflores.

Central Lima

The original city of Lima (laid out in the checkerboard pattern that characterized most Spanish Colonial cities) is bordered by Av. Abancay on the E, Av. Tacna on the W, the Rímac River on the N, and Av. Nicolás de Piérola (or La Colmena) on the S. This was the first sector occupied by the Spaniards and still retains some of the oldest Colonial buildings in the capital along with handsome examples of Republican-era architecture. Because of its artistic and historical value, Unesco declared it a Cultural World Heritage and its most traditional buildings and monuments have been undergoing restoration.

Traditional Locales

Main Square and Cathedral.

Room in the Government Palace.

• *Plaza Mayor* (or Plaza de Armas): this is the spot where Francisco Pizarro founded the city in 1535. Here are the Cathedral, the Sagrario chapel, the Archbishop's Palace, Town Hall and Government Palace (on the site of the residence of Taulichusco, who ruled the valley when the Spaniards arrived). These buildings have been modified or rebuilt several times and differ from their original layout. The attractive bronze fountain in the center of the plaza is original; it dates from 1650. The changing of the guard in front of the Government Palace takes place every day at 12:45pm.

- *Plaza San Martín*, Av. Nicolás de Piérola: inaugurated on July 28, 1921, in honor of the first centennial of Peru's independence, this plaza has a monument dedicated to José de San Martín. Curiously, when this statue was ordered, the Catalonian sculptor Mariano Benlliure was asked to include a votive flame (called a *llama*) over San Martín's head. He misunderstood and the hero is now topped with a small, bronze Andean llama.

Plaza San Martín.

Around the plaza are the Club Nacional, the Hotel Bolívar, and the Art Nouveau construction of the Teatro Colón and a building between Jr. Quilca and Av. Nicolás de Piérola.

Churches

- *The Cathedral*, Plaza Mayor. Tel 427 1600: construction of this church began in 1564 and was completed in 1622. After the 1746 earthquake it was rebuilt by Jesuit Juan Rehr. Gothic, Renaissance, Baroque, and Neoclassic styles have all left their mark. Its principal doorway is a lovely example of the Spanish Plateresque style, while its two svelte towers are Neoclassic. Highlights in its interior are the chapel holding the remains of Francisco Pizarro, the choir stalls by Pedro Noguera, the Baroque chapel of La Inmaculada, carvings in the holy scene of St. John the Baptist, a crucifix, a statue of Santa Apolonia by Spanish sculptor Juan Martínez Montañés (1568–1649), a sixteenth-century statue of the Madonna and Christ Child by Roque de Balduque, a beautiful seventeenth-century carving of the Holy Family and a sixteenth-century relief of the Adoration of the Shepherds attributed to Alonso Gómez. A museum of religious art exhibits splendid paintings, such as the Zodiac series by the Bassanos (sixteenth and seventeenth centuries), sculptures, chalices, and chasubles.

Façade of the Cathedral.

Baroque altarpiece of the Cathedral.

  Visiting hours: daily, 10am to 1pm, and 2 to 5pm.
- *Santo Domingo*, corner of Jr. Conde de Superunda

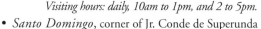

and Camaná. Tel 427 6793: the oldest church and convent in Lima, where Santa Rosa de Lima (1586–1617) is buried, along with San Martín de Porras (1579–1639) and San Juan Masías (1585–1645). This was the first site of the San Marcos University in 1551. The church has three naves laid out in a Gothic cross, a splendid Rococo tower and a magnificent statue of Christ-crucified by the artists from the sixteenth-century circle of Juan Bautista Vásquez, a handsome, seventeenth-century, marble image of Santa Rosa by Melchor Caffa, a Virgin of the Rosary by Roque de Balduque from the sixteenth century and choir stalls carved with reliefs and dating from the early seventeenth century. It also has a painting of San Jerónimo that is a copy of the original by Mateo Pérez de Alesio (sixteenth century) and some works by Matías Maestro from the seventeenth and eighteenth centuries. The convent has a fine Moorish ceiling from the sixteenth century, handsome tilework in its main cloisters, oil paintings attributed to Francisco Pacheco and Mateo Pérez de Alesio (1547–c.1615), a Baroque salon and a notable library.

Visiting hours: daily, 7am to 1pm, and 3:30 to 8:30pm.

- *San Francisco*, corner of Jr. Lampa and Jr. Ancash. Tel 427 1381: the convent and church of San Francisco, along with the adjacent churches of La Soledad and El Milagro, form the most notable group of Colonial buildings in the city. The church was rebuilt between 1657 and 1674. It is a mix of Mannerist, Moorish and Baroque elements. The most important are its main doorway, large towers and dressed walls. Inside are some of the

Church of San Francisco.

best Baroque and Neoclassic holy scenes, an eighteenth-century carving of La Dolorosa (Our Lady of Sorrows) attributed to Baltazar Gavilán and a sixteenth century crucifix by Roque de Balduque. The convent's main cloister has fine tilework and notable paintings; there is a unique wooden cupola of Moorish design over the imperial staircase. It also has impressive underground catacombs, a museum of religious art and a good library.

Museum and catacomb visiting hours:
daily, 9:30am to 5:45pm.
Church visiting hours:
daily, 8am to noon, and 4:30 to 8pm.

Library of the San Francisco Convent.

- *San Pedro*, corner of Jr. Azángaro and Jr. Ucayali. Tel 428 3017: this Jesuit church was consecrated in 1638. Its exterior is Renaissance, contrasting with a sumptuous Baroque interior containing some of the best Baroque holy scenes in Lima. It has extraordinary paintings of the life of San Ignacio de Loyola by the seventeenth-century Sevillan master Juan de Valdés Leal, a series of angels by Madrid artist Bartolomé Román (1596–1659), the Coronation of the Virgin and other sixteenth-century works by Bernardo Bitti and seventeenth-century works by Diego de la Puente. No less impressive are the sculptures: the Family of the Virgin Mary from the school of Gregorio Fernández, an anonymous Holy Family, two polychrome images of San Francisco Javier and San Francisco de Borja, a crucifix by Martín de Oviedo (c.1565–c.1615), a seventeenth-century painting of Christ («Cristo de la Buenamuerte») by Juan de Mesa, and an *Ecce Homo* and a Dolorosa by Pedro de Mena, from the seventeenth century. Only part of the convent, once a Jesuit school, is original.
  Visiting hours: daily, 7am to 1pm, and 5 to 8pm.
- *La Merced*, corner of Jr. de la Unión and Jr. Miró Quesada. Tel 427-8199: this church was rebuilt after 1628 with a layout similar to that of San Pedro. It has Baroque and Neoclassic holy scenes, magnificent choir stalls, and its sculptures include a splendid Cristo del Auxilio attributed to Juan Martínez Montañés (1568–1649) as well as a *Pietá* and a one of Christ's suffering at Geth-

Church of La Merced.

Santa Rosa de Lima.

semane. It has notable murals in the Captain Villegas chapel, attributed to Mateo Pérez de Alesio (1547–c.1615). The convent has wide cloisters; the main one, two stories high and finished in 1781, combines Moorish, Baroque, and Rococo design. A series of oil paintings on the life of San Pedro Nolasco by Julián Jayo, José Joaquín Bermejo and Juan de Mota Coronado date from the eighteenth century. On the main altar stands the effigy of Our Lady of Mercy, patron saint of Peru's armed forces. Here is also the venerated cross of Father Pedro Urraca (1538–1657), who dedicated his life to the poor.

Visiting hours: daily, 6:30am to 1pm, and 4:30 to 8pm.

- *Santa Rosa de Lima*, Av. Tacna, block 1. Tel 425-1279: this was the first church built in honor of this Lima-born saint, patroness of Lima, America and the Philippines. The sanctuary, built in 1699 next to the house where she was born in 1586, conserves the hermitage that Santa Rosa built with the help of her brother and the well where she threw the key to the chain girdling her waist. Tradition has it that the first rose grown in Lima flowered here. The convent holds the famous portrait of the saint by Angelino Medoro (c.1547–c.1629).

Visiting hours: daily, 9:30am to 1pm, and 3:30 to 7pm.

- *Las Nazarenas*, corner of Jr. Huancavelica and Av. Tacna. Tel 423 5718: this church, dedicated to the Lord of Miracles, patron of the city, is a good example of eighteenth-century Rococo in its layout, doorway, and pulpit. On the wall of its main altar is an image of Christ-crucified painted by an African slave. This image is venerated because this was the only wall left standing after the violent earthquake of 1655.

Visiting hours: daily, 6am to noon, and 5 to 8:30pm.

- *San Agustín*, corner of Jr. Ica and Jr. Camaná. Tel 427 7548: rebuilt in the late eighteenth century, although there remain from the original a sumptuously decorated doorway, a sacristy of wood crafted in 1643, fragments of its notable, seventeenth-century choir stalls and an impressive sculpture entitled The Archer of Death, by Baltazar Gavilán.

Visiting hours: daily, 7 to 11am,
and 4 to 7:30pm.

- *San Marcelo*, corner of Jr. Rufino Torrico and Av. Emancipación: one of the oldest churches in Lima, founded in the mid-sixteenth century by the Augustine order. Highlights are its Baroque façade and its Baroque and Rococo holy scenes.

Visiting hours: daily, 8am to noon, and 4 to 8pm.

Detail of façade,
Church of San Agustín.

Historical Homes and Buildings

- *Casa del Oidor*, Plaza Mayor: built a short time after the founding of Lima, this is considered the oldest manor house in the city. Tradition has it that society ladies of Lima hid behind the lattices on its balconies to watch events in the Plaza without being seen.

Closed to the public.

- *Osambela Palace*, Jr. Conde de Superunda 298. Tel 427 7987: this house was completed in 1807. Neoclassic in style, it has five balconies and a lookout from which Martín de Osambela, its first owner, watched galleons arriving in the port of Callao. Today it houses the Centro Cultural Inca Garcilaso de la Vega.

Visiting hours: Mon-Fri, 9:30am to 5pm.

- *Casa de Aliaga*, Jr. de la Unión 224: this private home was built in 1535 over what had been a large pre-Hispanic construction, the ceremonial pyramid of Taulichusco, who ruled the Rímac Valley when the Spaniards arrived. It has beautiful rooms, furniture, paintings and tiles, and is the oldest home on the continent still family-owned, as it has been for seventeen generations. It is in an excellent state of conservation.

Contact Lima Tours for a visit.
Tel 424 7560.

THE BALCONIES OF LIMA

Some experts assert that Colonial-era Lima resembled a Moorish city due to the many balconies adorning its manor houses.
There were many types of balconies, but those equipped with *celosías*, or wooden slats which allowed one to see the street without being seen, uniquely characterized this viceregal capital. A balcony with *celosías* is Moorish in origin.

Entrance and main patio of Torre Tagle Palace.

Main patio of the Casa de Riva Agüero.

- *Casa de Pilatos or Casa de los Jarava y Esquivel*, Jr. Ancash 390. Tel 427 5814: this is one of the oldest mansions in Lima. It has a stately, arched patio, a grand staircase and one of the best, Herrera-style Renaissance doorways in Lima. Currently the offices of the Constitutional Court of Peru.

  Visits with the permission of the Public Relations office of the Constitutional Court.

- *Torre Tagle Palace*, Jr. Ucayali 363. Tel 427 3860: a splendid mansion built in 1735, considered the best-preserved Colonial home in Lima. It is a work of Lima art in the Baroque, Moorish and *criollo* styles and has a lovely façade with a stone doorway between two beautifully carved balconies, excellent furniture, tilework, and paintings. Currently the offices of the Ministry of Foreign Affairs.

  Visits with the permission of the Public Relations office of the Ministry.

- *Casa de Riva Agüero*, Camaná 459. Tel 427 9275: this nineteenth-century home belonged to the line of the Marquis of Montealegre de Aulestia and was donated to the Pontificia Universidad Católica by its final heir, historian José de la Riva Agüero y Osma. It has an historical archive, library, and museum with the most complete collection of popular art in Peru.

  Visiting hours: Mon-Fri, 11am to 1:30pm, and 2 to 8pm.

- *Casa de la Riva*, Jr. Ica 426: one of the most prestigious residences of Lima during the Viceroyalty. It has elegant, eighteenth-century balconies, windows barred in wrought iron, elegantly stuccoed salons, a large patio, tilework, and a Neoclassic entrance in the main salon. Currently the offices of Entre Nous, a cultural association.

  Closed to the public.

Barrios Altos ❖

Across Av. Abancay from Lima's city center is the district of Barrios Altos, one of the city's most traditional neighborhoods. It owes its name to the gentle rise crossing it. Until the 1960s it was a haven for musicians, intellectuals and bohemians. Its origins are Colonial but the layout varies as its streets do not keep to the rigid checkerboard pattern that characterizes the center of Lima, giving this district a very special charm. Although it has not been maintained or restored for years, it is still possible to see some extraordinary specimens of Colonial and Republican architecture.

Traditional Locales

- *Plaza Bolívar*, Av. Abancay, block 2: this plaza is also known as the Plaza of the Holy Inquisition or of Congress, as the building that housed the Court of the Holy Inquisition until 1813 *(see Museums, p. 323)* borders it, and next to it lies the Congress of the Republic. It became the Plaza Bolívar when a bronze monument was erected to the Liberator, Simón Bolívar in 1859, a replica of the original monument in Caracas, Venezuela.

Plaza Bolívar and Congress.

- *Plaza Italia*, Jr. Junín, block 9: at the center of this plaza rises a monument to celebrated Italian naturalist Antonio Raimondi (1826–1890), a gift from the Italian community of Lima. To one side is the church of Las Descalzas de San José, built in 1604 and housing beautiful Baroque holy scenes, and the church of Santa Ana, built in 1550 over one of the largest pre-Hispanic constructions in Lima. The plaza also has a beautiful bronze fountain dating from 1611.

- *The Chinese quarter:* Calle del Capón is the main thoroughfare through this traditional Lima district and seems to have acquired its name because capon pigs were sold there. In the late nineteenth century it became the home of Chinese immigrants who moved to Lima after completing their work contracts on the coastal haciendas. It has a picturesque Chinese arch built in 1971 and three traditional Asian temples. Some of the best Chinese food restaurants (*chifas*) in the city are found here. The quarter celebrates the Chinese New Year in January.

- *Parque Universitario*, Av. Nicolás de Piérola, block 12: this small plaza served as entrance to the San Marcos university (its old building faces the plaza) founded in 1551 by the Dominican order. A clock tower in the center of the plaza that plays the national anthem at midday and midnight was a gift from the German colony in Lima. It has three monuments, in honor of the Arequipa-born bishop and educator Bartolomé Herrera (1808–1864), the Spanish historian and teacher Sebastián Lorente (1813–1884), and the Arequipa-born philosopher José Hipólito Unanue (1755–1833).

Parque Universitario.

Historical Homes and Buildings

- *Casa de Las Trece Monedas*, Jr. Ancash 536: built in 1787, this mansion (now closed to the public) owes its name to the thirteen coins in the coat-of-arms gracing its façade. Facing the mansion is the Ruiz Dávila home, a beautiful specimen of Republican architecture, built as a shelter for the widows of poor merchants. Since 1808 it has housed the Public Welfare offices.

- *Escuela Nacional de Bellas Artes*, Jr. Ancash 681: this began as the San Ildefonso school, run by Augustine fathers since 1606. It was the birthplace of a native school of painting founded by the Cajamarca-born artist José Sabogal in the 1920s.

  Visiting hours: Mon-Fri, 8am to 3pm.

- *Casa Canevaro*, Jr. Ancash 769: a stately home in the Republican style, built in the nineteenth century. It has exquisite balconied windows, large patios, and a magnificent staircase leading the visitor to the splendor of Lima's past.

- *Quinta Heeren*, Jr. Junín 1201: built in the second half of the nineteenth century by German engineer Oscar Heeren, this is considered one of the most charming corners of Barrios Altos.

Monument to José Hipólito Unanue, Parque Universitario.

It is a large garden surrounded by homes in the Neo-Gothic, German, and English styles.

- *Casona de San Marcos*, Parque Universitario. Tel 428 0052: this mansion housed the Universidad de San Marcos, the first university in America (1551). It has an ancient chapel to Nuestra Señora de Loreto with a beautiful wooden nave built in the eighteenth century and decorated with important paintings.

    Visiting hours: Mon-Sat, 8am to 2pm.

Rímac

This district, inhabited since pre-Hispanic times by natives who earned a living catching shrimp, lies on the right bank of the Rímac River. In early Colonial times this district had a large population of Negroes and Mulattos. It was also home to natives, craftsmen and poor Europeans. In the eighteenth century, the aristocracy of Lima began to take an interest in the area and sought to convert it into a center for recreation. This was when the Paseo de Aguas, the Plaza de Toros and the Quinta Presa were built and the famous Alameda de los Descalzos was rebuilt. With its strong *criollo* tradition, this «Abajo el Puente» («Under the Bridge») district retains much of the charm of Colonial Lima but is in a very poor state of conservation today.

Traditional Locales

- *Alameda de los Descalzos:* Viceroy Marqués de Montesclaros built this promenade in 1611 and Viceroy Manuel de Amat rebuilt it in 1770. In 1856, President Ramón Castilla gave it a newer, final layout with a handsome wrought-iron fence brought from England. There are also large British vases and 12 marble statues from Italy representing the months of the year. On each side are the Colonial churches of Santa Liberata and La Virgen del Patrocinio and at the far end is the church and convent of Los Descalzos. On one of the corners was the home of actress Micaela Villegas (better known as *La Perricholi*), famous for her scandalous romance with Viceroy Amat.

Alameda de los Descalzos.

Paseo de Aguas.

- *Paseo de Aguas:* a unique, peaceful locale, French in style. It is said to have been built by Viceroy Manuel de Amat to win the favor of his mistress, *La Perricholi.* One highlight is the handsome arch with markedly Neoclassical influence, crowned by a frieze pierced by a round hole, or *oeil-de-boeuf.*
- *Cerro San Cristóbal:* this hill is a natural lookout point that offers an impressive view of the city and its surroundings. Its summit, which can be reached via a paved road, has a cross and a small site museum. The first highland people to migrate to Lima settled here, founding the first districts called *pueblos jóvenes,* or «young towns.»

Churches

- *Los Descalzos,* Alameda de los Descalzos n/n. Tel 481 0441: this church and convent, first built as a house of meditation and penitence, was founded in 1565 at the foot of the San Cristóbal hill. It houses a valuable collection of paintings from the Lima, Quito, and Cusco schools, including works by the Sevillan Bartolomé Esteban Murillo (1617–1682), the Cusco artist Diego Quispe Tito (1611–1681), the *criollo* Leonardo Jaramillo (seventeenth century), and the Italian Angelino Medoro (c.1547–c.1629).

Visiting hours: daily (except Tue), 9:30am to 1pm, and 3 to 6pm.

Convent of Los Descalzos.

Historical Homes and Buildings

- *Plaza de Acho*, Hualgayoc 332: inaugurated in 1766 by Viceroy Manuel de Amat, this is the oldest bullring in America. In October and November, the Señor de los Milagros bullfights are held here. At its entrance is one of the most important bullfighting museums of its kind and quite close to the plaza is a tower called Ingunza's lookout, a handsome example of the various observation towers (*miradores*) built in the capital during the eighteenth century. Tradition holds that it was built by a bullfighting fan who had been forbidden to enter the plaza.

Bullfight in Acho.

- *Quinta Presa*, Jr. Chira 344: the most eloquent example of a Rococo, rural villa of the eighteenth century. It was the home of the Royal Spanish Army Colonel, Pedro Carrillo de Albornoz, and can be considered a *criollo* version of a small French chateau.

Closed to the public.

Ingunza's Tower.

Callao ❖

The port of the constitutional province of Callao, 14km from the center of Lima, is also the main port of the country. Founded in 1537, it contains the famous Fortaleza del Real Felipe from the eighteenth century, a pentagonal, stone fortress designed

Republican-era home in Callao.

by architect Luis Gaudin and finished by Viceroy Amat in 1773.

Another place of interest in this district is the tip of the Callao peninsula, known as La Punta. This is a beautiful beach where the moneyed families of Lima resided from the 1920s to the 1950s. It has pebbled beaches and a picturesque promenade along the beach, ideal for strolling and taking in the ocean breeze. Across from La Punta and accessible by boat are the islands of San Lorenzo, Palomino (with colonies of sea lions), Cabinzas (with natural caves and seabirds) and El Frontón, once the site of a prison.

Callao is a district of intense commercial activity and many seafood restaurants, which many consider to be the best in the city *(see Restaurants, p. 335)*.

❖ Barranco and Chorrillos

Puente de los Suspiros, Barranco.

Costa Verde.

A favorite beach resort among nineteenth-century and early twentieth-century Lima aristocrats, Barranco is one of the most beautiful districts of Lima, a spot preferred by artists, writers and bohemians due to its tranquil, idyllic ambiance (except at night, when the streets become a meeting point for Lima young people). Its highlights are the famous Puente de los Suspiros (Bridge of Sighs), a romantic spot in the shadow of ancient trees and much frequented by couples; its older mansions and ranch homes in the Republican style (many of these are now converted into cafes and restaurants); and a beautiful cliffside with views over the beaches of the Costa Verde.

Like Barranco, Chorrillos (whose name comes from the streams, or *chorrillos*, that issue from its cliffs) was a favorite beach resort among Lima residents during the mid-nineteenth century. During the

War of the Pacific (1879–1883), most of its beautiful homes were burnt down. Only a few buildings of old Chorrillos remain, along with the cliffside drive that affords a great view of the bay of Lima.

San Isidro • Miraflores

These are the «garden districts» of Lima, characterized by their green areas and lively commerce. Here are the best restaurants, hotels, and entertainment centers of Lima. While San Isidro maintains some of the solemnity of the luxurious suburb it used to be, Miraflores is the city's modern district, colorful and lively, and has a string of beaches as well.

Main Square at Miraflores.

Both districts also have some of the few pre-Hispanic constructions remaining in Lima. In San Isidro there is the Huaca Huallamarca *(corner of El Rosario and Nicolás de Rivera. Tel 440 2145)*, an ancient ceremonial center of the Lima culture (AD 100–600), a pyramid of stacked terraces with a wide access ramp. It has a site museum *(visiting hours: Mon-Fri, 9am to 5pm; Sat-Sun, 11am to 5pm)*. In Miraflores you can visit Huaca Pucllana, or Huaca Juliana *(Gral. Borgoño, block 8. Tel 445 8695)*, a ceremonial complex of the same culture, also with a site museum *(visiting hours: Wed-Sun, 9am to 5pm)*.

Museums in Lima

- *Museo Nacional de Arqueología, Antropología e Historia*, plaza Bolívar n/n, Pueblo Libre. Tel 463 5070: the largest collection of artifacts from pre-Hispanic cultures in Peru, exhibited in a stately colonial mansion that was once the country home of Viceroy Joaquín de la Pezuela and the leaders of the struggle for independence, José de San Martín and Simón Bolívar. The museum's ex-

St. James the Indianslayer, anonymous. Collection of the Museo Nacional de Arqueología, Antropología e Historia.

hibits include Chavín stone sculptures, textiles from Paracas, Nasca and Mochica ceramics and Chimú metalwork. There are also paintings, documents, and objects relating to prominent individuals in the Conquest, the Viceroyalty, and the Republic of Peru.

Visiting hours: Tue-Sun, 9am to 5:30pm.

- *Museo Arqueológico Rafael Larco Herrera*, Av. Bolívar 1515, Pueblo Libre. Tel 461 1312: houses some 50 000 ceramics of the Mochica culture, most unearthed by its founder at his hacienda in Chiclín, Trujillo. Especially unique are the erotic ceramics from the north. There are also Mochica and Chimú metalwork, mummies, and textiles.

Visiting hours: Mon-Sat, 9am to 6pm; Sunday, 9am to 1pm.

- *Museo de la Nación*, Av. Javier Prado Este 2465, San Borja. Tel 476 9875: exhibits a select collection of archeological pieces especially arranged to illustrate the primary cultural expressions of ancient Peru. Has a good replica of the tomb of the Lord of Sipán with informative displays.

Visiting hours: Tue-Sun, 9am to 8pm.

- *Museo Pedro de Osma*, Av. Pedro de Osma 421, Barranco. Tel 467-0141: a good display of Colonial art, paintings from the Cusco school, silver, sculptures, and furniture.

Visits by appointment, daily, 10am to 6pm.

- *Museo Amano*, Retiro 160, Miraflores. Tel 441 2909: a select collection of pre-Columbian ceramics and textiles, primarily from the Chancay culture.

Visits by appointment, Mon-Fri, 3pm, 4pm, and 5pm.

- *Colección Enrico Poli*, Lord Cochrane 466, San Isidro. Tel 422 2437: an extraordinary and controversial private collection of pre-Columbian and Colonial pieces. Visits guided by E. Poli himself.

Visits by appointment, daily, 10am to 7pm.

- *Museo del Banco Central de Reserva*, corner of Jr. Lampa and Jr. Ucayali, Lima. Tel 427 6250: a spectacular display of ceramics from the Vicús and Mochica cultures, as well as coins and paintings from the Republican and contemporary periods.

Visiting hours: Tue-Fri, 10am to 5pm; Sat-Sun, 10am to 1pm.

- *Museo de Arte*, Paseo Colón 125, Lima. Tel 423 4732: pre-Columbian ceramics and textiles, Colonial silverwork, paintings, and furniture, and the largest collection of Republican and contemporary paintings in Peru, in a beautiful, nineteenth-century mansion.

Visiting hours: Tue-Sun, 10am to 5pm.

- *Museo de Arte Italiano*, Paseo de la República 250, Lima. Tel 423-9932: displays paintings from the Italian school and by other contemporary artists.

Visiting hours: Mon-Fri, 9am to 5pm; Sat-Sun, 10am to 2pm.

- *Museo de la Cultura Peruana*, Alfonso Ugarte 650, Lima. Tel 423-5892: a display of art, folklore and popular handicrafts of ancient and modern Peru. Extensive collection of traditional costumes.

Visiting hours: Mon-Sat, 10am to 5pm.

- *Museo de la Inquisición*, Junín 548, Lima. Tel 427 0365: a display of the holding cells, furniture and instruments of torture used by the Court of the Holy Inquisition.

Visiting hours: Mon-Fri, 9am to 5:15pm; Sat, 9am to 12:15pm.

- *Museo de Historia Natural Javier Prado*, Av. Arenales 1250, Jesús María. Tel 471 0117: a collection of Peruvian fauna begun by the Italian naturalist Antonio Raimondi (1826–1890). The specimens are in a fair state of conservation.

Visiting hours: Mon-Fri, 9am to 7pm; Sat, 9am to 4:30pm.

Excursions

Beaches • Sea Resorts

)

During the summer months, Lima's beaches and seaside resorts are synonymous with amusement and water sports. The beaches most frequented by Lima residents are south of the city. The first string of beaches begins at km 37 and consists of Los Pulpos, El Silencio, Caballeros, Señoritas, Punta Hermosa and Punta Rocas. These can be accessed from the old South Panamericana highway (running parallel to the new highway). During the summer, the beaches are teeming with life and restaurants specializing in fish and seafood, discotheques, pubs and hostels in all price ranges. A second string of beaches begins at km 48 and the most popular are San Bartolo, Santa María and Embajadores. Here there are also many restaurants and lodgings for the season. Somewhat further south are the beaches of Asia (Las Brisas, Las Palmas, Caima, Los Cocos). These are mostly private beaches and entrance is restricted. Lastly, near km 100 (quite close to the Cañete Valley) there is a long stretch of lovely beaches (Sarapampa, Chepeconde, Gallardo), ideal a day or overnight camping.

Punta Rocas.

Lomas de Lachay National Reserve

150M / 492FT ON AVERAGE ◯

This is one of the most unique spots on the Peruvian coast, located at km 105 of the North Panamericana highway, 1 hour N of Lima, after Chancay. The Pacific trade winds push the fog up against the coastal mountains and here it is trapped by the *lomas,* or hills. The resulting humidity during the winter months (June-August) fosters plant growth on the normally desert terrain. Established in 1977 with an area of 5 070 hectares, this reserve protects a significant variety of native flora and fauna, some in danger of extinction. There are well-marked trails, barbecue pits, camping areas, and restrooms. The best season for

Lomas de Lachay.

Totora-reed groves in the Villa wetlands.

visiting is August to October, when the flowers are in bloom.

Pantanos de Villa Reserved Area

)

This protected area is 18km (15 minutes) S of the center of Lima. With an area of 396 hectares, these wetlands are a vitally important rest and feeding area for many species of migratory birds traveling from various points on the planet. The area has trails and observation towers. The best times for bird watching are in the early morning or late afternoon. To reach the Villa wetlands, take the turn-off for Av. Huaylas, on the way out of Lima via Chorrillos, or right off km 18 of the South Panamericana highway.

Pachacámac

35M / 115FT)

An archeological site 31km (20 minutes) S of Lima in the Lurín River valley, right off the old South Panamericana highway. This was one of the most important ceremonial centers in pre-Hispanic America, a mecca that drew many worship-

THE BIRDS OF VILLA

Its strategic location (on the route of intercontinental migrations) and its abundant food supply make the Villa wetlands a resting place for 160 species of birds from all over. In addition to the resident species, each summer the wetlands receive birds from North America (escaping the cold winter) and from the Caribbean. Species native to southern Chile and Argentina make use of Villa for the same reason. Completing this legion of seasonal visitors are the migrant birds that descend from the heights of the Andes (July to September) to seek food and shelter on the coast during periods of scarcity in their usual habitat.

**A MOSQUE
ON THE PLAINS**

Obsessed by the wars of
Reconquest in Spain which
had pitted Spaniard against
Moor for eight centuries, the
conquistadors believed
they were seeing some
of the elements of
Islam in America. For
example, while
Francisco Pizarro was
holding the Inca Atahualpa
prisoner, he sent his brother
Hernando to capture the
treasures at the Pachacámac
temple on the coast.
Hernando recorded that:
«... these lands on the plain,
and much further, do not
send tribute to Cuzco but
to the mosque...».

From a letter from Hernando
Pizarro to the Real Audiencia de
Santo Domingo,
November 23, 1533.

pers from far away to consult its prestigious oracle. Although its construction dates approximately from the third century AD, it continued to be an important religious center during Inca rule. The sanctuary was first a set of temples, but in time it became a sacred city with walled sectors, where homage was paid to Pachacámac, an Andean creation deity whose name comes from the Quechua words *pacha* and *camac*, meaning 'Lord of the world.' One of this deity's attributes was the power to control earthquakes.

A number of adobe structures remain today. The most interesting are the Old Temple, or Temple of Pachacámac, the Temple of the Sun, the Temple of Urpi Wachak and the Temple of the Moon or Acllawasi. Inside this ancient city, visitors can see the remains of walls, canals and patios, as well as wide streets connecting the different districts. Much of the gold ransom that Atahualpa paid to Francisco Pizarro for his release is said to have come from this sanctuary. There is a site museum. Highly recommended.

*Visiting hours: Mon-Thu, 9am to 4pm;
Fri-Sun, 9am to 5pm.*

Lomas del Lúcumo

380M / 1 247FT   )

34km (30 minutes) S of Lima. This area is accessed via the town of Pachacámac. From here, take a packed dirt road for 2,5km to the town of Quebrada Verde at the foot of the *lomas*, or hills. Lomas de Lúcumo is one of the few surviving coastal hill ecosystems in the Peruvian coastal desert. From August to October the prevailing humidity turns the hills green and covers them with yellow *ortiga* flowers (*Ipomoea sp.*) and wild tobacco (*Nicotiana sp.*), and wild bird song fills the canyons. This is an area often frequented by mountain bikers and hang-gliders.

Lunahuaná

250M / 820FT ○

178km (2 hours) S of Lima. A peaceful town in a small, sunny canyon ideal for adventure sports (rafting, kayaking, mountain biking, and hang-gliding). There are several hotels *(including Río Alto, Tel 463 5490; Embassy, Tel 472 3525, and El Abuelo)* and restaurants serving traditional Peruvian food. Don't miss the local shrimp, wines and pisco brandies. Nearby is Inca Wasi, an ancient Inca citadel. Take insect repellent.

Rafting at Lunahuaná.

Cerro Azul

○

A traditional beach resort km132 (1 hour, 30 minutes) on the South Panamericana highway. This beach has become a favorite among surfers and has some good restaurants and hotels *(Hostal Cerro Azul. Tel 271 1302)*. On the slopes of Centinela hill, on the south side of the beach, are some pre-Hispanic constructions once painted in bluish green, thus the name, Cerro Azul, or «blue hill.» Ideal beach for a day's outing.

Chincha

97M / 318FT ○

196km (2 hours) S of Lima on the South Panamericana highway, this town is known as the «Black Soul of Peru» as most of its residents are descendants of hacienda slaves. This is one of the best places to spend an idyllic weekend near Lima. Located in a fertile valley of cotton fields, Chincha has beautiful beaches (Jahuay) and several hotels *(we recommend the Casa Hacienda San José. Tel 221 1458, reservations in Lima Tel 444 5524)*. To enjoy Afro-Peruvian music and dance, the ideal town is El Carmen, a short 15km from Chincha.

Chaclacayo • Chosica

660M / 2 165FT CHACLACAYO
860M / 2 822FT CHOSICA)

27km and 35km (some 45 minutes) from Lima, respectively. This area was settled when the trans-Andean railway was built in the late nineteenth century. It became a favorite country retreat for the aristocratic families of Lima. It has old manor houses and restaurants, and is very popular among Lima residents for its invariable sunshine and the warm, dry climate at the foot of the mountains. It is also the point of departure for seeing the towns and scenery along the Central highway into the Andes.

Cieneguilla and the Lurín Valley

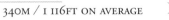
340M / 1 116FT ON AVERAGE)

Lurín Valley.

20km (30 minutes) E of Lima via paved road. Its sunny, pleasant climate, its numerous hostels and amusements, along with its proximity to Lima, make Cieneguilla one of Lima's favorite weekend destinations, especially in winter. From Cieneguilla, a packed dirt road climbs steeply up the Lurín River valley to Huarochirí (6 hours). Numerous turn-offs from this road lead to friendly towns well worth visiting. Sunicancha, Orcototo and Cruz de Laya are only a few of the more interesting.

Another road out of Cieneguilla ascends the Tinajas Canyon to the W, crossing an arid valley of cacti to finally reach Santo Domingo de los Olleros and Repartición (5 hours). From this last town the road rejoins the first road and continues on to Huarochirí.

Cajamarquilla

500M / 1 640FT)

One of the most important archeological sites on the central coast of Peru, considered the largest archeological complex in the Rímac River valley, 15km (30 minutes) E of Lima via the Central highway. This spot is reached by a packed dirt road that starts from Huachipa towards the zinc refinery at Cajamarquilla. Built entirely of adobe, the complex contains walled palaces separated by long, wide streets. Its construction began around the sixth century AD and it was inhabited until approximately the thirteenth century.

Visiting hours: daily, 9am to 5pm.

Puruchuco

200M / 656FT

An archeological site in the Rímac River valley at km 5 of the Central highway. Remains of an administrative center for the ancient kingdoms of the valley (the Ichma culture followed by the Inca culture). There is a site museum (Tel 494 2641).

Visiting hours: daily, 9am to 4pm.

Santa Rosa de Quives

1 550M / 5 086FT

65km (1 hour, 30 minutes) NE of Lima, overlooking the Chillón River valley (turn-off N of Lima). Santa Rosa de Lima was confirmed in this town. With its pleasant climate, it is a popular destination among Lima residents seeking sun and relaxation. There are hotels and country restaurants.

Canta • Obrajillo

2 819M / 9 246FT CANTA
2 764M / 9 069FT OBRAJILLO

Two charming towns 105km (2 hours) NE of Lima, past Santa Rosa de Quives. Access is by a paved road along the Chillón River. Both towns have restaurants and amusements often enjoyed by Lima residents, especially during winter as the sun shines here year round. Horses can be hired and fresh trout is on the menu. Obrajillo has beautiful countryside along its river, ideal for camping. Near Canta are the rock carvings of Checcta.

Outskirts of Obrajillo.

Marcahuasi

4 000M / 13 124FT ON AVERAGE

A high mesa located E of Lima in the mountain range rising on the right (or north) bank of the Rímac River. A series of gigantic, granite blocks on the mesa have been eroded by wind and

«Monument to Humanity,» Marcahuasi.

rain and carved into such curious shapes and designs as the famous «Monument to Humanity.» There are interesting archeological remains, including canals and dams for irrigating the terraces built in the canyons below. Marcahuasi can be reached from the town of Santa Eulalia, located at km 39 of the Central highway (2 hours from Lima). A packed dirt road from here leads to San Pedro de Casta (3 350m, or 10 991ft), from which a horse trail (3 to 4 hours) leads to the mesa.

Marcahuasi has no services; if you wish to camp you must take along all of your equipment and provisions (tent, food, water, and lots of warm clothing). San Pedro de Casta (which has some simple hostels) breaks from its quiet pace every October for the lively festivities and music of its Water festival. Town residents turn out for the traditional celebration and cleaning of the irrigation canals prior to the rainy season.

Outskirts of Andajes.

Hot spring baths in Churín.

Churín

2 085M / 6 841FT ◐ ◗

217km (5 hours) NE of Lima, this picturesque spot is accessed via the North Panamericana highway to a turnoff at km 103 (where it crosses the Seco River) that leads to town. Churín has several hotels and restaurants and is famous for its hot spring baths, with facilities for visitors.

From here, you can also visit Andajes (famous for its *manjarblanco*, or sweet milk paste) and archeological sites at Ninash, Kukun, Antasway, Huacho Sin Pescado and Kuray. Lake Wayo awaits trout fishing fans and the towering summits of the Raura cordillera invite mountain climbers.

Others

See p. 470, 498 and 512.

Hotels

Lima cuadrada

Hotel Sheraton ★★★★★
  Paseo de la República 170, Cercado. Tel 315 5000.
  Reservations 433 6358. Fax 315 5030.

Hotel Rivera ★★★★
  Garcilaso de la Vega 981, Lima. Tel 424 9438.
  rivera@terra.com.pe

Barranco

Park Suites Hotel ★★★
  Medrano Silva 396.
  Tel 477 1355. Fax 477 4064.

San Isidro

Hoteles Libertador ★★★★★
  Los Eucaliptos 550, San Isidro. Tel 421 6666.
  hotel@libertador.com.pe

Hotel Los Delfines Summit ★★★★★
  Los Eucaliptos 555, San Isidro. Tel 215 7020.
  reservas@losdelfineshotel.com.pe

Los Tallanes ★★★★★
  Jorge Basadre 325, San Isidro. Tel 222 5032.
  tallanes@hoteltallanes.com.pe

Plaza del Bosque ★★★★★
  Paz Soldán 190, San Isidro. Tel 441 8818.
  hotel@libertador.com.pe

Country Club de Lima ★★★★★
  Los Eucaliptos 590, San Isidro. Tel 611 9000.
  country@hotelcountry.com

Roosevelt Hotel & Suites ★★★★
  Álvarez Calderón 194, San Isidro. Tel 222 0012.
  informes@hotelroosevelt.com.pe

Sofitel Royal Park Lima ★★★★★
  Av. Camino Real 1050, San Isidro. Tel 215 1616.
  sofitel@sofitelroyalpark.com.pe

Sonesta Posada del Inca ★★★★★
  Pancho Fierro 194, San Isidro. Tel 221 2121.
  posada@el-olivar.com.pe

★★★★★ Swissôtel
Av. Central 150, Centro Empresarial Real; San Isidro.
Tel 421 4400. Fax 421 4422.
reservations.lima@swissotel.com

★★★★★ Las Palmeras de San Isidro
Av. Las Palmeras 240, San Isidro. Tel 422 3887.
postmast@hotpalmeras.com.pe

★★★★★ Hotel Meliá Lima
Av. Salaverry 2599, San Isidro. Tel 411 9000.

★★★★ Garden Hotel
Rivera Navarrete 450, San Isidro. Tel 442 1771.
reservas@gardenhotel.com.pe

★★★ Hotel San Isidro Inn
Av. Pezet 1765, San Isidro. Tel 264 2019.
Fax 264 3434. US$ 65

★★★ Hotel Collacocha
Andrés Reyes 100, San Isidro. Tel 442 3900.
Fax 442 4160. US$ 50

Lince

★★★★★ Hotel Carrera Las Américas
Jr. León Velarde 123, Lince. Tel 472 8666.
carrera@hoteleslasamericas.com

Corpac

★★★★ Prince Hotel
Av. Guardia Civil 727, Corpac. Tel 225 3025.
reservas@princehotel.com.pe

Miraflores

★★★★★ Hotel Las Américas
Av. Benavides 415, Miraflores. Tel 444 7272. US$ 250
hotel@hoteleslasamericas.com

★★★★★ Residencial Las Américas
Bellavista 216, Miraflores. Tel 242 6600.
residencial@hoteleslasamericas.com

★★★★★ Apart Hotel Las Américas
General Borgoño 116, Miraflores. Tel 241 3350.
aparthotel@hoteleslasamericas.com

María Angola   ★★★★★
   Av. La Paz 610, Miraflores. Tel 444 1280.

Marriot and Stellaris Casino-Lima   ★★★★★
   Malecón de la Reserva 615, Miraflores. Tel 217 7171.

Miraflores Park Hotel   ★★★★★
   Malecón de la Reserva 1035, Miraflores.
   Tel 242 3000. Fax 242 3393. US$ 255.
   mirapark@perouorientexpress.com.pe

Sol de Oro   ★★★★★
   San Martín 305, Miraflores. Tel 446 9876.
   ventas@soldeoro.com.pe

Suites Las Américas   ★★★★★
   Alcanfores 475, Miraflores. Tel 444 7272.
   suites@hoteleslasamericas.com

Double Tree El Pardo Hotel   ★★★★★
   Jr. Independencia 1412, Miraflores. Tel 241 0410.
   Fax 444 2171. US$ 210.
   pardohot@doubletreeelpardo.com.pe

La Hacienda Hotel   ★★★★
   Av. 28 de Julio 511, Miraflores. Tel 242 0109.

Hotel José Antonio   ★★★★
   Av. 28 de Julio 398, Miraflores. Tel 445 7743.

Apart Hotel El Condado   ★★★★
   Alcanfores 465, Miraflores. Tel 444 3614. US$ 190.
   condado@condado.com.pe

Gran Hotel Miraflores   ★★★★
   Av. 28 de Julio 151, Miraflores. Tel 241 3468.
   reservas@granhotelmiraflores.com.pe

Del Pilar Miraflores Hotel   ★★★★
   Pardo and Martir Olaya 141, Miraflores. Tel 242 7999.
   hotel@delpilarmiraflores.com.pe

Las Suites Apart Hotel   ★★★★
   Av. Grau 466, Miraflores. Tel 447 6415.
   suites@terra.com.pe

Camacho

   Golf Los Incas   ★★★★★
   Av. Cerro de Camacho 500. Tel 437 7701.
   hotel@golfincahotel.com

Central Highway

★★★★ El Pueblo Inn

Carretera Central km 11,2, Santa Clara.
Tel 446 6396. Fax 356 0024. US$ 115.

★★★ Los Cóndores Tambo Inn

Garcilaso de la Vega 900, Chaclacayo.
Tel 497 1783. US$ 60.

★★★ La Casona de los Cóndores

Las Begonias 243, Chaclacayo.
Reservations Lima Tel 497 2557. Fax 497 2538. US$ 40.

Cieneguilla

★★ Loma Linda

Av. Nueva Toledo s/n (highway to Cieneguilla, km 26).
Tel 479 8635.

★★ El Colono Inn

Av. Nueva Toledo 132 (highway to Cieneguilla, km 23).
Tel 479 8118. Fax 479 8224.

> RATES ARE APPROXIMATE AND, UNLESS OTHERWISE NOTED,
> ARE FOR DOUBLE OCCUPANCY.

Restaurants

Internacional Cuisine

✔ Costa Verde

Circuito de playas s/n, Barranco. Tel 247 1244.

✔ Astrid y Gastón

Cantuarias 175, Miraflores. Tel 444 1495.

✔ La Rosa Náutica

Espigón N.º 4, Costa Verde, Miraflores. Tel 445 0140.

✔ Rafael

San Martín 300, Miraflores. Tel 242 4149 / 444 4342.

✔ Le Bistrot des mes filles

Av. Conquistadores 510, San Isidro. Tel 422 6308.

✔ Ambrosía (Miraflores Park Hotel's Restaurant)

Malecón de La Reserva 1075, Miraflores. Tel 242 3000.

✔ La Gloria

Atahuallpa 201, Miraflores. Tel 446 6504.

Peruvian Food

José Antonio   ✔
Bernardo Monteagudo 200, San Isidro. Telefax 264 0188.

Las Brujas de Cachiche   ✔
Bolognesi 460, Miraflores. Tel 447 1883.

El Señorío de Sulco   ✔
Malecón Cisneros 1470, Miraflores. Tel 441 0183.

Manos Morenas   ✔
Av. Pedro de Osma 409, Barranco. Tel 467 0421.

A Puerta Cerrada   ✔
Bolognesi 752, Barranco. Tel 477 9277.

Restaurante Huaca Pucllana   ✔
General Borgoña 8th block, Miraflores. Tel 445 4042.

Grills and Roast Chicken

La Carreta   ✔
Rivera Navarrete 740, San Isidro.

La Tranquera   ✔
Av. José Pardo 285, Miraflores. Tel 445 4523.

Cuarto y Mitad   ✔
Comandante Espinar 798, Miraflores. Tel 446 2988.

Pardo's Chicken   ✔
Av. Benavides 730, Miraflores. Tel 446 4790.

La Granja Azul   ✔
Carretera Central km 4,5, Santa Clara. Tel 356 0082.

Rincón Gaucho   ✔
Av. Armendariz 580, Miraflores. Tel 447 4778.

El Rancho   ✔
Av. Benavides 2650, Miraflores. Tel 449 6036.

Mediterráneo Chicken   ✔
Comandante Espinar 194, Miraflores. Tel 242 3333.

Fish and Seafood

Segundo Muelle   ✔
Conquistadores 490, San Isidro. Tel 421 1206.

Alfresco   ✔
Las Begonias 560, San Isidro. Tel 222 2730.

Punta Sal   ✔
Conquistadores 948, San Isidro. Tel 441 7431.

✔ El Ceviche del Rey
    Av. Aramburú 979, San Isidro. Tel 441 5269.

✔ Don Beta
    José Gálvez 667, Miraflores. Tel 445 8370.

✔ Francesco
    Malecón de La Marina 526, Miraflores. Tel 442 8255.

✔ El Catamarán
    Av. República de Panamá 225, Barranco. Tel 477 0077.

✔ Costanera 700
    Costanera 700, San Miguel. Tel 506 0670.

✔ Rana Verde
    Plaza Gálvez s/n, Callao. Tel 429 5279.

✔ Cebichería Mateo
    Miller 386, Callao. Tel 465 8320.

✔ Hawaiano
    Av. República de Panamá 258, Barranco. Tel 477 0111.

Chinese Food

✔ Titi
    Av. Javier Prado Oeste 1212, San Isidro. Tel 224 8189.

✔ Lung Fung
    Av. Paseo de la República 3165, San Isidro.
    Tel 441 8817.

✔ Internacional
    Av. República de Panamá 5915, Miraflores. Tel 445 3997.

✔ 5 Estrellas
    Av. San Borja Sur 708, San Borja. Tel 476 8161.

✔ Omei
    Javier Prado Oeste 5902. Tel 437 0188.

Pastas

✔ San Ceferino
    Av. 2 de Mayo 793, San Isidro. Tel 422 8242.

✔ La Pizzería
    Malecón de La Reserva 610, Miraflores. Tel 444 3262.

✔ Antica Pizzería
    Av. 2 de Mayo 728, San Isidro. Tel 222 8437.

✔ La Romana
    Av. San Borja Sur 241, San Borja. Tel 476 6746.

Donatello ✔
  Av. Encalada 551, Monterrico. Tel 437 7229.
Trattoría de Mambrino ✔
  Manuel Bonilla 106, Miraflores. Tel 445 2862.
La Linterna ✔
  Caminos del Inca 489, Surco. Tel 372 5914.
Don Vitto ✔
  Martín Dulanto 111, San Antonio.

Japanese Food
Matsuei Sushi ✔
  Manuel Bañón 260, San Isidro. Tel 422 4326.
Fuji ✔
  Av. Paseo de la República 4090, San Isidro.
  Tel 440 8531.
Ichiban ✔
  Diagonal 220, Miraflores. Tel 446 5144.

Cafes • Pubs
Café Olé ◆
  Pancho Fierro 115, San Isidro. Tel 440 1186.
News Café ◆
  Av. El Polo 706, Surco. Tel 435 7935.
Café Café ◆
  Mártir Olaya 2250, Miraflores. Tel 445 1165.
Bohemia Café y Más ◆
  Av. Santa Cruz 805, Miraflores. Tel 446 5240.
Vivaldi ◆
  Av. Ricardo Palma 258, Miraflores. Tel 446 1473.

Folk *Peñas*
Rompe y Raja ◆
  Manuel Segura 127, Barranco. Tel 247 3271.
Don Porfirio ◆
  Manuel Segura 115, Barranco. Tel 477 3119.
Las Rocas ◆
  Vellavista 241, Miraflores. Tel 421 2605.
Peña Poggi ◆
  Av. Luna Pizarro 578, Barranco.

- ◆ Las Guitarras
    Manuel Segura cdra.2, Barranco.
- ◆ La Candelaria
    Bolognesi 292, Barranco. Tel 247 2941.
- ◆ Brisas del Titicaca
    Jr. Wakulsky 168, Lima. Tel 332 1881.
- ◆ Del Carajo!
    San Ambrosio 328, Barranco.
    Tel 247 7023 / 812 0733.

Useful Facts

AREA CODE **01**

☎

Basic Information
IPERÚ:

Information and Assistance for Tourists

Jorge Chávez International Airport.   574 8000

Open daily: 24 hours a day

E-mail: *iperulima@promperu.gob.pe*

Jorge Basadre 610, San Isidro.   421 1227

Open daily: Mon-Sun, 8:30 am to 6 pm.   421 1627

E-mail: *iperu@promperu.gob.pe*

Tourism Police Aid

Jr. Moore 268, Magdalena.   460 0921

Instituto Nacional de Cultura:

Av. Javier Prado este 2465. Museo de la Nación.   476 9890

Travel Agencies
Nuevo Mundo: Av. 28 de Julio 1220, Miraflores.   242 7272

Lima Tours: Av. Belén 1040, Lima.   424 5110

Explorandes: San Fernando 320, Miraflores.   445 0232

Cóndor Travel: Armando Blondet 249, San Isidro.   442 3000

Folkcraft Stores
Alpaca 111: Av. Larco 671, Miraflores

Mercado Indio Miraflores:

Av. Petit Thouars 5245, Miraflores

AREA CODE **01**

☎

Antisuyo: Tacna 460, Miraflores
Mercado Indio de La Marina:
Av. La Marina, San Miguel.

Post Offices
Main Post Office: Conde de Superunda 170, Lima. 428 0026
Open: Tue-Sat, 8am to 8pm;
Sun, 8:30am to 2pm.
Miraflores Post Office: Av. Petit Thouars 5001.
Open: Mon-Sat, 8am to 8pm;
Sun, 8:30am to 2pm.
San Isidro Post Office: Libertadores 325, San Isidro.
Open: Mon-Fri, 8am to 8pm;
Sun, 8:30am to 1pm.

Taxi Service
Taxi Real 470 6263
Taxi Seguro 275 2020

Car Rental
National Car Rental:
  Los Eucaliptos 555, San Isidro. 222 1010
Inka's Rent a Car:
  Cantuarias 160, Miraflores 445 5716
Budget:
  Av. Canaval y Moreyra 476, San Isidro. 442 8703
Avis Rent a Car:
  Av. Javier Prado Este 5235, Camacho, La Molina. 434 1111

2 400 M / 7 874FT
I 270 KM
SE OF LIMA

Machu Picchu

P. 345   P. 345

ROUTE MAP
11

The Sanctuary

Located 120km NW of Cusco, overlooking the Urubamba River valley (also known as the Vilcanota), the Inca citadel of Machu Picchu is one of the world's archeological jewels and a principal travel destination in Peru. Few works of man integrate so harmoniously with their natural surroundings as do this citadel and its peripheral sites.

Machu Picchu was revealed to modern-day science by the

Panoramic view of the citadel, through orchids and bromeliads.

North American explorer Hiram Bingham in 1911, thanks to information provided by local residents. Archeologists estimate that it was built in the second half of the fifteenth century and there are several hypotheses about the function and history of the citadel.

A typical sub-tropical climate, warm and humid during the day and cool at night. Showers and downpours are common (especially between November and April), followed by bright, intense sunshine. The best months for visiting are May and June. We recommend taking an umbrella or raincoat, sunblock and a bag to protect your camera equipment from the rain.

It could have been a military outpost strategically placed for the conquest of the jungle (or *antisuyo*) and to help contain potential insurrections of the native *antis* of the region. It is also said to have been a secret shelter for the *acllas* or «virgins of the Sun», who were dedicated to the service of the Inca, as, in one sector of the citadel, Bingham discovered a burial ground containing only female remains. Other specialists believe it was a favorite rest area of the Inca ruler's, or that it was a major sanctuary built in honor of the Inca Pachacútec, who saved Cusco's population from an invasion by the Chancas. Despite all these theories, its exact function remains a mystery.

The archeological complex is strategically located on the summit of the Machu Picchu mountain (its name means 'old mountain' in Quechua), which gives the citadel its name and its spectacular setting. Behind it rises the towering peak of Huayna Picchu ('young mountain') whose flanks and summit also hold archeological ruins. The torrential Urubamba River passes the feet of both peaks as it flows eastward some 400m (1 312ft) below the citadel.

In Machu Picchu it is possible to distinguish two well-defined areas: an agricultural sector that is a

HIRAM BINGHAM'S DISCOVERY

«I soon found myself before the ruined walls of buildings built with some of the finest stonework of the Incas. It was difficult to see them as they were partially covered over by trees and moss, the growth of centuries; but in the dense shadow, hiding in bamboo thickets and tangled vines, could be seen, here and there, walls of white granite ashlars most carefully cut and exquisitely fitted together [...]. I was left truly breathless...»

Hiram Bingham, *La Ciudad Perdida de los Incas.*

The urban zone and Huayna Picchu.

vast network of terraces and an urban sector that is further divided into a sacred area (temples, monuments, and burial chambers) and a secular area (with housing, miscellaneous enclosures and grain silos). The fact that the terraces provide the only cultivable land in the area suggests that Machu Picchu didn't have a very large permanent population. The design of the buildings and surroundings, with elements that were part of the Inca world view (huge mountains and rocks, caves and springs) leads some specialists to view Machu Picchu as a sanctuary or commemorative construction.

Perhaps the main attraction of Machu Picchu is the astounding degree of technology that its builders achieved in working

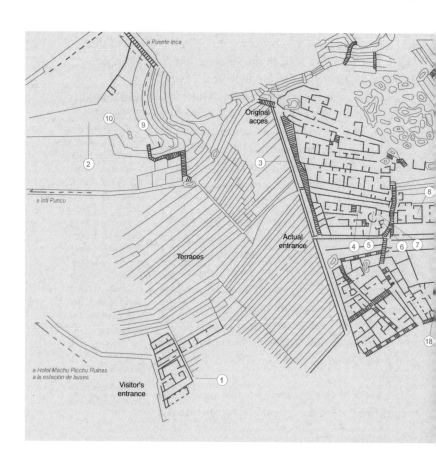

stone. The joins between the stone blocks in some of its buildings are so snug that it is impossible to insert even the tip of a needle between them. Some of the most interesting constructions are those labeled the Royal Tomb, close to the entrance to the citadel, the Temple of the Sun, the Tower (the only circular structure in the complex), the Priests House, the Temple of the Three Windows, the Central Temple, the Sunken Plaza, and the fountains form-

Inca trapezoidal windows.

ing the Baths of the Inca. Water channels and staircases carved from the living rock are some of the predominant constructions in the citadel. There are also stones that seem to have had a strong ritual significance. The most fascinating is the Intihuatana (a name that means 'hitching post of the sun'), which served as an astronomical calendar.

THE CITADEL OF MACHU PICCHU

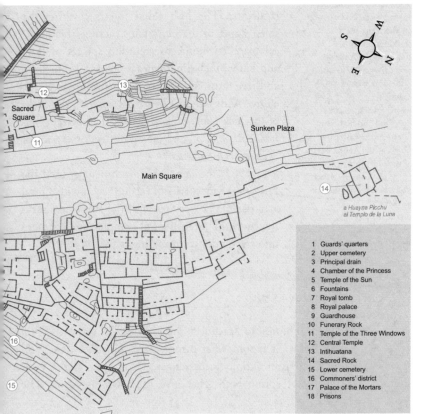

Sacred Square

Sunken Plaza

Main Square

a Huayna Picchu
al Templo de la Luna

1 Guards' quarters
2 Upper cemetery
3 Principal drain
4 Chamber of the Princess
5 Temple of the Sun
6 Fountains
7 Royal tomb
8 Royal palace
9 Guardhouse
10 Funerary Rock
11 Temple of the Three Windows
12 Central Temple
13 Intihuatana
14 Sacred Rock
15 Lower cemetery
16 Commoners' district
17 Palace of the Mortars
18 Prisons

Buildings on the slopes of Machu Picchu.

Machu Picchu's archeological significance is enhanced by the natural beauty of the surrounding landscape. The lush cloud forests covering the steep slopes of the mountains framing this magical place are home to countless species of flora and fauna, including delicate orchids, bromeliads and tree ferns. These forests are also home to the elusive Andean bear (*Tremarctos ornatus*), the cock-of-the-rock (*Rupicola peruviana*), the quetzal (*Pharomacrus auriceps*) and the dwarf deer or *sachacabra* (*Pudu mephistopheles*).

In 1981, the Peruvian government created the Historical Sanctuary of Machu Picchu with a total area of 35 592 hectares with the aim of conserving both the archeological complex and its magnificent natural surroundings.

Routes from Cusco

The town nearest to Machu Picchu is Aguas Calientes (1 700m, or 5 578ft). It is somewhat disorganized, but does have food and lodging in various price ranges. There are also the well-known hot spring baths that give the town its name. The baths are open from 5am to 8pm and the entrance fee is US$ 3.

By Rail

The most common approach to Machu Picchu is by rail. The train to Machu Picchu leaves Cusco every day from the San Pedro station (Tel 22 1313), next to the central market. Be very careful with your belongings in this area as theft is quite common. There are several levels of service: the *Vistadome-Autovagón* train (the most comfortable); the *Tourist Train* (Inka, Backpacker and Vistadome cars); and the *Local Train* (Social and Social Cerrojo cars). They all stop briefly at Ollantaytambo; Qorihuayrachina, at km 88 where the Inca Trail begins; Aguas Calientes, at km 112; and Puente Ruinas, at km 115, where buses must be boarded to ascend to the citadel.

- *Vistadome-Autovagón:* leaves daily 6am and costs US$ 73 (round-trip, bus to the ruins, entrance fee and lunch included). The trip takes 3h 35min. The return train to Cusco leaves at 3pm.
- *Inka:* leaves daily at 6h 15min and costs US$ 70 (roundtrip). The trip takes 3h 35min. The return train to Cusco leaves at 3:25pm.

Aguas Calientes.

- *Tourist Train:* Two kinds of services (Backpacker and Vistadome). The first one makes the full trip departing from Cusco and a short version (Cerrojo) between Ollantaytambo and Machu Picchu. The second one goes only from Ollantaytambo to Machu Picchu. Both leave daily and its cost vary from US$ 35 to US$ 55 (roundtrip).
- *Local Train (Social and Cerrojo services)* is also available daily from Cusco.

By Air

There is an helicopter service (Heli Cusco) available at the Cusco airport. It can comfortably transport up to 24 passengers and reaches Aguas Calientes in 25 minutes. The flight offers unique panoramic views of the fortress at Sacsayhuamán, Ollantaytambo and the Sacred Valley. The helicopter does not fly over the Sanctuary, so as not to damage the site or disturb the environment.

> *Reservations Lima Tel 444 7104.*
> *Approximate cost per person: US$ 90 one way*
> *and US$ 150 round trip.*

Getting Up to the Citadel

Buses leave the town of Aguas Calientes for Machu Picchu every half hour, with a brief stop at the Puente Ruinas train station. Another bus service leaves from Puente Ruinas every fifteen minutes. In either case the cost is US$ 6 per person, round trip. From Puente Ruinas, the bus makes the 700m (2 297ft) climb via 6km of winding road to reach the citadel. The first bus in the morning leaves Puente Ruinas at 8:30am, and the last one, at 5:30pm. It is best to get in line for the buses as soon as you get off the train at the Puente Ruinas station. You can also hike up to Machu Picchu (about one hour).

The Intihuatana.

Costs • Recommendations

Stairs, buildings and terraces in the secular zone.

Entrance to the Sanctuary costs US$ 20 per person for the first day and US$ 10 per person for each subsequent day. Overnight camping in the area is rarely allowed; only by special permission from the Instituto Nacional de Cultura office at Machu Picchu. There is a restaurant at the entry to the citadel, but if you wish to save money you should take along your own meals, but remember that eating is not permitted inside the ruins, neither are animals or audio equipment. There are restrooms and public telephones at the entrance.

The trail up Mount Huayna Picchu starts from the north end of the Machu Picchu citadel. The hike takes 30 to 90 minutes depending on the physical condition of the walker and the condition of the trail (rain makes the rocks very slippery). It is important to register at the entrance to the trail, and entrance is only allowed until 1pm.

This path is not recommended for children, the elderly, or those in poor physical condition. We suggest bringing along water and hiking shoes.

Archeological remains on Huayna Picchu.

Trekking to Machu Picchu

Inca Trail

Considered one of the most spectacular trekking routes in the world, the Inca Trail to Machu Picchu (40km, or 3 days of travel) attracts thousands of adventurers every year who are seeking its special combination of history and nature. Walking the same paths that the Incas once traveled and gazing over the same landscape of incomparable beauty, you can easily imagine yourself transported into the past.

Andenes or farm terraces in the agricultural zone.

To do this route, you must take the Cusco-to-Machu Picchu train and get off at Qorihuayrachina (km 88), where the train stops for several minutes. The Inca Trail begins on the other side of a suspension bridge over the Urubamba River. It first climbs alongside the ruins of Llaqtapata, between terraces planted to corn and quinoa, then heads towards the Cusichaca Valley and the town of Huayllabamba (2 750m, or 9 023ft). This is the last populated area on the route and is located at the confluence of the Cusichaca and Llullucha rivers. It is also the last place to find provisions.

From here on, there is only open countryside. The path continues to climb through the Llullucha Valley to the Warmiwañuska Pass, the highest point of the route at 4 200m (13 780ft). Its name means 'where the woman died' in Quechua, possibly based on a local legend. In the eighteenth and nineteenth centuries, merchants frequently used this part of the Inca Trail for

High Andean plain on the way to Warmiwañuska Pass.

contraband and commerce. From here you can see the Runtu-racay ruins and the Pacamayo River.

Once over the cold, windy pass, the trail descends sharply to the Pacamayo River valley and its stands of trees and cacti. It then begins to climb again, providing hikers with an idea of the magnificence of Inca engineering, as it becomes a path that is perfectly paved in white granite slabs and follows the zigzagging line of the cliffs and mountainside. For several hours the trail winds among the mountains until it reaches a second pass at 3 950m (12 959ft) and finally descends a stepped slope of almost 1 600m (5 250ft) to the ruins of Sayacmarca and the mysterious cloud forest.

The dense vegetation here conceals exquisite examples of Inca architecture: Phuyupatamarca (3 650m, or 11 976ft) and Wiñay Wayna (3 hours further down) with its spectacular system of terraces, and Inca way stations called *tambos* and observation platforms rising out of tree fern forests with dozens of orchids growing among their polished stones. The final descent is quick (30 minutes), through the Inti Punko gateway to the citadel of Machu Picchu.

The fee for hiking the Inca Trail is US$ 17 per person. There are no food or supply services available along the path and you must take along ev-

Phuyupatamarca.

erything you will need for three days of hiking. You can hire porters at Qorihuayrachina (where the trail begins). The approximate cost of this service is US$ 4 per porter, per day, plus food.

There are some restrooms along the path, as well as designated camp sites. Respect these areas and, above all, do not discard trash along the route. The climate varies as you cross the *cordillera* (intense cold) or descend into the cloud forest (hot and humid). Take layered clothing and at least two pairs of hiking shoes.

Royal Trail

A section of the Inca Trail sets out towards Phuyupatamarca from km 104 on the railway, shortly before the stop at Aguas Calientes. This route is shorter than the Inca Trail and climbs stone steps to join the last section of the main Trail, also crossing the Wiñay Wayna ruins and reaching Machu Picchu via the Inti Punko gateway. It does not require exceptional physical condition but does take about 6 hours. This section is free of charge.

Resting at the Warmiwañuska Pass.

Path of Purification

Recently discovered by archeologists, this section of the Inca Trail starts at km 107 of the railway, only 3km before Aguas Calientes. To reach it, you must walk 3km upriver from the Machu Picchu Pueblo Hotel (where the train stops at Aguas Calientes) to the water intake for the hydroelectric station. After crossing the river on a suspension bridge, you continue to the Choquesuisui Canyon (Quechua for 'where they wash gold'). The Path of Purification, named for the succession of pools formed by the stream alongside it, climbs the canyon and joins the main Inca Trail at the Wiñay Wayna ruins, reaching Machu Picchu via the Inti Punko gateway. Highly recommended for a short hike (four to five hours). This trail is free of charge.

Hotels

Machu Picchu

★★★ Machu Picchu Lodge

At the entry to the Machu Picchu site.
Reservations Cusco Tel 24 1777. Fax 23 7111.
Reservations Lima Tel 221 0826. Fax 440 6179.
reservas@peruorientexpress.com.pe

Aguas Calientes

★★★★ Machu Picchu Pueblo Hotel

Railway km 110. Tel 21 1032. US$ 180.
Reservations Cusco Tel 24 5314. Fax 24 4669.
Reservations Lima Tel 422 6574. Fax 422 4701.
reservas@inkaterra.com.pe

★★★ Hotel Machu Picchu Inn

Av. Pachacútec s/n. Tel 21 1056. Fax 21 1057.
Reservations Lima Tel 221 0826. US$ 75
peruhotel@peruhotel.com.pe

★★★ Hatuchay Tower Machu Picchu Hotel

Carretera Puente Ruinas Mz.4. Tel 21 1200. US$ 170
mapi@hatuchaytower.com.pe

RATES ARE APPROXIMATE AND, UNLESS OTHERWISE NOTED,
ARE FOR DOUBLE OCCUPANCY.

Restaurants

✔ **Toto's House**

Av. Imperio del Sol s/n.

✔ **Indio Feliz**

Yoque Yupanqui s/n. (nex to the plaza).

✔ **Inti Killa**

Av. Imperio del Sol 147.

✔ **Costa Verde**

Road to Machu Picchu.

✔ **Pizzería Clave de Sol**

Av. Pachacútec 156.

Manu

I 400　KM
SE ⅔　LIMA

P. 355　P. 355

P. 355

ROUTE MAP
11

History

Manu National Park, covering 1 532 806 hectares, is the largest national park in Peru and one of the largest parks on earth in a tropical region. The park, along with the Manu Reserve Zone and the Manu Cultural Zone, comprises the Manu Biosphere Reserve (recognized by Unesco in 1977), with an area of 1 881,200 hectares (about half the size of Switzerland). It is located partially in the department of Cusco and partially in the

Ficus trigona (*Ficus sp.*) in Cocha Cashu.

department of Madre de Dios and contains the entire basin of the Manu River, a tributary of the Madre de Dios. This protected area extends from the high Andes at over 4 000m (13 124ft) down to 365m (1 198ft) in the Amazon basin.

The first historical references to the region date from the time of the Inca Túpac Yupanqui, who discovered the Madre de Dios River in the fifteenth century and named it Amarumayo, or 'snake river.'

A typical tropical climate, warm and humid during the dry season (May to October) and rainy during the summer (December to March). Cold spells lasting several days are common between May and August.

In the late nineteenth century, the region became unusually important as a consequence of the rubber boom. In 1890 rubber baron Carlos Fermín Fitzcarrald discovered a pass between the Ucayali and Madre de Dios river basins, through an isthmus (that bears his name) between the Serjali (a tributary of the Mishagua River) and the Cashpajali (a tributary of the Manu River). Over the following decades, many adventurers used the new route to exploit the newly accessible forests.

After years of overexploitation —in which the rubber barons brutally used the indigenous population— the number of rubber trees began to decline. At the same time, the success of Asian rubber tree plantations, which were more productive and less costly, put the Peruvian and Brazilian rubber industry out of business. But the exploitation of the jungle's natural resources did not stop. Trappers seeking furs and loggers in search of cedar, mahogany and other valuable hardwoods penetrated further and more frequently into the area. They even went so far as to finance the construction of a landing field at the village of Boca Manu, at the confluence of the Manu and Upper Madre de Dios rivers. Nonetheless, over time man's intrusion became less noticeable as the difficult access

THE THREE AREAS OF MANU

The Manu Biosphere Reserve is comprised of three areas:
1. The Nucleus, strictly untouchable, comprised of the National Park and devoted to the protection of wildlife and natural resources.
2. The Buffer Zone or Reserve Zone, devoted to indirect use of resources, such as scientific investigation and controlled tourism.
3. The Cultural Zone, comprised of lands of the public domain, where there are villages and direct use of resources.

and rising costs of operation made exploitation of this distant region less worthwhile. The forests began to regenerate. In 1967, the British advisor Ian Grimwood came to Peru at the request of the Forest Service department of the Peruvian Ministry of Agriculture. An expert naturalist, Grimwood's task was to find three areas on Peruvian soil that were rich in natural diversity and where man's influence was still minimal or nil. Grimwood traveled tirelessly through the entire country, but never found what he was looking for. He was about to leave when he was contacted by Celestino Kalinowski, a Polish naturalist who invited him along on a trip to Manu. His reaction was immediate. In light of the area's exceptional characteristics and abundant flora and fauna, Grimwood recommended that the Peruvian government establish a large national park in the Manu River basin.

In 1973, the government set the park's definitive boundaries.

Cocha Cashu.

Native Community of Tayakome.

Geography

Given its geographical location and its steep terrain, Manu has a wide range of climates and environments, which give rise to its extraordinary natural diversity. The flora of Manu is as heterogeneous as it is abundant: over 2 000 species of plants have been recorded in its forests. Its territory is classified into five well-defined plant ecosystems: the high Andean grasslands at more than 4 000m (13 124ft); at a lower altitude, the dwarf tree forests, mysterious and almost unknown to science; the cloud forests between 2 800m (9 187ft) and 1 600m (5 250ft), with a myriad of orchids, tree ferns and giant begonias; the subtropical forests between 1 600m (5 248ft) and 800m (2 625ft),

Malvaceae in bloom.

Jaguar (*Panthera onca*).

Young Machiguenga.

containing species with varied uses in medicine, human consumption, and pharmacology; and the tropical forest below 800m (2 624ft) in the Amazon basin, with many forest species of commercial value that have almost disappeared from the rest of the Amazon (cedar, mahogany and others).

The fauna of Manu is some of the most diverse and most studied in the jungle. Biologists have established that there are more species in the immediate vicinity of the Cocha Cashu biology station than exist on the entire continent of Europe. They have identified as many as 13 species of primates, five of felines, a thousand bird species, close to a hundred species of bats, and as yet unknown quantities of fish, amphibian, reptile, and insect species. Manu is also home to vulnerable species that are in danger of extinction, such as the Andean bear (*Tremarctos ornatus*), the *taruca*, or Andean deer (*Hippocamelus antisiensis*), the black lizard (*Melanosuchus niger*) and the river otter (*Pteronura brasiliensis*). All of these are almost extinct on the rest of the continent but still in considerable numbers in Manu. Seeing river otters at play, observing a jaguar as it rests peacefully on a tree branch, or watching hundreds of macaws congregate at riverbank clay licks called *collpas* are just some of the exceptional experiences awaiting visitors to Manu.

Manu also shelters many indigenous communities who have lived in harmony with nature for thousands of years. The Upper Madre de Dios, the Manu and other rivers are the ancestral territory of diverse ethnic groups: Machiguengas, Yoras or Yaminahuas, Mashcopiros and Amahuacas. Some are very small and maintain very little contact with the modern world. Their customs, knowledge, techniques for using forest resources, and vision of nature are an invaluable cultural wealth. Today, the inhabitants of Manu live in protected territories that ensure their ability to continue to live as their ancestors did. They can travel freely throughout the park and directly use its resources as long as they do not alter the balance of the ecosystem. Some have organized into communities and are increasingly participating in modern society, by making canoes, cultivating agricultural products and taking part in scientific and tourist activities.

Access Routes • Costs

Visits to the national park are not permitted. The adjacent Manu Reserve Zone and Manu Cultural Zone, however, offer the same attractions and several lodges for visitors.

To travel to Manu you must hire the services of one of the agencies in the Ecotur Manu consortium, as they are the only ones officially authorized to operate in this region. (They can process the permits you need for a visit.) These agencies are: Inka Natura Travel, Manu Nature Tours, Expediciones Manu, Pantiacolla Tours, Selva Sur Expediciones and Aventuras Ecológicas Manu *(see Useful Facts, p. 358)*.

There are various access routes to Manu. The main ones leave from the city of Cusco, either overland (12 hours) to Atalaya or Shintuya and then by river (6 hours via the Upper Madre de Dios and Manu rivers), or by air (a 30 minutes flight) to the town of Boca Manu and then by river (4 hours) up the Manu River.

Visitors entering the Manu Reserve Zone must register at a park ranger's post, pay a US$ 10 entry fee, and respect the strict regulations protecting the natural environment. There are heavy penalties for infractions.

Because of its inaccessibility and the high cost of travel, the minimum duration of a visit to Manu is generally four days and three nights, and a five- to seven-day trip is most recommended. These travel packages cost from US$ 700 to US$ 1 250, per person, depending on whether you choose the

**BASIC EQUIPMENT FOR
A TRIP TO THE MANU***

- Binoculars
- Photographic equipment
- Two pairs of long cotton pants
- Two pairs of shorts
- Two light, long-sleeved shirts
- Four T-shirts
- Four pairs of socks
- Two pairs of comfortable boots or shoes
- Waterproof jacket
- Hat
- Swimsuit
- Towel
- Water bottle, full
- Sunblock
- Insect repellent
- Sunglasses
- Photocopies of personal documents
- Flashlight and batteries

* *Three to five days*

shorter or longer stay. The package includes travel (by air, overland or by river), lodging, meals, and expedition equipment. The cost of getting there from Cusco, either overland or by air, is not included. There are 10% to 20% discounts for groups of more than six. The entry fee to the park is generally included in the cost of the tour package.

The trip into the reserve is done only by boat with outboard engines via the Manu River. There is scarcely any infrastructure inside the reserve and tours must take all of their supplies and equipment for camping.

Lodges

Manu Lodge.

• *Amazonia Lodge:* 3km from the town of Atalaya on the Cusco–Paucartambo–Kosñipata–Shintuya highway. A former tea plantation converted to a meeting center for scientists and nature lovers. Managed by the hospitable Santiago Yábar and his family.

Approximate cost per person/day is US$ 40 for meals and lodging.

• *Pantiacolla Lodge:* 30 minutes from the town of Shintuya, on the banks of the Upper Madre de Dios River. Managed by Gustavo Moscoso, one of the people most knowledgeable about this region, and the Dutch biologist Mariana van Vlardigen. Has a number of bungalows and good trails, with abundant wildlife in the surroundings, including several rare species such as the black *huapo* monkey and the Andean bear.

Tel 23 8323.

Approximate cost per person/day is US$ 50 for meals and lodging.

• *Manu Lodge:* the only lodge actually located inside the Manu Reserve Zone. On the shores of Cocha Juárez, a beautiful lake, located four hours by boat from the airstrip at Boca Manu. Has a good trail system, abundant wildlife, experienced guides and all of the amenities of a hotel, in the middle of the Amazon jungle.

Reservations in Cusco:
Manu Nature Tours. Tel 25 2721.
Approximate cost per person/day
is US$ 80 for meals and lodging.

- *Manu Wildlife Center:* 90 minutes from the town of Boca Manu downstream the Madre de Dios River. Built by the environmental organization Inka Natura. It has an excellent trail system, two lakes of tremendous beauty nearby (Blanco and Blanquillo), the largest and most accessible *collpa* of macaws in the region, and a singular *collpa* of tapirs, pecaries and deers. Unique in the Amazonia.

    Reservations in Lima:
    Inka Natura Travel. Tel 271 8156.
    Approximate cost per person/day
    is US$ 50 for meals and lodging.

- *Tambo Blanquillo:* 2 hours from the town of Boca Manu, down the Madre de Dios River. Its principal attraction is its proximity to the spectacular *collpa* of macaws at Blanquillo and to Lake Blanquillo (only 5 minutes from the lodge). Has bungalows and a catamaran-blind for observing macaws unobtrusively from the river.

    Reservations in Lima:
    Explorandes. Tel 445 0532.
    Approximate cost per person/day
    is US$ 50 for meals and lodging.

Collpa of macaws.

Useful Facts

AREA CODE OF CUSCO

AND PUERTO MALDONADO **84**

☎

Offices of the Manu Natural Park
and the Manu Reserve Zone:

Micaela Bastidas 310, Wanchaq, Cusco — 23 4179

Authorized Tour Operators

Inka Natura Travel:

Plateros 361, Cusco. — 25 5255

Manuel Bañón 461, Lima — 440 2022

postmaster@inkanatura.com.pe

Manu Nature Tours:

Av. Pardo 1046, Cusco. — 23 4793

Pantiacolla Tours:

Plateros 360, Cusco. — 23 8323

pantiac@terra.com.pe

Manu Expeditions:

Paseo de los Héroes 895, Cusco. — 23 6706

Manu Ecological Adventures:

Plateros 356, Cusco. — 22 5562

Air Atlantic:

Aeropuerto de Cusco — 24 5857

Nasca

Nasca lies in a fertile valley surrounded by some of the most inhospitable desert on earth. The region's primary crops are cotton, grapes, and fruit.

Between the second and fifth centuries AD the Nasca culture flourished in this region and was able to control its arid environment by means of ingenious agricultural techniques. The Nasca built irrigation systems that not only managed surface water (building canals and dams and diverting rivers) but also utilized underground water via subterranean aqueducts. Some

P. 78

ROUTE MAP
7

Fields of cotton in the Nasca Valley.

of these constructions are still used today. The Nasca are also famous for their ceramics, beautiful polychrome pieces decorated with mythical and natural motifs (plants and animals). For their textiles, they spun cotton and the wool of camelids, then dyed them with vegetable dyes, using skilled techniques. Around the eighth century AD, this coastal culture came under the influence of the Wari, centered in Ayacucho. In the fifteenth

A typical desert climate, dry and warm, with a yearly mean temperature of 19°C (66°F). Sunny most of the year, but cold at night, especially during winter, when the temperature can drop to 10°C (50°F). Windy afternoons; it almost never rains.

century AD, the Nasca territory was incorporated into the Inca Empire.

The founding of the Spanish villa of Nasca dates from 1591, when Viceroy García Hurtado de Mendoza, Marquis of Cañete, ordered a city founded on the site of a small native village. It very soon became famous for its considerable production of wine and a grape liquor (similar to pisco) that was for the consumption of the slave population and which the locals called *nasca*.

Struck regularly by strong earthquakes (and almost entirely rebuilt after the earthquake of 1942), the city has no important architecture. It is nonetheless the departure point for those who want to see the famous Nasca lines, and it is also the starting point for a road to Puquio, Abancay, and Cusco (at 128km, 460km, and 660km, respectively).

Zapotes (*Capparis sp.*) in the desert.

Local Dishes

Soups
- Sopa de garbanzos: garbanzo soup, with bacon and aromatic herbs.

Main Dishes
- Picante de camarones: shrimp in a spicy sauce, served with potatoes.

Dessert
- Chapanas: a dessert made of yucca root sweetened with a cane molasses called *chancaca*.

Festivals

The most important festivals celebrated in Nasca are Tourism Week (the second week of May); the birthday of María Reiche (May 15); and the Feasts of the Virgen de Guadalupe, patroness of Nasca (October 8) and of the Virgen del Carmen (September 19).

Excursions

Nasca Lines and Geoglyphs

550M / 1 804FT

25km (20 minutes) N of Nasca on the South Panamericana highway. Etched over some 1 000km² on the San José *pampas*, or plains, and on some hillsides in the Grande River valley, these lines are some of the greatest archeological enigmas in the world. They were first described by the chronicler Pedro Cieza

Hummingbird drawn on the Pampas de San José.

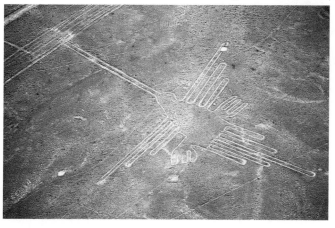

THE MEANING OF THE LINES

Although no theory can yet scientifically explain the meaning of the Nasca lines, they are thought to have formed a sort of gigantic astronomical calendar closely linked to the cult of water. They describe the movement of heavenly bodies, perhaps helping priests to predict the weather and plan farming activities. Another theory holds that they were *ceques* or ritual walkways. María Reiche, a German mathematician who devoted her entire life to studying and conserving the lines, put together an exact map of the figures, guided by the idea that they were drawn for practical and religious purposes.

Lookout tower at km 420 of the South Panamericana.

de León in 1550 and later studied by German archeologist Max Uhle in 1901. In 1926 they were the subject of a presentation by the Peruvian scientist Toribio Mejía Xesspe before the Congress of Americanists. In 1939, they were revealed to the rest of the world by archeologist Paul Kosok from the University of Long Island, New York, after he flew over the area in search of land suitable for agricultural use. It was through Kosok that German citizen María Reiche learned of the lines in 1940. She was born in Dresden in 1903 and came to Peru as a governess at the age of 31. Some time later, Kosok hired her to translate some of his writings about the geoglyphs. From that time until her death in 1998, the lines were her great passion. She became known as the Lady of the Lines and produced the first drawings and measurements of these mysterious figures.

The geoglyphs, which depict animals (several species of birds, a monkey, a spider, and fish, to name a few) and stylized plants, are set within an enormous labyrinth of straight lines, trapezoids, triangles, and spirals etched into the ground as shallow, 20cm deep, canals. Some figures are as long as 300m (984ft). Scholars have calculated that the lines were created between 200 and 500 BC by the inhabitants of the area.

There is an observation tower at km 420 on the South Panamericana highway, which affords a partial view of several figures. Morning flights (approx. 45 minutes) over the lines can be chartered in Nasca, Lima or Ica (Hotel Las Dunas) at an average cost of US$ 40 per person. It is forbidden to camp on the plains; there are heavy fines and penalties for doing so.

María Reiche Museum

550M / 1 804FT   )

25km (20 minutes) N of Nasca on the South Panamericana highway (km 416,5). A small but interesting display of archeological artifacts and photographs of the Nasca lines.

Visiting hours: Mon-Fri, 9am to 2pm.

Aqueducts of Cantayoc

600M / 1 968FT   )

Canals and subterranean aqueducts built by the Nasca culture, 4km (10 minutes) E of the city, on fields now farmed
by the Cantay cooperative. They are laid out in a vast network and are built with both river rock and stone slabs. Every so often along the subterranean canals there are water
boxes with openings for maintenance of the canals. This mas-

NASCA EXCURSION MAP

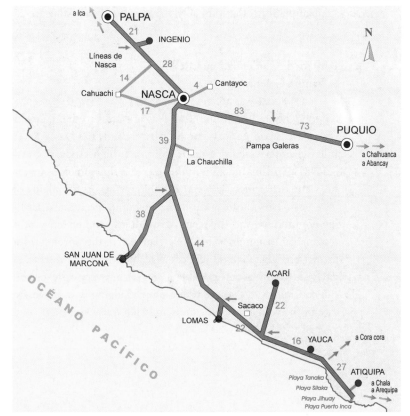

Aqueduct of Cantayoc.

terpiece of water engineering is still in use today.

Nearby are the remains of other pre-Hispanic buildings, including Paredones, an archeological site recently excavated by archeologists from Ica.

Cahuachi • La Estaquería

580M / 1 902FT

Archeological sites 17km (20 minutes) N of Nasca via the South Panamericana highway. At Cahuachi you can see the ruins of what was probably one of the most important religious and administrative centers of the Nasca culture and, according to some, its capital. It has two adobe pyramids (against the hillsides), large plazas and cemeteries. Nearby, at the site known as La Estaquería, several posts of carob wood can still be seen on a square, stepped platform that probably served as a ceremonial center.

Bárbara d'Achille National Reserve at Pampa Galeras

3 800M / 12 468FT ON AVERAGE

83km (1 hour, 30 minutes) E of Nasca. Access to the reserve is via a paved road (Nasca–Puquio) that ascends the Nasca River valley. Pampa Galeras extends over vast, high Andean grasslands. The main attraction in the reserve is the numerous graceful vicuñas (*Vicugna vicugna*) calmly grazing on the plains of *ichu* grass. This territory, mostly belonging to the Lucanas farming community, was the scene of an intense and effective protection campaign in the 1960s that saved the species from extinction. There are no services available within the reserve. A day visit from Nasca is possible if you set out very early, or you can continue E to Puquio, where simple lodging is available. Be careful to avoid altitude sickness and take warm clothing.

Punta San Juan de Marcona Reserved Area

77km (1 hour) S of Nasca. A paved road leaves the South Panamericana highway at km 481, heading SW for 38km to the mines at Marcona, the largest iron deposit in Peru. The reserve zone is 3km S of here and is under the supervision of the Fertilizer Division of PescaPerú. It is home to the largest population of Humboldt penguins (*Spheniscus humboldtii*) in the country, as well as an enormous colony of sea lions and other sea birds. To enter the reserve zone you will need authorization from the Fertilizer Division of PescaPerú. It is an ideal place for fishing and deep sea diving. The town of Marcona has some simple hotels and restaurants.

Humboldt penguins
in San Juan de Marcona.

Lomas

92km (1 hour, 15 minutes) S of Nasca. A picturesque fishing inlet with a residential area frequented by residents of Nasca and Acarí (in the department of Arequipa) during the summer. Ideal for fishing and diving. Access is via a 9km paved road off the South Panamericana highway at km 528. There are restaurants and hotels *(we recommend the Hostal Lomas. Tel 21 0282)*.

Hotels

Hotel Nazca Lines *(ex Hotel de Turistas)* ★★★★
  Bolognesi s/n (1st block). Tel 52 2293.
  Reservations Lima Tel 261 0240. US$ 75.
  hnazca@derramajae.org.pe
La Maison Suisse ★★★★
  Panamericana Sur 447. Tel 52 2434.
  Reservations Lima. Tel 445 0859. US$ 60.
  maison@terra.com.pe
El Huarango ★★★
  Av. Circunvalación 1082.
  Tel 52 2931.

★★★ Sol de Nasca
      Callao 568. Tel 52 2730.

★★★ Hotel Las Líneas de Nasca
      Arica 299, main square. Tel 52 2488. US$ 40.

★★ Hostal Nasca
      Lima 438. Tel 52 2085. US$ 10.

> **RATES ARE APPROXIMATE AND, UNLESS OTHERWISE NOTED, ARE FOR DOUBLE OCCUPANCY.**

Restaurants

✔ La Taberna
   Lima 321.

✔ Restaurant of the Hotel Nasca Lines
   Bolognesi s/n.

✔ Pizzería La Púa
   Lima, 1st block.

✔ Restaurant of the Hotel Las Líneas de Nasca
   Arica 299, plaza de armas.

✔ Sudamérica
   Lima 688.

Useful Facts

AREA CODE **34**

☎

Basic Information

IPERÚ:
  Information and Assistance for Tourists
  Tel 01-541-8000 Lima.

Instituto Nacional de Cultura:

Prolongación Ayabaca cdra.8, Urb. San Isidro.	23 4383
Post Office: Fermín del Castillo 379.	52 2016
ESSALUD: Juan Matta 613.	52 2876
Farmacia Señor de Luren: Lima 360	52 2299
Alegría Tours: Lima 168	52 2444
Nasca Trails Tours: Bolognesi 550.	52 2858

AREA CODE **34**

☎

Aerotaxis (offering flights over the Nasca lines)

Aero Nasca: Bolívar 225.	52 2297
Aero Cóndor: Panamericana Sur km 447 (at the edge of town).	52 2424
Aero Ica: Panamericana Sur km 447 (at the edge of town)	52 2376

5 M / 16FT ON AVERAGE
261 KM
S OF LIMA

Paracas

P. 78

ROUTE MAP

6

The Paracas National Reserve is located 22km (20 minutes) S of the city of Pisco (or 261km from Lima) and is the only reserve protecting a section of Peruvian coastline and cold-water ocean. Its 335 000 hectares extend from the Paracas peninsula to the point at Morro Quemado, south of La Independencia bay. It includes many salt flats, beautiful beaches, rocky points, and some of the richest ocean waters on earth. The species finding refuge here include seals and sea lions (*Arctocephalus australis* and *Otaria byronia*), Humboldt penguins (*Spheniscus humboldtii*),

Black skimmers (*Rhynchops nigra*) flying over Sequión.

sea otter or *chingungo* (*Lutra felina*), dolphins and porpoises, and over two hundred species of seabirds, both resident and migratory. Some of the latter are the Andean condor (*Vultur gryphus*), flamingoes or *parihuanas* (*Phoenicopterus chilensis*) and the biggest producers of *guano*, or bird dropping fertilizer (cormorants, boobies, and pelicans).

> *A temperate climate, with a yearly mean temperature of 22° C (72° F). Sunshine most of the year, although drizzle is common in winter and nights can be very cold. Strong, early afternoon winds from the SW (called* paracas*) are common.*

The reserve also contains considerable remains of the Paracas culture which inhabited the Chincha, Pisco and Ica valleys from 600 BC to the first centuries AD. This culture, revealed to modern-day science by Peruvian archeologist Julio C. Tello in 1925, has become famous for its fine polychrome textiles made from cotton and camelid wool. Artifacts from this ancient culture can be viewed at the Julio C. Tello site museum, some at Cerro Colorado and at Cabezas Largas, quite close to the site museum.

The reserve itself has no tourist services. What it does offer is natural scenery of incomparable beauty which can be visited by car or even by mountain bike. If you wish to camp, remember to bring drinking water, sunblock and warm clothing as the nights can be very cold. It is recommended to never navigate coastal waters after 1pm.

Next to the reserve, 18km (15 minutes) S of Pisco via paved highway, is the small beach resort of Paracas bay. This was the spot where the patriot forces under General José de San Martín landed in 1820.

The activity at the resort is mainly centered around its hotels (a great option for non-campers)

FLAMINGOES

Parihuanas, as flamingoes are known in Peru, are birds with a very unique appearance: they have duck's feet, stork's legs, a heron's neck, and an upside-down beak specially designed for feeding on microscopic water creatures without swallowing a single drop of water. In Peru there are three flamingo species: two live exclusively in the Andes, while the third regularly descends to the coast. The first two species, the James flamingo and the Andean flamingo, are in danger of extinction. The common flamingo (*Phoenicopterus chilensis*), the one seen at Paracas, is fortunately quite abundant.

Humboldt penguins.

and the beaches of the adjacent reserve. The bay is calm, but not good for swimming because of the quantity of kelp and small rayfish and the muddy seafloor.

The nearby port of El Chaco has restaurants serving typical dishes of the region. Expect mosquitoes at night.

Excursions

Punta Arquillo

)

Located on the S end of the Paracas peninsula, this tall cliff is an ideal viewpoint for observing the sea lion rookeries below and the majestic Andean condors that come in search of carrion. The best time to come here is in summer, when condors appear more frequently and the rookeries are at the height of the reproductive season. There is parking and a viewing area; don't forget binoculars and a jacket. Access is via the packed dirt road from Lagunillas (15 minutes from the entrance booth). This excursion takes about 1 hour, 30 minutes, round trip.

La Mina • El Raspón

)

To many, these are the most beautiful beaches of Paracas (they are certainly the most frequented). They can be reached via the packed dirt road from Lagunillas (15 minutes from the entrance booth to the reserve). The area has vehicle parking and a beverage stand (during the summer). It is ideal for camping, diving, swimming or simply enjoying the sea. To reach El Raspón (to the left of La Mina), you must descend a steep trail over the sand and rocks. The place takes its name, El Raspón, or «the abrasion,» from the hazards of the trail.

La Mina.

Ballestas Islands

)

A group of small islands, shaped by wind and water, that shelter an enormous sea lion and seabird rookery. They are located approximately 1 hour, 30 minutes from the coast and are protected by the Fertilizer Division of PescaPerú. Excursions here can be organized from the Paracas bay hotels or from the El Chaco beach; they take approximately 4 to 5 hours (round trip). Warm clothing and sunblock are recommended; overnight stays not allowed.

Atenas

)

One of the reserve's most easily accessible beaches (10 minutes from the entrance booth); shallow, with a stony, muddy seafloor. Its calm waters and constant winds make it an ideal place for sports like water-skiing and wind-surfing. It has a small restaurant (El Griego). During the summer there are more restaurants and guarded parking. The beach can be reached via the paved road from the Paracas bay resort to the northern sector of the peninsula, known as Punta Pejerrey (Puerto San Martín).

SEA LIONS

Two important sea mammals that inhabit the Peruvian coast can be seen at Paracas: sea lions (*Otaria byronia*) and seals (*Arctocephalus australis*). Their territory extends from Bayóvar in the department of Piura to southern Chile. They do not compete for habitat. While sea lions lie out in the sun on sandy or pebbled beaches, seals prefer rocky spurs and less accessible shores. Both reproduce during the summer months (December to March), when they gather by the thousands on islands and rocky points of the coast.

El Candelabro

)

An enigmatic, candelabra-shaped etching in the sand on a hill at the far N end of the Paracas peninsula, facing the ocean. Some believe it is related to the Nasca lines, but that is unlikely as it has been proven to be more recent. Some believe it was a signal used by pirates. It is usually seen from the ocean (on the way to the Islas Ballestas), although it is also possible to see it from land by following the packed dirt road that goes NW from the Atenas beach. It is absolutely forbidden to ap-

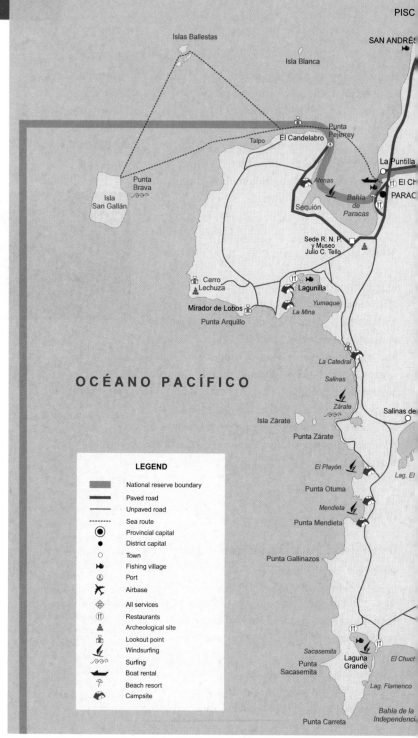

PARACAS NATIONAL RESERVE

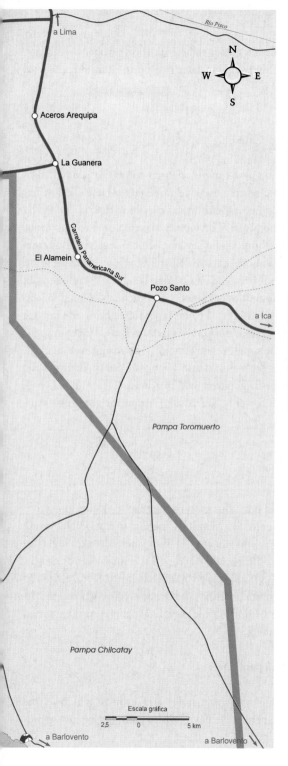

Río Pisco

a Lima

N
W   E
S

Aceros Arequipa

La Guanera

Carretera Panamericana Sur

El Alamein

Pozo Santo

a Ica

Pampa Toromuerto

Pampa Chilcatay

Escala gráfica
2,5   0   5 km

a Barlovento

a Barlovento

Blackish Oystercatchers
(*Haematopus ater*).

Sandcrab
(*Ocypode gaudichaudii*).

El Candelabro.

La Catedral.

proach closer than 20m (66ft) from the carving. The excursion lasts one hour, 30minutes, round trip.

La Catedral

This is a unique, natural formation carved from the seacliff by wind and waves. Here erosion has formed an enormous cupola with a tower facing the ocean. The outer walls are home to numerous seabirds (peruvian boobies, red-legged cormorants and inca terns), and the interior is accessible on foot from the La Catedral beach (a 15-minute walk along the shoreline). This beach, abounding in kelp and algae, is the best place for sighting the rare sea otters or *chingungo* (*Lutra felina*). Watch out for the small stinging rayfish. The road is well marked, there is parking for vehicles and a lookout point. To reach the area, take the partially paved road that heads S from the reserve's entrance booth towards Salinas de Otuma for about 30 minutes.

Mendieta

One of the most beautiful parts of the reserve, 45 minutes from the entrance booth. At Mendieta there is sandy beach, strong wind and waves and an area of hills and salt flats ideal for camping. Good fishing and diving off the small islands nearby. Access via the partially paved road that heads S from the entrance booth towards Salinas de Otuma; you will pass the La Catedral beach turnoff on the way. Don't forget to take a coat, water and sunblock.

Bahía de la Independencia

Anyone wanting to escape noise and crowds will find the beaches of Independencia bay ideal for camping or just spending a beautiful day on the beach. To reach the bay, take the partially paved road that heads S from the entrance booth for 2 hours, 30 minutes, passing through Mendieta and Salinas de Otuma. One of the best places is Cruz de Carhuas, wich has wide sandy beaches, good swimming, fishing and diving, and areas sheltered from the wind. Although a four-wheel drive vehicle is not strictly necessary, a vehicle with good ground clearance would be advisable. Avoid driving this route at night as there are numerous tracks which can confuse even the most experienced traveler.

Playón.

San Gallán Island

)

5km off the Paracas peninsula, this island has a large sea lion and seabird rookery. It also has an area of intense wave action, ideal for surfing. Access the island by hiring a boat from the port of El Chaco in the Paracas bay. The trip should take about an hour. Camping on the island is not recommend due to the strong afternoon winds. Remember to take water and sunblock along, and avoid disturbing the wildlife.

Sequión.

Day's end on the penninsula.

Barlovento

○

An area of beautiful, although somewhat windy beaches at the far S end of the reserve, much frequented by surf fishermen for the abundance of delicious species such as sole or sea bass. Antana, El Negro, Gallinazo and Boca del Río are just a few of the beaches in this area. Access the area by following tracks which lead S from Laguna Grande 3

hours). This is only for experienced off-road drivers. We also suggest taking sufficient water, clothing and supplies.

 ## Hotels

Pisco

★★★ Embassy Suites
Av. San Martín 202. Tel 53 5215 / 53 2040. US$ 30.

★★★ El Candelabro
Corner Callao and Piedemonte. Tel 53 2620. US$ 25.

★★ Hostal Pisco
San Francisco 115. Tel 53 2018. Fax 53 6669. US$ 20.
hostalpisco@latinmail.com

★★ Hotel Las Palmeras
Las Américas 816. Tel 53 5122.

★★ Hotel Regidor
Calle Arequipa 201. Tel 53 5220. Fax 53 5219.
regidor@terra.com.pe

Paracas

★★★★ Hotel Paracas
Rivera del Mar s/n. Tel 22 1736.
Reservations Lima Tel 446 5079. US$ 75.

★★★ Hostería Paracas
Av. Paracas 169 (next to the Hotel Paracas).
Reservations Lima Tel 447 4400. US$ 35.

★★ Hotel Paracas Reserva Natural
Av. Paracas 172. Tel 54 5100.
Reservations Lima Tel 445 9376. US$ 30.
hparacas@terra.com

★★ Hostal El Mirador
At the turnoff towards the Paracas resort bay.
Tel 22 0212. Reservations Lima Tel 423 8618. US$ 20.

RATES ARE APPROXIMATE AND, UNLESS OTHERWISE NOTED,
ARE FOR DOUBLE OCCUPANCY.

Restaurants

Pisco

As de Oro   ✔
  Av. San Martín 472.

Restaurant del Embassy Beach   ✔
  Av. San Martín 1119.

Restaurant Turístico Las Palmeras   ✔
  Las Palmeras 810.

Restaurant del Hotel Embassy Suite   ✔

Paracas

Restaurant del Hotel Paracas   ✔
  Rivera del Mar s/n.

El Chorito   ✔
  Nearby the entry to Paracas.

Otros

  The port of El Chaco has several small, inexpensive
  seafood restaurants. You will also find some in
  San Andrés, a fishing village halfway between Pisco
  and the Paracas bay resort.

Piura

P. 82

P. 78

ROUTE MAPS
① ②

The city of Piura, capital of the department of the same name, is located in the Chira River valley at the far north end of the Sechura desert, the largest desert in Peru. Mention of this region calls to mind carob trees and fertile fields, generous coastal waters with beautiful fishing villages, *tondero* music, elegant horses, and a people as warm as their region.

The region was originally ruled by two great cultures known for their skill in metalworking and ceramics: the Vicús and the Mochica. Around the seventh century AD it came under the

Rice fields in the Sullana Valley.

control of the Lambayeque, or Sicán culture, and later was governed by the Chimú (from the tenth to fifteenth centuries AD). One Chimú ethnic group, the Tallán, built important urban and ceremonial centers in the area. Forty years before the arrival of the Spaniards, the Tallán were conquered by the Inca Túpac Yupanqui and the region became part of the Inca Empire, or Tawantinsuyo.

> *A subtropical climate, sunny and warm year round, with little rain during the summer but significantly more with the El Niño phenomenon. Yearly mean temperature of 24°C (75°F).*

Piura was the first city the conquistadors founded in Peru. Its creation dates from the year 1532, when Francisco Pizarro bestowed the name of San Miguel on a small native town on the ancient site of Tangarará. Later the town was moved to a site «25 leagues from the sea», but because of poor soil conditions this site was abandoned and the town was again moved, first to the coast (to a spot that is now the port of Paita) and then inland in 1588 to the city's present site, known as Tacalá.

Dry woods vegetation, Amotape.

Sechura Desert.

Piura is the birthplace of Admiral Miguel Grau, Peru's most important naval hero in the War of the Pacific (1879–1883). It is a vigorous city that blends the traditional and the modern with very good results. Various Colonial buildings and locales share the city center with newer, well-appointed hotels. Agriculture plays a predominant role in the region, and cotton (second in the nation), rice and fruit (such as mango and lemons) are the most important crops.

Local Dishes
Entrées
- Majado de yuca: cooked, puréed yucca root spiced with *ají* pepper.

- Tamalito verde: shortened corn dough spiced with cilantro and wrapped in corn leaves.

Soups
- Caldo de siete carnes: broth of various meats and trimmings.

Main Dishes
- Copús: roast goat kid and banana.
- Seco de cabrito: stew of goat kid with cilantro, *chicha de jora* and squash.
- Seco de chabelo: stew of jerky and mashed banana.

Drinks
- Chicha de jora: a beer-like drink based on corn, fermented in earthen jugs.

Festivals

One of the most important festivals celebrated in Piura and its surroundings, is the Feast of the Captive Lord of Ayabaca (October 4 to 13), an image of Christ that draws thousands of pilgrims from northern Peru and Ecuador, some carrying crosses or walking on their knees. Other important festivals are: the Feast of the Señor de Chocán and the day of the Magi, in Sullana (January 1 through 12); the regional *marinera* dance contest (third week of January); Holy Week especially as celebrated in Catacaos (March or April); Tourism Week, in Piura (September 3 through 11); the Feast of Nuestra Señora de las Mercedes in Paita (September 22-26); the Peru-Ecuador Border Integration festival (September, exact date varies), and the *tondero* dance festival (October, exact date varies), an excellent opportunity to enjoy this typical dance of Piura, considered a vigorous variant of the north Peruvian *marinera*.

Folkcrafts

Some of Piura's best handicrafts are made in the town of Ca-

THE BLESSED CAROB

The *algarrobo* or carob tree (*Prosopis pallida*) is one of the most representative trees of the dry northern forests of Peru and one of the most common in the department of Piura. This blessing of nature germinates and grows in incredibly dry areas by utilizing any chance year of rain. When its roots reach the water table, it needs no further irrigation. Its leaves are excellent forage for livestock. Its fruit, which grows in pods, hangs by the thousands from every branch and contains a large amount of proteins, sugars, minerals, fiber and vitamin B complex. The fruit is boiled down to produce a syrup called *algarrobina*, an excellent food supplement and fortifier.

tacaos, known for its fine workmanship: filigree in gold and silver, and diverse objects carved from *zapote* wood. S of Piura 5km is the town of Simbilá, the leading pottery center of the department, where famous jars called *tinajas* are made to hold the *chicha* (corn beer) of Piura. Chulucanas is another town famous for its potters. Other highlights are the weavings and brooms of the artisans at Viviate.

Points of Interest in the City

Churches

- *The Cathedral*, Plaza de Armas: the construction of this building dates from 1588. Remodeled several times, today its mix

PIURA CITY MAP

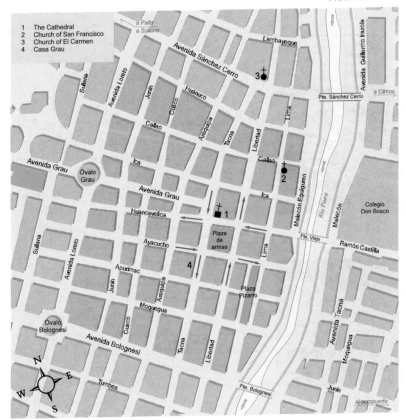

1 The Cathedral
2 Church of San Francisco
3 Church of El Carmen
4 Casa Grau

of styles gives it a rather eclectic character. It has lovely Baroque holy scenes and various works by the famous Piura painter Ignacio Merino (1817–1876).

- *Others:* San Francisco (the oldest church in Piura) and El Carmen.

Historical Homes and Buildings

Old Piura manor house.

- *Casa Eguiguren*, Lima 749: one of the oldest houses in Piura. With large, wrought iron gates and stately patios, this is a good example of the past opulence of the mansions of northern Peru.
- *Casa Grau*, Tacna 662: birthplace of Admiral Miguel Grau, July 17 in 1834. It has lovely salons and valuable objects that belonged to this eminent citizen.

  Visiting hours: Mon-Fri, 10am to 3pm.

Excursions

Colán

Colán beach resort.

The Cross of Colán.

A fishing village 65km (50 minutes) W of Piura, accessed by a branch off the paved highway to Paita. Colán is a favorite beach resort of the residents of Piura and Sullana. Homes stand on pilings all the way down the long beach, the modern ones interspersed with older ones that have survived the various El Niño storms, and many palm trees. It is said that the prettiest sunsets in the region can be seen from the balconies of these homes. If you go in the water, keep an eye out for the small rayfish. You can avoid them by dragging your feet as you enter the water. Close to Colán is the town of La Esmeralda, home to the church of San Lucas, built by the Dominican order in 1536 and by tradition the oldest in Peru. Colán has several hostels and restaurants specializing in such dishes as *cebiche*, *sudado*, and *tamalitos verdes*. Don't miss the traditional Macaria.

Catacaos
47M / 154FT)

9km (15 minutes) SW of Piura via paved road. With its old cane houses and river bank lined with *pájaro bobo* trees, this town, known as the «Indian heart of Piura,» remains the most traditional of the department. This is the land of *chicha* made in giant clay jugs and of the famous *toquilla* straw hats that were in great demand in the nineteenth century and were marketed around the world as Panama hats. This is also where artisans work gold and silver filigree and make carvings in *zapote* wood. There are many *chicherías* where you can taste typical dishes, *claritos* (young wines) and *entreverados* (mixed drinks) in the purest northern style.

Chulucanas
192M / 630FT)

60km (45 minutes) E of Piura via the old North Panamericana highway. A warm and lively city, Chulucanas is known as the «guitar of Piura.» A land of golden lemons, leafy mango trees, and the best *chicherías* of the north, it is also well-known for its works in clay that brought fame to local potter Gerásimo Sosa.

Paita
)

A fishing and industrial port 55km (1 hour) W of Piura. Nicknamed «port of the viceroys and temptation of pirates,» it was one of the most important ports of the Viceroyalty of Peru. Manuelita Sáenz, Simón Bolívar's mistress, died here in 1856. This «city of the loveliest moon» has lost much of its ancient splendor to the realities of the modern-day fishing industry. For lunch in Paita, we recommend the Club Liberal (at Jorge Chávez 161), with excellent fish and other seafood. S of Paita 5km is Yasila, a beautiful, sandy beach with lovely homes and, farther south, the popular beach of Cangrejos, with restaurants, bungalows,

The port of Paita.

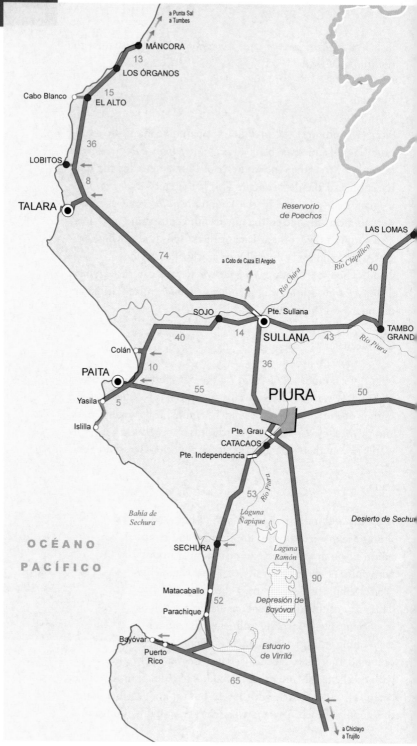

PIURA EXCURSION MAP

N

ECUADOR

a Macará

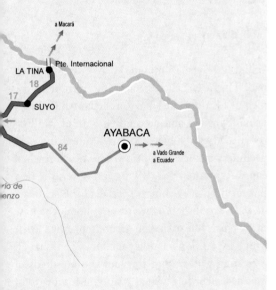

Pte. Internacional

LA TINA

18

17

SUYO

AYABACA

84

a Vado Grande
a Ecuador

río de
enzo

JLUCANAS

0

7 MORROPÓN

HUANCABAMBA

66

69

a Olmos

CANCHAQUE

Wagon, Chulucanas.

Weaver in Puerto Eten.

MARLIN

It was at Cabo Blanco that the US fisherman Alfred Glossell Jr. caught the world's largest marlin, weighing in at 702kg. The marlin is a close relative of the swordfish. It lives in the warm, open waters of northern Peru and southern Ecuador. Because of its large size, its speed and, above all, the ferocity with which it fights when it feels threatened, sport fishermen considered it their greatest trophy. They fish for it on the open sea using light, fast boats and artificial lures.

and one of the loveliest sunsets on the northern coast.

Cabo Blanco

153km (2 hours, 15 minutes) N of Piura via paved road. This area is accessed via the turnoff to the town of El Alto (km 1 137 on the North Panamericana highway) and descending 8km of winding paved road through rusted pipes and abandoned machinery to the beach below. This beach reached its greatest fame in the 1950s and 60s as the best spot for deep-sea fishing, especially for black marlin and swordfish. The welcoming hotel (the base from which the rich and famous planned their fishing expeditions) is still functioning and has an interesting gallery with trophies and hundreds of photos. Celebrities such as Marilyn Monroe, John Wayne, Nelson Rockefeller, and Ernest Hemingway have passed through. Cabo Blanco is said to have inspired Hemingway to write *The Old Man and the Sea*.

When there are big swells, Cabo Blanco beach is an ideal spot for surfing (the north side, or «Panic Point»), but is a little used during the rest of the year because of strong winds. The small beach of El Restín to the S is usually a better choice for beginning surfers.

Fishing for tuna in Cabo Blanco.

Los Órganos

171km (2 hours, 30 minutes) N of Piura at km 1 152 of the North Panamericana highway (30 minutes from Máncora). This was one of the favorite beach resorts among the people of Piura until the arrival of the 1983 El Niño storms, which damaged the homes built by North American oilmen and the seaside promenade. The sunny, warm beaches and the coconut palms still survive, however. S 6km is the lovely beach of El Ñuro, a favorite break for surfers, and next to it is the fishing village of Puerto Rico. Between the two is Cerro Encantado, a hill said to be haunted by ghosts. Its odd shape like an old church organ gave the town of Los Órganos its name.

Sechura Bay

Approximately 55km (1 hour, 30 minutes) SW of Piura via paved highway lies the largest bay in Peru. It contains a string of beautiful, warm-water beaches. The most frequented are in a 25km stretch between Bocana de San Pedro (with the southern-most mangroves of the American Pacific coast) and the Virrilá estuary. Access is from the Bajo Piura highway. Strong winds blow in the afternoon. The town of Sechura has an imposing Colonial church, San Martín de Sechura, with notable murals from the eighteenth century.

Sechura Bay.

Bayóvar

Beautiful northern coastline 105km (2 hours) SW of Piura via paved highway. The zone of Bayó-var, known as the area between the Virrilá estuary, Punta Tric-Trac, Punta Aguja, and Punta Bapo, is famous among underwater fishermen for its clear water and abundant marine life. On the south side of Cerro Illescas starts a long string of big-wave beaches, ideal for surfing (Reventazón and Punta Nonura or Shode). The dunes and enormous gran-ite boulders along its shores give this landscape a very special beauty.

Pelicans (*Pelecanus thagus*) at Bayovar Sea.

Facing these beaches is the island of Lobos de Tierra, a sea-bird paradise and ideal for fishing. Access to Bayóvar is re-stricted; to maintain one of the last virgin beaches of Peru, you must obtain permission to enter (a simple transaction with the PetroPerú authorities in Piura). Travel along this coastal region

Nonura Bay, Bayóvar.

requires an all-terrain, four-wheel-drive vehicle, and knowing how to drive it.

Ayabaca

2 709M / 8 888FT

213km (3 hours, 30 minutes) NE of Piura via a partially paved road from Sullana, difficult at times but worthwhile for the

Ceiba tree.

beautiful scenery. The birthplace of Piura natives known for their courage and fighting spirit, it is called the «fierce land of Piura.» Here is one of the most important meccas in Peru: the sanctuary of the Captive Lord of Ayabaca. Typical of the Ayabaca dry forest countryside are the aged ceiba tree (*Bombax sp.*) and *porotillo* (*Erythrina sp.*) trees. The town has some simple restaurants and lodgings. The ruins of Aypate are nearby.

Huancabamba

I 957M / 6 24IFT

214km (5 hours) E of Piura. A picturesque town in the mountains of Piura, surrounded by waterfalls and lush vegetation. It is accessed by traveling up through the spurs of the western cordillera on a road that passes through the town of Canchaque and over the Cruz Blanca pass (3 090m, or 10 138ft). It has the narrow, steep streets typical of an Andean town, and a hostel and restaurant with very moderate prices.

Las Huaringas
4 000M / 13 124FT

A series of lakes approximately 300km (a day and a half) from Piura. Located in the Huamaní cordillera, almost a full day's walk from Huancabamba (past the town of Salalá), this is considered the main center for shamanistic healing in northern Peru. The Inca is said to have traveled here when seeking a cure for his ailments. Here are a succession of 20 small lakes that are the source of the Quiroz (or Huancabamba) River. The largest, known as Laguna Blanca (or Shimbe) is the most famous for its curative powers. Others are the Negra, Amarilla, Roja, Los Patos, and Siete Pozos. Las Huaringas are still a popular destination for the thousands of pilgrims seeking a cure for diverse ailments. The lakes can visited by contacting the «mystical guides» who abound in Huancabamba and its surroundings.

Arqueological Sites

One of the best is Cerro Vicús, a necropolis that has yielded many ceramic, gold, and silver artifacts from the Vicús culture. It is located on what used to be the Huápalas (or Morropón) hacienda, some 35km SE of Piura. Other sites are: Narihualá (4km SW of Catacaos), with an imposing structure believed to be a fortress and place of worship of the Tallán culture; Chulucanitas; Chusis, and Santa Rosa de Frías.

Hotels

Piura
Hotel Río Verde   ★★★★
  Av. Ramón Mujica s/n, Urb. San Eduardo. Tel 32 8486.
  Reservations Lima Tel 442 5961. US$ 90.
Hotel Los Portales *(ex Hotel de Turistas)*   ★★★
  Libertad 875, plaza de armas. Tel 32 2952.
  Reservations Lima Tel 211 9000. US$ 80.

★★★ Hostal El Angolo
  F. Chirichigno 661, El Chipe. Tel 32 6461.
  Reservations Lima Tel 224 2431. US$ 65.

★★★ Costa del Sol
  Av. Lorreto 649. Telefax 30 2864. US$ 35.

★★★ Hostal Latino
  Huancavelica 720. Telefax 33 5123. US$ 35.

★★★ Hostal Américas
  Óvalo Bolognesi s/n. Tel 32 2006. US$ 35.

  ★★ Hotel Tangarará
  Corner Ica and Arequipa. Tel 32 6479. US$ 30.

  Hotel San Miguel Apurímac
  Plaza Las Tres Culturas. Tel 30 5192. US$ 20.

Colán

Bocatoma Resort
  Av. Costanera Norte s/n. Colán Piura.
  Tel 97 0100. Fax 61 1553.

  ★★ El Sol de Colán
  Malecón de Colán s/n. Reservations Piura Delta Reps.
  Tel 32 1784. US$ 20.

  ★★ Hotel Playa Colán
  Playa Sur (Las Palmeras). Tel 64 1449. US$ 35.

Cabo Blanco

★★★ Hotel Cabo Blanco Fishing Club
  Lobitos-El Alto road km 40. US$ 40.

  ★★ Hotel Merlín
  Caleta Cabo Blanco. Tel 85 6188. US$ 30.

Los Órganos

★★★ Hotel Nautillus
  Panamericana Norte km 1154. Tel 24 3162. US$ 45.

  Las Pirámides Surf Point
  Punta Los Órganos km 1153. Tel 61 8397.

RATES ARE APPROXIMATE AND, UNLESS OTHERWISE NOTED,
ARE FOR DOUBLE OCCUPANCY.

Restaurants

Piura

La Granja ✔
  Av. Guardia Civil 1001.
El Puente Viejo ✔
  Huancavelica 167.
Puente Nuevo ✔
  Av. Panamericana D-17.
La Isla ✔
  Av. Marcavelica G-21, Urb. La Alborada.
Los Percebes ✔
  Prolongación Grau 4133.
La Isla II ✔
  Tacna 761.
Romano ✔
  Ayacucho 580.

Useful facts

AREA CODE 74

☎

Basic Information

IPERÚ:
  Information and Assistance for Tourists
  Tel 01-541-8000 Lima.
Instituto Nacional de Cultura:
  Jr. Huancavelica 344.   32 1434
Tourism Police Aid: 30 7650
Post Office: Corner of Libertad and Ayacucho.   32 7031
Piura Tours: Ayacucho 585   32 6778
Hospital IPSS Cayetano Heredia:
  Av. Independencia s/n, Urb. Miraflores   34 2420
Clínica San Miguel: Los Cocos 111   30 9300
Inka Farma: Grau 278.   30 8228
Farmacia Americana: Grau 1147   30 1303
Piura Rent a Car: Av. Arequipa 504.   32 5510
Automóviles & Servicios: Corpac s/n. Stand 4,
  airport.   34 6111

155 M / 508FT
172 300 POP.
802 KM
E OF LIMA

Pucallpa

P. 82

P. 78

ROUTE MAP

10

Located on the left bank of the Ucayali River, in the heart of the Amazon jungle, the city of Pucallpa takes its name from the Quechua words *puca*, meaning red, and *allpa* meaning earth, for the red, clay soil abounding in the region. It was originally the territory of the Cashibos and Shipibos and remained mostly unexplored until the end of the nineteenth century, with only a few missionaries venturing into the area. The first colonists arrived in 1883 and established a small settlement at the present-day site of Pucallpa, officially founding the city in 1888. This is

Merchants on the Ucayali River.

the city's only history. Until the beginning of the twentieth century, Pucallpa was a small outpost of explorers, hunters and rubber traders. Not until the highway was built, connecting it to Huánuco and Lima, did the city experience sustained growth and a drastic and disorganized increase in commerce, although not in other infrastructure such as hotels and restaurants. It became the capital of the newly-formed department of Ucayali in 1980.

A warm and humid, tropical climate, typical of the Amazon jungle, with a yearly mean temperature of 25° C (77° F). Pucallpa has two distinct seasons: a rainy season from December to March and a dry season from May to October. The dry season is best for visiting.

Today, the city of Pucallpa is lively and still somewhat disorganized. It is the second largest city in the Peruvian Amazon. It receives most of its income from basic commerce, hardwoods, beer brewing and river port activities with the city of Iquitos (590km down river).

While the immediate natural environment has been changed considerably by agricultural ventures, it is still possible to enjoy the beautiful scenery of the Amazon basin (lakes, winding rivers and lush forests), especially in the area of Yarinacocha. Most of the population is engaged in fishing and farming (especially rice, yucca and bananas). In recent years, the exploitation of petroleum and natural gas at nearby Aguaytía have brought new growth to the region.

Natural gas extraction in Aguaytía.

Main Square.

Local Dishes

Entrées
• Juane: a mix of rice and meat wrapped in *bijao* leaves and steamed.Platos de fondo

SHAMANISM

In Peru there are areas where *curanderismo*, or shamanism, is still very active. One of these is Pucallpa, where masters consume *ayahuasca* (*Banisteropsis caapi*), a hallucinogenic vine that is also known as «the vine of the dead,» to establish contact with the supernatural world. Although there are many charlatans, some shamans have wide knowledge of medicinal plants and produce surprising healings. Some masters use *ayahuasca* to help patients with psychological problems or those who want a mystical experience.

Main Dishes

- Majás al horno: oven-baked *majás*, a large, Amazon rodent.
- Picadillo de paiche: a preparation of *paiche* fish with onion, tomato and *ají* pepper.
- Tortuga guisada: turtle stew, with peas, yucca flour and vegetables.

Drinks

- Guarapo: fermented cane liquor.

Festivals

The most important festival in Pucallpa is San Juan on June 24, celebrated throughout the region. On this occasion, crowds of pilgrims visit the nearby rivers and lakes for the ritual bath to commemorate St. John the Baptist. According to popular belief, he came down to the jungle near here, bringing with him a mix of rice and jungle fowl, wrapped in *bijao* leaves, thus initiating the *juane*.

Other festivals celebrated in Pucallpa and its environs are: Carnival (February 15 to 25); Tourist Week (July 23 to 31); the Regional Fair (September, exact date varies); Pucallpa's anniversary (October 9 to 13); the anniversary of Yarinacocha (October 10 to 16); and the Feast of Feasts in Pucallpa (November 19 to 23).

Shipibo native.

Folkcrafts

Some of the region's best handicrafts are made by the Shipibo people of the indigenous community of San Francisco on Lake Yarinacocha. Their textiles with geometric motifs are quite popular, as are their hand-painted ceramics. Other typical handicrafts are baskets and rugs woven with plant fibers such as *chonta* and *huicungo*, and decorations made with carved wood, seeds, *paiche* fish scales, bird feathers, bones and teeth of wild animals.

Points of Interest in the City

Museums

- *Museo Regional*, Jr. Inmaculada n/n, block 9: contains an interesting display of paleontological artifacts, Shipibo-Conibo ceramics over 200 years old, paintings by the Pucallpa artist Agustín Rivas and sculptures by Felipe Lettersten.
- *Casa de Agustín Rivas:* the workshop of the famous sculptor who creates Amazon-inspired works from roots and wood.
- *Casa de Pablo Amaringo:* the workshop of the shaman and artist known for his paintings depicting his visions seen under the influence of *ayahuasca*, a natural hallucinogen traditionally used by the indigenous people of the Amazon. Amaringo is the founder of the Usko Ayar art school.

Excursions

Lake Yarinacocha

200M / 656FT

7km NE of Pucallpa. Access is via paved road (10 minutes) or by river, through the Pao Caño channel. Considered the main attraction of the region, this lake has a small port (Puerto Callao), which is a good base from which to make excursions on the lake and visit the settlements on its shores. The lake is 18km long and covers an area of 1 340 hectares, making it one of the largest lakes in the Amazon. The good number of Shipibo settlements dotting its shores are well-frequented by tourists and offer handicrafts of great beauty and fine workmanship (especially in the communities of Santa Rosa and San Francisco). The Summer Institute of Linguistics also

Squirrel monkey (*Saimiri sciureus*).

has its center on the lake shore, from which it carries out missionary work and has contributed significantly to conserving the native Amazon languages since the 1940s. The islands and beaches of this lake are well-frequented in summer for fishing and water sports. (We recommend a visit to the Isla del Amor, a 15-minutes

Lake Yarinacocha.

boat ride.) There are restaurants, hostels and boat rentals, where you can hire a *peque-peque* boat. Nearby are the Botanical Gardens of Chullachaqui, with over 3 000 varieties of native ornamental and medicinal plants, and the Shipibo community at Santa Clara, considered the best organized in the region.

Cashibococha Lake

Late afternoon on the Ucayali.

200M / 656FT)

This lake, about 45 minutes from Pucallpa by river, to the west of Lake Yarinacocha, to which it is connected by a small channel. Its 10km length is best seen by *peque-peque* boat.

Although some Cocama and Shipibo families used to live on its shores, most of its population is now *mestizo*, a mix of indigenous and non-indigenous races.

 Hotels

Pucallpa

★★★ Hotel Sol del Oriente *(ex Hotel de Turistas)*
San Martín 502. Tel 57 5154. US$ 55.
★★★ Gran Hotel Mercedes
Raimondi 610. Tel 57 1191. US$ 45.

Ruiz Hotel   ★★★
   San Martín 475. Tel 57 1280. US$ 45.
Hostal Arequipa   ★★★
   Progreso 573. Tel 57 1348.
Hostal El Gran Dorado   ★★★
   Jr. Independencia 205. Tel 57 3330.
Albergue Turístico Divina Montaña   ★★
   Carretera Federico Basadre km 11,3.
   Tel 57 4030. US$ 45.
Cusco   ★★
   Antonio Raimondi 671. Tel 57 1120. US$ 15.
   divina-montaña@terra.com.pe

Yarinacocha
La Cabaña   ★★
   On the shores of the lake, 10 minutes from Puerto Callao.
   Tel 57 1120. US$ 45.
Pandisho Club   ★★
   On the shores of the lake, 15 minutes from Puerto Callao.
   Tel 57 5041. US$ 35.
Hospedaje Los Delfines
   Corner of Aguaytía and Circunvalación.
   Tel 59 6424. Fax 59 6761.

RATES ARE APPROXIMATE AND, UNLESS OTHERWISE NOTED,
ARE FOR DOUBLE OCCUPANCY.

Restaurants

El Golf   ✔
   Huáscar 545.
El Establo   ✔
   Carretera Federico Basadre km 3,7.
Los Rosales   ✔
   Mariscal Castilla 389.
Restaurante del Hotel Sol del Oriente   ✔
   San Martín 502.
Restaurante del Hotel América   ✔
   Coronel Portillo 357.

Useful Facts

Basic Information

IPERÚ:
Information and Assistance for Tourists
Tel 01-541-8000 Lima.

Instituto Nacional de Cultura:
Av. San Martín 644.   57 5110
Ecology and Tourism Police Aid: 59 1975
Post Office: Av. San Martín 418.   57 1382
Hospital regional de Pucallpa: 9 de Octubre s/n   57 1870
Clínica Santa Rosa: Inmaculada 529   57 5218
Botica San Borja: Ucayali 596   57 1666
Farmacia Los Ángeles: Raimondi 514   57 6065

Fuerza Aérea del Perú: Av. Yarina s/n.   59 6787
Transportes Aéreos S.A.: Progreso 547   57 5221

TRAVELING FROM PUCALLPA TO IQUITOS

In Pucallpa's river port of La Hoyada (2,5km from the city) you can board a boat to travel down the Ucayali River to Iquitos. The trip lasts three to six days and can be organized through one of the many local companies offering this type of service. All have their office in the port. Before departure, it is best to go to the harbormaster's office (Capitanía permiso de zarpe. Durante el recorrido, la embarcación se detiene en Contamana y Requena, que cuentan con alojamientos y restaurantes rústicos. Si bien estas embarcaciones llegan hasta Iquitos, en Requena se puede contratar otra embarcación más veloz, aunque algo más cara, para completar el recorrido.

Puerto Maldonado

183 M / 600FT
31 200 POP.
1 619 KM
SE OF LIMA

P. 82

P. 78

ROUTE MAP
11

The city of Puerto Maldonado, capital of the department of Madre de Dios, is located at the confluence of the Tambopata and Madre de Dios (or Amarumayo) rivers. This part of the Amazon jungle is home to more plant and animal species than any other zone in the tropics. This is why Puerto Maldonado is known as the «biological capital of the world» and is considered one of the largest gene reserves on the planet.

During Colonial times, the area remained unknown, save for a few explorations. Only recently, in 1861, did explorer Faustino

Tambopata River.

Maldonado travel down the Madre de Dios River to its junction with the Madeira River in Brazil, where he died when his craft capsized. In his honor, his companion, the famous rubber baron Carlos Fermín Fitzcarrald, carved Maldonado's name on the trunk of a large tree, precisely on the present site of the city of Puerto Maldonado. In 1902, the installation of a military

A tropical climate, warm and quite humid, with a rainy season from December to March and a yearly mean temperature of 26° C (79° F). From May to June there are cold spells lasting three to five days, when masses of cold air move up from the south, dropping temperatures down to 8° C (46° F) to 10° C (50° F). The months of May through October are best for a visit.

Main Square.

Ese'eja native.

garrison ensured the name would be perpetuated and Puerto Maldonado became a stopover for rubber traders. In 1963, Lima poet Javier Heraud died near the city and was buried here.

Maldonado, as its inhabitants call it, is a small, but growing city. Its expansion has accelerated with the arrival of immigrants from the highland departments of Cusco and Puno. The region's economic activity centers on basic commerce, hardwoods, extracting gold from the rivers (wich supply 20% of Peru's gold production), and harvesting the only forests of Brazil nut trees (*Bertholletia excelsa*) in Peru, a resource that provides the region with a large part of its income.

Although the city itself may have little of interest to tourists, it is the port of entry to some of the most beautiful forests in the country, particularly those in the Tambopata–Candamo Reserve and the Bahuaja–Sonene National Park. From Puerto Maldonado, a packed dirt road leads to Iñapari on the border with Brazil.

Soups
- Timbuche: a soup of fish, banana and *sachaculantro*, a native variety of cilantro.

Main Dishes
- Patarashca: fish wrapped in banana leaves and grilled over coals.
- Picuro asado: grilled *picuro*, a tasty Amazon rodent.

Folkcrafts

It is possible to find handicrafts typical of the Peruvian Amazon, such as bows and arrows, feather decorations and mobiles made with the beautiful scales of the huge *paiche* fish. However, these handicrafts are generally not made in Puerto Maldonado, but are brought from larger cities such as Iquitos or simply copied from the artisan's originals. We do not recommend purchasing handicrafts in this city because it can encourage illegal hunting of macaws and other birds with lovely plumage

Excursions

Tambopata–Candamo Reserved Area
• Bahuaja–Sonene National Park

200M / 656FT ON AVERAGE

This reserve was established in 1990, to protect some 1,8 million hectares in the departments of Puno and Madre de Dios. The area is accessed by traveling S, down the Tambopata River from Puerto Maldonado for about 4 hours. It is home to an extraordinary diversity of flora and fauna and, along with the Manu Reserve, it is one of the richest natural areas on Earth. Along the way, about 3 hours from Puerto Maldonado, is the native community of Infierno, home of the Ese'eja people, ancestral inhabitants of this territory. There are extensive Brazil nut forests in the area, lakes of great beauty and several hostels. Deep in the reserve, some 8

Las Piedras River.

CLAY LICKS

In Quechua, *collpa* means 'salty earth.' It is also the name that natives use for certain parts of the tropical forest —generally cliffs of clay and mud— that many animals, mammals as well as birds, use to supplement their diet with vital salts and minerals. Each morning, the *collpas* in the department of Madre de Dios host a gathering of hundreds of colorful parrots and macaws in one of the most beautiful natural spectacles on Earth.

Tree frog
(*Hyla geographica*).

hours upriver, is the famous *collpa*, or clay lick, of macaws. In June 1996, part of the reserve was named the Bahuaja–Sonene National Park, using the original names of the Tambopata and Heath rivers.

Because the lodges are located in remote areas, the minimum recommended length of a trip to the reserve is three days and two nights. The average cost of a trip varies from US$ 200 to US$ 350, which generally includes river transport, room and board and camping equipment, but not the flight to Puerto Maldonado. There are 10% to 20% discounts for groups of more than six people. The ideal basic equipment for an excursion to this reserve is the same as for Manu *(see p. 355)*.

Pampas de Heath

180M / 590FT ON AVERAGE ◯ ◗

About one and a half days from Puerto Maldonado by river, these pampas are the only savanna ecosystem in Peru, deep in the tropical forest. They are also a refuge for unique forest species such as the tall marsh deer (*Blastocerus dichotomus*) and the elusive maned wolf (*Chrysocyon brachyurus*). The pampas are located on the left bank of the Heath River, which marks the border with Bolivia, and can be accessed by traveling the Madre de Dios River to its confluence with the Heath River (Puerto Maldonado) and up the Heath to the entrance at the Quebrada Juliana control station. This area has recently become part of the Bahuaja–Sonene National Park. The ideal basic equipment for an excursion to this reserve is the same as for Manu *(see p. 355)*.

Sandoval Lake

180M / 590FT

40 minutes E of Puerto Maldonado via the Madre de Dios River, this is one of the most beautiful lakes in the region. It can be reached is by walking a 5km trail lined by lush, tropical vegetation. Surrounded by numerous ponds, the lake is an ecosystem containing the *aguaje* palm (*Mauritia flexuosa*) and protecting several species in danger of extinction, such as the black lizard (*Melanosuchus niger*) and the river otter (*Pteronura brasiliensis*). This is an ideal place for observing the tropical forest and navigating its waters by canoe. There are two tourist lodges on the lake.

Butterfly (*Heliconius sp.*).

Valencia Lake

180M / 590FT

Some 3 hours from Puerto Maldonado by river, towards Bolivia. On this great lake lives a group of immigrants engaged in fishing and harvesting Brazil nuts (*Bertholletia excelsa*). The lake was stocked with the well-known *paiche* fish (*Arapaima gigas*), providing an important food source, and it is ideal for sport fishing. There is no tourist infrastructure; visitors have to camp or rent a room from one of the inhabitants. Mr. Yarikawa is an excellent guide to the area.

Lake Chuncho.

Manu National Park

see p. 351.

Hotels

Cabaña Quinta Hotel   ★★★
Cusco 535. Tel 57 1864.
Fax 57 1890. US$ 25.
cabañaquinta@webcusco.zzn.com

★★★ Don Carlos *(ex Hotel de Turistas)*
León Velarde 1271. Tel 57 1029. Fax 57 1323. US$ 25.
dcarloslim@tci.net.pe

★★★ Wasaí Lodge
Plaza Grau s/n. Tel 57 2290. Fax 57 13255. US$ 20.

> RATES ARE APPROXIMATE AND, UNLESS OTHERWISE NOTED,
> ARE FOR DOUBLE OCCUPANCY.

Jungle Lodges

Lake Sandoval.

- *Cusco Amazónico Pueblo Hotel:* about 45 min by boat on the Madre de Dios River.
  Reservations Lima: Tel 422 6574.
  Reservations Cusco: Tel 24 5313.
  amazonico@inkaterra.com
- *Sandoval Lake Lodge:* located on the shores of beautiful Lake Sandoval, about 30 minutes by river from Puerto Maldonado.
  Reservations Lima: Tel 440 2022.
  Reservations Cusco: Tel 25 5255.
  postmaster@inkanatura.com.pe
- *Explorer's Inn:* 3 hours by boat on the Tambopata River from Puerto Maldonado. This inn is a favorite among birdwatchers.
  Reservas Lima: Tel 447 8888.
  Reservas Cusco: Tel 23 5342.
  safaris@amauta.rcp.net.pe
- *Posada Amazonas:* 3 hours by boat on the Tambopata River from Puerto Maldonado. On the Ese'eja Native Community at Inferno.
  Reservations Lima: Tel 421 8347.
  rainfore@amauta.rcp.net.pe
- *Tambopata Research Center:* 8 hours by boat on the Tambopata River from Puerto Maldonado. In the famous *collpa* de guacamayos.
  Reservations Lima: Tel 421 8347.
  rainfore@amauta.rcp.net.pe
- *Corto Maltés:* about 30 minutes by river from Puerto Maldonado, on the shores of the Madre de Dios River.
  Reservas Puerto Maldonado: Tel 57 3831 / 68 6147.
  cortomaltes@terra.com.pe

Restaurants

El Califa ✔
Piura 266.

Restaurant of the Hotel Cabaña Quinta ✔
Dos de Mayo s/n.

Brombus Café Bar ✔
Nearby the airport.

Cevichería el Tigre ✔
Jr. Tacna 456. Tel 57 2286.

Pizzería El Hornito ✔
D. Alcides Carrión 271, plaza de armas. Tel 57 2082.

El Sitio ✔
Plaza de armas.

Useful Facts

AREA CODE **84**

☎

Handicraft Stores

Shabuya:
Jr. Arequipa 279, plaza de armas. 57 1856

Inotawa:
Av. León Velarde 315. 57 2511

Post Office: León Velarde 675 57 1088
ESSALUD: Cajamarca 341. 57 3529
Hospital Santa Rosa: Cajamarca 171 57 1019
Farmacia Santa Inés: Dos de Mayo 690 57 1524

ENTERING THE RESERVE ZONE

To enter the Tambopata–Candamo Reserve Area, the Bahuaja–Sonene National Park and the Pampas de Heath, you must obtain authorization from the offices of the Dirección Subregional Agraria Madre de Dios (INRENA) at 28 de Julio 482, Puerto Maldonado. Tel 57 1604. To plan your excursion, we recommend hiring the services of one of the tourism companies operating in the area. (They will take care of obtaining the entrance permit.) You also have the choice of hiring the services of a private guide in the city of Puerto Maldonado. (The airport or the port on the Tambopata River are good places for this.)

3 830 M / 12 562 FT
91 900 POP.
1 320 KM
SE OF LIMA

Puno

P. 82   P. 85

P. 78

ROUTE MAP

8

The city of Puno, capital of the department of the same name, is located on the Altiplano, or high plateau, of Collao, a vast tableland lying at an average altitude of 4 000m (13 124ft) above sea level. The terrain is mainly grassland, with *ichu* grass (*Stipa ichu*) predominating. Located at the southern tip of Peru, this plateau stretches N to Cusco and S to Lake Poopó in Bolivia. Peru shares the region with Bolivia, as evidenced by the strong cultural interchange occurring between Puno and its neighboring country. Located on the shores of Lake Titicaca, the highest

En route to Azángaro.

navigable lake in the world, Puno is a city of modest appearance, fitting well into the sparse landscape surrounding it.

The Collao Altiplano is the ancestral territory of the Quechuas, Aimaras, Uros, Pacajes, and Puquinas. It was the cradle of one of the most influential pre-Hispanic cultures in the Andes: Tiawanaco (AD 100-700), which had its capital in present-day

The climate on the Altiplano is typical of the high Andes, dry and extremely cold, with bright sunshine during the day and the temperature sometimes dropping to -10°C (14°F) at night. Within the city the temperature changes are not so drastic. The yearly mean temperature is 6°C (43°F). The region's rainy season is from December to March. Because of the altitude, we recommend resting or taking only short walks on your first day here, as well as drinking frequent cups of **mate de coca** *(coca-leaf tea).*

Bolivia, Tiawanaco (AD 100-700), which had its capital in present-day Bolivia, only a few kilometers from the Peru-Bolivia border. Around the ninth century AD, many independent kingdoms arose on the Altiplano to compete with each other. The most well-known are those of the Colla and Lupaca cultures. Both were successful because they combined agricultural efforts (primarily tubers) with the herding of camelids. The Spanish chroniclers recorded that they were «wealthy Indians.»

Woman of Taraco.

Towards the mid-fifteenth century, the Incas conquered the kingdoms of the Altiplano and named the region the Collasuyo, meaning 'territory of the Collas' in Quechua. The Incas highly valued the Altiplano. It contained many herds of camelids, ensuring an unfailing supply of wool and, according to Inca creation mythology, their own ancestors had emerged from the island of the Sun in the Bolivian portion of Lake Titicaca.

A downtown street.

When the Spanish arrived in Peru, the Altiplano was one of the richest and most populated regions in the Andes and the inhabitants of the area, the Lupacas, were thus designated as belonging directly to the King of Spain and not indentured to a conquistador, as was almost always the case. Until the end of the seventeenth century, Puno was a small town named San Juan Bautista de Puno, a stopover for travelers heading to the silver mines at Potosí (today in Bolivia). It was not until 1668, when rich silver mines were discovered at nearby Laicacota, that Viceroy Conde

Pier in Puno Bay.

de Lemos renamed the city San Carlos de Puno and made it the capital of the province of Paucarcolla. The many churches scattered along the lake shores, with architecture quite similar to the *mestizo* style of Arequipa, reflect the wealth of the region during that period.

Once Peru gained its independence in 1824, the Altiplano began to supply camelid wood to the British market, becoming part of a renowned, wool trade that had its Peruvian headquarters in Arequipa.

Today, Puno continues to be a predominantly agricultural region, in which the farmers still carry out age-old rites venerating the earth. Its main economic activities are cattle, sheep and camelid herding, as well as cultivating potatoes, barley, quinoa and *cañihua*.

The city of Puno is called the Folk Capital of Peru, as it displays the multiple cultural expressions of the people of the Altiplano in such dances as the *diablada* and the *morenada* or *sikuri*, and dances to the music of instruments such as *sikus*, *quenas*, *tarkas*, *charangos*, and *pinkullos*. These are only some of the many attractions for visitors to this small, Andean city with its ancient churches and long tradition.

Buttresses of the Cathedral.

Local Dishes

Soups

- Chairo: a soup of beef or lamb, potatoes, broad beans, squash, cabbage, *chuño* (potato flour), wheat and *chalona* (dried mutton).

- Thimpo: lamb stew cooked with onions, *ají mirasol* (a type of hot pepper) and *chuño* (potato flour).

Main Dishes

- Cancacho al horno: veal or lamb marinated in *ají* pepper and oil, then baked.
- Alpaca meat: prepared in several fashions, and highly valued for its high protein and low fat content.
- Huarjata: pig's head stew with *chuño* and *ají mirasol*.
- Fish: trout, *pejerrey*, *ishpi*, and other local fish, prepared in various fashions.
- Pesque: quinoa stewed with butter, milk and fresh cheese.
- Sajta de pollo: chicken stew with potatoes and peanuts.

The most spectacular of all the festivals celebrated in Puno and its environs (and one of the most important in the southern Andes) is the Feast of the Virgen de la Candelaria or the Candlemas Virgin, patroness of Puno. The main day is February second, but the celebrations begin on the previous Sunday with a presentation of the regional ensembles that will participate in the dance competition. This is unfailingly an impressive display of masks, music and typical costumes of the Altiplano, accompanied by fireworks. The dancers are organized in special groups called *comparsas*, which follow the Virgin in a procession through city streets, along with the crowd of worshippers. On the Sunday following February 2 is the competition of the *trajes de luces*, or costumes of lights, named for the small mirrors sewn into the dancers' outfits. The festival ends with the image of the Virgin returning to the church of San Juan Bautista.

LLAMAS, ALPACAS, VICUÑAS AND GUANACOS

In Peru there are four species of camelids: two domesticated (llama and alpaca), and two wild species (vicuña and guanaco). Ideally conditioned for life at high altitudes, these camelids have developed a number of adaptations that make them some of the best-prepared creatures in the Andes: the finest natural wool in the world, cushioned toes that prevent the compacting and subsequent erosion of the ground they travel on, teeth that continue growing all their lives, and a stomach that can digest a great variety of the plants native to the Andes. Peru has the largest population of alpacas and vicuñas in the world. The department of Puno is home to almost 80% of Peru's camelid population and has the most alpacas.

Feast of La Candelaria.

Taraco market.

Another, quite curious festival celebrated in Puno is the Alacitas handicrafts fair (May 2 to 4), in which miniature replicas of everyday animals and objects are sold (including trucks, houses, livestock, and even university degrees and passports). These are meant to be presented as gifts, in hopes the recipient will get the real thing, and they include the *ekekos*, small figures representing prosperity.

If you are crossing to Bolivia in August, enter through Copacabana, where many are making their pilgrimage to Our Lady of Copacabana on the shores of Lake Titicaca (August, exact date varies).

Other important festivals are the Virgen del Carmen in Pucará (July 16); Santiago Apóstol, celebrated in all the towns of the Altiplano (although the best is on Taquile Island), adorning the livestock with colored ribbons (July 25); Nuestra Señora de la Alta Gracia in Ayaviri (September 12 to 16); and the Fiesta Jubilar in Puno (November 3 to 9).

Folkcrafts

Some of the highlights among Puno handicrafts are the textiles made in alpaca, llama and lamb's wool, ideal for the intense cold of the region. Very beautiful, although quite delicate and difficult to transport, are the masks worn by the Altiplano dancers. You can also acquire musical instruments typical of the region, such as the *siku* and *charango*. Well known for their beauty and quality are the small ceramic bulls of Pucará. The rugs, necklaces and other handicrafts of woven *totora* reed made by the residents of the floating islands of Lake Titicaca have become popular in recent years. So have stuffed waterfowl, unfortunately. We do not recommend purchasing these, as the indiscriminate hunting of these birds endangers the ecosystem of the lake.

Points of Interest in the City

Traditional Locales

- *Lookout:* there are two places from which to enjoy excellent panoramic views of the city and of Lake Titicaca. One is Parque Waqsapata, on the hill of the same name, 10 minutes from the center of town. The other is the Arco Deustua, in the center of town (Independencia n/n).

Churches

- *The Cathedral*, Plaza de Armas: built of stone in 1756, this church has an impressive façade with lovely reliefwork linking it to the *mestizo* style of southern Peru, while the solidity of the building itself links it to the Cusco architecture of the eighteenth century. It has splendid, gilded altars. Be sure to stop and admire the painting called *Cristo de la Bala*.
  Visits during Mass.
- *San Juan Bautista*, next to Parque Pino: this church is home to the image of the Candlemas Virgin and has interesting paintings.
  Visits during Mass.

THE ARCHITECTURE OF THE ALTIPLANO

Some impressive churches survive from the years when the Jesuits first evangelized on the shores of Lake Titicaca. The Colonial architecture of the Altiplano has many similarities to that of Arequipa, from which it inherited a style known as *mestizo*, the highly original current that first mixed American native motifs with Western ones. Given their proximity to Cusco, the churches of the Altiplano exhibit some of its architectural style also.

A traditional crucifix draws worshippers in the Cathedral atrium.

Excursions

Lake Titicaca

3 808M / 12 494FT

)

This is the highest navigable lake in the world, with a surface area of 8 300km², a length of 195km (935ft), an average width of 50km and a maximum depth of 285m. It was formed when an even larger lake gradually dried up, the prehistoric Lake Ballivián, which contained Lake Titicaca, Lake Poopó (in Bolivia) and all the territory between them. Peru and Bolivia share Lake Titicaca. Despite the altitude, the lake temperature remains near 10°C (50°F) to 12°C (54°F), allowing the proliferation of considerable flora and fauna. It is fed by some

View of Lake Titicaca from Pomata.

PUNO EXCURSION MAP

twenty rivers and drained by the Desaguadero
River, which flows into Lake Poopó. Legends tell
of how Manco Cápac and his sister-wife, Mama
Ocllo, emerged from its dark waters to found the
empire of the Incas.

Today, the lake is an important trade route for
the communities on its shores and an area of great
tourist potential. It is also a refuge for the wildlife
of the high Andes, as many species of resident and
migratory birds, several native species of fish (*ca-
rachi* and *suche*), frogs, twelve species of water plants
and other species that are economically important
to the region are protected in the Titicaca National

Women of the Altiplano.

Reserve. Established in 1978, with an area of 36 108 hectares,
this reserve protects all the *totorales* (groves of *totora* reeds) in
the Puno and Huancané bays. The purposes of the reserve include promoting tourism and combining the socio-economic
development of the surrounding communities with a rational use
of the lake's natural resources.

Uros' floating islands

3 808M / 12 494FT)

20 minutes from the city of Puno by boat. These are not truly
floating islands, nor are they inhabited by Uro people. Their

residents are Aimaras who have inherited the customs and way of life of the long-gone Uros. Legend
tells that the members of this ancient community,
who disappeared sometime in the 1950s, had black
blood flowing in their veins and none of them
could drown or feel the cold. Today, the inhabitants of these «islands» have organized themselves
as the Uros-Chulluni Community and, although
they still hunt and fish, they manage tourist-di-
rected activities in their territory. Their livelihood
is based on the benefits of a unique plant: the *totora* reed (*Scyrpus totora*). They use it to build their
homes, boats and even the floating islands they

Small Uro boatman.

live on, periodically adding new layers of reeds. *Totora* reed is a source of food for man and animals, a refuge for their hunting quarry and a vital tool for everyday activity.

In recent years, however, the intense growth of tourism has given highly commercial overtones to a visit to these islands. The people may beg for money or even charge for having their photo taken. We recommend offering fresh fruit instead of money. An excursion to these islands can be organized from Puno for a moderate price (US$ 3 to US$ 5 per person) and takes 2 hours to 3 hours in all.

Taquile Island
3 808M / 12 494FT

Taquile Island.

About 35km (4 hours) from the city of Puno by boat, this island is unique for many reasons. Although it is located in an almost exclusively Aimara region, its inhabitants speak only Quechua. Farmers, fishermen and weavers, they wear distinctive outfits: for men, black pants, a white shirt of homespun cloth and the requisite, colorful, woven sash, or *chumpi*; for women, traditional skirts and long black tunics called *llicllas*. On the island there are no vehicles, roads, police officers or electricity, and, curiously enough, no dogs.

Taquile is 6km to 7km long and has several hills and many archeological ruins. Perhaps the most interesting aspect of the people of Taquile is their solid sense of community. Heirs of the ancient, commune-like system called *ayllu*, the people of Taquile offer room and board to visitors in their own homes, thus ensuring efficiency and security at moderate prices (about US$ 3 per night) and, most of all, an opportunity to share in their customs and way of life. Boats leave Puno for Taquile Island at 8am and 9am, and leave for Puno at 2:30pm. The trip costs US$ 15 per person.

Amantani Island

3 808M / 12 494FT

40km (4 hours, 30 minutes) from Puno and 30 minutes from Taquile Island by boat, this island has lovely landscapes and a community organized like that of its neighbor. It is less visited, making it attractive to those seeking peace and quiet. It has simple lodgins and food.

Sillustani

3 950M / 12 960FT

This archeological site is 34km (30 minutes) from Puno on the paved highway to Juliaca. It contains the famous *chullpas*, round burial towers built of stone, some standing as tall as 12m (39ft). They were used by the Collas and later by the Incas. Lake Umayo, in front of the archeological site, only adds to the beauty of the place, especially at

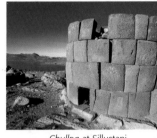

Chullpa at Sillustani.

sunrise. In the vicinity you can also see some *waru-waru*, the artificial hillocks of earth designed for protecting crops from frost and floods. Sillustani is also a good place to observe wild guinea pigs, birds and other wildlife of the high Andes. There is a small site museum.

Juliaca

3 824M / 12 547FT

45km (1 hour) N of Puno via paved highway. With a population of more than 100 000, this is the largest city in the department of Puno and has the region's only commercial airport. It is also an important junction on the railway linking Arequipa, Puno and Cusco. As the commercial emporium of the south Peruvian Andes, it teems with activity, wich accentuates its urban disorder. «While Puno dances, Juliaca advances,» is the motto of its inhabitants, proud of their enterprising character. Its highlights are the churches of Santa Catalina and La Merced, the Franciscan convent and the nearby *chullpas* (pre-

Church of Santa Catalina, Juliaca.

Hispanic burial structures) of Esquén, as well as the lake and hot springs at Chacas. Several packed dirt roads lead out of the city to towns in the high jungle (Sandia and San Juan del Oro) and the Bolivian border at Patascache.

Chimú

3 850M / 12 632FT)

8km (15 minutes) SE of Puno along the paved road bordering the lake southwards towards Juli, Pomata, Zepita and Yunguyo. This spot is known for the boats built of *totora* reed.

Church of San Pedro, Zepita.

You can see the bundles of reeds drying in the sun and the many other steps in the fabrication of these graceful crafts.

Chucuito

3 793M / 12 445FT)

16km (20 minutes) SE of Puno via paved highway, this was an important town during the Colonial era because it was the site of the Royal Treasury. It was this era of splendor that produced the churches of Santa Bárbara (with Renaissance doorways) and Santo Domingo. On the outskirts of town is the Inca

Shrine of Inca Uyo, Chucuito.

Uyo shrine, with several phallus-shaped, stone sculptures, suggesting it was devoted to the cult of fertility. There is a charming hotel here.

Juli

3 870 / 12 694FT

80km (1 hour, 15 minutes) SE of Puno via paved highway. This was one of the region's most important towns during the Colonial era, as it was the point of departure for the Jesuit and Dominican missionaries who evangelized the native Guaraní of Paraguay, and a meeting point for caravans traveling between the Altiplano and the coast with loads of silver. Today, its principal attractions are the four Colonial-era churches: San Pedro in the Plaza de Armas, with a lovely Renaissance façade, and beautiful Baroque altar and paintings by Italian master Bernardo Bitti (sixteenth century) and artists of the Cusco school; San Juan Bautista (a few blocks from the former and today the site of the religious museum), with a sacristy door that is considered a jewel of native craftsmanship, lovely altars, seventeenth-century paintings by Diego de la Puente and artists of the Cusco school; Santa Cruz, with magnificent doors and carved interior structures; and lastly, Nuestra Señora de la Asunción, which, despite being in ruins, still has a beautiful side doorway, a splendid tower and a magnificent stone arch in its atrium.

Every Thursday in Juli, there is a fair that is highly recommended.

Pomata

3 845M / 12 614FT

104km (1 hour, 30 minutes) SE of Puno via the paved highway to Desaguadero. One highlight of this town is the Dominican church of Santiago Apóstol, also known as Nuestra Señora del Rosario, with doorways decorated in native motifs and a carved cupola considered one of the best examples of *mestizo* art.

Pomata.

From Pomata, a detour of 22km takes you to Yunguyo (on the Bolivian border), on the shores of the Tiquina strait.

Continuing S, you will reach Zepita (30km from Pomata) before arriving at the Desaguadero border crossing (40km from Pomata). Zepita has a magnificent stone church (San Pedro).

Lampa

3 842M / 12 602FT)

35km (1 hour) NW of Juliaca via packed dirt road, this town is known as the «Rose-colored City.» One of its highlights is the church of Santiago or La Inmaculada, built of stone in 1683. It contains an exact duplicate of the original Michelangelo's *Pietá* sculpture, one of only two in the world. Near town is the *queñual* tree forest of K'ello K'ello, a chinchilla farm (*Chinchilla laniger*) and the cave paintings at Lensora.

Church of La Inmaculada, Lampa.

Pucará

3 996M / 13 107FT)

107km (1 hour, 45 minutes) N of Puno via the paved highway to Cusco. This is a town of skilled potters, famous for their small ceramic bulls called *toritos de Pucará* and which are reminiscent of Baroque art and intimately linked to the magical and religious beliefs of the countryside. One curious aspect of these handicrafts is that they do not originate in Pucará itself, but rather in the nearby Quechua community of Cheqa-Santiago de Pupuja, in the province of Azángaro. They have taken their name from Pucará because they have always been sold here at this railway station only 15km from Pupuja. One of the most splendid Colonial churches in the region can be found in Pupuja and on the outskirts of Pucará there is an important archeological site of the pre-Columbian Pucará culture (c. 200 BC - AD 300). It consists of six, stepped, stone pyramids, including one particularly pyramid called Kalasaya. Pucará also has a beautiful Colonial-era church, Santa Isabel, and a small archeological museum.

Azángaro

3 859M / 12 658FT ○

130km (3 hours) NW of Puno (via Pucará and Pupuja) on a partially paved road. Here is the famous Templo de Oro, or Church of Gold, considered one of the most beautiful in the southern Andes. It contains a number of important paintings by Isidoro Francisco de Moncada, dating from 1758. Near town there is an area where *puya* Raimondi grow. In the town of Asillo (23km NW), you can visit the church of San Jerónimo, with its splendid Churrigueresque doorway carved with angel and siren motifs (eighteenth century); Lake La Calzada, mineral water springs, the burial *chullpas* at Paucarpata and some interesting pre-Hispanic system of terraces and irrigation works at Catahuicucho. Azángaro has some simple hostels.

The Peru–Bolivia Border
3 800M / 12 464FT

There are two main routes leading overland to Bolivia from Puno, both of them partially paved. The first goes through Yunguyo (2 hours, 30 minutes), turning off at Pomata, and is perhaps the more attractive, as it includes a boat crossing of the Tiquina straits to reach the Bolivian town of Copacabana. The border near Yunguyo is open from 8am to 6pm. Copacabana is a pleasant place to spend the night, with good hotels and restaurants.

The second route, via Desaguadero, can be faster (2 hours) but has a tendency to deteriorate rapidly when it rains. The border at Desaguadero is open from 8am to noon and 2 to 5pm. Busses that go by the ruins at Tiawanaco depart daily from here for La Paz.

It is also possible to cross the border by lake. Some boats with a capacity of 5 or 10 passengers leave from Puno for Copacabana and cost about US$ 100.

Oat harvest.

A passport is required for any border crossing. Some transport companies will help you with the border-crossing formalities and change about US$ 10 for the whole trip. It is easy to obtain Bolivian pesos from moneychangers on the street around the Plaza de Armas in Puno or in Yunguyo. One last note: Bolivian time is one hour ahead and you should take this into account when making travel plans.

Titicaca Island or Isla del Sol (Bolivia)

3 808M / 12 490FT

Some 20km from Copacabana *(see Peru-Bolivia Border, p. 419)* by boat. According to Inca mythology, this was the place of origin of their people and a holy place which they made a sanctuary. The name of the island (which comes from the Aimara words, *titi*, meaning wildcat, and *caca*, meaning stone) can be translated as 'the rock of the puma' or the 'stone puma.' The name clearly alludes to a large stone on the island, which had a strong ritual significance to both the Quechuas and the Aimaras. This stone was especially venerated by the last Inca rulers, as they believed that the Sun and Manco Cápac, founder of their empire, had emerged from this site. The island has many archeological remains of Inca origin.

Tiawanaco (Bolivia)

3 800M / 12 464FT

An archeological complex about 18km from Desaguadero *(see Peru-Bolivia Border, p. 419)*. Built by the Tiawanaco culture (AD 100-700) as their primary urban and ceremonial center, it contains drainage systems, a network of underground canals and streets joining its buildings. One of the most impressive of its monumental constructions of fine stonework is the temple of Akapana, a pyramid about 15 meters (49ft) high, with the remains of a sunken plaza on its summit. There is also the Kalasasaya temple, a large rectangular plataform bordered by monolithic pillars. Nearby is the renowned Gateway of the Sun, a stone doorway carved from a single block of andesite and decorated with bas-reliefs.

Hotels

Puno

Hotel Libertador Isla Esteves *(ex Hotel de Turistas)*
  Isla Esteves s/n. Tel 36 7780. Fax 36 7879. ★★★★★
  Reservations Lima Tel 442 2988. US$ 130.
  hotel@libertador.com.pe

Hotel Hacienda
  Deustua 297. Tel 35 6109. US$ 55. ★★★

Hotel Sillustani
  Lambayeque 195. Tel 35 1881. US$ 35. ★★★

Hotel Don Miguel
  La Torre 545. Tel 36 8228. Fax 36 4066. US$ 30. ★★★

Hotel Italia
  Teodoro Valcárcel 122. Tel 35 2521. US$ 30. ★★★

Hotel Las Islas
  Carlos B. Oquendo 178. Tel 36 9091. US$ 20. ★★★

Conde de Lemos
  Jr. Puno 675. Tel 36 9898. ★★

Juliaca

Don Carlos *(ex Hotel de Turistas)*
  Manuel Prado 335. Tel 32 1571. Fax 32 2635. US$ 65.

Royal Inn Hotel ★★★
  San Román 158. Tel 32 1561. Fax 32 1572. US$ 40.

Hotel Samari ★★★
  Noriega 325. Tel 32 1870. US$ 40..

La Maison Hotel ★★★
  Jr. 7 de Junio 535. Telefax 32 1444. Fax 32 1763. US$ 30.

  ★★

Suasi

Albergue Rural Isla Suasi
  Isla Suasi, 2 hours from the city of Puno. ★★★
  Recommendable.
  Consorcio de Ecoturismo y Hotelería Suasi.
  Tel 62 2709. Fax 35 1417.
  islasuasi@terra.com.pe

RATES ARE APPROXIMATE AND, UNLESS OTHERWISE NOTED,
ARE FOR DOUBLE OCCUPANCY.

Restaurants

- ✔ La Casona
    Lima 517.
- ✔ Restaurante of the Hotel Sillustani
    Lambayeque 195.
- ✔ Don Piero
    Lima 364.
- ✔ Internacional
    Corner of Libertad and Moquegua.
- ✔ El Portón Colonial
    Jr. Lima 346.

Useful Facts

AREA CODE 54

☎

Basic Information

IPERÚ:
  Information and Assistance for Tourists
  Corner of Jirón Deustua and Jirón Lima.
  Open daily: 8:30am to 7:30pm.

Tourism Police Aid:	36 4735
Instituto Nacional de Cultura:	
Av. La Torre 367.	36 8278
Bolivian Consulate: Arequipa 136, 3th. floor	35 1251
Post Office: Moquegua 269.	35 1141
PerúRail S.A.: Av. De la Torre 224.	35 1041
ESSALUD, Hospital III: Rinconada Salcedo.	36 7385
Hospital Regional: Av. Sol 1022.	36 9696
Botica Santa Fe: Lima 427.	36 4247

Tacna

562 M / 1 843
174 300 POP.
1 273 KM
S OF LIMA

P.
P. 78

ROUTE MAP
8

The city of Tacna overlooks the narrow valley of the Caplina River. In the local native language, *caplina* meant 'unending' or 'not reaching the ocean.' Only 49km from the border with Chile, Tacna is the southernmost city of Peru. Its buildings are predominantly Republican and some still have their characteristic gabled roofs. This is one of the most patriotic cities in Peru. Contributing to the patriotic air are its numerous streets and monuments named for the fathers of Peru's independence (1821–1824) and heroes of the War of the Pacific (1879–1883).

Alameda Bolognesi.

In pre-Hispanic times, the inhabitants of the Tacna Valley were Aimaras from the Altiplano, or high Andean plateau, who came to exploit and trade coastal resources such as corn, *ají* peppers, fish and other seafood. The first Spaniards arrived in 1535, led by Diego de Almagro on his southern explorations. They brought grapevine cuttings and viticulture spread quickly. In the mid-nineteenth century, a wave of Italian immigrants

A warm climate in the summer and cold in the winter, with a yearly mean temperature of 22°C (74°F), and lows around 10°C (50°F). From June to August there are occasional camanchacas, *or low fogs accompanied by light rain.*

came to Tacna, attracted by the success of local trade and agriculture (and providing many of today's *Tacneños* with their Italian surnames). This period of economic bonanza was abruptly brought to a halt by the War of the Pacific. After the defeat of

Old homes of Tacna.

the Peruvian army at the battle of Alto de la Alianza in 1880, Tacna was sacked and the region became a «captive province,» annexed by Chile against its will. It wasn't until 1929, after half a century, that Tacna was restored to Peru.

Today, Tacna is an eminently commercial city (a vocation inherited from its Aimara ancestors), containing many immigrants from Puno. Its economy centers on trade over the border with the cities of Arica and Iquique in northern Chile. It is also a duty-free zone for Peruvians and enjoys certain tax privileges. This is why hundreds of merchants stock up on imported products from the numerous open markets of Tacna

Local Dishes

Entrées
- Salpicón a la tacneña: shredded beef with olives, cilantro and lemon.
- Cebiche made from fish and seafoods.

Soups
- Patasca tacneña: a soup of different meats, beans, kerneled corn, wheat and broad beans.

Main Dishes
- Cordero a la tacneña: lamb seasoned with wine, peanuts and nutmeg.
- Cuy frito: guinea pig breaded in corn flour and fried, served with fried potatoes.
- Picante a la tacneña: a stew of organ meats, jerky, potatoes and oregano.

Festivals

The city's most important festival is Tacna Week (August 25 to 30). On the 28th, the city celebrates the anniversary of the department's reincorporation into Peru, with the Paseo de la Bandera (Flag Procession), one of the most important patriotic events in the country. As part of the celebrations, there are agricultural and industrial fairs.

> **THE FLAG OF PERÚ**
> Every July 28 a gigantic flag sewn by the women of Tacna makes the rounds of the city. This custom began in 1901, during the Chilean occupation, when a group of Tacna residents defied the Chilean authorities' prohibition against the displaying of Peruvian flags in the city.

Folkcrafts

Tacna produces bowls, tables, chairs and other items carved from olive wood, which has a lovely grain and is highly resistant to insects.

Points of Interest in the City

Traditional Locales

- *Plaza de Armas:* in contrast to other central plazas in Peru, this one extends for several blocks in what is known as the Paseo Cívico. It has three monuments: the Cathedral; the Arco

Heros' Arch.

Main square.

The Cathedral.

de los Héroes, the symbol of the city and honoring the heroes of the War of the Pacific, and an elegant, ornamental, bronze fountain brought from Brussels as a gift to the government of José Balta in 1869, by Gustaf Eiffel's construction firm.

- *Alameda Bolognesi:* a few meters from the Plaza de Armas, this is Tacna's best-known promenade. Built on what was once the bed of the Caplina River, it has a beautiful monument to Christopher Columbus, donated by the Italian community.
- *Parque de la Locomotora:* this park was built to house Locomotive N.° 3 (built in Pennsylvania in 1859), which brought back the Peruvian soldiers who fell defending El Morro de Arica on June 7, 1880.

Churches

- *The Cathedral,* Plaza de Armas: construction on this neo-Renaissance-style church began in 1875, under the prestigious French firm of Gustaf Eiffel. The war with Chile stopped the works. On August 28, 1929, a bell temporarily placed in one of its towers rang out the liberation of Tacna after half a century of Chilean occupation. The church was finally inaugurated in 1954. It has a fine, stained glass window and a main altar of onyx.

Museums

- *Casa de la Cultura or Museo Histórico Regional,* Apurímac 202: exhibits an ample archeological collection and has an historical section with bronze busts of the heroes of the War of the Pacific and paintings by Lima artist Juan Lepiani (1864–1932), who produced many works depicting crucial events at the height of the war with Chile.

> *Visiting hours: Mon-Fri, 9am to 5pm.*

- *Museo Ferroviario*, Av. Dos de Mayo (at the train station): an interesting historical documentary on the Tacna-Arica railway and a library specializing in the railways of Peru.

> *Visiting hours: Mon-Fri, 8am to 1pm.*

- *Museo de la Reincorporación*, corner of Zela and Pasaje Calderón de la Barca: a nineteenth-century home where the decree restoring Tacna to Peru was signed in 1929.

Excursions

Boca del Río

)

A beach resort frequented by the people of Tacna during the summer. Access is via the South Panamericana highway, turning off at km 1 303 and following a paved road W for 50km (45 minutes). Open beaches with strong waves and rocky outcrops along the shoreline. Various restaurants are set up on the beach during the summer.

Alto de la Alianza

640M / 2 010FT)

8km (15 minutes) N of Tacna via the South Panamericana highway. This was the site of the battle of the same name, fought on May 26, 1880 between the Peru-Bolivia alliance and the Chilean army, and ending with the fall of Tacna. It has a site museum displaying uniforms and weapons of the soldiers, as well as several documents and a large diorama of the battle. Only a few meters away is the battlefield, dotted with hundreds of white crosses.

El Alto de la Alianza monument.

Calientes

1 850M / 6 070FT)

A picturesque Andean town located 22km (35 minutes) E of Tacna via the partially paved dirt road leading to Palca. Hot

Countryfolk from the Tacna highlands.

Guanacos (*Lama guanicoe*) on the outskirts of Miculla.

mineral springs considered beneficial in treating rheumatism, gout and other ailments. It is best to bring food and drinking water, although there are some vendors near the baths.

Petroglifos de Miculla
900M / 2 953FT

These are rock carvings located at km 24 (45 minutes) out of Tacna, on the packed dirt to Collpa and La Paz, in the district of Pachía. Follow a turnoff, also packed dirt, for 3km as it descends into the Palca Canyon. This road is well marked and has a parking area, with an Inca suspension bridge at the far side. At Miculla, there are about 500 identified rock carvings, apparently related to the cults of water and fertility, worked in low relief on the surface of the rocks scattered around the site. They are calculated to be some 1 500 years old.

Paso de la Concordia
(The Peru-Chile Border Crossing)
560M / 1 837FT

The paperwork necessary for entering Chile is easy and quickly done. Let one of the *colectivo* transport companies covering the

Tacna-Arica route help you (at an approximate cost of US$ 5 per person). They know exactly how to obtain the safe-conduct pass required by Peruvian citizens for travel to Arica. For any travel further, a passport and visa are necessary. The border crossing opens at 8am and closes at 10pm. Remember that Chilean time is one hour ahead in the winter and two hours ahead in the summer.

Hotels

Gran Hotel Tacna *(ex Hotel de Turistas)* ★★★★
Av. Bolognesi 300. Tel 72 4193. Fax 72 2015.
Reservations Lima Tel 261 0240. US$ 75.
htacna@derramaje.org.pe

Camino Real Hotel ★★★
Av. San Martín 855. Tel 72 8091. Fax 72 6433.
Reservations Lima Tel 440 0914. US$ 45.

Holiday Suites Hotel ★★★
Alto de Lima 1476. Tel 74 1201. Fax 74 1159. US$ 35.
holidaysuites@terra.com.pe

El Mesón ★★★
Hipólito Unanue 175. Tel 72 5841. Fax 72 1832. US$ 30.
mesonhotel@terra.com.pe

Damasco Inn ★★★
Av. San Martín 982. Tel 72 1141. US$ 20.

RATES ARE APPROXIMATE AND, UNLESS OTHERWISE NOTED, ARE FOR DOUBLE OCCUPANCY.

Restaurants

Gerólamo ✔
Av. San Martín 981.

Rancho San Antonio ✔
Coronel Bustíos 298.

El Gaucho ✔
Av. Pinto 100.

Génova ✔
Av. San Martín 649.

✔ Sur Perú
   Ayacucho 80.
✔ Muelle Sur
   Arias Aragüéz 135.
✔ Il Pomodoro
   Av. San Martín 521.

Useful Facts

AREA CODE **54**

☎

Basic Information

IPERÚ:
   Information and Assistance for Tourists
   01-574-8000 Lima
Tourism Police Aid: 71 4141
Instituto Nacional de Cultura:
   Calle San Martín 405.   71 1171
Chilean Consulate:
   Corner of Presbítero Andia and Coronel Albarracín.   72 3063
   Open: Mon-Fri, 9am to 3pm.   Fax 72 4391
Post Office: Av. Bolognesi 361.   72 4221

Tacna Travel: Av. Bolognesi 754.   72 3625
Business Travel: Alto de Lima 1480   74 6609

IPSS: Carretera Tacna-Pachía s/n, Calana.   72 3181
Hospital de Apoyo Hipólito Unanue:
   Hipólito Unanue s/n   74 2121
Farmacia Caplina: Av. Bolognesi 611   71 5101
Inka Farma: Av. San Martín 537.   74 6821

Tarapoto

P. 82

P. 78

ROUTE MAP

9

Tarapoto is located in the department of San Martín, at the foot of the Cordillera Azul and at the confluence of the Cumbaza and Shilcayo rivers, very near where the two flow into the Lower Mayo River. This area is considered a transition zone between the high rain forest and the low, Amazon jungle plain because it has abrupt changes in relief and a unique flora and fauna.

With no exaggeration, it could be called the «land of waterfalls,» because of the many gorges in which orchids and tree ferns

Tununtunumba Falls.

reign and streams and torrents of crystalline waters leap in cataracts, forming landscapes of extraordinary natural beauty.

Founded in 1782 by Baltazar Martínez de Compañón, bishop of Trujillo, the city is named for the *tarapoto* palm tree (*Iriartea ventricosa*) that abounds in the area. Throughout its history, the

A classically tropical climate with a yearly mean temperature of 26° C (79° F) that can reach a maximum of 38° C (100° F) on some days from January to March. The rainy season generally starts in December and lasts until March and the ideal season for visiting the city is from June to September.

region has experienced cycles of wealth and poverty, as the prices of its principal commodities fluctuated: tobacco, cotton, rice, fine woods and coca leaf. With the construction, in the 1960s, of the Marginal highway that runs along the edge of the jungle, Tarapoto became an important nexus for commerce between the towns of the Amazon basin and those of the high rain forest. During the following decades, however, a large influx of immigrants from the higher Andean regions and improper land use (deforestation, livestock breeding and coca-leaf cultivation) plunged the region into economic crisis, accentuated by the appearance of drug trafficking and terrorism.

Today, peace has returned to Tarapoto and ecotourism is considered an alternative with great potential for this city that has some of the most beautiful surroundings in the Peruvian jungle. We encourage you to visit.

ORCHIDS

Considered by many to be the most beautiful flowers in the world, orchids belong to the largest family of flowering plants, with close to 20 000 species. In Peru there are some 3 000 registered species of orchids, from the tiny *Pleurotalis*, measuring only a few millimeters, to the large *Cattleyas*, which are exported worldwide. Besides its lovely appearance, it is the orchid's unique relationship with its pollenizers that makes it a true wonder of nature.

Local Dishes

Entrées
- Sarajuane: a dough of corn and peanuts, stuffed with pork, wrapped in *bijao* leaves and steamed.

Soups
- Lamisto: yucca soup with pieces of *paiche* fish.

Main Dishes
- Chunchulijuane: a yucca dough with cilantro and chicken organ meats, wrapped in *bijao* leaves and steamed.
- Chontajuane: dough of palm heart (*chonta*) with *paiche* fish, wrapped in *bijao* leaves and steamed.

Tarapoto palm
(*Iriartea ventricosa*).

Festivals

Tourism Week of Tarapoto (August 11 to 18) and Santa Rosa (August 30) are the most interesting festivals.

Excursions

Aguashiyaku Waterfalls
465M / 1 526FT

Located 14km (45 minutes) NW of the city, along the packed dirt road to Yurimaguas. The native name of this spectacular waterfall on the La Escalera mountain means 'laughing waters' and perfectly describes the natural beauty and harmony of the scene. Many tours set out from Tarapoto for this place. Quite close by are the San José hot spring baths, which do not have any formal facilities for visitors but are ideal for restoring the body after the discomforts of days on the road. Along this same route (at km 35) are the Carpishoyaku falls, also quite beautiful.

Aguashiyaku Falls.

Sauce Lake
650M / 2 133FT

45km (2 hours) S of the city via packed dirt road, following the right bank of the Huallaga River. Also known as Laguna Azul, this is a lovely lake about 5km in length, some 1,4km wide and

Lindo Lake.

over 35m (115ft) deep. It is divided into two sections joined by a narrow canal. The southern body is called Lago Lindo. It is ideal for swimming, canoeing, photography or just relaxing and observing the tropical jungle. There are a few restaurants and hotels. *(We recommend the Puerto Patos Sauce Lodge, Tel 52 3978. Reservations Lima Tel 242 3850. E-mail: Ctareps@puertopalmeras.com).*

Lamas

835M / 2 739FT

21km (40 minutes) NW of Tarapoto via the packed dirt road to Moyobamba. This is perhaps the only town in the Peruvian Amazon not located on the banks of a river. Its population is a

TARAPOTO EXCURSION MAP

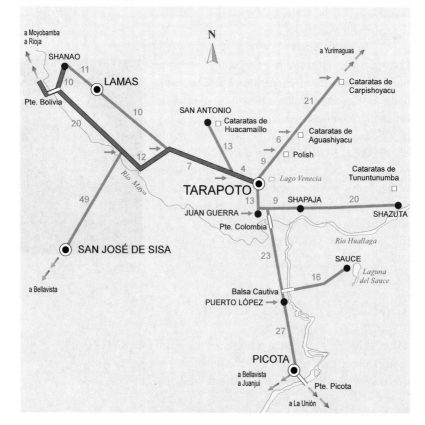

mix of natives and *mestizos* (the inhabitants speak a singular blend of Quechua and jungle languages). The town is divided into three districts lying at different heights. Lamas is famous for its music, handicrafts and traditional dance and is considered the folk capital of the high jungle. The tremendous increase in tourism in recent years has somewhat affected the authenticity of the display of the town's traditional customs.

Huallaga Valley.

Huacamaíllo Waterfalls
408M / 13 386FT

These waterfalls are located 18km N of Tarapoto, in the district of San Antonio de Cumbaza, where a locally popular wine is made. The falls can be reached by a walk of about 2 hours from the town of San Antonio, 30 minutes from Tarapoto via packed dirt road. Set within in a gorge of exuberant beauty, they are perhaps the most beautiful falls in the region. To find out about local road conditions, ask at travel agencies in Tarapoto.

Tununtunumba Waterfalls
280M / 919FT

45km (2 hours) E of Tarapoto on the left bank of the Huallaga River, in the district of Chazuta, about 1 hour, 30 minutes of walking through the jungle from the village of Chazuta. An impressive series of waterfalls over 6m (20ft) wide and over 40m (131ft) tall that drop into a crystalline pool. Its name comes from the deafening sound of the falling water. The spot is ideal for photography and a refreshing swim. To find out details and conditions of the roads to Chazuta, ask at travel agencies in Tarapoto.

Cebu cattle in Saposoa.

Children of Tarapoto

Venecia Lake
307M / 1 007FT

5km (15 minutes) N of Tarapoto on the packed dirt road to Yurimaguas. This lake is reached by

walking 200m (66ft) off the right side of the road. Set in a lovely tropical landscape, its calm waters are ideal for fishing, swimming or just puttering around in one of the small boats for rent nearby. Information at travel agencies in Tarapoto.

Moyobamba
850M / 2 789FT

Capital of the department of San Martín, 105km (2 hours, 30minutes) N of Tarapoto via partially paved road. This town is located in the high rain forest, in a region that is considered a paradise of orchids and tropical flowers. There are good hotels and restaurants. Nearby are the spectacular Gera waterfalls (21km from the city) and some hot spring baths amid lovely natural scenery.

Orchid
(*Odontoglossum sp.*).

Hotels

★★★★ Puerto Palmeras Tarapoto Resort
Carretera Marginal Sur km 3, Banda de Shilcayo (10 minutes from Tarapoto). Tel 52 3978. Reservations Lima Tel 242 5551. US$ 50 and package rates (consult). ctareps@puertopalmeras.com

★★★ Hotel Río Shilcayo *(ex Hotel de Turistas)*
Psje. Las Flores 224, Banda de Shilcayo (2km from Tarapoto). Tel 52 2225. Reservations Lima Tel 436 9214. US$ 50. hotelsh@telematic.com.pe

★★ Hotel Nilas
Moyobamba 173. Tel 52 7331. Fax 52 5175. US$ 15.

★★ Hotel Lily
Jr. Jiménez Pimentel 405. Tel 52 3154. US$ 15.

★★ Hotel Edison
Jr. Jiménez Pimentel 115. Tel 52 4010.

★★ La Posada Inn
San Martín 146. Tel 52 2234. Fax 52 6768.

Jungle Lodges ★★★

Puerto Patos*: Laguna El Sauce, a 2 h de Tarapoto.
Puerto Pumas*: Laguna Pomacochas, a 6 h de Tarapoto.
Puerto Pericos*: On the shores of the Paranapura river, Yurimaguas.
All managed by Corporación Turística Amazónica.
Reservations Tarapoto: Tel 52 3978. Reservations Lima: Tel 241 5551.
ctareps@puertopalmeras.com.pe

Restaurants

Restaurant	
Real Grill	✔
Plaza de armas.	
La Pizzería	✔
Martínez de Compañón 301.	
Chifa Tay Pay	✔
Rioja 252.	
Restaurante del hotel Puerto Palmeras	✔
Carretera Marginal Sur km 3, Banda de Shilcayo.	
Restaurante del Hotel Río Shilcayo	✔
Psje. Las Flores 225, Banda de Shilcayo.	
Restaurante Regional La Patarashca	✔
2 blocks from the plaza de armas.	

Useful Facts

AREA CODE **94**

☎

IPERÚ:
Information and Assistance for Tourists
01-574-8000 Lima
Instituto Nacional de Cultura:
Jr. Óscar Benavides 3, Moyobamba.

Post Office: San Martín 482.	52 3706
Selva Tours: San Martín 153.	52 6668
Hospital II IPSS: A. Delgado cdra. 3.	52 2071
Clínica San Marcos: A. B. Leguía 604.	52 3838
Farmacia Guadalupe: Jr. Maynas 300.	52 8154
Farmacia San Pedro: Pedro de Ursúa 163.	52 2652

3 053 M / 9 991FT
40 000 POP.
241 KM
E OF LIMA

Tarma

P. 78

ROUTE MAPS

⑤ ⑩

Located on the left bank of the Tarma River, the city of Tarma lies in a valley that serves as a gateway to the nearby, high rain forest and the Amazon jungle. It is called the Pearl of the Andes for the beauty of its countryside and the mountains surrounding it. Its other byname is City of Flowers, for the expanse of land planted to flowers for the markets of Lima.

The Tarma region was well populated before the Spanish arrived, as evidenced by the quantity of archeological ruins near the city.

Outskirts of Palcamayo.

The most significant site is the citadel of Tarmatambo (see Excursions, p. 442).

Francisco Pizarro himself founded Tarma in 1538. Its strategic location soon made it an advanced base for colonists and Franciscan missionaries hoping to conquer the jungles beyond. Until the mid-seventeenth century, it was a tranquil city, known for the homespun cloth made by its artisans. Its proverbial calm was shattered when a rebellion broke out, led by Juan Santos Atahualpa, in the central jungle (1742–1752). One of the con-

> *A dry climate with warm days and cold nights and a yearly mean temperature of 26° C (79° F). It has a distinct rainy season from December to March.*

sequences was the interruption of commerce with the jungle, through which Tarma had obtained fruit, coca leaf and salt. While the rebellion lasted, and until the end of the eighteenth century, the city became a sort of military base from which many rebellions in the Andes were repressed.

When Peru gained its independence, peace was restored to Tarma. The city reached its height during the administration of President Manuel A. Odría (1948–1956). He was a native of Tarma, who loved his hometown and had important buildings put up here.

Today it is one of the most popular tourist destinations among the people of Lima because of its proximity to the capital, its idyllic countryside and pleasant climate. Red-tiled roofs and narrow, cobblestone streets give the city a marked Andean character.

Acobamba.

Main Square and Cathedral.

Local Dishes

Soups
• Sancochado: mutton soup with potatoes, vegetables and rice.

- Wallpa chupe: chicken soup with noodles and potatoes.

Main Dishes
- Gallina a la tarmeña: chicken stew with potatoes, eggs and vegetables.

Festivals

The primary festival in Tarma is unquestionably Holy Week, one of the most known and receptive festivals in Peru. Its night processions on Holy Thursday and Good Friday are a long-time tradition. Images of saints are carried though the city streets, accompanied by the light of thousands of candles. Also renowned is the Easter Sunday procession. After a crowded, 6am Mass, the image of Christ is borne through the streets over carpets of flower petals.

Other important events are the feasts of the Lord of Muruhuay, one of the most colorful pilgrimages in Peru (May 3) and of San Sebastián (January 20).

Holy Week procession.

Points of Interest in the City

Churches

- *The Cathedral*, Plaza de Armas: this plainly designed church was built in 1965 and dominates the city center. Former President Manuel A. Odría (1897–1974), a native of Tarma, is buried here.

Excursions

Santuario del Señor de Muruhuay

3 350M / 10 991FT

A shrine on Mount Shalacoto, in the nearby district of Acobamba, 9km (15 minutes) NE of Tarma. It is a modern chapel where an image of Christ crucified is venerated. One of the larger pilgrimages in the central Peruvian Andes is made to this chapel.

Acobamba Valley.

Cueva de Huagapo

3 550M / 11 648FT

28km (40 minutes) N of Tarma via the packed dirt road from Acobamba (9km E of Tarma) to Palcamayo. This fascinating cave has been declared a National Speleological Zone and has an opening over 30m (98ft) tall, from which a cold, underground river issues. Inside are stalactites, stalagmites and other curious formations produced by the water erosion. It is considered one of the deepest cave systems in America. In the environs are some simple restaurants and plenty of guides. We recommend hiring the services of one and taking along a headlamp.

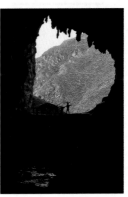

Huagapo Cave.

San Pedro de Cajas

3 700M / 12 140FT

This is a picturesque town 40km (1 hour, 30 minutes) N of Tarma, home to skilled weavers. The town can be reached via

San Pedro de Cajas.

Field of wallflowers.

the same packed dirt road from Acobamba (9km E of Tarma) that leads to the Huagapo cave. The town can also be reached from the paved highway to Junín by taking an 11km detour *(see Route 7, p. 507)*.

Tarmatambo

3 700M / 12 140FT)

An archeological site 6km (10 minutes) S of the city via a packed dirt road that climbs to the district of Tarmatambo. The site is an extensive Inca settlement (that gave Tarma its name), consisting of stone and adobe buildings on a hillside. It has administrative areas, domestic structures, plazas, farming terraces, storage chambers called *colcas*, burial chambers called *chullpas*, and a large network of canals.

Valle de Chanchamayo (San Ramón • La Merced))

See p. 212.

Hotels

★★★ Hotel Los Portales *(ex Hotel de Turistas)*
     Av. Ramón Castilla 512.
     Tel 32 1411 / 32 1410. US$ 65.

★★★ Hostal Hacienda La Florida
     Carretera central, 6km from Tarma.
     Reservations Lima 424 6969. US$ 40 (includes breakfast).

★★★ Hostal Internacional
     Dos de Mayo 307. Tel 32 1830. Fax 32 3324. US$ 30.

★★★ Hostal Restaurante La Casona del Rey
     Av. Pacheco 596. Tel 32 2311. US$ 30.

★★★ Hostal Vargas
     Dos de Mayo 627. Tel 32 1460. Fax 32 1721. US$ 25.

★★ Hostal Central
     Huánuco 614. Tel 32 1334. US$ 20.

Hostal Campestre Albergue Normandie
Muruhuay. Tel 34 1028. Reservations Lima: Tel 349 5440.
hostalnormandie@yahoo.com

RATES ARE APPROXIMATE AND, UNLESS OTHERWISE NOTED,
ARE FOR DOUBLE OCCUPANCY

Restaurants

Lo Mejorcito de Tarma ✔
  Huánuco 190.
Chavín ✔
  Lima 270, plaza de armas.
Restaurant of the Hotel Los Portales ✔
  Av. Ramón Castilla 512.

Useful Facts

AREA CODE **64**

☎

Basic Information

IPERÚ:
  Information and Assistance for Tourists
  01-574-8000 Lima
Post Office: Callao 356.   32 1241

ESSALUD: Av. Vienrich.   32 1380
Policlínico Tarma: Av. Pacheco 362.   32 1400

34 M / 112 FT
509 300 POP.
560 KM
N OF LIMA

Trujillo

P. 82

P. 78

ROUTE MAP

③

Trujillo, capital of the department of La Libertad, is located in the fertile Moche River valley, which is mostly devoted to the cultivation of sugar cane, asparagus and cereals. Along with the Chicama River valley to the north, this is one of the main areas of archeological interest in Peru.

Inhabited since ancient times by fishermen and farmers, between the first and seventh centuries AD these territories were the dominion of one of the most famous ancient cultures of Peru: the Mochica, whose many impressive remains can still be seen

«The Executioner,» detail of a frieze, Huaca de la Luna.

around Trujillo. In the late sixth century AD, the region became the center of power of the Lambayeque culture, and was later ruled by the Chimú during the ninth to fifteenth centuries. The citadel of Chan Chan, only 4km from Trujillo, was the Chimú capital. The Moche River valley was finally incorporated into the Inca empire during the reign of Inca Túpac Yupanqui in the fifteenth century.

The Spanish conquistador, Diego de Almagro, founded the city

> *With a sunny and agreeable climate year round,*
> *Trujillo is known as the land of eternal spring.*
> *It has a yearly mean temperature of 18° C (64° F),*
> *although it can climb to 28° C (82° F) in the summer.*
> *Drizzle is common in the winter.*

of Trujillo on December 6, 1534, naming it in honor of the homeland of Francisco Pizarro, Trujillo de Extremadura. Shortly after its founding, the city was surrounded by new plantings of sugar cane, corn and wheat. These crops, along with the abundant fish from its rich seas, allowed the inhabitants to live in lordly wealth and leisure. In 1557, Trujillo was made the seat of a bishopric and the city's wealth was soon turned to the construction of many churches and splendid mansions, which incorporated elements of various styles over the years. One of these has become the architectural mark of the city: the window barred in wrought iron so intricately curled that it resembles lace and capped by a «coronet.»

Fishermen in Salaverry.

Old manor house
with barred window.

In 1680, in defense against the constant attacks of pirates and corsairs, the city was walled. In 1790 it was made the capital of an *intendencia* and 30 years later the Marquis of Torre Tagle, the *intendente* of Trujillo, summoned his town council and announced that Trujillo was joining the cause of independence.

Soon after Peru became an independent nation, large sugar cane and cotton haciendas were formed,

HORSES OF PERU

The city of Trujillo has one of the longest traditions in Peruvian Paso horse breeding. Esteemed for their graceful movement in combination with marinera dancers, these horses descend from Berber, Arabian, and Andalusian horses that the conquistadors brought to America. Nevertheless, natural selection and environment have created a different animal with a unique stride. As opposed to other breeds which only walk in a crossed manner (moving right foreleg with left hindleg), Peruvian Paso horses can also amble, that is, advancing both legs on the same side at the same time.

devoted exclusively to exportation. Economic growth was interrupted by the War of the Pacific (1879–1883). It wasn't until the late nineteenth century that the local economy stabilized and the haciendas began to flourish again.

In the city of Trujillo, the new economic bonanza was accompanied by a strong cultural movement. In 1920, a group of Trujillo artists and intellectuals formed the renowned *Bohemia de Trujillo* group. Among them was painter, sculptor and musician Macedonio de la Torre, political thinker Víctor Raúl Haya de la Torre and César Vallejo, one of the renowned poets of the twentieth century.

With its stately residential neighborhoods and many commercial zones, Trujillo is today the principal economic and cultural center of the Peruvian north. Capital of the marinera, tondero and resbalosa dances, land of fine Peruvian paso horses and beautiful beaches where fishermen still put out to sea in reed crafts, Trujillo is an ideal destination at any time of the year.

Local Dishes

Soups

- Shámbar: a soup of wheat, pork, beans and cilantro. Considered *the* Monday lunch.
- Sopa teóloga: chicken soup with soaked bread, potatoes, milk and cheese.

Main Dishes

- Frejoles a la trujillana: black beans with sesame seeds and hot *ají mirasol* pepper.
- Pepián de pava: turkey stewed with rice, grated tender corn, cilantro and *ají* pepper.
- Pescado a la trujillana: steamed fish with an egg-and-onion sauce.
- Seco de cabrito: lamb stewed with cilantro and *ají panca*.

Desserts
- Tajadón: a dessert of egg yolks and port wine.

Festivals

Among the festivals in Trujillo and its environs is the national marinera competition (last two weeks of January). This is the best occasion for enjoying the marinera norteña, one of the most traditional dances of Peru. Spanish in origin, this dance has an undeniable *criollo* flavor and some say it has African influence as well. Partners dance separately, each waving a handkerchief, and the man courts the woman gracefully until he gets her to look into his eyes. Other events are the Beach Festival in Huanchaco, with a surfing contest and an exhibition of building and handling the small reed crafts known as *caballitos de totora* (July 26 to 29); the International Spring Festival (September); and the festival of La Mamita de la Puerta in Otuzco, 72km from Trujillo, one of the most touching and important festivals of the north, celebrated since 1664 (December 12 to 15).

MARINERA

Although this dance has its northern, Lima and Andean varieties, most people believe the northern variety is the most beautiful. The marinera was known by other names until well into the nineteenth century: *mozamala, resbalosa, tondero,* and *chilena.* This last name became embarrasing to Peru when the country entered into war with Chile in 1879. The name was consequently changed to marinera in honor of the Peruvian Navy and its heroic campaign during the War of the Pacific. The first marinera music written as such was *La concha de perla* (1899), by Lima composer Rosa Mercedes Ayarza de Morales.

Folkcrafts

Some of Trujillo's best handicrafts are its hats, baskets and other woven straw items, its *caballitos de totora*, and works in embossed leather, silver filigree and bronze and copper. The town of San Pedro de Lloc produces *pellones sanpedranos*, fine wool saddle blankets used for the Paso horses. The higher regions around Trujillo (Otuzco, Santiago de Chuco, Huamachuco and Pataz) are well-known for their woolen ponchos and shawls.

Points of Interest in the City

Traditional Locales

- *Plaza de Armas:* laid out by conquistador Martín de Estete, it is framed by the Cathedral, the archbishop's palace, the church

Main Square.

The Cathedral.

of La Compañía, the municipal palace and stately Colonial and Republican mansions. In the center stands a monument of granite and bronze in honor of the fathers of Peru's independence and created by the German sculptor E. Moeller in 1929.

Churches

- *The Cathedral*, corner of Jr. Independencia and Jr. Orbegoso, Plaza de Armas: the building of this church began in 1647 and finished in 1666. It was partially destroyed by an earthquake in 1754 and again in 1970. With three naves, a cupola and brick walls, it is similar to its counterparts in Lima and Cusco. It has a handsome main altar, beautiful polychrome statues of St. Peter and St. John the Evangelist and a splendid Agony of Christ from the eighteenth century. It also has valuable oil paintings from the Cusco and Quito schools and a religious museum in the basement with murals painted in the sixteenth century.

  Visiting hours: Mon-Sat, 7:50 to 9:30am, and 5:30 to 8:30pm; Sun, 7:30am to 1pm, and 5:15 to 7pm.

- *El Carmen*, corner of Jr. Colón and Jr. Bolívar: this monastery and church comprise the main religious complex of the city. It contains an important collection of works from Quito, with images of St. Joseph and the Christ Child attributed to the Baroque sculptor of Quito, Manuel Chili, also known as Caspicara. The church's highlights are its main altar, the plain pulpit, carved wooden gratings and the Baroque side altars. Don't miss the Last Supper in the art gallery. Its was painted by Otto Van Veen, who taught Peter Paul Rubens.

  Visiting hours: daily, 7 to 8pm.

- *Belén*, corner of Jr. Ayacucho and Jr. Almagro: this church was built by the Bethlemite order and one of its most notable features is the large Byzantine cupola decorated with paintings of the Evangelists. Other highlights are its façade with images of St. Joseph, Mary and the Christ Child, a lovely white and gold pulpit with statues of the great scholars of the Church and some valuable paintings portraying different scenes from the life of Christ.

Visiting hours: daily, 7 to 8pm.

- *La Merced*, Jr. Pizarro 550: this church dating from the seventeenth century was built by the Portuguese artist Alonso de las Nieves. It has a beautiful reproduction of the life of San Pedro Nolasco in its cupola, a sculpture of the Virgen de la Merced by Alonso de Mesa dating from 1603 and a lovely Rococo organ.

Visiting hours: Mon-Sat, 8am to noon, and 5 to 8pm.

- *Santo Domingo*, corner of Jr. Pizarro and Jr. Bolognesi: the only church in Trujillo with twin towers. Inside, it has a holy scene of the Virgin of the

1 Cathedral
2 Church and Monastery del Carmen
3 Church of Bethlehem
4 Church of Santa Clara
5 Church of San Agustín
6 Church of San Francisco
7 Church of La Compañía de Jesús
8 Church of Santo Domingo
9 Casa Bracamonte
10 Casa Urquiaga
11 Casa del Mayorazgo de Facalá
12 Church of La Merced
13 Casa del Mariscal Orbegoso
14 Casa de Madalengoitia
15 Iturregui Palace

TRUJILLO CITY MAP

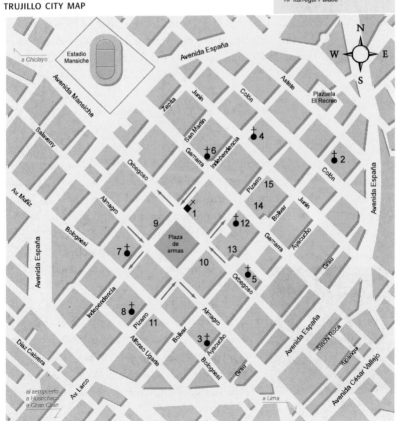

Church of Santo Domingo.

Rosary, the most representative of the Baroque style in Trujillo. The sculptures are wooden panels instead of three-dimensional figures. The murals in the main crypt are also notable.

> *Visiting hours: daily, 6:30am to noon, and 4 to 8:30pm.*

- *Santa Clara*, corner of Jr. Junín and Jr. Independencia: once named Santa María de la Gracia de Santa Clara la Real, this church has a beautiful golden altar. Its pulpit is notable for its carved figures. It has a beautiful Crucifixion by artists from the circle of Juan Martínez Montañés (seventeenth century) and there is beautiful relief-work in its cupola depicting the life St. Clair.

> *Visiting hours: daily, 8am to noon, and 4 to 6pm.*

- *San Agustín*, Jr. Bolívar 508: although building started in the sixteenth century, most of this church dates from the seventeenth century. It has a gilded main altar with polychrome carvings attributed to the eighteenth-century, Black artist Fernando Collado. Its celebrated Rococo pulpit of carved and gilded wood is considered one of the Colonial-era jewels of Peru.

> *Visiting hours: daily, 7am to noon, and 4 to 7:30pm.*

- *San Francisco*, corner of Jr. Independencia and Jr. Gamarra: dating from the seventeenth century, this church of three naves and an octagonal tower has a main altar with a magnificent tabernacle and profuse carvings framed in Baroque details, evidence of the influence of the Lima and Quito schools. It houses a pulpit dating from the early seventeenth century (one of the oldest in Latin America) from which San Francisco Solano (1549–1610) preached.

Church of La Compañía.

> *Visiting hours: Mon-Sat, 6:30 to 8:30am, and 6 to 8pm; Sun, 7 to 11am, and 7:30 to 8:30pm.*

- *La Compañía de Jesús*, corner of Jr. Independencia and Jr. Almagro: built in 1640 in the form of a basilica with two side chapels, a cupola and a two-part doorway, this church is Baroque in style but has Mannerist elements. It is the work

of the Portuguese artist Alonso de las Nieves. Inside it has beautiful murals attributed to the seventeenth-century, Jesuit artist Diego de la Puente. The cloisters of the Jesuit seminary are now the La Libertad university.

Visiting hours: Mon-Fri, 7:30am to 7pm.

• *Others:* San Lorenzo, Santa Ana.

Historical Homes and Buildings

• *Casa Bracamonte*, Jr. Independencia, Plaza de Armas: built in the eighteenth century, this home underwent many changes in the nineteenth century. It has large salons and beautiful patios, a Neoclassic portico on its façade and windows barred in beautifully wrought iron.

Visiting hours: daily, 7am to 7pm.

• *Casa Urquiaga or Calonge*, Jr. Pizarro 446, Plaza de Armas: built in the eighteenth century, and with considerable modifications in the nineteenth, this house had the honor of receiving General Simón Bolívar during the war of independence. It conserves his stately desk of mahogany, various objects of silver and other furniture of the era. It also has a display of pre-Hispanic ceramics.

Visiting hours: Mon-Fri, 9:15am to 3:15pm.

Inner patio of an old manor house.

• *Casa del Mayorazgo de Facalá*, corner of Jr. Pizarro and Jr. Bolognesi: this mansion was built in the eighteenth century by Pedro de Tinoco, founder of the Facalá estate. Its large main patio is framed by wooden columns with Corinthian capitals. It also has an old well.

Visiting hours: Mon-Fri, 9am to 1pm,
and 4:30 to 6:30pm; Sat, 9:30am to 12:30pm.

Trujillo balcony.

• *Casa Ganoza Chopitea or Portada de los Leones*, Jr. Independencia 630: this home has a beautiful Baroque façade, barred windows and notable remnants of murals. It is a good example of an eighteenth-century mansion, although it did undergo some changes in the nineteenth century.

Visiting hours: Mon-Sat, 8am to 6:30pm.

- *Palacio Iturregui*, Jr. Pizarro 688: this home is Italian Neo-Renaissance in style and dates from the nineteenth century. It belonged to General Juan Manuel Iturregui, who had it built in 1855. Around its three large patios are arranged bedrooms, salons and a dining room. The first patio is two stories high; the others are only one. It is now the site of the Club Central de Trujillo and has some magnificent furniture.

  Visiting hours: Mon-Sat, 8am to 6pm.

- *Casa del Mariscal Orbegoso*, corner of Jr. Bolívar and Jr. Orbegoso: this home, built during the eighteenth and nineteenth centuries, is sober, elegant and midway between urban and rural in appearance. It holds furniture and relics that belonged to Marshal Luis José de Orbegoso y Moncada (1795–1847), one of the fathers of independence and president of Peru. There is also a crypt where he is buried.

  Visiting hours: Mon-Sat, 9am to 1pm, and 4 to 8pm.

- *Casa de Madalengoitia or De la Emancipación*, Jr. Pizarro 610: in this eighteenth-century home the document was signed declar-

Casa Risco.

ing Trujillo's commitment to the cause of independence. It also holds an older document in which the king of Spain granted a coat-of-arms to the city, and an invaluable collection of watercolors painted for Trujillo's Bishop Martínez Compañón (1737–1797) during his visits to the diocese.

  Visiting hours: Mon-Fri, 9:15am to 1pm, and 4 to 6:30pm; Sat, 9:30am to 1pm.

- *Others:* the Casa Pinillos (Plaza de Armas), the Casa Risco and the Casa de los Condes de Aranda.

Museums

- *Museo Arqueológico de la Universidad de Trujillo*, Jr. Junín 338, Tel 24 9322: housed in a very modern locale, this museum exhibits many archeological artifacts found in the region. The most important are from the Huaca de la Luna, where this museum directs excavations.

  Visiting hours: Mon-Fri, 8:30am to 2:30pm; Sat, 9am to noon.

- *Museo José Casinelli*, corner of Av. Mansiche and Av. Víctor Raúl Haya de la Torre: located, curiously enough, in the basement of a gas station, this museum houses an interesting exhibit of Mochica and Chimú archeological artifacts, as well as some very interesting pieces from the Recuay culture.

Visits by appointment: Mon-Sat, 9am to 1pm, and 3 to 6:30pm.

Excursions

Chan Chan
18M / 59FT

An archeological site 4km (10 minutes) W of the city in the Moche River valley, following the paved highway to Huanchaco. It was the capital of the Chimú culture, built between the twelfth and fourteenth centuries AD by the rulers of the Tacaynamo dynasty. Considered the largest adobe city in pre-Hispanic America, it covers an area of more than 20km² and it housed some 100 000 people. The city has a maze of streets, canals, water reservoirs, *wachaques* (sunken plazas), silos, plazas, terraces and truncated pyramids.

Adobe wall at Chan Chan.

It also contains nine walled palaces named after famous archeologists and other celebrities. The Tschudi citadel, named for Swiss scholar Juan Diego Tschudi (1818–1889), is the one is the best state of conservation today. After years of intense resistance, Chan Chan fell to the Incas around 1450. When the Spaniards arrived, they found the city abandoned. Unesco has declared the site an Historical and Cultural World Heritage. There is a modern site museum.

Visiting hours: daily, 9am to 4pm.

The Tschudi citadel.

Huacas del Sol and de la Luna
30M / 98FT

An archeological site 4km (15 minutes) S of Trujillo in the Moche Valley. It consists of enormous adobe constructions over 20m (65ft) high built by the Mochica culture. The Huaca del Sol is considered the largest adobe pyramid in Peru. The Huaca de la Luna, 500m (1 640ft)in front of the other, has an extensive burial ground and some fine polychrome murals in which a deity is often repeated.

Although there are remains of domestic activities at the Huaca de la Luna, there are none at the Huaca del Sol, leading many to believe that they were complementary in character, one administrative and the other religious.

Visiting hours: daily, 9am to 2pm.

El Brujo

15M / 49FT)

An archeological complex near the town of Magdalena de Cao in the Chicama Valley, 34km (30 minutes) N of Trujillo via partially paved road (taking a turnoff at km 603 on the North Panamericana highway). It contains three large buildings constructed in different eras: Huaca Prieta (for many, the oldest construction on the coast of Peru), Huaca el Brujo (a Mochica pyramid), and Huaca Cao Viejo, where you can see the remains of an old Christian church. Excavations in the Huaca Cao Viejo have brought to light enormous carved and painted figures of dancers and murals portraying warriors and prisoners.

Visits by appointment only.

Huanchaco

)

A beach resort 13km (10 minutes) NW of Trujillo, well frequented by beach-goers and surfers and famous for its *caballitos de totora*, the small reed crafts used for fishing. On a hillside is a Baroque church housing an image of the Virgen de Perpetuo Socorro, flanked by *caballitos de totora*. It is also the burial place of Antonio Saavedra y Leyva (1707), venerated in the region as a benefactor to local fishermen.

CABALLITOS DE TOTORA

Few water craft were as frequently portrayed by ancient Peruvian artists as these small reed boats, which the Spaniards dubbed «little *totora*-reed horse» after seeing natives astride them with their feet dangling in the water. Depictions of them appear on many Mochica and Chimú ceramics.

These show two kinds of open-sea fishing using the little boats: individuals fishing with hook and line, and pairs of men fishing with nets. Some archeologists believe they were used along the entire coast in ancient times. Today they are only used in the departments of La Libertad and Lambayeque.

Huaca del Dragón or del Arco Iris

15M / 49FT)

One of the best-conserved Chimú ceremonial centers, 4km (15 minutes) NW of Trujillo in the La Esperanza district of the Moche River valley. Enclosed by a solid wall of 3 000m², it contains a myriad of lovely friezes of anthropomorphic and zoomorphic figures, one of a two-headed serpent representing the rainbow. It has a site museum.

Visiting hours: daily, 9am to 4pm.

Port and Beaches of Chicama

)

94km (1 hour, 30 minutes) NW of Trujillo. Access via a paved turnoff at the town of Paiján (km 613 on the North Panamericana highway). A paradise for surfers, its waves are considered «the longest left breaks in the world.» The port has always been called Malabrigo, or 'inhospitable' due to the difficulty of docking boats here. In Colonial times, this was one of the ports where African slaves, brought to work the coastal haciendas, were disembarked. It was also the end of the line of a railway that carried sugar cane from the Casagrande hacienda. Its old dock, built in 1921, and the old wooden houses on its seaside promenade bring to mind the long past of the picturesque spot. Near Chicama there are empty beaches of great beauty, such as Malpaso.

Chicama.

Guañape Islands

○

Across from Puerto Mori, 45km (45 minutes) S of Trujillo via the North Panamericana highway. These islands are an important and beautiful refuge for sea lions, sea birds and dolphins. They can be accessed by hiring a launch from the fishermen at Puerto Mori. The trip will take some 30 minutes. Take food, water and sunblock.

Hoteles

Trujillo

★★★★★ **Hotel El Golf**
Av. Los Cocoteros 500. Tel 28 2515. US$ 100.
granhotelgolf@terra.com.pe

★★★★ **Hotel Libertador Trujillo** *(ex Hotel de Turistas)*
Independencia 485, plaza de armas.
Tel 23 2741. Fax 23 5641. US$ 100.

★★★★ **Hotel El Gran Marqués**
Díaz de Cienfuegos 145-147-151, Urb. La Merced.
Tel 24 9366. Fax 24 9582. US$ 85.
hotel@elgranmarquez.com

★★★ **Los Conquistadores Hotel**
Diego de Almagro 586.
Tel 20 3350. Fax 23 5917. US$ 65.
losconquistadores@viabcp.com

★★★ **El Brujo Hotel**
Santa Teresa de Jesús 170, Urb. La Merced.
Tel 22 3322. US$ 60.

★★★ **Los Jardines Bungallows Hotel**
Av. América Norte 1245. Telefax 22 2258. US$ 50.
losjardinesra@terra.com.pe

★★★ **Hotel Las Terrazas**
Av. Manuel Vera Enríquez 874, Urb. Primavera.
Tel 23 2437. US$ 35.

★★★ **Hotel Continental**
Gamarra 663. Tel 24 1607. US$ 30.

★★★ **Hotel Opt Gar**
Av. Grau 595. Tel 24 4997.
Reservations Lima Tel 438 3321. US$ 25.

★★★ **Hotel Country**
Av. El Golf 857, Las Palmeras. Tel 28 3956.
countryhotel@pmail.net

★★★ **Saint Germain Hotel**
Jr. Junín 585. Tel 20 0574. Fax 20 8102.
saintgermainhotel@pmail.net

Huanchaco

Las Palmeras ★★★
> Av. Larco 1150, Sector los Tumbos. Tel 46 1199.
> hpalmeras@terra.com.pe

Hostal Huanchaco ★★
> Víctor Larco 287. Tel 46 1272. Fax 46 1688. US$ 25.
> huanchaco_hostal@terra.com.pe

Sol y Mar ★★
> Los Ficus 571. Tel 46 1120. Fax 20 6647.

Caballito de Totora ★★
> Av. La Rivera 219. Tel 46 1004. US$ 30.
> totora@terra.com.pe

Hostal Bracamonte ★★
> Los Olivos 503. Tel 461 112. Fax 46 1266. US$ 25.
> hostalbracamonte@yahoo.com

Hostal La Rivera ★★
> Av. La Rivera Sur 197. Tel 46 1003. US$ 20.

RATES ARE APPROXIMATE AND, UNLESS OTHERWISE NOTED,
ARE FOR DOUBLE OCCUPANCY

Restaurants

Trujillo

Romano ✔
> Pizarro 747.

Demarco ✔
> Pizarro 725.

El Mochica ✔
> Bolívar 462.

Chifa Ham Muy ✔
> Av. Juan Pablo II 155-157.

Fiesta ✔
> Av. Juan Pablo II 1110.

Il Valentino ✔
> Orbegoso 224.

Parrillada Ramiro ✔
> Estados Unidos 396.

Huanchaco

✔ Club Colonial

Grau 272, plaza de armas. Outstanding cuisine
by belgian *cheff* Anne Deverte.

✔ Wachaque

La Rivera 323.

✔ Don Pepe

Av. Larco 502.

✔ Café Bar La Tribu

Plaza de armas. Only during summer.

Useful Facts

AREA CODE **44**

☎

Tourist Information

IPERÚ:

Information and Assistance for Tourists

Jr. Pizarro 412, Trujilo.   29 4561

iperutrujillo@promperu.gob.pe

Open daily: 8:30am to 7:30pm.

Instituto Nacional de Cultura:

Independencia 572.   24 8744

Post Office:

Independencia 286.   21 6119

Hospital IPSS Víctor Lazarte E.:

Corner of Av. América Sur and Prolong. Unión.   22 4159

Clínica Peruano-Americana:

Av. Mansiche 702-810   23 1261

Farmacia Grau: Grau 501.   24 2341

Inka Farma: Jr. Gamarra 770.   23 3124

C.M. Rent a Car: Prolong. Buenos Aires 293.   42 0059

Tumbes

P. 82

P. 78

ROUTE MAP

① 1

Located at the extreme NW of Peru, this capital of the department of Tumbes is a peaceful, tropical city of friendly, relaxed inhabitants. A steel bridge leads into the city, crossing the Tumbes River that flows down from the tropical forests in the east of department. It is the largest river on the coast of Peru. Near the city, it flows slowly, forming meanders and lagoons surrounded by extensive fields of rice and *guineos*, the local name for bananas.

In pre-Hispanic times, the inhabitants of the area maintained

Boats at Puerto Pizarro.

close cultural ties with territories that are today part of Ecuador. They were great merchants, using a system by which the products of the region were carried north on rafts with sails, to be bartered there for others. It was a group of native merchants on one of these rafts that first met the Spanish conquistadors. In 1527, Francisco Pizarro disembarked onto the shores of Tumbes and set out from the stone fortress of Tumbi to conquer the Inca empire.

A warm, humid climate, with a yearly mean temperature of 26° C (79° F), makes this city and its environs a favorite destination to those seeking year round sun and sand. It has a rainy season from December to March, which becomes more intense during El Niño years.

Today, the economy of the department of Tumbes is based on agriculture, fishing, shrimp farms, or aquaculture and commerce with Ecuador.

The city seems to have been impulsively modernized and has

Mud and cane façade.

El Ñuro Beach.

few attractions for visitors. One of its few locales still exhibiting something of the traditional northern style is the Plaza de Armas, with its leafy trees known locally as *matacojudos* (fool-killers), for the large, heavy fruit that hangs precariously from their branches. A stroll along the old Benavides promenade, a dike built in 1935 to protect the city from continual flooding of the Tumbes River, or a walk down the Paseo Peatonal, lined with stores doing a lively business, are the only recommended points of interest in the city.

The tourism infrastructure of Tumbes is underdeveloped as well. For this reason, most visitors almost immedictely turn south towards Zorritos, Punta Camarón, Punta Sal, Máncora and other beaches and resorts. We recommend a visit to them.

Local Dishes

Entrées
- Cebiche de conchas negras: black shellfish from the mangrove swamps, marinated in lime.
- Oysters, clams and lobster in abundance.

Soups
- Caldo de bolas: soup of green banana stuffed with meat, olives and raisins.

Main Dishes
- Ají de langostinos: crayfish in a sauce of milk and breadcrumbs with *ají* pepper.
- Majarisco: banana puree in a seafood sauce.
- Fish (*congrio, mero, fortuno, cherela*) prepared in a variety of fashions.

Festivals

Some of the most interesting festivals celebrated in Tumbes and its environs are the feasts of San Pedro in Caleta La Cruz and Puerto Pizarro (June 28 and 29) and of Santa Clara in Zorritos (August 12 and 13); Tourism Week in Tumbes and the Zarumilla Fair (second week of September); and the Tumbes Trade Fair (December 8).

Folkcrafts

Although there is not a great variety of handicrafts in Tumbes, there are lovely hanging mobiles made of mother-of-pearl and necklaces, bracelets and other jewelry made from the shells that abound in the warm waters off Tumbes.

NATURE IN TUMBES

Despite its small size, the Tumbes department has been naturally blessed with a wide variety of ecosystems: mangrove swamps, dry forest, Pacific coast tropical forest (unique in the country), and a warm ocean bathing its numerous beautiful beaches. Evidence of this variety lies in the protected natural areasthat cover almost 50% of the department: the Tumbes National Mangrove Sanctuary (with restricted access and under the custody of the Peruvian Navy), Cerros de Amotape National Park, and the Tumbes Reserve Zone.

Excursions

Puerto Pizarro

)

A small fishing village 13km (15 minutes) NW of Tumbes via the North Panamericana highway, located at the far north end

MANGROVE SWAMPS

Mangrove swamps are considered to be some of the most productive ecosystems on the planet. Formed by as many as 40 botanical species, including the *Rhizopora mangle* or mangrove tree, these forests prosper in warm regions near Ecuador, where ocean and river waters meet. As well as providing refuge to an enormous variety of wildlife, the mangrove swamp has the ability to «reclaim» land from the ocean, depositing greatamounts of sediment and organic material.

of the Tumbes River delta, in an area where the sea mixes with the fresh river water, giving rise to the unique ecosystem of the mangrove swamp. From the swamps, the fishermen of town extract the black shellfish known simply as *conchas negras* (*Anadara sp.*). This town is a good starting point for a visit to the mangrove forests, known for their beauty and wild birds (cormorants, pelicans, herons and other migratory birds). Guided boat tours to the islands of Amor, Hueso de Ballena and Los Pájaros are available. Don't forget insect repellent, as mosquitoes reign supreme in the afternoon. In town there are various simple restaurants whose specialties are shrimp omelets and fish. Be sure to inquire about the tides, as you can only get into the mangrove swamps during high tide.

Aguas Verdes and the Peru–Ecuador Border

10M / 32FT)

27km (45 minutes) from Tumbes via the North Panamericana highway. Aguas Verdes is an area of intense commerce between Peru and Ecuador, a veritable emporium of small temporary shops and street venders. We recommend hiring a taxi, as traffic can be chaotic. The hub of town is the international bridge over the Zarumilla River, crossing to the Ecuadorian town of Huaquillas. It is usually simple to cross the border. Peruvian citizens can obtain a safe-conduct pass by presenting their identify card in Aguas Verdes. This serves for a visit to Huaquillas and the surrounding area, including the Ecuadorian city of Machala. Any travel further requires a passport. The border is open from 8:30am to noon and 2 to 6pm. Remember that Ecuadorian time is one hour behind Peruvian time when making your travel plans.

Zorritos

)

28km (30 minutes) S of Tumbes via the North Panamericana

highway. It was the beach resort of choice for the well-to-do of Tumbes at the height of oil drilling in the area. Here there are lovely beaches from wich you can still see the twisted structures of abandoned oil platforms off the shore. Nearby, the Complejo Turístico Punta Camarón lavishes attention on summer beach-goers. There are other small hotels and many restaurants specializing in fish and seafood. Also nearby is the town of Bocapán (point of departure for Cerros de Amotape National Park), and the Hervideros hot springs (4km E via packed dirt road), with some simple restaurants and changing rooms. Zorritos is the favorite summer spot among the young people of Tumbes.

Shrimp nets at Zorritos.

Villages to the East and the Tumbes Reserved Area

350M / 1 148FT ON AVERAGE

To visit these traditional villages of Tumbes you must take one of the two roads along the banks of the Tumbes River. The road along the north bank is the best, as it is paved. It will take you to the towns of Limón (with its old hacienda house) and Pampas de Hospital (15km). The latter is the point of departure for the Tumbes Reserve Area(60km or 3 hours via packed dirt road), which protects the last remaining Pacific coast tropical forest in Peru and has spectacular landscapes and abundant wildlife.

El Limón hacienda house.

Rafting the Tumbes River.

The road along the south bank of the Tumbes River, entered from the town of Corrales (35km S of Tumbes on the North Panamericana highway) also has picturesque villages, beautiful riverside scenery and extensive fields of bananas and rice and stands of carob trees. Other nearby villages are Cabuyal, Casitas, Tamarindo and Plateros (with another hacienda house). The Tumbes Reserve Area does not have tourist infrastructure. We recommend taking supplies and equipment, especially if you wish to camp there. Access to the park requires a permit, issued by the office for the Tumbes Reserve Zone *(see Useful Facts, p. 468)*.

Cerros de Amotape National Park
350M / 1 148FT ON AVERAGE

About 50km (3 hours) SE of Tumbes, via Zorritos–Bocapán. Covering 91 300 hectares, this protected area of dry, equatorial forest spreads over the slopes of the Amotape mountain range. It is the refuge of varied wildlife, including white-tailed deer (*Odocoileus virginianus*), the northwest Peruvian otter (*Lutra longicaudis*), puma (*Puma concolor*), ocelot (*Leopardus pardalis*), anteater (*Tamandua mexicana*) and the white-necked squirrel (*Sciurus stramineus*). It also has unique flora, including the ceiba (*Ceiba trichistandra*), the *guayacán* (*Tabebuia sp.*), the *hualtaco* (*Loxopterygium huasango*) and the *porotillo* (*Erythrina sp.*).

Amotape mountain range.

There is no tourist infrastructure in the park. We recommend taking food supplies for the day and complete equipment or if you wish to camp there.

Access is complicated as there are many dirt paths leading into the park. You must have the aid of a local guide for this excursion. Ask at local towns and villages for one.

Ceiba tree.

Punta Sal

Many feel this is the most beautiful series of beaches in the department of Tumbes and perhaps in Peru. Located 79km (1 hour, 15 minutes) S of Tumbes via the North Panamericana highway, the beaches all have warm, clear waters.

The resort of Punta Sal, also known as Punta Sal Grande, has a number of private bungalows, many for rent year round. There is no piped water nor electricity (an added attraction to many). The beach is ideal for sport fishing (*mero*, *robalo*, *sierra* and *agujilla*) and diving.

There are some hostels and restaurants in the area. The Punta Sal Club Hotel is located 5km N of Punta Sal Grande. It is an excellent place for leaving the urban world behind and enjoying sun, good food and water sports such as wind surfing, deep-sea fishing, diving, parasailing and others.

Undersea fishing at Punta Sal.

Máncora

106km (1 hour, 45 minutes) S of Tumbes via the North Panamericana highway (and 34km S of Punta Sal). This is a typical northern roadside town. It is actually located in the department of Piura, but most people reach it via Tumbes. A paradise for surfers who have made it into a sort of Peruvian Hawaii, with the arrival of a good swell, the streets become a noisy meeting point for young people in search of the perfect wave. It has good restaurants specializing in shrimp, lobster and fresh fish, and hotels for every taste and price range. N of town is Quebrada Fernández with carob tree forests and picturesque villages. This is the point of departure for going to Cerros de Amotape National Park (35km or 1 hour, 30 minutes via packed dirt road). Don't miss the salty mineral springs known as El Barro, 15 minutes from Máncora.

Day's end at Máncora.

Hotels

Tumbes

Hotel Costa del Sol *(ex Hotel de Turistas)*   ★★★★
   San Martín 275. Tel 52 3992. Fax 52 5862.
   Reservations Lima Tel 472 8227. US$ 55.

Hostal Chilimasa   ★★★
   Panamericana Norte km 1272. US$ 40.
   Tel 52 4555. Fax 52 1946.

Hostal Lourdes   ★★
   Mayor Bodero 118. Tel 52 2966. US$ 15.

★★ Hotel Roma
Corner Grau and Bolognesi, plaza de armas.
Tel 52 4137. US$ 10.

Zorritos

★★ Hotel Punta Cocos
Panamericana Norte km 1 243. Tel 54 4002. US$ 60.

★★ Hostal Playa Florida
Panamericana Norte km 1 222. Reservations Tumbes
Tel 52 5207. US$ 50 (for meals and lodging)
o US$ 25 (meals not included).

★★ Hostal Turístico Zorritos
Faustino Piaggio 202. Tel 54 4045.
Reservations Lima Tel 472 8227. US$ 35.

★★ Hotel Punta Camarón
Panamericana Norte km 1 235. Reservations Lima
Tel 445 6592. Fax 447 3238. US$ 35 (includes breakfast).

★★ Hostel Casa Grillo
Los Pinos 563, playa Los Pinos. Tel 54 4206.
Reservations Lima Tel 446 5488. US$ 10.

Punta Sal

★★★★ Punta Sal Club Hotel
Panamericana Norte km 1 192. Tel 52 1386.
Reservations Lima Tel 442 5961.
US$ 90 (for meals and lodging).

★★★ Hostal Caballito de Mar
Tel 60 8077. Reservations Lima Tel 994 0624. US$ 30.

★★★ Hotel Blue Marlin Beach Club
Panamericana Norte km 1 190,5. Reservations Lima
Tel 445 8068. US$ 60 (for meals and lodging).

★★ Hostal Los Delfines
Playa Punta Sal s/n. Tel 32 0251. US$ 25.

★★ Hostal Guá
Playa Punta Sal s/n. Tel 60 8365. US$ 20.

★★ Casa de Mar Sunset Punta Sal
Tel 68 8413. Resertvations Lima Tel 475 2739. US$20.

Máncora

Máncora Beach Bungallows ★★★
    Section Las Pocitas. Tel 85 8125.
    Reservations Lima Tel 241 6116.
    david@peru-hotels-inns.com

Casa de Playa ★★★
    Section Las Pocitas. Tel 85 8085.
    Reservations Lima Tel 241 0889.
    casadeplaya@latinmail.com

Puerto Palos ★★★
    Section Las Pocitas. Tel 85 8199.
    puertopalos@terra.com.pe

Los Corales ★★★
    Section Las Pocitas. Tel 85 8309.
    Reservations Lima Tel 882 7556.
    sandrar@ec.red.com

Sunset Residencia Restaurante ★★★
    Section Las Pocitas. Tel 85 8111.
    sunset@amauta.rcp.net.pe

Hotel Punta Ballenas ★★★
    Panamericana Norte km 1164. Tel 85 8136.
    Fax 68 4538.

Las Pocitas Beach Club ★★★
    Section Las Pocitas. Tel 69 2033.

Hotel Las Arenas de Máncora ★★★★
    Southern section of Las Pocitas. Tel 85 8240.
    Reservations Lima Tel 441 1542.
    krysia@terra.com.pe

Hospedaje Playa Bonita ★★★
    Section Las Pocitas. Tel 85 8113.
    Reservations Lima Tel 326 1262.
    playabonita@terra.com.pe

Hotel Guagua (el Point) ★★★
    Km 1165 Panamericana Norte.

RATES ARE APPROXIMATE AND, UNLESS OTHERWISE NOTED,
ARE FOR DOUBLE OCCUPANCY.

Restaurants

Tumbes

✔ El Estadio
  Francisco Ibáñez 312.

✔ Classic
  Teniente Vásquez 185.

✔ El Algarrobo
  Huáscar 505.

✔ El Curich
  Bolívar 121, main square.

✔ Restaurant of the Hotel Costa del Sol
  San Martín 275.

Useful Facts

AREA CODE 74

☎

Basic Information

IPERÚ:
  Information and Assistance for Tourists
  01-574-8000 Lima.

Post Office:
  San Martín 208.   52 3886

Office of Reserva de Biosfera del Noroeste:
  Av. Tarapacá 427.   52 5489

Ecuadorian Consulate: Bolívar 155, plaza de armas.   52 1739
  Open: Mon-Fri from 9:00am to 1:00pm.

Tumbes Tours: Av. Tumbes 3521   52 2481
Rosillo Tours: Av. Tumbes 293.   52 3892

Hospital Tumbes: Av. Teniente Vásquez s/n,   52 2222
  (cuadra 8)
ESSALUD: Av. Panamericana Norte s/n.   52 4983
Botica Nazareth: Av. Tumbes 600.   52 3321
Farmacia Rodrich: Av. Piura 1004.   52 3604

ROUTES

Concerning the wondrous
routes crossing the great plains,
mountains and jungles of this
misterious land.

North

Lima-Tumbes

1

- ➤ DISTANCE: 1 267KM
- ➤ ESTIMATED TIME: 14 TO 16 HOURS
- ➤ PAVED ROAD
- ➤ ROAD MAPS: 5–4–3–2–1

This route is truly an odyssey through Peru's coastal desert. The route begins on a highway (*autopista*) to Huacho, then changes to a paved road in very good condition (save for the periodic damage caused by the El Niño rains). Few people actually drive the Lima-Tumbes route in one day; the ideal is to take two days and spend the night in Trujillo or Chiclayo, both of which have good hotels and restaurants. On this trip observe the following recommendations: avoid speeding, as speed limits on this route are enforced by the highway police; when passing through a populated area decrease your speed to 40KM/H; take advantage of large gas stations and hotels on the way to use restrooms and obtain drinking water; and lastly, keep an eye on your levels of gasoline, oil and coolant, as the desert can be treacherous and quite deserted.

Lima to Pativilca

- ➤ 202KM   ➤ 2 HOURS 30 MINUTES
- ➤ 150KM OF HIGHWAY
- ➤ 52KM OF PAVED ROAD

The route leaves Lima, heading N on the North Panamericana

highway. We recommend the route through Ventanilla as the quickest way out of town, with the least traffic *(see map on following page)*. After passing Zapallal KM 36, the beaches of Santa Rosa and San Francisco, and the beach resort of Ancón KM 43, you will sight the first significant geographical feature: Pasamayo, an enormous, mountain-sized sand dune along the coast between the Chillón and Chancay river valleys.

Ancón Beach.

Here a road designed for light vehicle traffic, the Pasamayo alternate route, starts at KM 47 and climbs the great dune to an altitude of 600M/1 968FT. It was built to avoid the congestion and accidents caused by curves and sandslides on the original route several hundred meters below, today designated for heavy vehicle traffic. Fog and drizzle are common on the upper course, which is why we recommend decreasing speed, turning headlights on and keeping to the right-hand side of the road.

The descent from the dune is rapid and reveals the Chancay Valley, the site of an important culture (also called Chancay) that flourished between the eleventh and fourteenth centuries AD and which is still renowned for its textiles.

On the right side KM 71 we find the turnoff to **Huaral,** sunny land of fruit orchards whose seedless oranges made the former Huando hacienda famous. This city has many services. We recommend the hospitable Hostal Las Dalias (Las Dalias 370, Tel 75 1387).

• A packed dirt road starting from Huaral passes through Huando and climbs up to the Andes to Cerro de Pasco 202KM ➤ 5H FROM HUARAL. On the way, you can enjoy the simplicity and beauty of Acos, La Florida, Pirca, Pacaraos and many other highland towns. From the village of La Florida, a horse trail leads 14KM ➤ 3H, 30MIN to the impressive archeological site at Rúpac 3 400M/11 152FT, where numerous *chullpas* (burial towers) are in an excellent state of preservation. Another packed dirt road leaves the town of Aucallama (a few kilometers E of Huando), heading S and connecting the Chancay and Chillón valleys •

Continuing on the North Panamericana, you will reach **Chancay** KM 82, a peaceful town of farmers and ranchers who produce

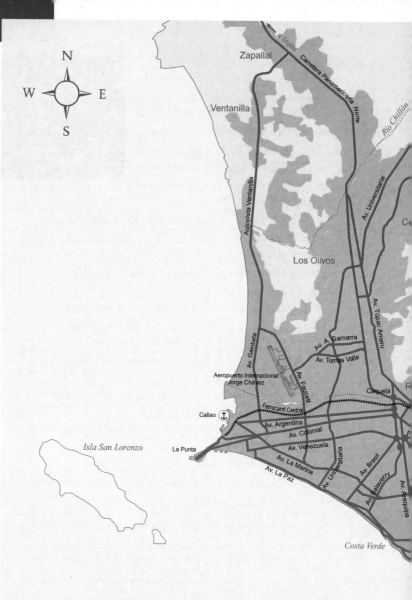

LIMA ACCESS AND BYPASS ROUTES

a large part of the poultry and eggs consumed in Lima. There is also a small port devoted to fishmeal production. Chancay has a pretty Plaza de Armas where there is a small, but educational site museum and several fish and seafood restaurants (we recommend El Parque, Av. Primavera 130, La Rivera). Don't miss the curious castle near the ocean, now converted into a comfortable hostel and restaurant.

If you are serious in your search for a restaurant, the best in the region are found on the roadside here. El Marcelo KM 81,5 has a varied menu locally renowned for its flavor. Its *tacu-tacu con lomo* (grilled beef loin over refried beans and rice) is, quite simply, delectable. If you don't have time for a large meal with all the trimmings, there is another, first-rate alternative: the Del Pino restaurant (near the Del Pino service station at KM 77,5), offering the best *tamales* and fried pork (*chicharrón*) sandwiches around.

After Chancay and **Chancayllo** KM 91 you will come to the **Río Seco** intersection KM 103, where a paved road heads to **Sayán** 52KM ➤ 1H, and continues, partially paved, to **Churín** 62KM ➤ 2H BEYOND SAYÁN.

Climbing again, this time towards the flat land called Pampa de Doña María, you will find the turnoff to the **Reserva Nacio-**

nal Lomas de Lachay KM 105, a unique ecosystem in the coastal hills that blooms every year from August to October. To the N of Lachay are the Huacho salt flats KM 131 and lovely beaches and flatlands at **Paraíso** KM 136 and Playa Chica KM 140, formed by irrigation runoff from nearby La Unión and which have become a vital stopover for birds migrating south.

Lomas de Lachay.

The highway (*autopista*) ends at **Huacho** KM 150, a city engaged in commerce with many towns in the Andes. There are many hotels (Pacífico, Garden and Centenario, all on Av. 28 de Julio) and restaurants (we recommend the excellent breakfasts at Las Brasas, Av. 28 de Julio 550). Huacho is also a port and home to fishermen.

The nearby inlets of Carquín and Végueta are the best known. From here you can visit some lovely beaches (Hornillos, Colorado) and archeological sites (Hualmay, Runtur Cochas, El Colorado and the walls at Mazo and Acaray). For more information call 32 3521 or 32 3512.

Further N of Huacho is **Huaura** KM 152, the land of a cherry called *guinda*, where you can visit the old balcony from which José de San Martín proclaimed the independence of Peru in 1821, the **Centinela** beach that is ideal for surfing and the hacienda house of Rontoy.

Hornillos Beach.

• From Huaura, a partially paved road runs through farmland in the direction of Sayán 45KM ➤ 1H, Churín 107KM ➤ 3H and Oyón 3 620M / 11 874FT, 139KM ➤ 4H •

A bit further along, you will come to **Medio Mundo** KM 174, a saltwater lagoon 7,5km long and parallel to the ocean. It is a wildlife refuge for a large number of waterfowl (ducks, plovers and coots). It is also one of the favorite recreation areas of Huacho residents. It has an hostel owned by the municipality, with a restaurant and boat rental agency.

Continuing N, there is a lovely beach at Caleta Vidal KM 180 and, around a dangerous curve, the city KM 186 and port of **Supe** KM 189, with its beaches of La Isla and El Faraón and an impressive pre-Hispanic ruin, the Chupacigarro pyramid. Soon afterwards, you will arrive in **Barranca** KM 193, a city engaged in vigorous commerce with mountain towns in the southern part of the department of Ancash. Barranca has good hotels and restaurants (El Chavín and El Tumi, on the side of the highway). Towards the coast there are popular beaches (Chorrillos, Cerro Colorado) and a couple of pleasant, hospitable hotels: Chorrillos Beach (Av. Chorrillos 101, Tel 35 3729) and Casa Blanca (Av. Chorrillos 440, Tel 994 3184). **Pativilca** KM 202 is the next town on the route and has the last service station for more than 80km if you are headed N.

Pativilca to Chimbote

➤ 225KM   ➤ 3 HOURS
➤ PAVED ROAD

• From Pativilca a packed dirt road leads to Congas, Ocros, Chiquián and many other picturesque towns of the Huayhuash and Raura mountain ranges. The paved road that is the main route to Huaraz and the Callejón de Huaylas also begins at Pativilca (at KM 206 of the Panamericana, *see Route 4, p. 495*) •

Continuing N from Pativilca, the desert gives way to the fertile Fortaleza River valley, where sugar cane plantations predominate. The extensive fields have been farmed for centuries, producing the raw material for the sugar factory at **Paramonga** KM 210 in the Fortaleza River valley. Don't forget to visit the pre-Inca fortress (visible from the road) located on the border between the departments of Lima and Ancash. Coincidentally, this was also the southern border of the territory of the ancient Chimú civilization. This imposing pyramid for ceremonial purposes seems to have been the last bastion of the Chimú before they fell to the armies of the Inca Pachacútec in the mid-fifteenth century.

The Panamericana continues across the desert sand dunes that conceal some beautiful beaches such as **Punta Bermejo** KM 222, an inlet with perfect waves appreciated by fishermen and surfers alike; Punta Colorado KM 231; San Francisco KM 237; and Gramadal KM 251. At Pampa de Las Zorras, an area of large dunes, there is a turnoff to the charming inlet of **Tamborero** KM 258 and the beaches of La Cocinita and Punta Las Zorras KM 262, ideal for camping.

Corralones Beach.

Continuing on the Panamericana, you will reach **Huarmey** KM 293, a very small town (but with all basic services) that makes its living catering to business on the highway. Huarmey's main attraction is unquestionably its lovely beaches and bays: Tuquillo KM 301, Punta Muñi KM 305, Corralones KM 306 and Punta Culebras KM 308. These are small, easily accessible, cold water beaches with small islands off-shore and are known for clear waters and good fishing (the result of submarine, cold-water springs).

A bit further N, is the beach and fishing village of **La Gramita** KM 345, and N of that there is a pretty inn (Las Aldas. Reservations Lima Tel 440 3221) with bungalows and a restaurant. La Gramita is a favorite among campers and an ideal point of departure for visiting lovely beaches nearby (Punta El Huaro) and the ruins at Las Aldas.

The next town on the highway is **Casma** KM 375 in the Casma Valley. The stately, red-flowered *ponciana* trees seem to welcome the visitor to this small, sunny town. There are impressive ruins at **Sechín** (2KM from the highway turnoff at KM 374). This area is thought to have been the first center of civilization on the Peruvian coast. Sechín is known for its hundreds of stone monoliths (stone was rarely used in pre-Hispanic coastal construction). Almost 3500 years old, the outer walls still exhibit bas-reliefs of warriors in bloody combat. There is also a site museum. In the outskirts of Casma KM·375,5 you'll find a new and comfortable hotel: Las Poncianas.

Ponciana flower (*Delonyx regia*).

• For the more daring, the same packed dirt road to Sechín KM 374 goes on to cross the Cordillera Negra to the Callejón de Huaylas 149 KM ➤ 5H, offering a spectacular view of the mountains, especially at the highest point, Punta Callán, 30 KM from Huaraz. The road is in poor condition •

Leaving the Casma Valley (take care on the dangerous curves in this area) and entering the desert once again, there is a turnoff to the beach resort at **Tortugas** KM 392, a splendid bay with clear waters and lovely beaches ideal for fishing and diving. There are restaurants and hostels —we recommend El Farol, with a restaurant and bar (Tel 71 1064). Only a few minutes to the N is the beach and inlet known as Los Chimú. The next valley on the route is **Nepeña** KM 404, where sugar cane is also the primary crop. Its port and fishing harbor, **Samanco** (in a bay of the same name) supplies the entire region with seafood. Very close by (9KM on the Nepeña Valley turnoff) is a Mochica pyramid at **Pañamarca** that has uncommonly large frescoes.

A few kilometers further on the Panamericana are roads to **Vesique** KM 412, a favorite beach resort among the people of

Fishing with a dragnet in Samanco.

Chimbote, and El Dorado ᴷᴹ 424, located at the far S end of a curious peninsula shaped like a whale's tail, the southern tip of Chimbote Bay.

The road finally leads to the city of **Chimbote** ᴷᴹ 427, Peru's main fishing port. The innumerable round buoys floating off shore have become part of the scenery. Seriously affected by pollution, Chimbote is constantly growing, spurred by a large number of industries (including the old HierroPerú iron and steel plant) and a large influx of immigrants from the Andes.

Chimbote to Trujillo

> 142KM > 2 HOURS
> PAVED ROAD

Moving on from Chimbote, N on the Panamericana, you will enter Coishco ᴷᴹ 438 and the valley of the **Santa** River (the same river that flows through the Callejón de Huaylas).

• From the town of Santa ᴷᴹ 443 a packed dirt roads leads to the Callejón de Huaylas, through the spectacular Cañón del Pato gorge and the town of Huallanca. This stretch of road through the gorge, passing through 35 tunnels and bordering sheer precipices, is simply spectacular, but the road condition is only fair. This route is also the main means of access to the towns of Corongo and Pallasca on the border of the department of La Libertad, and Sihuas and Pomabamba in the northern part of the Callejón de Conchucos. The distance from Santa to Huaraz is 277KM or 6 HOURS •

Crossing a bridge over the Santa River ᴷᴹ 445 and reentering the desert, you will see the asparagus fields of the **Chao** River valley ᴷᴹ 496, then San José ᴷᴹ 505 and next the **Virú** Valley ᴷᴹ 514. Today a large agroindustrial center, the Virú Valley was the site of important pre-Inca communities. You can still see the remains of large pyramids among the sugar cane fields and modest homes. Continuing through the desert, which by now will be growing monotonous, you will encounter turnoffs to the small fishing village of **Puerto Mori** ᴷᴹ 526 and the bustling industrial port of

Salaverry KM 552. A couple of kilometers further N, you will enter the Moche River valley and pass the turnoff to the beach resort of **Las Delicias** KM 554, an old and somewhat neglected spot, but still quite popular among the people of Trujillo.

You will be about to enter **Trujillo** KM 569, the principal city of north-central Peru. Just before entering the city there is a turnoff to the pyramids, or huacas, **Huaca del Sol** and **Huaca de la Luna** KM 556 and the circle that is the city's traffic interchange. If you are going on to Chiclayo and prefer not to enter downtown Trujillo (it's your loss), take the road to the right (towards the sea), which passes very close to **Huanchaco** and **Chan Chan** (*see map on following page*).

Trujillo to Chiclayo

> ➤ 213KM ➤ 2 HOURS 30 MINUTES
> ➤ PAVED ROAD

Leaving Trujillo (we recommend filling the gas tank), the highway enters the desert, crossing the extensive flats of Pampa El Alto guarded by the immense Campana hill. Further along are the towns of **Chicama** KM 590, **Chiclín** and the turnoff to **Cartavio** KM 594, and **Chocope** KM 603, from which one road leads to the town of Magdalena de Cao and the pyramid called Huaca **El Brujo** to the W, and another to **Casagrande, Ascope** 18 KM and **Contumazá** 117 KM, to the E. **Paiján** appears next KM 613, with its

Totora-reed boats in Huanchaco.

Trujillo balcony.

Sunset at Huanchaco.

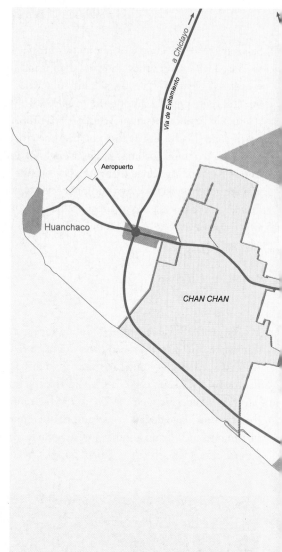

a Chiclayo

Vía de Evitamiento

Aeropuerto

Huanchaco

CHAN CHAN

OCÉANO PACÍFICO

TRUJILLO ACCESS AND BYPASS ROUTES

red-flowered ponciana trees and narrow streets. From Paiján, a road leads to the port of **Malabrigo**, also known as **Puerto Chicama** [15 KM], an area of lovely beaches with hostels and restaurants, where surfers say you can find the longest left breaks in the world.

Back into the desert and continuing N, you will cross the Pampa Urricape flats and come to **San Pedro de Lloc** [KM 657], a small town where the renowned Italian traveler and savant, Antonio Raimondi (1826–1890) died. This town is also known for offering a unique dish: *pacaso*, or iguana. The road then divides, one fork leading to the coast and the town of **Pacasmayo** [KM 667] and the other continuing directly N. Both courses reunite a bit further along at the town and pampas of San José, to continue towards the rice fields of the Jequetepeque Valley.

• At KM 682,5 you can enjoy excellent dishes prepared with shrimps (Restaurant El Gordo). At KM 683 is the turnoff to Cajamarca *(see Route 2, p. 488)* •

Soon afterwards there appear the towns of **Guadalupe** [KM 691], founded in 1550, **Chepén** [KM 696], San José del Moro [KM 702], Pacanguilla [KM 705], a road to the fishing port of Chérrepe [KM 731], then **Mocupe** [KM 730], now in the department of Lambayeque. The highway enters the **Zaña** River valley (turnoff at KM 734), with its spectacular ruins (Pueblo Viejo) and cotton fields, then the **Reque** River valley [KM 757], the entry way to **Puerto Eten** (9KM away by paved road), the fishing and industrial center of the department of Lambayeque. Continuing N, you will pass a turnoff to the town of **Monsefú** [KM 760], known for its accomplished artisans; the fishing village of **Santa Rosa**; and the port and beach resort at **Pimentel**, the main industrial zone of Chiclayo.

Having reached **Chiclayo** [KM 773] *(see map on following page)*, you will be in one of the main economic hubs of the north, strategically situated at the junction of many roads. One leads W to the port of Pimentel [10KM], the fishing villages and boatyards of **San José** [12KM FARTHER N] and Santa Rosa [13KM S]. Another, to the E, leads to Pomalca [7KM], Tumán [16KM] and Chongoyape [62KM], on the way to Cutervo in Cajamarca. Another leads NE to Ferreñafe [28KM] and another N to **Lambayeque** [10KM].

CHICLAYO ACCESS AND BYPASS ROUTES

Chiclayo to Piura

- ➤ 213KM   ➤ 3 HOURS
- ➤ PAVED ROAD

Leaving Lambayeque (10 KM N of Chiclayo), you will come to an important fork in the road. The right-hand road leads to the old Panamericana (km 784) and **Olmos** and the left-hand road to the new Panamericana, a section known as the **variante de Sechura**. Both roads will take you on to Piura.

The former is in a fair state of conservation, but allows for a visit to the traditional towns and rich archeological sites at **Túcume** [24KM], Motupe [66KM], Olmos [92KM] and Ñaupe [141KM], also with a turnoff to Huancabamba [192 KM] and another to **Chulucanas** [216 KM], a town known for its artisans. Estimated time to Piura is 3 HOURS 30 MINUTES.

The alternate road, the variante de Sechura, is in very good

Lake Ramón.

Chira River.

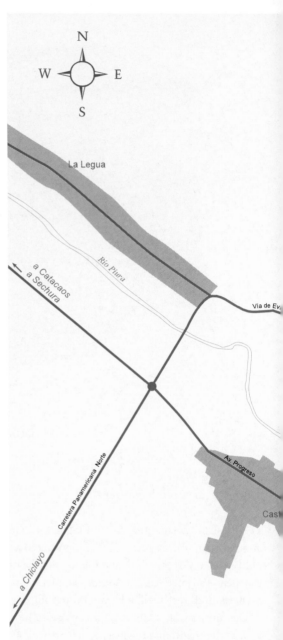

La Legua

a Catacaos
a Sechura

Río Piura

Vía de Ev

Carretera Panamericana Norte

a Chiclayo

Av. Progreso

Cas

PIURA ACCESS AND BYPASS ROUTES

condition and is faster and more direct. You must take some precautions in crossing the vast desert of Sechura. Fill your gas tank in Chiclayo or Lambayeque $^{KM\,781}$, as there are no service stations for the next 180km. You will be able to find some informal venders selling diesel fuel and 84-octane gasoline, but

Artisan of Chulucanas.

do not count on them. In the afternoons (generally after 2pm), wind from the south becomes a factor to be considered if you are traveling S, as visibility decreases and fuel consumption increases. The estimated time to Piura by this route is 2 HOURS 30 MINUTES. On this road, you will pass the town of Mórrope $^{KM\cdot804}$ and, afterwards, a traffic circle in the middle of nowhere $^{KM\,886}$. This is the turnoff to Bayóvar. Take the right lane to continue on to Piura.

• The left lane will take you to Bayóvar ^{65KM} and joins a road that comes from the Lower Piura Valley and goes on to the Virrilá estuary (a stopover for hundreds of flamingoes and other migratory birds), the fishing villages of Parachique and Matacaballo, the small town of Sechura (be sure to visit the church), mangrove swamps at San Pedro, and some of the most beautiful beaches on the coast •

Back on the Panamericana highway, the next natural points of interest on the road are lakes Ramón and Ñapique $^{KM\,932}$, natural depressions in the desert that become, quite literally, inland seas upon the arrival of the rains accompanying the El Niño phenomenon. A few kilometers N of the turnoff to **Catacaos** $^{KM\,976}$, is the entrance to the city of **Piura** $^{KM\,982}$ *(see map on previous page)*.

Piura to Tumbes

> ➤ 285KM ➤ 3 HOURS 30 MINUTES
> ➤ PAVED ROAD

Leaving Piura and continuing N, you will pass a turnoff to the left that leads to the port of **Paita** ^{55KM}, the beach resorts of **Colán** ^{65KM} and **Yasila** ^{60KM}, and other very beautiful beaches (Cangrejos, La Grama, Islilla and Tortuga).

Continuing on the Panamericana, after passing through a tunnel 35KM from Piura that opens onto a bridge over the Chira

River, you will be rewarded with a view of the palm trees and rice fields of the lovely Sullana country-side.

Rice fields in Querecotillo,
Sullana.

You will feel you have been transported instantly to a distant Asian country, perhaps Cambodia or Laos. The small city of **Sullana** KM 1 020 is known as the «city of *guayaberas*,» for the style of light, summer shirts worn by the men. It is also known as the «pearl of the Chira,» for its fertile fields. Sullana has many hotels and restaurants. Be sure to try the *pipas heladas* (fresh coconut milk) sold by the side of the road.

• From Sullana, paved roads go E to Las Lomas 77KM and La Tina 143KM, on the Ecuadorian border, and W to the port of Paita 64KM •

The Panamericana leaves the fertile Sullana Valley to reenter the desert through a series of rolling hills. **Talara** KM 1 093, an area rich in petroleum, is the next turnoff on the highway. Although it is disorderly and dusty, it has all the basic services for travelers. Continuing N, you will reach the turnoff to the port and beaches of **Lobitos** KM 1 102, which was occupied successively by British, then North Americans and lastly by a garrison of Peruvian soldiers, but is all but abandoned today. Access to Lobitos is through a complicated web of dirt roads; it is best to ask directions of local oil company employees to avoid ending up at an oil well.

The Panamericana then climbs to the Pampa de El Atascadero and, after a series of hills and curves requiring caution, reaches **El Alto** (the turnoff to **Cabo Blanco** KM 1 136). The highway soon descends again, offering a lovely view of the coastline, and reaches **Los Órganos** KM 1 152 and **Máncora** KM 1 163, developing tourist areas with some of the most beautiful beaches in the country (Las Pocitas, Vichayito). As you drive out of Máncora, you will be surprised by a large building. Don't be startled;

Punta Sal Beach.

it is simply the new customs terminal, situated in the hollow of Quebrada Pajaritos. Proceeding N along the shoreline, you will pass the beach resort of **Punta Sal** KM 1 187 and, a few kilometers further, the hotel-resort of the same name KM 1 192. Next to appear are the small town of **Cancas** KM I 193 and the rustic ports of **Punta Mero** KM I 204 and **Acapulco** KM I 225. With the ocean still in view, you will pass **Bocapán** Canyon KM I 232 and the turnoff to the town of Casitas, the hot springs of Hervideros KM 233 and the access road to the **Parque Nacional Cerros de Amotape**.

At KM I 240 is **Zorritos**, with its lighthouse, dock and homes built in the 1950s. Today it is the favorite beach resort of the people of Tumbes.

Leaving town, there is a very dangerous curve in the road. Finally, almost at the entrance to Tumbes, there appears the tranquil fishing village of Grau and the more active one of **La Cruz** KM I 250, serving as prelude to the fertile valley of unending fields of rice, bananas and leafy mango trees. La Cruz is said to be the place where Francisco Pizarro and his men encountered their first group of coastal natives and where the conquest of the Inca Empire began in 1532. La Cruz has several restaurants. We especially recommend El Challe for its excellent *cebiches* and *majariscos*.

Finally, a bridge over the **Tumbes** River KM I 267 leads into the capital of the department. End of route.

• From Tumbes, the Panamericana continues N, passing the turnoff to Puerto Pizarro KM I 278 and its beautiful mangrove swamps, Zarumilla KM I 289, and the border town of Aguas Verdes KM I 293, one step from the Ecuadorian border •

Sunset at Puerto Pizarro.

---

2 Trujillo-Cajamarca

➤ DISTANCE: 308KM
➤ ESTIMATED TIME: 5 HOURS
➤ PAVED ROUTE
➤ ROAD MAP: 3

This is a short, but beautiful trip suitable for any type of vehicle and with a combination of dry, coastal countryside and the steep terrain of inter-Andean valleys. After turning off the Panamericana highway, the ascent into the Andes can be divided into two sections, one with a straight, slow rise APPROX. 100KM, the other with many curves and steep climbs APPROX. 65KM. After this second part, the descent into the Cajamarca Valley is easy. We recommend taking warm clothing (the pass is at a chilly 3 000M OR 9 843FT) and topping off the gas tank at San Pedro de Lloc or Chilete before continuing. The route deteriorates with the arrival of the rainy season (December to March). Although it is paved, potholes or rock slides onto the edge of the road are not uncommon.

Trujillo to Pacasmayo

- ➤ 123KM ➤ 1 HOUR 30 MINUTES
- ➤ PAVED ROAD

For travel from Trujillo to Pacasmayo, *see Route 1, p. 479-482.*

Pacasmayo to Cajamarca

- ➤ 185KM ➤ 3 HOURS 30 MINUTES
- ➤ PAVED ROAD

The road to Cajamarca starts at a turnoff at KM 683 of the Panamericana (past **Pacasmayo**) and heads E following the flow of the Jequetepeque River. (Subsequent kilometers are measured from the turn-off.) Along the way, you can see the reservoir formed by the **Gallito Ciego** KM 35, contrasting with the dry surroundings. There are picturesque towns such as **Tembladera** KM 49, devoted to rice and fruit farming, where there is also a small site museum in the San Isidro Labrador school, housing an extraordinary collection of pre-Columbian artifacts, and **Chilete** KM 90, which is known for the mangoes it exports and is the starting point for two packed dirt roads, one S to Contumazá 40KM ➤ 2H 30MIN and one N to San Miguel de Pallaques 64KM ➤ 3H 30MIN.

Mango tree, Chilete.

• From Chilete, you can turn off onto the packed dirt road that leads N to San Miguel de Pallaques and climbs

24KM 25MIN to the town of San Pablo 2 365M / 7 760FT. From here the road continues to the summit of La Copa mountain. At the top is Kunturhuasi, an important archeological site from the Formative Period (1200 to 200 BC) and contemporary to the Chavín culture. Along with the ceremonial center at Chavín de Huántar (in Ancash), Kunturhuasi was one of the most important ceremonial centers of the Peruvian highlands. There is a site museum (perhaps one of the best in the country) organized by the Japanese archeologists who excavated here and now managed by the local farming community at San Pablo. You must bring your own equipment if you wish to camp in the area. *For more information on access, see excursion map, p. 149* •

Continuing on the paved road from Chilete you will come to the towns of **Magdalena** KM 114 and Choropampa KM 125. From the latter, an 8KM jeep trail leads to the lovely Llagadén hacienda. The road continues to climb moderately to reach the town of **San Juan** KM 141. After this, it makes a serpentine climb to the **El Gavilán** Pass 3 000M/9 843FT, the highest point on the route, where the road winds between enormous walls of rain-eroded granite. From the pass, it descends through stands of pine and eucalyptus towards the green countryside of Cajamarca. End of route.

Panoramic view of the Cajamarca Valley.

Chiclayo~Tarapoto

3

- ➤ DISTANCE: 710KM
- ➤ ESTIMATED TIME: 12 TO 15 HOURS
- ➤ PARTIALITY PAVED ROAD
- ➤ ROAD MAPS: 2–9

This route is an extraordinarily beautiful trip that for a long time was only for adventurers with an all-terrain vehicle during the dry season (May to October), due to the poor road conditions. The road can be divided into three sections. The first, to Bagua Chica, is not very difficult, except for the potholes and the heat.

The second, to Pedro Ruíz, has many curves and lovely scenery and the third is typical of the jungle and its last part is almost impassable during the rainy season. We recommend taking appropriate clothing (ranging from shorts for the tropical heat to coats for the high Andean passes), drinking water and some food and driving only during the day. The best way is to stop for the night in Bagua Chica or Chachapoyas. You should have no problems with altitude sickness.

Chiclayo to Bagua Chica

- ➤ 239KM ➤ 4 HOURS 30 MINUTES
- ➤ PAVED ROAD

Leaving Chiclayo, head N to **Lambayeque** 10KM *(see map, p. 483)*. On the outskirts of Lambayeque (KM 865 on the Panamericana) you will encounter an important fork in the road. The left-hand road is the *variante*, or alternate route, of Sechura, heading NW (the road to Piura via Mórrope on the new Panamericana). The right-hand road is the older Panamericana heading NE and will take you to Piura via the town of **Olmos**. Take the latter, right-hand road. (Subsequent kilometers are counted from this point.)

Taking the route to Olmos, you will enter the desert, where the singular scenery of the northern plains is broken only by the towns of Mochumí KM 9, **Túcume** KM 16, Illimo KM 24, **Jayanca** KM 33 and **Motupe** KM 66. Solitary carob trees, *zapote* trees, and herds of goats dot the landscape. A few kilometers before Olmos, take a paved turnoff to Bagua Chica and Jaén. (Subsequent kilometers are now measured from this point. Place your odometer in 00). The paved road winds up through a narrow valley to the **Porculla** Pass 2 144 M/7 034FT, 38KM ➤ 1H FROM THE LAST TURNOFF, the lowest pass over the Andes and also the shortest route from the coast to the Amazon jungle. The northern Peruvian pipeline also runs through this pass, carrying oil from the jungle of Loreto to Bayóvar on the coast.

At the pass, desert landscape disappears and vegetation covers the hills. After a quick descent, you will come to the town of **El Tambo** KM 67, the entrance to the department of Cajamarca, where the road will begin to follow the winding Huancabamba River. The road continues its slow descent to the town of **Pucará** KM 117, on the left bank of the Chotano River. Leaving Pucará and passing through the village of **Puerto Chiple** KM 148 (where there is a turnoff to Cutervo, Chota and Cajamarca), the road finally enters the Marañón River valley and the countryside again becomes extremely arid.

Among cactus-covered hills, the road continues to the town of **Chamaya** KM 182, where there is another important fork in the road. The road to the N goes to **Jaén** (on 17KM of paved road) and San Ignacio 126KM FURTHER on the banks of the lovely Chinchipe River. You should take the road to the E, which leads to a bridge that is variously called **Corral Quemado** or 24 de Julio

The Marañon River from Corral Quemado bridge.

KM 196 and crosses the Marañón River. This bridge has replaced the legendary raftsmen, who were once entrusted with the dangerous river crossing. You will have now entered the department of Amazonas, the third department on the trip from Chiclayo. Ten kilometers further, you will enter the area known as El Valor, the site of a military airstrip. At El Valor, the road forks KM 206. The left-hand route, to the N, will take you to **Bagua Chica** 12KM AWAY, a possible stop for the night.

• From Bagua Chica, a road continues to Aramango, Chiriaco, Imazita and Uracuza on the banks of the Marañón River. You can reach Iquitos from Uracuza by traveling the Marañón River through this territory of the Aguaruna-Huambisa people. This spectacular route is known as «the route of the *pongos*.» The *pongos* (the Quechua word for 'doors') are the deep, narrow gorges, through which the river cuts through the eastern ranges to join the Ucayali and then the mighty Amazon River on the Amazon jungle plain. The primary *pongos* on this route are Rentema (near Bagua Chica), Gangariza, Gamburama, Escurrebraga, Curva de Huaracayo, Cumuc-Yacu, Yulpa, Taquitiza and Manseriche ('the one that frightens'). The Manseriche breaches the Campanquiz mountain range, the last eastern reaches of the Andes, overlooking the Amazon basin •

Bagua Chica to Chachapoyas

➤ 140KM ➤ 3 HOURS
➤ PARTIALLY PAVED ROAD

To continue the trip to Chachapoyas, return to the fork at El Valor (subsequent kilometers will be counted from this point) and taking the road to the E. You will soon reach the austere town of **Bagua Grande** KM 227 and, further along, the Utcubamba River valley. After a few kilometers, the valley narrows and becomes the Utcubamba Canyon, with

Rice fields near Bagua Grande.

a cooler climate and lush vegetation. Here the crystalline waters of the river cascade precipitously over almost vertical rock walls, forming a scene of great beauty. The river valley leads to a village of **Magunchal** KM 263. Beside the road is the Tingo waterfall, with warm, sulfur waters put to good use by travelers.

The Utcubamba widens again at the small town of **Pedro Ruiz** KM 294, where life revolves around a military base and commerce with towns in the lower jungle. Two roads lead out of here, one E to Moyobamba 180KM ➤ 6H AWAY. Take the other S to Chachapoyas 52KM ➤ 1H 30MIN. (Subsequent kilometers are counted from Pedro Ruiz.)

The road follows the course of the Utcubamba River, passing through the small town of Churuja 1 470M / 4 823FT, 13KM. It continues another 26KM to pass a turnoff to Luya and Lamud, the point of departure for a visit to the sarcophagi at Karajía. Continue on the main road 5KM to another fork, taking the road to the E.

After about a 35-MINUTES' climb, this road enters the city of **Chachapoyas** 2 334M / 7 658FT, 13KM. The road to the S, following the

The fortress of Kuélap.

valley, leads to the town of Tingo ²¹ᴷᴹ, through which you can access the archeological site of Kuélap.

• You can also continue on the road past Tingo through Leimebamba ⁶⁶ᴷᴹ, Balsas ¹⁵⁰ᴷᴹ, where a bridge re-crosses the Marañón, and Celendín ²⁰⁴ᴷᴹ, to finally reach Cajamarca ³⁰⁴ᴷᴹ ➤ 7ʜ •

Chachapoyas to Moyobamba

➤ 236ᴋᴍ   ➤ 7 HOURS
➤ PARTIALLY PAVED ROAD

To reach Moyobamba from Chachapoyas, it is necessary to backtrack 56ᴋᴍ to the town of **Pedro Ruiz**. (Subsequent kilometers are measured from this point. Place your odometer in 00). Take the road ᴇ that enters the **La Florida** valley and the town of **Pomacochas** ² ¹⁵⁰ ᴍ/⁷ ⁰⁵⁴ꜰᴛ, ³¹ᴋᴍ, where there is a lovely, 12km² lake considered one of the most attractive in the region. (Don't miss it.) From here, the road ascends to the Pardo de Miguel Pass ¹ ⁹³⁰ ᴍ /⁶ ³³²ꜰᴛ, and then descends through lush cloud forest to the town of **Naranjos** ⁸¹ᴋᴍ and Nueva Cajamarca. It continues along the Mayo River valley to the town of **Rioja** ¹ ⁴⁰⁰ ᴍ/⁴ ⁵⁹³ꜰᴛ, ¹⁶⁰ᴋᴍ.

Rioja is known for handicrafts made of woven straw and for clothing made from colorful fabrics. It was the birthplace of the nineteenth-century rubber baron, César Arana, and has many natural attractions such as Lake Mashuyacu (5ᴋᴍ from the city, with a fish farm) and the grottos of La Unión, a complex of limestone caves in the midst of lush natural beauty.

From the city of Rioja, the remaining 21ᴋᴍ ¹ʜ of partially paved road lead to the city of **Moyobamba** ⁸⁵⁰ᴍ/² ⁷⁸⁹ꜰᴛ.

Tangarana Pass, Alto Amazonas.

Moyobamba to Tarapoto

➤ 105ᴋᴍ   ➤ 2 HOURS 30 MINUTES
➤ PARTIALLY PAVED ROAD

In contrast to the previous roads, the road from Moyobamba to Tarapoto is almost completely paved. (Subsequent kilometers are measured from Moyobamba.) It climbs along the Mayo River and passes through the village of **Jepelacio** to reach the **Tangarana Pass** 1 230M /4 036FT, the highest point on the route. Once this pass is crossed, the rest of the route is downhill.

The road returns to follow the Mayo River and passes through the towns of Tabalosos, Shanao, and **Lamas** 835M/2 740FT, 77KM, the cradle of the popular art of the department of San Martín. From here, continuing downhill, the road passes through small towns such as Rumisapa, Cacatachi and Morales, to finally enter **Tarapoto** 333M /1 093FT from the W side. End of route.

• From Tarapoto, a dirt road leads past the towns of Almendral, San Cristóbal and Punta Hermosa to Yurimaguas 181M/594FT, 135KM ➤ 5H FROM TARAPOTO, on the banks of the Upper Huallaga River in the department of Loreto. From Yurimaguas, where the road ends, Iquitos can be reached by river •

Lima-Callejón de Huaylas

4

- ➤ DISTANCE: 403 KM
- ➤ ESTIMATED TIME: 6 HOURS TO 7 HOURS
- ➤ PARTIALLY PAVED ROAD
- ➤ ROUTE MAPS: 5–4

This route is suitable for any type of vehicle; it is beautiful and uncomplicated even for those who are unfamiliar with the roads of the Peruvian highlands. The route begins in Lima on a highway (*autopista*) to Huacho, then becomes a two-lane road in very good condition (aside from periodic damage caused by El Niño rains). After a turn-off at Pativilca, the rest of the route consists of two quite different sections: the first climbs[122KM] to a pass at Conococha and the second gradually descends[81KM] to Huaraz in the center of the Callejón de Huaylas. We recomend taking warm clothing, not eating heavily beforehand (as the road climbs to an altitude of 4 100M /13 400FT), filling your gas tank in Pativilca and, once you are in the Callejón de Huaylas (after passing Cátac), keeping an eye out for potholes and reducing your speed in populated areas.

Lima to Pativilca

- ➤ 202KM ➤ 3 HOURS
- ➤ 150KM OF HIGHWAY
- ➤ 52KM OF PAVED ROAD

To travel from Lima to Pativilca, *see Route 1, p. 470.*

Pativilca to Huaraz

- ➤ 201KM ➤ 4 HOURS
- ➤ PAVED ROAD

The route from **Pativilca** (KM 202 of the North Panamericana) to Huaraz is the most commonly used route into the Callejón de Huaylas. It begins at KM 203 of the North Panamericana with an initial, straight section of 20KM along the Fortaleza River, bordering extensive sugar cane fields. The first town on the road is Huaricanga KM 21, where the valley starts to narrow progres-

Drying *ají* in Shauro.

Lake Conococha.

sively and the climb into the mountains begins. The grade is moderate and the curves are wide, allowing the traveler to enjoy the beautiful countryside and picturesque towns such as **Shauro** KM 32. The *ají panca* harvested in the neighboring valleys is brought to this region to be sun-dried, as it is known for its splendid climate.

Further along are the towns of **Chasquitambo** KM 48, where there is a police checkpoint, and **Chaucayán** KM 65, where the route begins to climb steeply and from where we recommend driving with extra caution. Next to appear are **Raquia** KM 80, **Colca** KM 81 and **Cajacay** KM 90, where fruit is said to grow like nowhere else.

The final climb leads to the pass at **Conococha** 4 100M/13 452FT, KM 120, at the summit of the Cordillera Negra. (Conococha means 'warm waters' in Quechua.) This is the highest point of the route. A few kilometers beyond the pass, you can see Lake Conococha. Lying at 4 000M/13 124FT, this beautiful lake is the source of the Santa River, which flows north through the Callejón de Huaylas to Huallanca, where it starts its final descent to the sea.

• From Conococha a packed dirt road leads NE to Chiquián 3 374M/ 11 070FT, 31KM, Huallanca, La Unión, and Huánuco 293KM ➤ 7H, passing near the cordilleras Huayhuash and Raura •

Once you leave the pass behind, the final 81KM are an easy descent, first across the high Andean plateau, or *puna*, and then through stands of eucalyptus and blossom-filled canyons, with the towering Cordillera Blanca always on the right (Mount Caulliraju 5 603M/18 383FT is the most impressive here.) The route crosses the towns of **Pachacoto** KM 159, the starting point for a packed dirt road to the Pastoruri glacier 26KM; **Cátac** KM 165, the starting point for a road to Chavín de Huántar 66KM and Huari 101KM at the entrance to the Callejón de Conchucos, and finally **Ticapampa** KM 170.

Mount Huascarán, seen from Ranrahirca.

Continuing on the paved road to Huaraz you will reach **Recuay** KM 174, the first of the picturesque towns of the Callejón de Huaylas.

• From Recuay it is possible to drive to Huarmey 132KM ➤ 5H, on the coast via a packed dirt road that climbs the Cordillera Negra and passes through the town of Aija 3 363M/11 034FT •

From Recuay to **Huaraz** KM 201 there are only 25KM of easy descent along the western flank of the Cordillera Blanca. End of route.

• From Huaraz the road continues N to the coastal town of Santa, 17KM N of Chimbote. To begin this trip, you must first drive to Caraz 2 256M/7 431FT (67KM from Huaraz). Here the paved road ends and continues N as a packed dirt road to Sucre. It passes through the spectacular Cañón del Pato on a narrow stretch of 25KM with 39 tunnels, following the river-carved gorge through the Cordillera Negra, and finally reaches Huallanca 1 590M/5 217FT (106KM from Huaraz) and Yuracmarca, where the Santa River changes direction abruptly to head W to the Pacific Ocean. From Yuracmarca, the road (in fair condition) follows the river in its steep descent, passing through the last towns of Chuquicara and Vinzos before completing the route at the town of Santa. The distance between Huaraz and Santa is 240KM and takes some 6 HOURS to complete •

5

Lima-Huancayo

- ➤ DISTANCE: 295KM
- ➤ ESTIMATED TIME: 5 HOURS 30 MINUTES
- ➤ PAVED ROAD
- ➤ ROUTE MAP: 5

This is a paved route in good condition. Its first section is marked by a spectacular climb into the Andes, from sea level up to the Ticlio or Anticona Pass at 4 818M / 15 808FT in little more than 2 HOURS. This part of the route, with narrow curves and steep grades, will test the most able driver and the best of vehicles. From Ticlio to La Oroya the descent is easy, but you must stay alert as your brakes may behave erratically

En route to Huancayo.

at altitude. Finally, the descent to the picturesque towns of the Mantaro Valley is delightful, easy in grade and well marked. We recommend making this trip during the day, taking plenty of warm clothing and (to avoid altitude sickness) a good quantity of liquids and *Coramina glucosa* tablets. There are good service stations on the route, but higher-octane gasoline is only available in Lima and Huancayo. Remember to check your oil and coolant levels and reduce your speed in populated areas.

Lima to La Oroya

> ➤ 175KM   ➤ 3 HOURS
> ➤ PAVED ROAD

The Central highway leaves the center of Lima and heads E. For those not familiar with this route, we recommend driving Av. Javier Prado to the cloverleaf interchange with the Ramiro Prialé highway and taking the Prialé to Huachipa *(see map, p. 472-473)*. You will be less likely to get lost this way. The first towns you will come to are **Chaclacayo**, **Chosica** and **Ricardo Palma**, sunny suburbs of the capital only 40 MIN from town and offering many pleasant ways to enjoy a day in the country. All have numerous restaurants specializing in typical dishes such as *pachamanca* and barbecues, along with family-oriented recreation (horses, swimming pools and sports fields).

Zárate forest.

• At KM 56 there is a turn-off to the town of San Bartolomé. From the town, you can reach the Bosque de Zárate 2 400M / 7 874FT by taking a winding horse trail for almost 5 HOURS. This is perhaps the last native forest on the western slopes of the Andes, predominantly old *chachacomo* and *calatillo* trees along with many pre-Hispanic ruins. There is a site for camping, water in the nearby Carnacha Canyon, and a beautiful waterfall at the village of Llancha •

Continuing on the Central highway you will pass **San Jerónimo de Surco** KM 66.

• From San Jerónimo de Surco, via another horse trail, you can reach the picturesque village of Huaquicha and the Pala Cala falls [3H], cascading over a 20m (66ft) cliff during the rainy season •

The highway winds E and the Rímac River valley narrows into a canyon as it climbs into the Andes between sheer cliffs and enormous walls of granite, natural obstacles that required impressive engineering efforts to conquer. Evidence of this work are the spectacular bridges on the Lima–La Oroya–Huancayo railroad in the area of **El Infiernillo** [KM 99]. You will pass the town of **Matucana** [2 380M/7 809FT, KM 74] with its orchards of apple and white peach trees. Next you will pass the turn-off to Tambo de Viso [KM 82,5], a town that seems to be suspended from the beautiful, surrounding peaks. Then you will come to **San Mateo** [3 240M/10 630FT, KM 93], site of the Hotel Andino, famous for its chicken soup and as one of the few hostels on the route.

The Central highway continues its dizzying ascent to **Chicla** [3 840M/12 600FT, KM 106] and finally reaches the mining town of **Casapalca** [4 200M/13 780FT, KM 117].

• At KM 120 a packed dirt turn-off to the left leads to Lake Marcapomacocha [4 800M/15 749FT] at the foot of the spectacular Cordillera La Viuda. From here, several dirt roads lead past beautiful emerald lakes, then down to the coast through the Santa Eulalia and Chillón valleys •

Ticlio Pass and Mount Anticona.

Only a few kilometers further uphill you will come to the Anticona Pass [KM 132], better known as **Ticlio** [4 818M/15 808FT], the highest railroad pass in the world. This place, generally snow-covered, lies on the continental divide and offers a beautiful view of lakes to the E, including Lake Huacracocha [KM 136] and towering snowy mountains such as San Andrés, Monte Anticona with its three peaks, and Monte Meiggs named in honor of the British engineer who designed the railway route.

From Ticlio the road begins its descent to the mines of **Morococha** [KM 140], **Yauli** and **Duvaz** [KM 142], finally reaching the mining city of **La Oroya** [3 750M/12 304FT, KM 175], a dismal mining town where soot and cold weather prevail. The town is divided by the Mantaro River into a «new town,» the site of metallurgical installations, and an «old town,» with the miners' old homes. La Oroya is a strategic crossroads between the coast, jungle and Andes. Roads from here lead to **Huancayo**, **Tarma**, and the **Chanchamayo** Valley, as well as **Junín**, **Cerro de Pasco**, **Huánuco**, **Tingo María**, and **Pucallpa**.

La Oroya to Huancayo

> ➤ 120KM   ➤ 2 HOURS 30 MINUTES
> ➤ PAVED ROAD

Mantaro Valley.

To reach Huancayo from La Oroya, take the right-hand road going S. (Subsequent kilometers are measured from the turn-off.) The road follows the winding course of the Mantaro River among bare limestone mountains, curiously smoky in color due to the constant foundry emissions of nearby La Oroya. As you advance, vegetation reappears and the scenery becomes more attractive. After 43KM there is a stone bridge, known as Matachico, over the Mantaro River.

• Matachico bridge is the entrance to the town of Canchayllo, seat of the former Pachacallo hacienda and an important center of production for the famous Cerro de Pasco breed of cows that was developed here in Peru. By this route, after 3 HOURS of travel crossing two high altitude passes, you can also reach the lakes that are the source of the Cañete River. Continuing W towards the Pacific, you also come to the picturesque towns of Vilca and Huancaya amid some of the most beautiful natural scenery in the Peruvian highlands. Because of its difficulty, this route should only be undertaken in an all-terrain vehicle •

Continuing on towards Huancayo, the altitude decreases and becomes more bearable, allowing contemplation of the grand scenery of the Mantaro Valley. Stands of eucalyptus, colorful broom sage bushes and fields of barley line the road on the descent.

At KM 77 (Stuart Bridge), the route divides into two roads, both paved, one on each side of the Mantaro River. The two meet again 45KM further on, at the city of Huancayo. It is here, in the area known as **Hatun Mayo** (town of Huaripampa), that the

Mantaro Valley is the widest. On clear days you can see the towering Huaytapallana range in the distance, its snowy summits guarding the horizon. Place your odometer in 00.

The road following the **left bank** (E bank) of the river is perhaps the most recommended, as it passes through the most im-

portant towns in the valley. Some 1KM after the Hatun Mayo fork you will pass the turnoff to **Jauja** 3 390M/11 123FT, the city chosen by Francisco Pizarro in 1534 to be the first capital of the Viceroyalty of Peru. Only 6KM beyond Jauja (if you take the turn-off) lies beautiful **Lake Paca**, with country restaurants and bucolic surroundings. Continuing on the left-bank road, after passing the towns of Ataura and **Huamalí** KM 9, you will reach **Matahuasi** KM 22, from which a road leads to the **Ocopa Convent** and down to Satipo in the jungle.

A few kilometers further is the city of **Concepción** 3 283 M/10 772FT, KM 27, capital of the department of the same name. From Concepción the road continues to **San Jerónimo de Tunán** KM 36 and **Hualhuas**, famous for its alpaca wool textiles, and finally

Eucalyptus in Orcotuna.

arrives at Huancayo KM 43. From La Oroya, the route following the left bank of the river is 120KM 2H 30MIN.

The route following the **right bank** (W bank) of the river is less traveled and more rural than the other. Locales of great beauty, with unique native names are found on the way: **Huaripampa** KM 2, Quechua for 'indomitable plain;' **Muquiyauyo** KM 4, or 'cunningly overcome;' **Huancani** KM 11, or 'has large stones;' **Sincos** KM 15, or 'round stone;' **Orcotuna** KM 27, or 'encircled by mountains'; **Sicaya** KM 30, or 'steep slope,' with its beautiful church of Santo Domingo and the sanctuary of the Virgin of Cocharcas; and finally **Pilcomayo** KM 32 at the entrance to the city of Huancayo.

From La Oroya, the route along this side of the valley is about 114KM 2H. Because it is shorter, it is the recommended route for returning from Huancayo to La Oroya.

• Several routes begin in Huancayo: a packed dirt road leads E to the town of Pariahuanca 93KM ➤ 3H, after crossing the Huaytapallana Pass 4550M/14929FT; another, partially paved, heads W to Chupaca, San José de Quero, Tomas and Yauyos in the Cañete River valley; a third, paved and perhaps the most traveled, heads S to Huancavelica 145KM ➤ 3H 30MIN and Ayacucho 255KM ➤ 9H *(see Route 9, p. 527)* •

Lima-Chanchamayo Valley

6

> ➤ DISTANCE: 310KM
> ➤ ESTIMATED TIME: 5 HOURS
> ➤ PAVED ROAD
> ➤ ROUTE MAP: 5

This is a paved route in good condition with sufficient service stations. Its first section is marked by a spectacular climb into the Andes, from sea level up to the Ticlio or Anticona pass at 4818M/15808FT in a little over 2 HOURS. This part of the route, with tight curves and steep grades, will test the most able driver and the best of vehicles. From Ticlio to La Oroya the descent is easy, but you must stay alert as your brakes may behave erratically when travelling at high altitude. The section between La Oroya and Tarma must also be driven with care because of its steep grades and tight curves. On the last stretch, from Tarma to the jungle valley of Chanchamayo, the descent is somewhat less steep, but still has many curves and runs along sheer precipices. Many believe the La Oroya–Chanchamayo section is one of the most beautiful roads in Peru. Despite the good condition of the route, we recommend driving with care because accidents are frequent due to crossing animals and careless pedestrians.

Lima to La Oroya

> ➤ 175KM   ➤ 3 HOURS
> ➤ PAVED ROAD

To reach La Oroya from Lima, *see Route 5, p. 499.*

La Oroya to Tarma

> ➤ 56KM   ➤ I HOUR
>
> ➤ PAVED ROAD

To reach the Tarma Valley from La Oroya, you must take the left-hand road towards Cerro de Pasco. This road runs along the Mantaro River to the town of **Paccha** KM 183, where it crosses the river and then climbs through rolling hills covered in *ichu* grass to the **Cochas** Pass 4 367M/14 328FT on the high Andean plateau or *puna*. Be alert for symptoms of altitude sickness (*soroche*) and dress warmly. At KM 196, a spot known as **Las Vegas**, the road divides, with the left fork leading to Cerro de Pasco and Huánuco and the right to Tarma and Chanchamayo.

Cochas Pass.

Valley of Huinco.

Taking the road to the right, you will continue the steep descent to the picturesque Tarma Valley, nestled among mountains carpeted with fields of barley and broad beans. Several kilometers of winding descent lead to the farming village of **Huinco**, from where you can observe the deep valley falling away to the east and its fields of flowers and vegetables. Tile roofs at the far end announce the city of Tarma. Place your odometer in 00.

Tarma to San Ramón and La Merced

> ➤ 77KM   ➤ I HOUR
>
> ➤ PAVED ROAD

Although it is short, the section of the route between Tarma and La Merced makes an impressive drop of 2 800M/9 200FT in altitude as it descends from Andean mountains to high rain forest. The Central highway leaves Tarma and passes through stands of eucalyptus and fertile fields of grain. The road leads downhill into **Acobamba** 2 750M/9 023FT, 7KM.

• From Acobamba a packed dirt road heads NW towards the towns of Palcamayo and the Huagapo cave 24KM ➤ 40MIN, and the weavers' town of San Pedro de Cajas 37KM ➤ IH. Continuing N on the same road you can reach the Bombón Mesa and a paved road to Junín, Cerro de Pasco, and Huánuco •

A few minutes further on you will come to **Palca** [17 KM], where a dramatic change in the surrounding vegetation is immediately noticeable. As the road winds its way downhill, clumps of *ichu* grass give way to small bushes and leafy ferns while the valley narrows considerably and its walls become covered in bromeliads and epiphytes. This is the edge of the high rain forest. The next valley on the route is that of the Palca River, with its towering cliffs and mountainsides. Halfway down there is a turn-off to the town of **Huasa Huasi** [27 KM], known for producing the best seed potatoes in the country. Next you will come to the area known as the descent (*bajada*) of **Carpapata** [31 KM], where landslides are common, especially in summer. To avoid them, several tunnels have been built in this section (including one known as Mal Alma, or Bad Spirit), along with substantial retaining walls. During the rainy season vehicles commonly have to wait in long lines on this stretch of the road as heavy machinery repairs the road from the damage of recurrent landslides (*huaicos*). A few kilometers further on, the bushy vegetation gives way to dense cloud forest.

The arrival in the Chanchamayo Valley is unmistakable and spectacular. The valley widens and steep mountains give way to rolling hills covered in lush tropical vegetation. Extensive orchards of orange and tangerine trees can be seen on all sides. They are the main source of supply for the cities of central Peru.

The next city on the route is **San Ramón** [60 KM], on the banks of the Chanchamayo River. It was built in 1847 as a fort to repel the frequent attacks by the natives. San Ramón has restaurants and hotels ideal for spending an enjoyable weekend.

Quimiri Bridge over the Chanchamayo River.

• From San Ramón, which has an airport, you can take an aerotaxi to the jungle cities of Izcosasín and Puerto Bermúdez. Also, a packed dirt road heading E crosses the Tulumayo River valley, leading to Vitoc and Monobamba [38KM] ➤ 1H 30MIN •

Beyond San Ramón, a [17KM] stretch of road runs through fruit orchards and coffee fields, crosses the Chanchamayo River on the La Herrería bridge (officially the Eduardo de Habich bridge) and enters the city of **La Merced** 77 KM. This bustling, tropical city has many tourist services. End of route.

• Eleven KM N of La Merced, by paved road, a turn-off to the E crosses the Chanchamayo River on an iron bridge and then follows the Perené River to the jungle villages of Pichanaki 75 KM and Satipo 110KM ➤ 3H 30MIN. Further N of La Merced, after passing San Luis de Shuaro 21 KM and its old avocado orchards, is Puente Paucartambo 30KM. From here you can continue, now by packed dirt road, NE to Villa Rica 21KM ➤ 1 H 30 MIN or NW towards Oxapampa 76KM FROM LA MERCED ➤ 2H 30 MIN and Pozuzo 152KM ➤ 6H •

7 Lima-Pucallpa

> ➤ DISTANCE: 802KM
> ➤ ESTIMATED TIME: 14 HOURS
> ➤ PARTIALLY PAVED ROAD
> ➤ ROUTE MAPS: 5–4–10

This route is long and grueling, but has great beauty. Its first section (paved and in good condition) is marked by a spectacular climb into the Andes, from sea level up to Ticlio or Anticona Pass at 4 818M / 15 808FT in a little over 2 HOURS. This part of the route, with narrow curves and steep grades, will test the most able driver and the best of vehicles. From Ticlio to La Oroya the descent is easy, but you must stay alert as your brakes may behave erratically at altitude. The La Oroya–Cerro de Pasco–Huánuco section of the route lies at very high altitude, crossing the high Andean plateau, or *puna* (dress warmly and be prepared for altitude sickness). The Huánuco–Tingo María–Pucallpa section, with many tight curves, is characterized by a dramatic change in scenery as well as in road conditions. The latter becomes a packed dirt road at Tingo María. Fuel is readily available along the entire route. We recommend driving during the day only (especially once you are in the jungle) and making the trip in winter, as road conditions deteriorate seriously in summer (December to March). We also recommend stopping for the night in Huánuco.

Lima to La Oroya

> ➤ 175KM   ➤ 3 HOURS
> ➤ PAVED ROAD

To reach La Oroya from Lima, *see Route 5, p. 499.*

La Oroya to Huánuco

> ➤ 245KM   ➤ 4 HOURS
> ➤ PAVED ROAD

To reach Huánuco from La Oroya, you must take the left-hand road towards Cerro de Pasco. This road runs along the Mantaro River to the town of **Paccha** KM 183, where it crosses the river and then climbs through rolling hills covered in *ichu* grass to the **Cochas** Pass 4 367M/14 328FT on the high *puna*. Be alert for symptoms of altitude sickness (*soroche*) and dress warmly. At KM 21, a spot known as **Las Vegas** KM 196, the road divides, with one fork leading to Cerro de Pasco and Huánuco and the other to Tarma and Chanchamayo. Take the former (left-hand) road, which winds alongside the Paccha River and then climbs to the La Cima Pass 4 280M/14 043FT to reach the vast mesa of Bombón.

• At KM 214 there is a turn-off to the right that heads E on a packed dirt road to the picturesque town of San Pedro de Cajas 11KM, home of skilled weavers, and to the towns of Huagapo (famous for its cave) and Acobamba 48KM ➤ 1H 30MIN, and finally links up with the route to the Chanchamayo Valley •

After a stretch of somewhat tight curves, the road passes the **Santuario Histórico de Chacamarca** KM 220, site of the famous Battle of Junín in 1824, and then Lake Junín, which is also known as Chinchaycocha or Lago de Los Reyes and is the center of the **Reserva Nacional de Junín**. This lake, with extensive *totora* reed groves at its south end, is an important refuge

Lake Junín or Chinchaycocha.

for high Andean wildlife, especially waterfowl. It is the home of endangered species such as the Lake Junín grebe (*Podiceps taczanowskii*) and two species of edible frogs in high demand. The

En route to Óndores

best spot from which to view the lake is its western shore, reached by circling it through the towns of **Óndores** and **San Pedro de Pari**. If you wish to know more about the birds of the area, be sure to look up the well-known guide, Francisco Tueros, in Óndores.

The road continues, with the great lake always on the left, past a turn-off leading to the city of **Junín** KM 228. The next populated area is **Carhuamayo** KM 259, just before the Pasco department border.

• From Carhuamayo, a difficult but beautiful packed dirt road heads E to the jungle towns of Oxapampa (via Chontabamba) and Puente Paucartambo (via Llaupi) •

The route continues past the mining towns of Ninacaca KM 266, Shelby KM 281, and **Vicco** KM 285.

• From Vicco and Tinyahuarco, packed dirt roads to the W lead to the stone forest of the Santuario Nacional Bosque de Piedras de Huayllay, ideal for day trips or overnight camping •

The road next enters an extensive area of small lakes and meadows where alpacas are raised (Yanamate KM 292). A bit further on is the turn-off to the mining center of **Cerro de Pasco** 4 338M/

Ambo Valley.

14 233FT, KM 296 and the town of La Quinua, from which you can see the Huagurunchu massif, the main summit of the region, towering to almost 6 000M / 19 700FT in height. The road, still paved, crosses a series of hills covered in stands of *queñual* trees KM 315, then the mining towns of **Chicrín** KM 324 and Cajamarquilla KM 329, and then descends to the towns of Huariaca KM 342, Pallanchacra KM 348 and **San Rafael** KM 355, the last in the department of Huánuco. It then enters an area of recurrent landslides (keep an eye out for debris) until it reaches the town of **Huaracalla** KM 379 amid stands of eucalyptus and *maguey*. The next place of interest is **Ambo** 2 064M/6 772FT, KM 385, with restaurants and service stations. It is followed by the picturesque **Tomayquichua** 2 350M/7 710FT, KM 391 district of Huánuco and the old **Quicacán** hacienda KM 392, where the landscape distinctly changes to become more mild and pleasant. The city of **Huánuco** 1 894M/6 214FT, KM 405 is next on the route.

Huánuco to Tingo María

> ➤ 120KM   ➤ 2 HOURS 30 MINUTES
> ➤ PAVED ROAD

This short section of 120KM is defined by its steep but spectacular drop of more than 2 000m / 6 500ft into the high rain forest. Once through the city of Huánuco, the road climbs to the towns of **San Andrés** KM 415, Taruca KM 423 and **Chullqui** KM 428 (a toll booth and a turn-off to Churubamba), to finally reach the heights of **Acomayo** KM 450 and the impressive **Carpish** Pass 2 700M/8 859FT, KM 461, the highest pass crossed before entering the high rain forest, with its characteristic cloud forest, waterfalls and innumerable orchids.

From here the road begins a sharp descent to the towns of Mesapata, **Chinchao** KM 478, known for its tea plantations, **Concordia** KM 493 and **Cayumba** KM 501, where the road continues, following the Huallaga River, to the city of **Tingo María** 652M/2 139FT, KM 525.

• From Cayumba you can reach the impressive, 100m-high cataracts of San Miguel, 2 HOURS away by horse trail. At Tingo María, a section of the Marginal highway begins and leads to Tarapoto after passing through the towns of Tocache, Juanjuy, Bellavista and Picota, all located along the Upper Huallaga River valley. Although this route is very beautiful, it is not presently recommended due to the violence and danger still prevailing on some sections of the route •

Tingo María to Pucallpa

➤ 262KM ➤ 4 HOURS
➤ PARTIALLY PAVED ROAD

Heading NE out of Tingo María on the Federico Basadre highway, 16KM leads to an intersection with the Marginal highway to Pucallpa (to the right). This is the end of the paved section of the route. (Remember that the kilometers on this part of the route are measured from Pucallpa.)

• The road N (to the left) leads to Aucayacu and the towns of Huallaga Valley (Pucayacu, Uchiza and Tocache) •

Continuing E through the high rain forest, the packed dirt road leads to the town of Hermilio Valdizán. It then climbs to a place known as **La Divisoria** 1 613M/5 292FT, 28KM, the border between the departments of Huánuco and Ucayali, in the heart of the Cordillera Azul. This spot, locally known as El Boche, marks the beginning of the final descent to the Amazon plain. Take the curves with caution, especially during the rainy season. Some 29KM further, past the town of Luyando, the renowned gorge called **Boquerón del Padre Abad** 420M/1 378FT opens before the traveler, a spectacular natural setting where crystalline waterfalls drop from the almost vertical granite walls towering 1 000m / 3 300ft on each side of the Yuracyacu River. It

was named in honor of the Franciscan priest, Alonso Abad, who discovered the pass on one of his journeys into the jungle in 1757. It provides access to the Amazon without the need of climbing to higher altitudes. The route remained unknown, however, until Abad's manuscripts were found during the presidency of Óscar R. Benavides. Based on Abad's information, the highway was laid out without great difficulties and the population of the lower jungle were linked to the rest of the country. Inaugurated in 1943, the highway was named after Federico Basadre, the engineer responsible for its construction.

Padre Abad falls.

Leaving the mountains and lush scenery behind, the Marginal highway is dotted with concrete obstacles placed to prevent the landing of light aircraft, which was common during the height of the drug-trafficking era. The next place of interest is the city and river port of **Aguaytía** 287M/ 942FT, 27KM. Leaving the city by the long bridge over the Aguaytía River, the road enters the wide plains, **Pampas del Sacramento**, passing rolling hills and streams. An hour of driving leads through towns such as **Huipoca**, **San Alejandro** and Humboldt.

Forests of Aguaytía.

• At the town of Humboldt, a right-hand turn follows the Marginal highway to the Bosque Nacional (national forest) Alexander von Humboldt and the towns of Puerto Inca 110KM, Puerto Bermúdez 222KM and Villa Rica 337KM •

Leaving Humboldt, the road becomes paved once again. The town of **El Milagro** (at KM 75 from Pucallpa) is followed by the jungle town of **Neshuya** (15KM further, at KM 60 from Pucallpa), with a turn-off to Curimaná. Next is **Campo Verde** (27KM further, at KM 33 from Pucallpa), with a highway police station, and the last is **Pucallpa** 155M/509FT. End of route.

8 Lima-Tacna

- ➤ DISTANCE: 1 292KM
- ➤ ESTIMATED TIME: 16 TO 18 HOURS
- ➤ PAVED ROAD
- ➤ ROUTE MAPS: 5-6-7-8

This is a long route (somewhat boring perhaps for those not used to road trips) that takes the traveler through the southern Peruvian coastal desert and its fertile valleys. The first 132KM are on a four-lane highway (   ) and the rest is paved road in good condition. This trip is generally done in two days, one long and one short (or vice-versa), because there are few cities with good hotels and restaurants on the way. If you want to make the first day a short one (Lima to Nasca 441 KM), you can spend the night in Nasca and go on to Tacna the next day. Others prefer to make the longer drive first (Lima to Arequipa 1 005KM), spending the night in Arequipa before continuing to Tacna. The inconvenience of this option is that it adds some 78KM to the drive (the side trip to Arequipa), but provides enjoyment of Arequipa's legendary hospitality and cuisine.

We recommend bringing a generous supply of drinking water and keeping an eye on your vehicle's fluid levels. Top off your gas tank before starting the Nasca to Arequipa section, as there are very few service stations.

Lima to Chincha

➤ 196KM   ➤ 2 HOURS 30 MINUTES
➤ 132KM OF HIGHWAY
➤ 64KM OF PAVED ROAD

Leaving Lima and getting on the four-lane, South Paname-ricana highway is considerably less complicated than the getting on the North Panamericana *(see map, p. 472-473)*. Once you have crossed the Atocongo bridge it is impossible to get lost. The highway is first rate and is very well marked. Be very care-ful for the first 20KM, as pedestrians cross the highway fre-quently and the lack of lighting is dangerous at night.

On the outskirts of Lima, you will pass the city's only nature re-serve, the **Reserve Zone Panta-nos de Villa**, a wetland that is a vital resting and feeding area for over 160 species of resident and migratory birds. You can reach it by taking a turn-off at KM 18 (toll booth).

Snowy egret (*Egretta thula*) at Villa marshes.

At KM 29, in the Lurín Valley, you will spot a promontory over-looking cultivated fields; this is **Pachacámac** ('Lord of the world' in Quechua) the most important pre-Hispanic sanctuary on the Peruvian coast and the most important archeological complex of the capital city of Lima. To visit it, take the turn-off to Lurín at KM 26.

A few kilometers further S, still on the Panamericana, are the favorite beaches among the people of Lima, ideal for surfing. Entrances to these begin from a road (the old South Panameri-cana) paralleling the new South Panamericana highway. To reach this road you must exit at KM 35 or KM 48.

• The first beaches on the southern route are Arica and the Los Pul-pos resort KM 35 TO KM 37, followed by El Silencio, Caballeros and Seño-ritas KM 38 TO KM 43, perhaps the most popular. Next come the resorts of Punta Hermosa, where thousands of young people congregate in summer, and the private beach of La Quebradita KM 40. Further S on the old South Panamericana are **Punta Rocas** KM 46, a favorite beach among surfers as its spectacular waves have put it on the international surfing circuit, then **Punta Negra** KM 45, and **San Bartolo** KM 48, two beach towns that were built in the 1960s and have been recently renovated. Santa María and Embajadores (turn-off at KM 51) appear next, with luxurious modern buildings and a yacht club. There are restaurants, pubs and discotheques along this entire portion of the route, operating primarily during the summer. There are also hostels and houses for short-term rent •

Continuing on the Panamericana, you will pass turn-offs to beautiful private resorts (La Honda, Pelícanos, La Quipa) and the picturesque resort and fishing village of **Pucusana** KM 58, an ideal place for spending the day, fishing and dining (boats are available for rent). N of Pucusana by 1KM is the turn-off to Naplo, a more exclusive resort with private areas.

Next come the turn-offs to **Chilca** KM 62, an old fishing village with a spacious beach, **Las Salinas** (with three lagoons that locals say have curative properties), and Lapa Lapa KM 67, an attractive private resort.

Continuing S, you will pass the turn-offs to the beaches of **Puerto Viejo** KM 72; San Antonio KM 79 (and the southern site of the Lima yacht club, Club Regatas); Boca León KM 79,5 (private); the popular **León Dormido** KM 80, the extremely popular **La Ensenada** KM 82 and **Totoritas** KM 86 (private).

Asia Beaches.

• At KM 86 (Totoritas) is the turn-off to the town and valley of Mala, renowned for its *chicharrones* and *tamales*. Some 35KM up the valley are the picturesque towns of Calango and La Capilla, with a clear river, grain and corn fields and apple orchards •

The highway continues S past the beaches of Bujama and Chocaya (turn-offs at KM 91 and KM 92) and the area known as **Asia** KM 97. Facing an island also called Asia are a number of recently built private resorts: Playa Blanca, Flamingos, La Isla, Las Brisas, Caima, Las Palmas, Los Cocos and Kapala, to name a few.

Next, cliffs and sandy mountains flank the enormous beach

of **Sarapampa** KM 105 and conceal the beautiful beaches of Chepeconde KM 119,5, Puerto Fiel KM 121, **Gallardo** KM 124 and Los Lobos KM 126. At KM 132 is the turn-off to the resort and fishing village of **Cerro Azul**, a high point on the route. According to chronicler Pedro Cieza de León [1550], there were some turquoise-colored, pre-Hispanic buildings on the slopes of Mount Centinela (at the S end of the beach) that belonged to the dominion of Huarco. Seen from the sea, these buildings gave the mountain a blue tone, and its the name. The highway ends at Cerro Azul, where there are numerous hotels and restaurants.

Tomato fields in Cañete.

A few minutes later you will enter the **Cañete** Valley KM 142 and its fields of cotton, asparagus, tangerines, sweet potatoes and orange marigolds. The city of Cañete has good restaurants, including Muelle 56 (Jr. Bolognesi 156), although the most popular is El Piloto, next to the highway at KM 137 in the San Vincente district, famous for its *lomo saltado* and its crepes.

• From Cañete, a paved road enters the valley and leads to Imperial (only 5KM away), where you can lunch at the popular Ñañón, a good restaurant specializing in crayfish. Following this paved road through a series of picturesque villages (Socsi, Paullo, Catapalla), you will come to the town of Lunahuaná 42KM, with good hotels and restaurants serving typical Peruvian food. This area is ideal for adventure sports (rafting, kayaking, mountain biking and hang-gliding). From Lunahuaná you can continue on a packed dirt road to the Mantaro Valley and Huancayo, crossing some of the most beautiful spots in the country. On the way to Huancayo, 120KM NE of Lunahuaná are the towns of Huancaya and Vilca 3650M / 11 976FT, with spectacular waterfalls (including those at Huallhua, 35m, or 115ft high) and emerald lakes. To find food and lodging in Huancaya, ask for the friendly Doña Aquila or seek out municipal employees •

Leaving Cañete, the Panamericana climbs and crosses a desert mesa. Drive with caution as this area has many tight curves and, in winter, dense fog. The road then descends to the seashore and the long beaches of **Wakama** KM 178, **Jahuay** KM 182 (at the entrance to the department of Ica), and Totoritas KM 189, favorites among the people of Chincha. After a few more kilometers of desert you will reach the valley and the city of **Chincha** KM 196.

Chincha to Pisco

➤ 39KM ➤ 30 MINUTES
➤ PAVED ROAD

Immediately after Chincha you will pass a turn-off to Chincha Baja and the port of Tambo de Mora KM 202. A bit further and to the left, just between two branches of the San Juan River (known as Chico and Matagente), there is a paved entrance that leads to the town of El Carmen 10KM AWAY and the beautiful hacienda house of San José 11KM AWAY, both enclaves of Peruvian Black art.

At KM 211 there is a packed dirt road that leads through cotton fields to the archeological site of Huaca Centinela and the beaches of San Pedro, Barranquito and Chamberí.

Leaving the valley, the road crosses 20KM of desert with dangerous curves and dense winter fog, to reach the town of San Clemente KM 227 (watch for pedestrians and local traffic).

Tambo Colorado.

• From San Clemente KM 228 a paved road leads to Pámpano and continues as a packed dirt road to Castrovirreyna (to the N) and Ayacucho (to the S) via the difficult, but spectacular Ruta de los Libertadores. 31KM along this road is the town of Humay, known as the birthplace of Luisa La Torre (1819–1869), the venerated beata, or lay sister of Humay. On this road is also the archeological site of Tambo Colorado, which many consider the best example of Inca architecture on the Peruvian coast •

Pisco (turn-off at KM 231) is around the next corner. To enter the city, take a paved road for 5KM that leads to the Plaza de Armas and the beachfront promenade.

• From Pisco you can reach the Paracas beach resort and Reserva Nacional de Paracas 22KM ➤ 20MIN via a paved road that follows the beach and passes through the fishing village of San Andrés (ideal for first-rate seafood). San Andrés is the last town on the way to have a service station (diesel and 84-octane gasoline), so we recommend top-ping off your tank before continuing. The road continues past an Air Force Base (try not to stop), fishmeal factories (try not to breathe), and a left-hand, paved turn-off that returns to the Panamericana at its KM 246. Finally, a small turn-off to the right will lead to the Paracas bay resort. Passing the turn-off and continuing S, you will reach the Paracas National Reserve entrance station •

Pisco to Ica

> 75KM   > 45 MINUTES
> PAVED ROAD

From Pisco the road continues through the desert, the site of in-teresting, crescent-shaped dunes, then crosses the arid and solitary flats or pampas of **Villacurí**, where date palms planted by Jesuit priests in Colonial times still grow.

Dunes of Comatrana, Ica.

At KM 257 is **Pozo Santo**, an oasis converted into a shrine with a small chapel to Franciscan fa-ther Ramón Rojas (1775–1839), known as el *Padre Guatemala* and venerated throughout the region. According to legend, his plea for divine intervention made water spring up in this desert spot, that has been called *pozo santo*, or holy well, ever since.

• From Pozo Santo a packed dirt road (recommended for all-terrain vehicles only) leads to beaches at the S end of the Paracas National Reserve (Carhuas, Barlovento, and Laguna Grande). We recommend driving this route only by day and with someone who knows it well •

Further along you will pass the towns of **Guadalupe** KM 292 and **Subtanjalla** KM 297, known for their dates, mangoes and pecans. In the wide Ica Valley, fields of cotton, lima beans, asparagus and kidney beans, vineyards and old ficus trees bordering the highway are the prelude to the city of **Ica** KM 302, the grape and wine capital of Peru, on the slope of an enormous dune.

Ica to Nasca

➤ 139KM   ➤ 1 HOUR 30 MINUTES

➤ PAVED ROAD

Leaving the city and valley of Ica behind and continuing S, you will find a turn-off KM 335 to the old hacienda of **Ocucaje** 2KM, today a charming hotel, and **Lomitas** beach 60KM. From here on, the scenery is dominated almost entirely by the Ica mesa, a desert covered in dunes crossed occasionally by small river valleys devoted to farming.

Palpa geoglyphs.

• At KM 384 there are turn-offs to the archeological site of Huayurí and the old beach resort and fishing village of Punta Caballas (to the right), accessed via a packed dirt road running parallel to the Grande River for TWO HOURS •

An enormous, stone mountain breaks the monotony of the scenery. Here is the extremely narrow (and dangerous) Santa Cruz tunnel KM 387 and the winding descent to the Grande River valley, now closed and replaced by the Santa Cruz alternate route.

The next town is **Palpa** KM 395, famous for fruit trees (oranges and plums) and cotton fields. It is well worth visiting during the grape and plum harvest festivals (first week of April) and during the Orange Festival (second half of August).

• At Hacienda Chichictara, 11KM S of Palpa, are a series of impressive rock carvings of stylized animals, presumably done by the Nasca culture (second to seventh centuries AD) •

Continuing S, you will pass a turn-off to the town of **Ingenio** KM 416, birthplace of Ángel Valdez, who was known as El Maestro and considered Peru's best bullfighter of all time. (Legend has it that he was able to fight twelve bulls in a single afternoon.) Starting at KM 420 you will enter the **Pampas de San José** plain, the site of the **Nasca lines and geoglyphs**. Remember that driving onto this area with any type of vehicle is strictly prohibited (and penalized with heavy fines). From a lookout tower beside the road at KM 420 you can observe several of the designs.

A turn-off from this point leads to the archeological site of Cahuachi [14KM]. Finally, like a mirage appearing on the wide desert plain, the city of **Nasca** [KM 441] appears.

Nasca to Arequipa

➤ 563KM ➤ 6 HOURS 30 MINUTES
➤ PAVED ROAD

• Just after leaving Nasca [KM 445], a paved turn-off climbs 100KM [1H, 30MIN] along the Nasca Valley to the Reserva Nacional Pampa Galeras Bárbara d'Achille [3 800M / 12 468FT] a paradise of vicuñas. This road leads to Puquio, continuing from there as a packed dirt road to Chalhuanca and the city of Abancay [460KM FROM NASCA]. The section from Abancay to Cusco [660KM FROM NASCA] is almost entirely paved. This road crosses landscapes of great beauty, but some portions are in poor condition •

Continuing on the Panamericana, you will pass the first turn-off to **Punta San Juan de Marcona** [KM 483].

• This paved road leads, after some 38KM, to the industrial port of Marcona, a ghost town at the site of the largest iron mine in Peru. THREE KILOMETERS from Marcona is Punta San Juan, known in former times as Punta Parada. It was the site of various shipwrecks, including that of the steamship Rímac in 1855, on which Ricardo Palma (1833–

Inca terns (*Larosterna inca*) at Punta San Juan de Marcona.

1919), author of the famous *Tradiciones Peruanas* was among the survivors. The point, now declared a reserve zone, is a paradise for sea lions and has the largest Humboldt penguin colony in Peru, along with millions of seabirds and other species of coastal marine fauna. Authorization from the Ministry of Agriculture is required to enter the zone •

At KM 528, now in the department of Arequipa, is the turn-off to **Lomas** (9KM of paved road), an almost obligatory stop on the trip through the southern desert. This small bay of friendly fishermen still conserves much of the flavor of old traditional ports. It has a beautiful beach of tranquil waters, several restaurants serving very good fish and seafood, and a pair of small hostels near the water (Hostal Lomas, Tel 21 0282). Highly recommended.

Further S you will pass the sand dunes of **Sacaco** KM 540, the largest pre-Historic whale graveyard in the world. Discovered by Italian savant Antonio Raimondi (1826–1890), it has abundant remains of mammals, birds and even giant sharks that disappeared from the Earth some 10 million years ago. There is a site museum built around a spectacular discovery, the Roque whale.

Still crossing the immense sand dunes of Sacaco, you will come to the turn-off to **Acarí** KM 550, a peaceful farming town known for its beans and olives as well as for the hospitality of its inhabitants.

Desert continues to prevail until you will reach the town and valley of **Chaviña** KM 553, whose name, derived from the expression «mucha viña,» refers to the extensive vineyards here. On the journey between Nasca and Arequipa, Chaviña is one of the few spots with a service station, so we recommend filling your gas tank here.

Olive trees in Yauca.

After a pronounced curve, you will be greeted by the striking olive grove of **Yauca** KM 566. Its leafy orchards were grown from a single tree, stolen from a grove planted around 1550 by conquistador Antonio de Rivera at his home in the San Isidro district of Lima. This small valley, entirely devoted to the production of olives and olive oil, is almost an obligatory stop on the route. Fresh local bread and crayfish are also available here.

After a long straight section through sand dunes that often intrude onto the road (which at this point runs alongside the beach), you will reach **Tanaka** KM 580, a small beach resort that is empty for most of the year. In this area, sandstorms are so frequent that house windows are commonly bricked up.

Tanaka Beach.

From Tanaka you will climb into mountains of erosion-carved rock (Morro Chala), the remains of an ancient coastal range. In the desolation of the almost-lunar landscape you will pass the turn-off to the rocky beach of **Silaka** KM 589, frequented by the inhabitants of the highland town of Jaquí (E of Yauca). Next appear a series of canyons with vegetation irrigated by water off the nearby hills. These are the hills or lomas of **Atiquipa** KM 594, the most extensive coastal hills in Peru and the source of pasturage for nomadic Peruvian shepherds since time immemorial. At KM 597 are the beautiful beaches of **Jihuay** (next to remains of the pre-Inca citadel of Ayparipa), Moca, Cascajal, Champeque and Los Lobos.

A discreet sign announces the turn-off to **Puerto Inca** KM 603. Also known as Quebrada de la Huaca (the name given by German archeologist Max Uhle), this beautiful beach has many archeological remains lying only a few meters from the water. They are the vestiges of the ancient fishing village of Llacpatera, which provided fresh fish to Inca nobility. It is said that *chasquis*, the empire's message runners, would carry fresh fish to the Inca in less than a day. In the surroundings are remains of living quarters, colcas or storage rooms, llama corrals and sections of the stone road that joined the coast to the Andes. There is a small hotel with a restaurant (Hotel Puerto Inka. Reservations Arequipa Tel 27 2663).

Only a few minutes from Puerto Inca is the port town of **Chala** KM 613, once an important center of trade and commerce for products of the southern Andes. In the late nineteenth century, many steamships from England and Denmark anchored here, which provides an idea of the extent of the local economic bonanza during the era. In 1948, a violent earthquake destroyed the town, the pier, the recently built Hotel de Turistas and the fishmeal factory. Today, the decades of prosperity are only a memory for its inhabitants, as Chala has undergone a long period of crisis. There are a few simple hotels and restaurants.

Continuing on the Panamericana you will reach the town of Puerto Viejo KM 646 and, a bit further S, the port of **Atico** KM 692 with a fishmeal factory and guano-producing promontory. In a narrow valley 10KM further is the town of Atico, an area of beautiful beaches (La Florida, Los Colorados, El Pato) with a myriad of islets and points. Continuing through the sand dunes, next to come is the industrial fishing center of **La Planchada** KM 754, then the green and fertile valley of **Ocoña** KM 776, truly a relief on the desolate southern coast. Ocoña, land of rice paddies and lima bean fields, has a port (actually a wide, rocky beach) where a few fishermen live.

From the desert, you will once again enter rice fields in the **Camaná** Valley KM 835, where the river of the same name empties into

Rice fields in the Camaná Valley.

the ocean. This river, famous for its crayfish, is known as the Majes River upstream, and, even further upstream, as the Colca River. The city of Camaná is small and quiet (too quiet for some), but there are many restaurants (don't miss El Rinconcito Trujillano, Jr. Pizarro 304), very good *chifas*, or Chinese restaurants, and an old, but comfortable Hotel de Turistas (Av. Lima 138, Tel 57 1113).

Leaving Camaná the road follows the shoreline and passes through some of the most beautiful areas on the coast (the beaches of Cerillos, La Dehesa, Primavera, Las Gaviotas, and the turn-off to the port and fishing village of Quilca KM 845). It then turns E towards the pampas of Sihuas and **Majes** KM 900 (and the turn-off to the rock carvings at Toro Muerto), crosses the town of Tambillo or El Alto KM 913 (and the paved turn-off to Huambo), **Vítor** KM 948 and El Cruce KM 958, arriving finally at **Repartición** KM 966. From here the left-hand road continues to Arequipa ^{39KM VIA TINGO AND UCHUMAYO} *(see map on following page)* and the right-hand road to Mollendo and Tacna.

Arequipa to Tacna

> ➤ 365KM   ➤ 3 HOURS
> ➤ PAVED ROAD

Leaving Arequipa, return to the Panamericana at Repartición KM 966. At KM 981 you will find the turn-off to the ports of **Matarani** and **Islay**. Matarani is the new port, Islay the old one.

• The turn-off at KM 981 also leads to beautiful beaches (Quilca, Punta Hornillos, La Huata, San José). Following the coast along this road, the next to appear is Mollendo, the principal industrial port of the area. This city, previously the site of a railroad to Arequipa, was bombed by a Chilean naval squadron during the War of the Pacific (1879–1883). Continuing S for about 16KM, you will reach the beach resort of Mejía, a favorite among the people of Arequipa since the early twentieth century. A few kilometers further S, the mouth of the Tambo River appears, and a series of lagoons and wetlands with extensive totora reed groves: the lagoons of Mejía, recognized in 1984 as a National Sanctuary due to their importance as a rest and feeding area for migratory birds. This area is the last refuge for fauna in the almost 2 000km of coastal desert between the feeding areas of Paracas near Pisco and the wetlands in northern Chile. A bit further S, a paved turn-off leads back to the Panamericana KM 1 035 (at the town of El Fiscal) •

Continuing on the Panamericana, you will enter a desolate section, climbing gradually among the rocky hills and vast sand dunes of Pampa de Guaneros until you reach a turn-off KM 1 140 leading to the valley and city of **Moquegua**. This road, only 6KM long, runs through the green Moquegua countryside, past vineyards and olive groves, to join a road from the right that heads towards the mining settlement of Cuajone, the heights of the Puno department, Mazo Cruz and, finally, Bolivia. The city of Moquegua, characterized by its gabled roofs, is famous for its sweets, preserved fruits, and its great pisco, unquestionably the best of its kind in the country.

Continue S until you cross the railroad line KM 1 182 that con-

Arequipa's main square.

Sumbay grasslands.

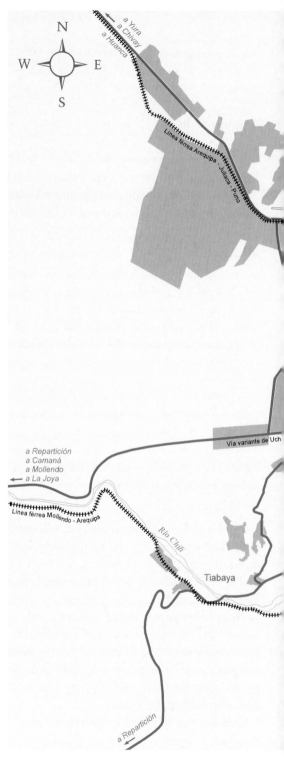

a Yura
a Chivay
a Huanca

Línea férrea Arequipa - Juliaca - Puno

Vía variante de Uch

a Repartición
a Camaná
a Mollendo
← a La Joya

Línea férrea Mollendo - Arequipa

Río Chili

Tiabaya

a Repartición

AREQUIPA. ACCESS AND BYPASS ROUTES

nects the Ilo coast to the Toquepala and Cuajone mines. Nearby KM 1 186, is the turn-off to **Ilo**, the former port of Moquegua that was the scene of violent events in the past. Attacks by the pirate, Bartholomew Sharp, in 1655, an earthquake and flooding in 1868 (that demolished the town), and battles of the War of the Pacific (1879–1883).

Today Ilo is the headquarters of the Southern Peru Copper Corporation and is an active center of commerce. With some of the most beautiful beaches on the Peruvian coast, this is a land of seafood: *cebiches* and *parihuelas*. The city offers all basic services, some of them surprisingly good. We recommend Hotel Chiribaya (Tel 054-78 4050) and Los Corales restaurant.

Punta Coles.

Ite wetlands.

• La Costanera, a paved road to Tacna, begins at Ilo and runs parallel to the ocean. A series of beautiful, calm beaches can be reached by this route (Tres Hermanas, Punta Coles, Pozo de Las Lizas, Ite, Meca Grande, Meca Chica), all ideal for sport fishing and diving. Further along on the Costanera, about 50KM from Ilo at the mouth of the Locumba River (in the bay of Ite), there are extensive, curious wetlands (formed as a result of two decades of mine tailings) that have become a refuge for waterfowl. This area, with beautiful small beaches, is recommended for camping. Further along the Costanera (70KM from Ilo), you will reach one of the largest hills on the Peruvian coast: Morro Sama, 700m (2 297ft) high, with enormous cacti on the ocean side, sea lion colonies, seabirds and a lighthouse. Past Morro Sama is the fishing village of Vila Vila 90 KM, at the mouth of the Sama River, and the resort of Boca del Río (with many services and a favorite among the people of Tacna). The final point on the Costanera is the beach of La Curva; there the road turns E to rejoin the Panamericana about 15KM S of Tacna •

Enormous sand dunes continue to dot a desert that, by now, will be driving even the most seasoned driver to despair.

At KM 1 210, you will cross the extremely narrow Locumba River valley.

• From the Locumba Valley a road heads E, passing through the town of Locumba and climbing to Lake Aricota $^{2\,783\,M/9\,131FT}$, the town of Candarave $^{3\,415M/11\,205FT}$ and beautiful Lake Suches $^{4\,750M/15\,585FT}$, to finally reach Puno and Desaguadero (on the Bolivian border) •

Next appears the equally tiny Sama River valley $^{KM\,1\,255}$, the site of a customs control point and some roadside restaurants. An enormous military base breaks the monotony at the pampa of Lagayache. This is **Alto de la Alianza** $^{KM\,1\,285}$, announcing the patriotic atmosphere of the upcoming southern city. You will climb to a small mesa and finally descend to the city of **Tacna** $^{KM\,1\,292}$. End of route.

• There are 49KM between the «Heroic City» of Tacna and the La Concordia Pass on the Chilean border. All vehicles must stop at the Santa Rosa Border Complex $^{KM\,1\,326}$, where the usual document checks are done. From Tacna, several packed dirt roads head into the Andes. One leads to the towns of Tarata $^{3\,075M/10\,089FT}$, Mazo Cruz (at over $4\,000M/13\,100FT$), and Puno, while the other climbs the Caplina River valley, crosses the impressive punas of Pachía, Palca, the La Monja Pass $^{4\,812M/15\,788FT}$, and Lake Blanca to the Peru-Chile-Bolivia border, the site of unique trade fairs •

Huancayo-Ayacucho

9

➤ DISTANCE: 255KM
➤ ESTIMATED TIME: 9 HOURS
➤ PAVED ROAD
➤ ROUTE MAP: 6

This route is a typical trip through the highlands of Peru, with the difficulties (potholes and dust) common to rural, packed dirt roads and the usual lack of service stations, but passing through truly unique landscapes. Altitude sickness should not be a problem, since you will have crossed higher altitudes on the way to Huancayo than you will encounter on this route. Be careful on curves, especially when descending, and ask directions frequently to confirm that you are on the right road (there are many side roads and signs are few).

deficiente). Recomendamos hacer este recorrido sólo de día, de preferencia durante el invierno (llueve de diciembre a marzo) y tener siempre agua a la mano y abrigo suficiente.

En route to Izcuchaca.

Huanta.

The road from Huancayo to Ayacucho is little used because of its poor condition. There are actually two roads between these two cities. The main one, running along the bottom of the Mantaro Valley, is more direct, but deteriorates rapidly in bad weather. The other one, along the mountains above the river, is in better condition and passes through more populated areas (Pucará, Pampas and Churcampa), but is considerably longer. The former road, in the lower valley, will be described here.

The main route leaves Huancayo on a short, paved section that descends the Mantaro Valley to the towns of Huayucachi 7KM, **Huacrapuquio** 12KM, Imperial 31 KM, **Acostambo** 38KM and **Izcuchaca** 2 900 M 9 515FT, 65KM, where it joins a road coming from Pisco and Huancavelica. Izcuchaca is a small town with a mild climate and a beautiful Colonial-era bridge. From here the road continues S past the town of Mejorada 75KM and the Tablachaca dam (which feeds the Santiago Antúnez de Mayolo hydroelectric plant).

After a long stretch along the Mantaro River, the road reaches the town of **Mayocc** KM 180, where it rejoins the other road from Huancayo.

It next crosses the Alcomachay bridge (which is continuously buffeted by the river) and, 8KM further, the Mayocc bridge over the Mantaro River, which at this point heads NW and away from the road. Some 20KM further on is the serene city of **Huanta** 2 628 M / 8 622FT, also known as the «garden of the Andes» for its excellent climate and profusion of cultivated fields. From Huanta to **Ayacucho** there are only 50KM of paved road in good condition, truly a blessing for suffering drivers. End of route.

Pisco-Abancay

10

- ➤ DISTANCE: 655KM
- ➤ ESTIMATED TIME: 13 TO 16 HOURS
- ➤ PARTIALLY PAVED ROAD
- ➤ ROUTE MAPS: 6–7

This is a long, somewhat arduous route with high altitude passes and poor conditions in some sections. This trip is generally done in two parts of similar distance and difficulty, spending the night in the city of Ayacucho. The first section (Pisco to Ayacucho) via the recently-paved Ruta de los Libertadores, is easy but somewhat tedious, crossing a couple of passes at over 4 000M/ 13 000FT. We recommend filling the gas tank at Huaytará and taking sufficient warm clothing. The second section (Ayacucho to Abancay) also crosses a high-altitude pass and has an area of tight curves and cliffs that must be driven with caution (between Andahuaylas and Abancay). We recommend driving this route only by day and preferably with an all-terrain vehicle. The route deteriorates to a great extent with the arrival of summer rains.

Pisco to Ayacucho

- ➤ 335KM ➤ 6 HOURS
- ➤ PARTIALLY PAVED ROAD

The turn-off to Ayacucho starts from the outskirts of Pisco at the town of **San Clemente** (KM 227 of the South Panamericana highway). Formally called the Route of the Free-dom Fighters (Ruta de los Libertadores), this road was long been known as «the route of the brave» due to its poor condition. Today, it is entirely paved.

Calquichico Valley.

The road slowly ascends the Pisco River valley, passing through the towns of Independencia [13KM] and **Humay** [404 M/1 326FT, 31 KM], known for having been the home of Luisa La Torre (1819–1869), the venerated *beata* of Humay. The road leads past the archeological site of Tambo Colorado (which many believe is the best example of Inca architecture on the coast) and the village of Huancano [66KM]. The town of **Pámpano** [81KM] is next, at an important fork in the road: the road to the right leads, by a more direct route, to Ayacucho via a stretch of road know as the *variante* de Huaytará, while the road to the left goes to Huancavelica.

• The road to Huancavelica passes through the town of Ticrapo 2 174M/7 133FT. From here, 41KM of difficult road, through numerous tunnels, tight curves, and precipices leads to Castrovirreyna 3 975M/13 042FT, KM 134. Next is the town of Santa Inés, with a turn-off to Pilpichaca (and the old road to Ayacucho) and surrounded by a beautiful series of lakes (Choclococha, Orcococha, Agnococha) that are the source of the Pisco River. FIVE HOURS 189KM from the turn-off at Pámpano,

the road reaches Huancavelica 3 675M/12 058FT. Continuing on this same route you can reach the Mantaro Valley (Huancayo 390KM) through the towns of Izcuchaca and Acostambo •

Inca palace of Huaytará.

The right-hand road crosses the valley and town of **Huaytará** 2 658 M/8 721FT, KM 109, a pretty Andean village with a beautiful church that was built over an Inca palace. The road then climbs steeply to a turn-off to Rumichaca and Pilpichaca. It crosses the Apacheta Grande Pass 4 460M/14 633FT, the highest pass on the route, then descends to Casacancha and enters the city of **Ayacucho** KM 335 from the W.

Ayacucho to Andahuaylas

> ➤ 205KM   ➤ 4 HOURS
> ➤ PAVED ROAD

From Ayacucho (subsequent kilometers are counted from the city), the packed dirt road continues S, passing a turn-off at KM 41 that leads to the regions of Cangallo and Vilcashuamán. It climbs to the Huamina Pass 4 400M/14 436FT, then descends dramatically to the towns of Ocros and the Pampas River valley 1 820M/5 971FT.

After crossing a bridge over the Pampas River, it climbs again to the picturesque town of **Chincheros** 2 772M/9 095FT amid fertile fields and towering mountains. Continuing on the road to Andahuaylas over plains and past steeply-cut precipices, you will reach Uripa, climb to the heights of Soraccocha, and descend once again to the town of **Talavera**, with its stone plaza, a curious clock-tower (still functioning) and, nearby, the hot spring baths of **Hualalache**. From Talavera, only 4KM remain to the city of **Andahuaylas** 2 899M / 9 512FT.

Andahuaylas to Abancay

- ➤ 140KM   ➤ 3 HOURS
- ➤ PACKED DIRT ROAD

Leaving Andahuaylas, the road enters the **San Jerónimo** district, surrounded by trees and bucolic countryside. It next climbs to **Kishuara** 3 450M / 11 319FT and the *ichu*-grasslands of the high Andean *puna*. Here it begins the steep descent to the **Pachachaca** River valley 2 000M / 6 562FT, where there is an attractive, Colonial-era, stone bridge. The warm climate of the area, in contrast to the enormous surrounding mountains, permits the cultivation of a great variety of crops including sugar cane and vegetables.

From Pachachaca the towering Mount Ampay marks the way to the city of **Abancay** at the end of the valley. This section along the Pachachaca Valley has many tight curves and is in poor condition. We recommend driving it during the morning to avoid the truck traffic that tends to be heavy at night. End of route.

Outskirts of Abancay.

11 Nasca~Cusco

- ➤ DISTANCE: 606KM
- ➤ ESTIMATED TIME: 14 TO 18 HOURS
- ➤ PARTIALLY PAVED ROAD
- ➤ ROUTE MAPS: 7–11

This beautiful route is little traveled due to its poor condition in some sections, but mainly because there is no lodging on the way. The road between Nasca and Puquio has been recently paved, but the next section is the most difficult, taking almost an entire day to cross the cold, high plateaus, or *punas*, of Ayacucho (be prepared for altitude sickness) to the town of Chalhuanca, where there is only one rustic hostel (El Zegarra) for spending the night. The following day you can fill your gas tank and continue to Abancay. This is the most beautiful part of the route; it has no high passes, road conditions are good, and the landscapes are lovely. The last section (Abancay to Cusco) is easy and almost entirely paved. We recommend driving the route unhurriedly, by day only, and during the dry season (May to December). Do not forget to reduce your speed when passing through the populated areas on the way.

Nasca to Abancay

- ➤ 465KM   ➤ 10 TO 12 HOURS
- ➤ PARTIALLY PAVED ROAD

There are several roads into the department of Apurímac. The most traveled is the paved road from Nasca to Puquio, that begins in the Nasca River valley and climbs to the vast Andean plateaus of the **Pampa Galeras Bárbara d'Achille National Reserve** 4 000M/13 000FT ON AVERAGE, refuge for thousands of graceful vicuñas. It next passes the turn-off to Lucanas 130KM, a community that plays a key role in protecting these camelids on the verge of extinction. It then descends to the valley and austere city of **Puquio** 3 214M/10 545FT, 175 KM (top off your gas tank here). From Puquio the road climbs to the Occe-Occe Pass 4 400M/14 436FT,

Vicuñas (*Vicugna vicugna*) in Pampas Galeras.

crosses the *pampas* of **Yaurihuiri** 203KM (on the shores of a beautiful lake) and passes a turn-off to the towns of Andamarca, Cabana, and Querobamba. Continuing on towards Abancay, now on packed dirt road, it climbs to the Huas-huaccasa Pass 4 350M / 14 272FT, then reaches the town of Cotaruse 2 936M / 9 633FT, 323KM on the bank of the Cotaruse River. The next town is **Chalhuanca** 2 888M /9 476FT, 345 KM, capital of the province of Aymaraes, is a good place to spend

Lake Yaurihuiri.

the night or take a rest before the long road remaining to Abancay. From Chalhuanca, the road follows the beautiful Pachachaca River valley, past the old haciendas of Ninaybamba, Amoray, and Purcay. Continuing along the Pachachaca, it leads to Santa Rosa 395KM and Casinchihua 422KM. From the old Pachachaca bridge 448KM, where the roads from Andahuaylas (to the W) and Chuquibambilla (to the SE) meet, only 17KM of gentle ascent remain to the city of **Abancay** 2 378M / 7 802FT.

Abancay to Cusco

➤ 195KM   ➤ 5 HOURS
➤ PARTIALLY PAVED ROAD

This section is considered one of the most spectacular in Peru. From Abancay, a partially paved road heads NE and climbs a series of switchbacks to the Carbonera Pass 4 000M / 13 124FT, from which you can see the city of Abancay beneath the towering colossus of Mount Ampay and, on clear

Apurímac Valley.

days, the majestic peaks (Sacsarayoc and Salcantay) of the Cordillera Vilcabamba. It then descends to the archeological site of **Saywite** KM 44 (where the paved road begins) and the picturesque **Curahuasi** Valley 70KM, Peru's anise capital, scattered with cultivated fields and tile-roofed adobe houses. The road continues to the narrow Huamanmayo Pass, between precipices and many curves, then crosses the Apurímac River 1 900M / 6 234FT on the **Cúnyac** bridge 95KM, the entrance to the department of Cusco. The impressive Apurímac River valley is unquestionably the highlight of the region.

The road, surrounded by vegetation typical of the inter-Andean valleys, climbs slowly around a series of curves until it reaches a turn-off to **Mollepata** [107KM]. The next point on the route is the **Limatambo** Valley [2 890M / 9 482FT, 116KM], from which it climbs again to the **Huillque** Pass [4 280M / 14 042FT]. It then descends to the wide plain of **Anta**, one of the most beautiful parts of the route, where cultivated fields alternate with hundreds of *pisonay* trees and old rural manor houses, and the Vilcanota range is always to the E. The plain, or *pampa*, of Anta (its name means 'copper flats' in Quechua) leads to the towns of Compone and Cotabambas. At Izcuchaca [KM 171] there is an important intersection. The road going N (to the left) leads to the **Urubamba** Valley (Huaro-condo, Maras) and the road going E (to the right) will take you 24KM into the city of Cusco *(see map, p. 538-539)*. End of route.

12 Arequipa-Cusco

- ➤ DISTANCE: 484KM
- ➤ ESTIMATED TIME: 10 HOURS
- ➤ PARTIALLY PAVED ROAD
- ➤ ROUTE MAPS: 8–11

This is a difficult route, even for those used to driving in the highlands of Peru. We recommend making the trip in dry season only (May to October) as road conditions deteriorate during rainy season. One alternative is to split the trip into two parts, one from Arequipa to Chivay or to Yanque in the Colca Valley [3H TO 4H], the other from Chivay to Cusco [6H TO 7H]. Take precautions against altitude sickness (*soroche*) as a large part of the route lies at very high altitudes. Take warm clothing and plenty of drinking water as well. Don't forget to fill your gas tank at Yauri (the halfway point).

The two primary roads leading N from Arequipa are the packed dirt road to Charcani, which passes between the Misti and Chachani volcanoes, and the partially paved road [26 KM] to Yura *(see map, p. 524-525)*. Both roads reunite at the town of **Patahua-**

Corn fields in Huasacache in view of El Misti.

si approximately 50KM from Arequipa and continue as packed dirt road to Cusco. Leaving Patahuasi, the road travels through the vast, high Andean grasslands of the **Reserva Nacional de Salinas y Aguada Blanca**, with its many flocks of vicuña and *yareta* plants. Some 22KM further on is **Viscachani**, a modest village with a side road going left to Chivay and the Colca Valley 60KM. Continuing on towards Cusco, you will cross the extensive plains of **Cañahuas** (in the sector known as La Pulpera) until you reach the town of **Callalli** 53KM and its impressive cliffs carved by erosion (its famous «castles»). Here there is a bridge and the road splits: the road to the left leads to Chivay 29KM and the Colca Canyon, while the road to the right continues to Cusco.

Taking the right-hand option, you will leave Callalli, heading to **Chichas** 30KM AWAY, a small village with a couple of simple restaurants that specialize in sheep's head soup. TEN KILOMETERS further on, there appears the beautiful **Condoroma** reservoir, gathering the waters of the Colca River before releasing them into the Colca Valley. The road resumes its climb to the **Negro Mayo** Pass 4764M /

Condoroma Dam.

15 631FT, 18KM which is actually a series of mountain passes along several kilometers of winding road. From here the route descends a bit, climbs again to cross the **Martín** Pass 4400M /14 435FT,

30KM, then descends once again to the plains and town of **Yauri** 3 927M / 12 884FT, 48KM. Yauri is a typical trading center that earns its living by providing services to the many mines nearby, including Tintaya. The town has simple hotels and restaurants and a beautiful church and is an ideal spot for refueling.

From Yauri, the road continues N crossing arid mesas, passing through the town of **El Descanso** 20KM and bordering the beautiful lake of **Languilayo**. The view here in the morning is impressive. The enormous body of water, emerald-blue in

color, has two small towns on its shores, Langui and Layo, which together give the lake its name. The road winds through a canyon to the town of **Maca**. From here, only 13KM remain to the city of Sicuani.

Sicuani 3 574M / 11 726FT, located midway between Puno and Cusco, is a peaceful, modest city in harmony with the austere landscape of the *puna*. It has all basic services (we recommend filling the gas tank here) and is the beginning of a paved road to Cusco (141KM).

Leaving Sicuani, you will pass a turn-off to **Raqchi** 16KM (on the right), where the splendid ruins of a temple, built by the Inca Pachacútec for the god Wiracocha, are well worth seeing. The road

Temple of Wiracocha at Raqchi.

continues NW following the course of the Vilcamayo River (known downstream as the Urubamba and Vilcanota) to reach the towns of **Tinta** 20KM, where the famous rebel chieftain Túpac Amaru II lived, Combapata 26KM, Cusipata 58KM and Quiquijana 74KM. From here it is only 24KM to the town of **Urcos** 3 150M / 10 335FT, 97KM, situated on the shores of a beautiful lake.

From Urcos, the road continues to **Andahuaylillas** 105KM with its lovely Plaza de Armas and spectacular church built in the seventeenth-century.

The remaining 35KM pass through picturesque towns such as **Oropesa** 119KM, home to consummate bread bakers who still use Colonial-era earthen ovens; **Choquepata** 121KM, the point of departure to the Tipón ruins; Lucre and its beautiful lake with its attractive groves of *totora* reeds; **Saylla** 121KM, emporium of *chicharrones*; **San Jerónimo** and, lastly, **San Sebastián**, the gateway to the city of **Cusco** KM141, *(see map, p. 538-539)*. End of route.

Cusco-Puno

13

- ➤ DISTANCE: 389 KM
- ➤ ESTIMATED TIME: 10 HOURS
- ➤ PAVED ROAD
- ➤ ROUTE MAPS: 11–8

This is a long, but relatively uncomplicated route with frequent gas stations. It passes through many beautiful towns (remember to reduce your speed through them) and considerable natural attractions. Take drinking water and plenty of warm clothing (especially if you travel early in the morning), and be alert for symptoms of *soroche*, or altitude sickness.

To travel overland from Cusco to Puno, take the paved road that heads SE to the district of **San Sebastián** KM 5, with one of the region's most beautiful seventeenth-century churches, and on to **San Jerónimo** KM 8 *(see map, p. 538-539)*. Soon afterwards the valley widens and there appear the cultivated fields of **Saylla** KM 17, a town famous for its country restaurants specializing in *chicharrones con mote* (pork with kerneled corn, quite popular among the people of Cusco). Next is the town of Huacarpay.

• On the outskirts of Huacarpay a paved road turns off to the left, heading E to another fork in the road. Here, the left-hand road leads to Písac and the Urubamba Valley, while the right-hand one leads to the towns of Huancarani, Paucartambo, and the Kosñipata Valley (on the way to the Reserva Nacional del Manu, *see Route 15, p. 545*) •

Lake Lucre or Huacarpay.

Continuing towards Puno, you will come to the lovely Lake **Lucre** or Huacarpay 3 150M / 10 335FT, KM 26,5, offering the spectacular view of the mountains reflected in its calm waters. Nearby are the Inca ruins of **Tipón** (**detour in Choquepata** KM 22, which have terraces, a temple dedicated to the sun and a wall of worked stone some 20m (66ft) high. Next you will pass the turn-off to the town of **Oropesa** 3 129M / 10 266FT, KM 22, whose old adobe ovens still produce bread for the city of Cusco.

Next on the route is **Andahuaylillas** 3 198M / 10 493FT, KM 36, a town whose church, known as the «Sistine Chapel of Peru,» has beautiful polychrome murals dating from the seventeenth century. After Andahuaylillas you will pass through **Huaro** KM 42, where witchdoctors called *waros* lived during the time of the Incas and read the future in fires by blowing on the coals with long silver tubes. In Huaro there is also a handsome Colonial-era church with interesting murals. A gradual ascent towards the hills leads to the town of **Urcos** 3 150M / 10 335FT, KM 44. On the outskirts of Urcos there is a beautiful lake where legend has it that a great Inca treasure is hidden.

CUSCO ACCESS AND BYPASS ROUTES

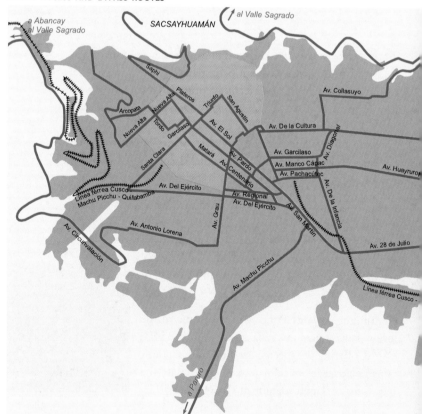

• From the outskirts of Urcos KM 47 a packed dirt road heads E (left-hand turn-off) towards the city of Puerto Maldonado in the jungles of the department of Madre de Dios *(see Route 14, p. 542)* •

Continuing S, you will follow the course of the Vilcanota River, through fields of barley and picturesque towns such as **Quiquijana** 3 216M / 10 552FT, KM 67, which means 'my property' in Aymara and has a pretty stone bridge. Then comes **Cusipata** 3 300M / 10 827FT, KM 83, or 'joyful heights' in Quechua, a name which well reflects the friendly character of its inhabitants. The road curves in tight switchbacks to reach **Checacupe** 3 585M / 11 762FT, KM 99. Curiously, its name means 'from left to right' in Quechua, perhaps alluding to the winding approach. Checacupe has a Colonial-era church with murals dating from the seventeenth century. When native chieftain Túpac Amaru II led his

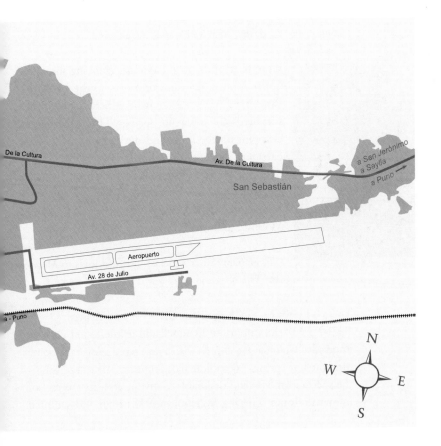

famous rebellion against the Colonial system (1780–1781), this town served as refuge for the rebels and, after his defeat, it protected Túpac Amaru, who reached it by swimming across the river.

The road continues climbing gradually along the valley, leading to **Combapata** 3 525M / 11 566FT, KM 115 and the historic town of **Tinta** 3 400M / 11 155FT, KM 121, home of Túpac Amaru II. A few kilometers further you will pass the turn-off to **Raqchi** KM 125, where there is a spectacular Inca sanctuary dedicated to the creator god Wiracocha and built by the Inca Pachacútec (don't miss it).

The next town of importance is **Sicuani** 3 552M / 11 654FT, KM 141, known for its busy, crowded markets. Here in 1836 a National Assembly convened by General Andrés de Santa Cruz agreed to create the Peru-Bolivia Confederation.

• After Sicuani a packed dirt road appears on the right that leads to Langui, Layo, Yauri, the Colca Valley and Arequipa •

From Sicuani the road continues climbing through upper Andean plateaus, or *punas*, to the **La Raya Pass** 4 312M / 14 148FT, KM 194, where there is a town of shepherds and a few hot springs. This is the highest point on the route and the gateway to the department of Puno.

Through the rolling hills of the *puna* you will continue, now in a gentle descent, to the town of **Santa Rosa** 3 993M / 13 101FT, KM 210 at the foot of snowy Mount Cunurana.

Hot springs at La Raya Pass.

• From Santa Rosa a packed dirt road leads to Macusani, Olaechea and other towns to the E of Puno •

The road leads on to **Chuquibambilla** KM 232 and **Ayaviri** 3 925M / 12 878FT, KM 255, an important livestock and textile center with an impressive Colonial-era church (San Francisco de Asís) and some pleasant hot springs (Pojpojquella). Some 30 MINUTES away is the spectacular Tinajani or Diablo Canyon, with its «forest» of immense stones standing over 60m (197ft) high and sculpted by erosion into curious shapes (ideal for hiking and photography).

Further along you will find the picturesque town of **Pucará** 3 996M / 13 111FT, KM 285, the home of potters who made their little ceramic bulls famous. The last section leads to the city of **Juliaca** 3 824M /12 547FT, KM 347, a vital center of commerce for the southern Andes and the junction of roads leading to Puno and towns on the north side of Lake Titi-caca (Huancané, Rosaspata, and Moho).

From Juliaca only ONE HOUR 45KM remains to the city of Puno, past the town of **Caracoto** 3 958M / 12 986FT, KM 356, a turn-off to the archeological site of **Sillustani** KM 372 and the town of Paucarcolla with its attractive Colonial-era church. You will be able to see your destination from the little hill that overlooks the city of **Puno**. Before you lays the majestic Lake Titicaca. End of route.

Colonial church in Paucarcolla.

• Several roads leave Puno to circle Lake Titicaca. The primary (paved) one heads S towards the towns of Chucuito, Ácora, Ilave, Juli, Pomata (the turn-off to Yunguyo), and Desaguadero (the Bolivian border and the road to La Paz) on a route well worth driving. From Ilave, a packed dirt road leads to a fork at Mazo Cruz. One of the roads goes to Tarata and Tacna, the other to Moquegua via Lake Aricota. From Puno another packed dirt road leads to Laraqueri and Moquegua •

14 Cusco~Puerto Maldonado

- ➤ DISTANCE: 530KM
- ➤ ESTIMATED TIME: 18 HOURS
- ➤ PACKED DIRT ROAD
- ➤ ROUTE MAP: 11

This route is only for seasoned travelers with all-terrain vehicles; it is a true odyssey for adventurers. Do not let be misled by the seemingly short distance from beginning to end, as the road is generally in deplorable condition. We recommend driving it only during dry season (May to October), as it could take as long as a month to make the trip during rainy season. In addition, there are not many service stations on the route, so we recommend filling your gas tank whenever possible (at Marcapata, Quincemil and Mazuco). The reward for these inconveniences is, unquestionably, getting to know one of the most beautiful areas in Peru. Take drinking water, warm clothing and food for the first part of the route.

To reach Puerto Maldonado from Cusco, you must iniatilly take the paved road towards Puno *(see map, p. 538-539)*. At **the outskirts of Urcos** (KM 47 from Cusco and KM 00 of this route), turn off on a packed dirt road that climbs to the towns of **Catca** 42KM through fields of barley and eucalyptus trees.

Next is **Ocongate** 78KM in the Mapacho River valley, where there is an important center of instruction operated by the Jesuit order (who have been here for several centuries), and **Tinqui** 87KM, the site of a colorful and well-attended Sunday fair. In this area, it is fairly common to spot columns of llamas carrying goods from their distant villages to trade here. At this point, below the towering Mount Ausangate, travelers could be said to be entering the past.

Continuing the ascent, you will reach the small town of **Mahuayani** KM 101, the point of departure for the popular pilgrimage to the sanctuary of the Lord of Qoyllur Ritt'i (which means 'star of the snow' in Quechua) that draws tens of thousands of countryfolk each May in what is considered the largest indigenous festival in America.

Leaving Mahuayani you will come to the **Hualla Hualla** Pass 4750M / 15585FT, KM 122 and descend switchbacks to the village of Coline at the headwaters of the Marcapata River, which the road will follow down to the high rain forest. The next town on the route, also called **Marcapata** KM 167, is perched on a sort of spur protruding from the surrounding mountains and covered in lush vegetation. Marcapata is a town of mists; it rains 300 days a year there, stimulating the growth of a rich and diverse flora, which includes a great variety of orchids. Its unique church is interesting (it has stubbornly resisted the weather and several lootings), built entirely of adobe and crowned with an attractive thatched roof that is changed every five years in a colorful festival that draws people from all points of the region. An additional attraction are its hot spring baths, the hottest in Peru (73°C, or 163°F).

Continuing downhill on a packed dirt road (in generally poor condition) you will pass through the village of San Lorenzo KM 208 and cross the «movable» bridge over the Araza River on the other side. Further along you will come to the small town of **Quincemil** KM 239, home of celebrated naturalist Celestino Kalinowski, who is credited with spurring the creation of Manu National Park. From here the road runs parallel to the beau-

Outskirts of Ocongate.

High rain forest at Quincemil.

tiful Nusiniscato River (a tributary of the Inambari) to the town of **Puente Inambari** KM 297, a modest group of homes (and a police station) located at the confluence of the Marcapata and Inambari rivers.

• From Puente Inambari, a packed dirt road heads S (right-hand road) to San Gabán, Olaechea, Macusani, and Puno •

Next to appear is **Mazuco** KM 312, the point of departure for Colorado and Huaypetue (gold mining centers of the region). Then you will climb a small chain of hills crowned by a lookout (and a small hermitage) offering a fabulous view of the vast Amazon plain (4 000km to the Atlantic Ocean).

The first town on the plains is **Santa Rosa** KM 342, followed by some small villages generally named for the kilometer at which they are located. The scenery on this part of the route is comprised of extensive pastures dedicated to raising livestock and portions of forest that are always dominated by the imposing Brazil nut trees (*Bertholletia excelsa*). Peruvian law prohibits felling these giants, which produce their highly appreciated nuts for the inhabitants of the region for decades.

After a long day, you will reach the beginning of an 10,5KM paved road that leads to the jungle city of **Puerto Maldonado**. End of route.

• From Puerto Maldonado there is a road heading N to the town of Iñapari on the Brazilian border 236KM ➤ 6H. To reach the road, you must first cross the Madre de Dios River on a motorized ferry (approx. US$ 7). This ferry service operates from 8am to 8pm. At night the port closes and you will have to contact the Capitanía, or harbormaster's office, if you wish to cross (you will probably have to locate the port watchman as well, who is the only person with the key). If it is Saturday or Sunday, forget it; you will simply have to wait until Monday.

Once across the river, the road (improved by the Army) is wide and well packed (as long as it doesn't rain). After passing through the villages of Planchón 39KM, Mavila 74KM and Alerta 107KM, you will cross a bridge over the Tahuamanu River to reach the towns of San Lorenzo and Iberia [169KM] ➤ [4H], home to settlers engaged in extracting mahogany, cedar and other hardwoods. There is also a large military base and airfield here.

At this point, only [67KM] [2H] remain to the town of Iñapari [365M] / [1198FT] on the right bank of the Acre River, very close to its junction with the Yaverija River on the Peru-Brazil border. This area of typical Amazon jungle has red clay roads that easily deteriorate with the arrival of rain. We do not recommend driving them in rainy season (December to March) as they can become a real nightmare.

If you wish to continue your trip across the border in Brazil, cross the Acre River to the city of Assis where there is an intersection of roads leading to Brasileia in Brazil and Cobija in Bolivia. Both cities have good hotels, restaurants and highway connections.

Remember: before crossing the border, stop at the Immigration office in Puerto Maldonado •

Madre de Dios River.

Cusco-Manu

15

➤ DISTANCE: 252KM

➤ ESTIMATED TIME: 12 HOURS

➤ PACKED DIRT ROAD

➤ ROUTE MAP: 11

This route crosses some of the most beautiful natural scenery of southern Peru, but is long and requires an all-terrain vehicle. After crossing the heights of the Andes, the road plunges into the lush, high rain forest of Kosñipata Valley and descends to the town of Shintuya on the banks of the Upper Madre de Dios River. This is the end of a route that makes one of the most impressive changes in altitude in all of Peru. Take warm clothing, food and water and be prepared to deal with poor road conditions and meager services (with the exception of Paucartambo, where there are rustic restaurants and hostels).

To travel overland from Cusco to Manu you must take the paved road towards Puno *(see map, p. 538-539)*, through the districts of **San Sebastián** ᴷᴹ 5 and **San Jerónimo** ᴷᴹ 8.

Soon afterwards the valley widens and there appear the cultivated fields of **Saylla** ᴷᴹ 17, a town known for its country restaurants specializing in *chicharrones con mote* (pork and kerneled corn, quite popular among the people of Cusco). Next is the town of Huacarpay.

On the outskirts of Huacarpay ᴷᴹ 26, take a left-hand, paved turnoff E to another fork. Here the left-hand road leads to Písac and the Urubamba Valley. Take the right-hand road, crossing an iron bridge over the Vilcanota River and continuing on a packed dirt road to the town of Huancarani and the top of Mount Ninamarca, where you will see a number of *chullpas*, or stone burial towers, built by the Lupaca culture. A few kilometers further, you will begin the descent to **Paucartambo** ⁶⁶ᴷᴹ , a town surrounded by stands of eucalyptus trees on the banks of the Mapacho River. With its narrow streets, tile-roofed houses and balconied homes, this town is known for its colorful celebrations (July 16) in honor of the Virgen del Carmen, affectionately called *La Mamacha*.

From Paucartambo, the road climbs to **Acjanaco** ⁹¹ᴷᴹ ➤ I H and a lookout point at **Tres Cruces**, the southern border of the Ma-

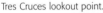

Tres Cruces lookout point.

nu National Park. It is said that the most beautiful sunrise in the world can be seen from this spot.

At Tres Cruces the road begins the steep and winding descent to the **Kosñipata** Valley (meaning 'smoky earth' in Quechua in allusion to the ever-present blanket of fog in the region). Amid dense cloud forests, the road passes through Pillahuata, **Atalaya**, Patria, Chontachaca and **Pilcopata** [197KM]. Now in the last reaches of the Andes, it comes to the towns of **Salvación** and **Shintuya** [252KM]. In this last town, where there is a Dominican monastery, the road ends.

You can only reach the Manu National Park by river [8H], traveling the Upper Madre de Dios to the town of **Boca Manu**, then following the Manu River upstream.

Upper Madre de Dios River.

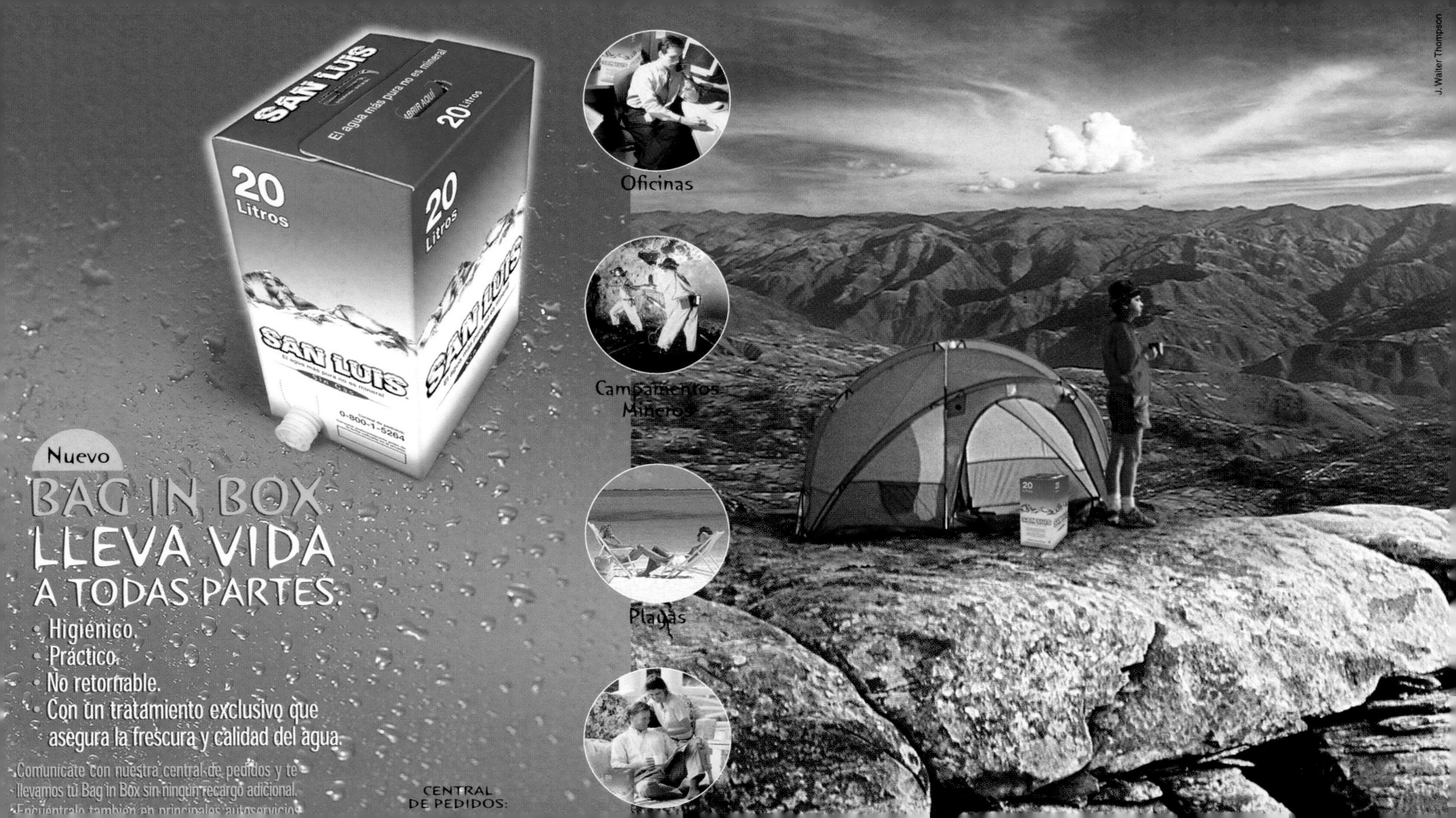

SAN LUIS
El agua más pura no es mineral
ABRIR AQUÍ
20 Litros
0-800-1-5264
Oficinas
Campamentos Mineros
Playas
Nuevo
BAG IN BOX
LLEVA VIDA
A TODAS PARTES.
• Higiénico.
• Práctico.
• No retornable.
• Con un tratamiento exclusivo que asegura la frescura y calidad del agua.
Comunícate con nuestra central de pedidos y te llevamos tu Bag in Box sin ningún recargo adicional.
CENTRAL DE PEDIDOS:
J. Walter Thompson

INDEX

Concerning all the rivers,
streams and lakes; mountain
ranges, plains and deserts; ports,
bays and principal towns named herein

Index of Place Names

This index lists, in alphabetical order, all the places mentioned in parts one, two, three and four of this guide.

Abajo el Puente, *see* Rímac
Abancay, 25, 65, 73, 79, 96-100, 105, 360, 519, 529, 531, 532, 533
Acapulco, 488
Acaray, 475
Acarí, 365, 520
Acjanaco, 195, 546
Acobamba, 439, 441, 442, 504, 507
Acomayo, 509
Acora, 541
Acos, 241, 471
Acostambo, 528
Acre, río, 545
Acuchimay, 130
Achoma, 159, 160, 161, 170
Aguaitando, 105
Aguas Calientes, 344, 345, 346, 349, 350
Aguas Verdes, 73, 462, 488
Aguashiyaku, waterfall, 433
Aguaytía, 89, 393, 511
Aguja, mount, 272
Aija, 497
Aishpachaca, 209
Alca, 120
Alcomachay, bridge, 528
Alerta, 544
Almendral, 495
Alpamayo, mount, 260, 272
Altiplano, 22, 28, 29, 108, 406, 407, 408, 409, 410, 411, 413, 417, 424
Alto Amazonas, río, 494
Alto de la Alianza, 427, 527
Alto Huallaga, bridge, 495, 509

Alto Madre de Dios, river, 352, 354, 355, 356, 545, 547
Amantaní, lake, 88, 415
Amarilla, lake, 389
Amarumayo, *see* Madre de Dios, río
Amazonas, department of, 84, 203, 492
 −río, 20, 21, 170, 172, 239, 286, 287, 288, 289, 292, 296, 493
Amazonia, 22, 23, 56, 87, 250, 286, 291, 293, 294, 354, 393, 395, 432, 434, 492
Ambo, 253, 508, 509
Amor (Tumbes), island, 462
Amor (Ucayali), island, 395
Amoray, hacienda, 533
Amotape, National Park Cerros de, 46, 379, 461, 463, 464, 465, 468, 488
Ampato, volcano, 108, 117, 156, 170
Ampay, mount, 94, 98, 99, 101, 531, 533
 − National Sanctuary, 98
Áncash, department of, 28, 46, 264, 301, 475, 476, 490
Ancón, 87, 471
Andabamba, 253
Andagua, 120
Andahuaylas, 25, 65, 79, 101-106, 138, 529, 530, 531, 533
Andahuaylillas, 195, 196, 536, 538
Andajes, 330
Andamarca, 533
Andamayo, river, 157
Andes, mountain range, 20, 21, 27, 60, 94, 96, 103, 141, 165, 203, 204, 205, 213, 232, 239, 268, 272, 287, 301, 352, 369,

407, 409, 432, 471, 492, 493, 498, 499, 503, 506, 547

Ankascocha, lake, 98

Anta, 259, 534

Antabamba, 96, 120

Antana, 283, 375

Antasway, 330

Anticona, *see* Ticlio, pass

Anticona, mount, 500

Añashuayco, 108

Apacheta Grande, pass, 530

Aplao, 120

Apurímac, department of, 29, 56, 94, 95, 101, 102, 532

– río, 29, 99, 533

Aramango, 492

Araza, river, 543

Arcopunco, 98

Arequipa, 24, 25, 48, 56, 65, 70, 76, 77, 79, 82, 85, 86, 107-126, 155, 156, 161, 163, 169, 171, 175, 199, 301, 408, 411, 415, 512, 519, 520, 523, 524, 525, 534, 540

– department of, 27, 48, 82, 119, 365, 520

– region of, 29, 30

Arica, 513

Aricota, laguna de, 541

Ascope, 482

Asia, 324

Asillo, 419

Assis, 545

Atalaya, 195, 355, 547

Ataura, 502

Atenas, 371, 374

Atico, 522

Atiquipa, Lomas de, 521

Atlántico, ocean, 544

Aucallama, 471

Aucayacu, 509

Ausangate, mount, 174, 177, 547

Ayabaca, 61, 65, 380, 388

Ayacucho, 23, 25, 29, 64, 65, 73, 79, 82, 127-140, 239, 503, 516, 527, 528, 529, 530, 532

– departament of, 27, 29, 34, 48, 59, 82, 109

– region of, 29, 128, 142, 360

Ayaviri, 410, 540

Aymaraes, province of, 533

Ayo, 171

Ayparipa, 521

Aypate, 388

Azángaro, 406, 418, 419

Azul, mountain range, 431, 510

Bagua Chica, 25, 73, 79, 491, 492, 493

Bagua Grande, 25, 73, 79, 493

Bahuaja–Sonene, National Park, 48, 400, 401, 402, 405

Bajo Mayo, river, 431

Bajo Piura, river, 387, 486

Balsas, 494

Ballestas, islands, 87, 371

Baños del Inca (Cajamarca), 143, 148

Baños del Inca (Cusco), *see* Tambomachay

Barlovento, 283, 375, 517

Barranca, 475

Barranco, 301, 308, 320, 331

Barranquito, 516

Barrios Altos, 304, 305, 308, 315-317

Batán Grande, Reserved Area, 46, 222, 227

Bayóvar, 89, 371, 387, 388, 486, 492

Belén, 289, 291

Bellavista (Loreto), 289

Bellavista (San Martín), 510

Blanca, mountain range, 47, 260, 262, 264, 265, 272, 497

Blanca, lake, 527

Blanco, lake, 357

Blanquillo, lake, 357

Boca del Río (Ica), 375

Boca del Río (Tacna), 427, 526

Boca Manu, 352, 355, 356, 357, 547

Bocana de San Pedro, 387

Bocapán, 463, 464, 488

Bolivia, border crossing to, 419

Bombón, mesa, 255, 504, 507
Boquerón del Padre Abad, 510
Borja, 287
Brasil, border crossing to, 294
Burgos, 269

Caballeros, 324, 513
Cabana, 533
Cabanaconde, 121, 155, 156, 157, 158, 159, 160, 161, 162, 165
Cabezas Largas, 369
Cabinzas, island, 320
Cabo Blanco, 386, 390, 487
Cabuyal, 463
Cacatachi, 495
Cachigaga, hacienda 253
Cahuachi, 364
Caima, 324, 514
Cajacay, 496
Cajamarca, 25, 30, 31, 64, 70, 73, 79, 82, 141-153, 300, 482, 488, 489, 490, 492, 494
– department of, 64, 82, 89, 482, 492
– region of, 29, 30, 128
Cajamarquilla (Lima), 300, 328
Cajamarquilla (Pasco), 509
Cajatambo, 273
Calango, 514
Calca, 177, 188, 189, 192, 193
Caleta La Cruz, 461, 488
Caleta Vidal, 475
Calientes, 427
Calquichico, valley, 529
Callalli, 157, 165, 535
Callao, 19, 300, 301, 305, 308, 313, 319-320
Camaná, 157, 522
Campana, hill, 479
Campanayoc, hill, 101
Campanquiz, mountain range, 493
Campo Santo, 271
Campo Verde, 511
Cancas, 488
Canco, 171

Canchaque, 388
Canchayllo, 21, 501
Candamo, river, 87
Candarave, 527
Cangallo, 530
Cangrejos, 386, 486
Canocota, 165
Canta, 329
Cantayoc, aquaducts, 363, 364
Cañahuas, plain, 155, 535
Cañete, 65, 324, 501, 503, 515
Cao Viejo, 454
Caplina, river, 423, 426, 527
Caracoto, 541
Caraz, 65, 259, 262, 263, 264, 271, 272, 274, 275, 497
Carbonera, pass, 533
Carhuacocha, lake, 258, 272, 273
Carhuamayo, 508
Carhuas, 282, 283, 517
Carhuaz, 262, 263, 269, 270, 274, 275
Carnacha, stream, 499
Carpa, 266
Carpapata, descent, 505
Carpish, pass, 509
Carpishoyaku, waterfall, 433
Carquín, 474
Cartavio, 479
Casacancha, 530
Casagrande, 455, 482
Casapalca, 500
Cascajal, 521
Cashibococha, lake, 396
Cashpajali, river, 352
Casinchihua, 533
Casitas, 463, 488
Casma, 259, 477
Castrovirreyna, 516, 530
Cátac, 260, 263, 264, 268, 269, 495, 497
Catacaos, 380, 380-381, 383, 389, 486
Catahuicucho, 419
Catapalla, 515
Catca, 542
Caulliraju, mount, 497

Cayhuayna, 253
Caylloma, 108, 158
Cayma, 111, 113
Cayumba, 509
Ccaccatapay, 162
Ccollpa, shelter, 169
Celendín, 494
Cenepa, river, 292
Centinela, beach, 327, 515
– hill, 516
– huaca, 475
Cerillos, 522
Cerro Azul, 327, 515
Cerro Baúl, 29
Cerro Colorado (Ica), 369
Cerro Colorado (Lima), 475
Cerro de Pasco, 25, 73, 249, 250, 253,
    471, 501, 504, 506, 507, 509
Cerro Encantado, 387
Cerro Illescas, 387
Cerro Vicús, 389
Cieneguilla, 328, 333
Cocha Cashu, 351, 353, 354
Cocharcas, 65, 103, 105
Cochas, 241, 244, 504, 507
Coishco, 478
Colán, 382, 390, 486
Colca, 64, 65, 108, 118, 119, 120, 121,
    155-171, 496, 522, 534, 535, 540
Coline, 543
Colombia, border crossing to, 294
Colombo, 214
Colorado (Cusco), 544
Colorado (Lima), 475
Colla-Cruz, 209
Collaguata, volcano, 157
Collao, mesa, 31, 406, 407
Collpa, 428
Comatrana, 282, 517
Combapata, 536, 540
Combayo, 152
Concepción, 242, 244, 247, 502
Concordia, 509
– Pass at, 73, 428, 527

Conchucos, Callejón de, 264, 266, 269,
    270, 271, 478, 497
Condorcocha, 138
Condorcunca, hill, 136
Condoroma, dam, 535
Congas, 476
Conococha, 258, 273, 495, 496, 497
Contamana, 398,
Contrahierbas, mount, 270
Contumazá, 482, 489
Copa, mount, 270
Coporaque, 158, 159, 160, 168
Corazón de Jesús, 209
Corire, 120, 121
Corongo, 264, 478
Coropuna, volcano, 120, 170
Corral Quemado, bridge, 492
Corrales, 463
Corralones, 476
Costa Verde, la, 320
Cotahuasi, 120, 121, 125
Cotaruse, 533
Cruz Blanca, pass, 389
Cruz de Carhuas, 375
Cruz de Hueso, 282
Cruz de Laya, 328
Cruz del Cóndor, see La Cruz
    del Cóndor
Cuajone, 523, 526
Cueva de las Lechuzas, 256
Cueva de las Pavas, 256
Cumbaza, río, 431
Cumbe, cerro, 150
Cumbemayo, 150, 151
Cumuc-Yacu, 493
Cunurana, nevado, 540
Cúnyac, puente, 533
Curahuasi, 97, 98, 533
Curimaná, 511
Curva de Huaracayo, 493
Cusco, 25, 30, 48, 56, 61, 64, 65, 70, 73,
    76, 79, 82, 84, 85, 86, 97, 98, 99, 102,
    108, 128, 129, 157, 172-200, 204, 233,
    239, 254, 340, 344, 345, 347, 355, 356,

360, 411, 415, 418, 448, 519, 532, 533, 534, 535, 536, 537, 538, 542, 545, 546
– department of, 29, 32, 48, 60, 61, 62, 64, 65, 82, 352, 400, 533
– region of, 128, 173, 406
Cusichaca, river, 347
Cusipata, 536, 539
Cutervo, 482, 492

Chacamarca, Historical Sanctuary at, 507
Chacas (Áncash), 270
Chacas (Puno), 416
Chacchán, 259
Chaclacayo, 327, 499
Chacraraju, mount, 260, 272
Chachani, volcano, 107, 108, 156, 534
Chachapoyas, 25, 79, 203-211, 491, 493, 494
Chachas, lake, 120
Chala, 521, 522
Chalhuanca, 519, 532, 533
Chamaya, 492
Chamberí, 516
Champará, mount, 265
Champeque, 521
Chan Chan, 29, 222, 445, 453, 479
Chancay, 324, 471, 474
Chancayllo, 474
Chancos, 269
Chanchamayo, 21, 65, 79, 212-220, 442, 501, 503, 504, 505, 506, 507
Chao, valley of, 478
Charcani, 119, 156, 534
Chasquitambo, 496
Chaucayán, 496
Chavín de Huántar, 28, 263, 266, 267, 268, 269, 490, 497
Chaviña, 520
Chazuta, 435
Checacupe, 539
Checcta, 329
Chepeconde, 324, 515
Chepén, 482
Chérrepe, 482

Chicama, 444, 454, 455, 479
Chichas, 535
Chichictara, hacienda, 518
Chicla, 500
Chiclayo, 25, 46, 56, 65, 73, 76, 79, 82, 221-231, 470, 479, 482, 483, 486, 491, 492
Chiclín, 322, 479
Chicón, mount, 188, 191, 193
Chicrín, 509
Chiguata, 119, 156
Chila, mountain range, 157, 170
Chile, border crossing to, 428
Chilete, 489
Chili, river, 107
Chillón, 62, 329, 471, 500
Chimbote, 25, 79, 259, 476, 478, 497
Chinancocha, lake, 271
Chincha, 25, 64, 79, 280, 327, 369, 513, 516
Chinchao, 509
Chinchaycocha, see Junín, lake
Chinchero, 177, 188, 191, 192, 193
Chincheros, 530
Chinchipe, river, 492
Chininia, 170
Chipuric, 208
Chiquián, 273, 476, 497
Chira, river, 484, 487
Chiriaco, 492
Chivay, 155, 156, 157, 159, 160, 161, 162, 163, 164, 165, 168, 169, 170, 171, 534, 535
Choclococha, 236, 530
Chocope, 479
Chongoyape, 482
Chontabamba, 508
Chontachaca, 547
Chopicalqui, mount, 260, 270
Choquepata, 536
Choquesuisui, ravine, 349
Choquetico, 170
Choropampa, 490
Chorrillos, 301, 308, 320-321, 325, 475

Chosica, 327, 499
Chota, 492
Chotano, river, 492
Chucuito, 416, 541
Chucura, mount, 158
Chulucanas, 381, 383, 385, 483, 486
Chulucanitas, 389
Chullqui, 509
Chumbao, river, 101
Chuncho, lake, 403
Chupaca, 242, 503
Chupacigarro, 475
Chuquibamba, 120
Chuquibambilla, 533, 540
Chuquicahuana, 536
Chuquicara, 259, 497
Churajón, 108, 119
Churcampa, 528
Churín, 330, 474, 475
Churubamba, 509
Churuja, 493
Chusis, 389,
Chuspi, nevado, 246

Desaguadero, 413, 417, 419, 420, 527, 541
Diablo, cañón del, see Tinajani, canyon
Doña María, pampa de, 474
Duvaz, 500

Ecuador, border crossing to, 462
El Alto (Arequipa), see Tambillo
El Alto (Piura), 386, 487
El Alto, plain, 479
El Atascadero, plain, 487
El Barro, 465
El Boche, 510
El Brujo, 454, 482
El Candelabro, 371, 374
El Carmelo, 278
El Carmen, 327, 516
El Colorado, 475
El Cruce, 522
El Chaco, 370, 371, 375, 377
El Descanso, 536

El Dorado, 478
El Faraón, 475
El Fiscal, 523
El Frontón, island, 320
El Gavilán, pass, 490
El Infiernillo, 500
El Limón, hacienda house, 463
El Milagro, 511
El Negro, 283, 375
El Ñuro, 387, 460
El Pato, 522
El Pedregal, 273
El Raspón, 20, 370
El Restín, 386
El Silencio, 324, 513
El Tambo, 492
El Tirol, waterfall, 214
El Valor, 492, 493
Embajadores, 324, 514
Ene, river, 239
Escurrebraga, 493
Esquén, 416
Eten, 224, 225

Ferreñafe, 224, 482
Flamingos, 514
Fortaleza, river, 258, 476, 496
Frailes, Stone Forest,
    see Frailones
Frailones, 150, 151

Gallardo, 324, 515
Gallinazo, 283, 375
Gallito Ciego, dam, 489
Gamburama, 493
Gangariza, 493
Gera, waterfall, 436
Gramadal, 476
Gran Pajatén, 47
Grande, river, 361, 518
Guadalupe (Ica), 517
Guadalupe (La Libertad), 482
Guaneros, plain, 523
Guañape, islands, 455

Hanan Jauja, 245
Hatun Mayo, 502
Heath, river, 402
Hermilio Valdizán, 510
Hervideros, 463, 488
Higueras, río, 254
Honcopampa, 273
Hornillos, 475
Huaca del Arco Iris, *see* Huaca del Dragón
Huaca del Dragón, 455
Huaca Prieta, 454
Huaca Rajada, 38
Huacachina, lake, 280, 281
Huacama, 516
Huacamaíllo, waterfalls, 435
Huacarpay, 196, 537, 546
Huacarpay, laguna, *see* Lucre
Huacracocha, lake, 500
Huacrapuquio, 528
Huachipa, 328, 499
Huacho, 25, 470, 474, 475, 495
Huacho Sin Pescado, 330
Huagapo, 441, 442, 504, 507
Huagurunchu, mount, 509
Hualalache, 531
Hualca-Hualca, mount, 158, 164
Hualcán, mount, 270
Hualgayoc, 142
Hualhuas, 241, 242, 502
Hualmay, 475
Hualla Hualla, pass, 543
Huallaga, 249, 253, 435, 509
Huallanca, 259, 260, 264, 478, 496, 497
Huallhua, waterfall, 515
Huamachuco, 447
Huamalí, 502
Huamaní, mountain range, 389
Huamanmayo, pass, 533
Huambo, 121, 161, 162, 171, 522
Huambocancha, 151
Huambutío, 195
Huamina, abra, 530
Huancabamba (Apurímac), 101

Huancabamba (Piura), 388, 389, 483
– río, 217, 389, 492
Huancané, 413, 541
Huancani, 502
Huancano, 529
Huancarani, 195, 537, 546
Huancavelica, 25, 64, 79, 85, 87, 102, 129, 232-237, 248, 503, 528, 530
– department of, 29, 56, 239
Huancaya, 501, 515
Huancayo, 25, 56, 65, 73, 77, 79, 85, 86, 236, 237, 238-248, 498, 499, 500, 501, 502, 503, 515, 527, 528, 530
Huanchaco, 65, 447, 453, 454, 456, 479, 480
Huando, 471
Huandoy, mount, 260, 271, 272
Huanta, 127, 131, 137, 139, 528
Huánuco, 25, 64, 73, 79, 249-257, 393, 497, 501, 504, 506, 507, 509
– department of, 272, 509, 510
– región de, 250
Huánuco Pampa, *see* Huánuco Viejo
Huánuco Viejo, 250, 254
Huanzocochá, lake, 120-121
Huápalas, 389
Huaquicha, 499
Huaracalla, 509
Huaral, 471
Huarán, 189
Huaraz, 25, 46, 64, 73, 77, 79, 259, 262, 263, 264, 266, 268, 269, 270, 271, 273, 275, 476, 477, 478, 495, 496, 497
Huari, 264, 268, 497
Huari Huillca, 246
Huariaca, 509
Huaricanga, 496
Huaripampa, 502
Huarmey, 41, 476, 497
Huaro, 194, 538
Huarocondo, 534
Huarochirí, 328
Huasa Huasi, 505
Huasacache, 111, 118, 535

Huascarán, mount, 21, 260, 265, 270, 271, 497
– National Park, 46, 265, 276
Huashuaccasa, river, 533
Huatanay, river, 172
Huatata, river, 127
Huaullac, 273
Huaura, 475
Huayanay, stone forest, 236
Huaychopampa, 209
Huayhuash, Cordillera, 76, 255, 258, 262, 269, 272, 273, 476, 497
Huaylas, Callejón de, 56, 64, 79, 258-276, 476, 477, 478, 495, 496, 497
– mount, 272
Huayllabamba, 347
Huayllay, 255
– National Sanctuary Stone Forest of, 46, 254, 508
Huayna Picchu, mount, 341, 342, 346, 347
Huaynacotas, 121
Huaypetue, 544
Huaypo, lake, 192
Huaytapallana, pass, 503
– Cordillera de, 246, 502
Huaytará, 529, 530
Huayucachi, 242, 528
Huayurí, 518
Huchuy Qosqo, 192
Hueso de Ballena, island, 462
Huillque, pass, 534
Huinco, 504
Huipoca, 511
Humay, 516, 529
Humboldt, 511
Humedades, hill, 229
Hurin Jauja, 245

Iberia, 545
Ica, 25, 48, 56, 64, 65, 79, 83, 277-285, 362, 369, 517, 518
– department of, 28, 33, 48, 74, 89, 233, 278, 516, 516, 517
Ichupampa, 159, 160, 161, 168

Ilave, 541
Ilo, 25, 80, 82, 526
Illimo, 491
Imata, 156
Imazita, 492
Imperial (Huancavelica), 528
Imperial (Lima), 515
Inambari, río, 544
Inca Uyo, 416
Inca Wasi, 327
Independencia, 529
– bay, 282, 368, 374
Indio, lake, 156
Infierno, 401
Ingenio, 518
Inti Punko, 348, 349
Iñapari, 400, 544, 545
Iquitos, 25, 46, 82, 83, 84, 87, 286-298, 398, 401, 492
Islandia, 294
Islay, 523
Islilla, 486
Itaya, river, 286, 289
Ite, 526
Izcosasín, 505
Izcuchaca, 528, 530, 534

Jaén, 492
Jahuacocha, lake, 272, 273
Jahuay, 327, 516
Jalca Grande, 205, 208
Janca, 273
Janku, 273
Jaquí, 521
Jauja, 25, 129, 238, 239, 241, 242, 245, 502
Jayanca, 491
Jepelacio, 494
Jequetepeque, 482, 489
Jesús, 118
Jihuay, 521
Jónoc, 98
Juanjuy, 510
Juli, 416, 417, 541

Juliaca, 25, 76, 82, 85, 86, 415, 418, 421, 541
Junín, 255, 442, 501, 504, 508
– department of, 21, 34, 46, 238, 239, 255, 301, 507
– lake, 255, 507
– fields, 34
– National Reserve, 46, 507
Juscallacta, 170
Juscubamba, valley, 209

K'ello K'ello, 418
Kahuish, 268, 269
Kancha Huanca, 245
Kapala, 514
Karajía, sarcophagi, 209, 493
Karwas, see Carhuas
Kekamarca, 273
Keyash, 273
Kishuara, 531
Kosñipata, 195, 356, 537, 545, 547
Kotosh, 254
Kuélap, 205, 206, 208, 494
Kukun, 330
Kunturhuasi, 490
Kuray, 330

La Calera, 159, 162, 170
La Calzada, lake, 419
La Catedral, 374
La Cima, 507
La Cocinita, 476
La Colpa, 149
La Copa, hill, 490
La Cruz del Cóndor, 156, 157, 165
La Cruz, see Caleta La Cruz
La Curva, 526
La Dehesa, 522
La Divisoria, 510
La Escalera, hill, 433
La Esmeralda, 382
La Esperanza, 455
La Estaquería, 364
La Florida (Amazonas), 494

La Florida (Arequipa), 522
La Florida (Lima), 471
La Grama, 486
La Gramita, 477
La Hoyada, 398
La Huata, 523
La Isla, 475
La Leche, valley, 222, 227
La Libertad, department of, 82, 444, 454, 478
La Merced, 25, 56, 73, 79, 212, 213, 214, 215, 216, 217, 218, 219, 220, 442, 504, 505, 506
La Mina, 370
La Oroya, 25, 73, 498, 499, 500, 501, 502, 503, 504, 506, 507
La Planchada, 522
La Pulpera, 535
La Punta, 308, 320
La Quebradita, 513
La Quinua, 509
La Raya, see Purgatorio, hill
La Raya, pass, 540
La Tina, 487
La Unión (Huánuco), 497
La Unión (Lima), 474
La Viuda, Cordillera, 500
Lachay, see Lomas de Lachay, National Reserve
Lagayache, plain, 527
Lago Lindo, 434
Laguna Azul, 433
Laguna Blanca, 389
Laguna Grande, 282, 283, 376, 517
Laguna Negra, 389
Laguna Shimbe, see Laguna Blanca
Lagunillas, 370
Laicacota, 408
Lalita, cerro, 229
Lamas, 434, 435, 495
Lambayeque, 25, 37, 39, 42, 221, 222, 225, 229, 482, 483, 486, 491
– department of, 46, 82, 454, 482
– region of, 42, 224

Lampa, 418

Lampas, plain, 268, 273

Lamud, 205, 209, 493

Langui, 536, 540

Languilayo, lake, 536

Laos, 487

Lapa Lapa, 514

Laraqueri, 541

Lares, valley, 192

Lari, 157, 159, 161, 168, 169, 170

Las Aldas, 477

Las Brisas, 324, 514

Las Delicias, 479

Las Gaviotas, 522

Las Huaringas, lakes, 389

Las Lomas, 487

Las Maravillas, canyon, 120

Las Palmas, 324, 514

Las Piedras, river, 401

Las Pocitas, 487

Las Rocas, 228

Las Vegas, 504, 507

Las Zorras, plain, 476

Lasuntay, mount, 246

Layo, 536, 540

Leimebamba, 494

León Dormido, 514

Levanto, 204, 209, 210

Libertad, hill, 246

Lilasca, hill, 229

Lima, 18, 19, 25, 26, 31, 32, 33, 34, 35,
    36, 46, 47, 54, 55, 56, 62, 65, 70, 71,
    72, 73, 74, 76, 77, 78, 80, 81, 82, 83,
    84, 85, 86, 90, 108, 109, 129, 174, 222,
    255, 259, 260, 279, 299-339, 393, 439,
    448, 450, 470, 473, 495, 496, 498, 499,
    500, 503, 506, 507, 512, 513, 520

– departament of, 46, 64, 65, 82, 301,
    476

Limatambo, valley, 534

Limón, 463

Lobitos, 487

Lobos de Tierra, island, 387

Locumba, 526, 527

Lomas, 365, 520

Lomas de Lachay, National Reserve,
    46, 324, 474

Lomitas, 518

Loreto, department of, 46, 82, 87, 286,
    492, 495

Los Cocos, 324, 514

Los Colorados, 522

Los Chimú, 477

Los Italianos, canyon, 214

Los Lobos, 515, 521

Los Órganos, 386, 390, 487

Los Pájaros, island, 462

Los Patos, lake, 389

Los Pulpos, 324, 513

Los Reyes, see Junín, lake

Lucanas, 364, 532

Lucerna, hill, 157

Lucre, 193, 536

– lake, 193, 537

Lúcumo, Lomas del, 326

Lucha, 120

Lucho, 120

Luna, Huaca de la, 444, 452, 453, 453-454,
    454, 479

Lunahuaná, 327, 515

Lurín, 300, 303, 325, 328, 513

Luya, 205, 208, 209, 493

Luyando, 510

Llacanora, 148, 149

Llacpatera, 521

Llactacucho, 163

Llagadén, hacienda, 490

Llámac, 261, 270, 273

Llancha, 499

Llanganuco, 265, 266, 271

Llaqtapata, 437

Llaupi, 508

Llullucha, river, 347

Llumpa, 271

Maca (Arequipa), 159, 160, 161, 164

Maca (Cusco), 536

Macusani, 540, 544

Machacancha, 192

Machu Picchu, Historical Sanctuary, 30, 48, 49, 84, 85, 86, 173, 175, 190, 195, 199, 340-350

Madre de Dios, department of, 48, 82, 87, 352, 399, 401, 402, 539

– river, 88, 195, 352, 357, 399, 400, 402, 403, 404, 544, 545

Madrigal, 159, 160, 161, 169

Magdalena (Cajamarca), 490

Magdalena (Lima), 301

Magdalena de Cao, 479-482

Magunchal, 493

Mahuayani, 542, 543

Majes, 110, 121, 157, 162, 171, 522

Mal Alma, tunel, 505

Mala, 25

Malabrigo, 482

Malpaso, 455

Mamacona, 64, 65, 303

Mamachocho, lake, 120

Manache, 476

Máncora, 386, 460, 465, 467, 487

Mancos, 271

Manseriche, 493

Mantaro, 30, 65, 79, 127, 238, 239, 240, 241, 245, 246, 499, 501, 504, 507, 515, 528, 530

Manu, 48, 195, 199, 351-358, 401, 402, 403, 543, 545, 546, 547

Mapacho, river, 542, 546

Marabamba, see Pilcomoso, hill

Marañón, river, 206, 209, 266, 287, 292, 492, 494

Maras, 192, 534

Marcahuasi, 329, 330

Marcapata, 542, 543, 544

Marcapomacocha, lake, 500

Marcará, 270

Marcona, Reserved Area Punta San Juan at, 365, 519

Marcún, 273

María Josefa, path, 271

Mariño, river, 94, 95

Marpa, 121

Martín, pass, 536

Mashcón, river, 141

Matacaballo, 486

Matachico, bridge, 501

Matahuasi, 502

Matarani, 523

Matucana, 500

Maucarquipa, stone forest, 156

Mavila, 544

Mayo, river, 494, 495

Mayocc, 528

Mazo, 475

Mazo Cruz, 523, 527, 541

Mazuco, 542, 544

Meca Chica, 526

Meca Grande, 526

Medio Mundo, saltwater lagoon, 475

Mejía, 523

Mejorada, 528

Mendieta, 283, 374, 375

Mesapata, 509

Miculla, rock carvingsde, 428

Minasmoqo, 192

Mirador de los Cóndores, 156

Miraflores, 299, 301, 305, 308, 321, 332

Mishagua, river, 352

Mismi, mount, 158, 170

Misti, volcano, 107, 109, 118, 119, 534, 535

Moca, 521

Mocupe, 482

Moche, 37, 444, 445, 453, 455, 479

Mochumí, 491

Moho, 541

Molino-Huayco, 210

Mollendo, 25, 109, 528

Mollepata, 534

Mollepunku, 169

Momón, río, 296

Monobamba, 505

Monsefú, 65, 224, 225, 228, 482

Monte Meiggs, mount, 500

Monterrey, 269, 274

Moquegua, 25, 79, 244, 523, 541
– department of, 48, 82, 119
Morales, 495
Moray, 192
Morococha, 500
Moronacocha, 292
Morro Chala, 521
Morro Quemado, point, 368
Morro Sama, 526
Mórrope, 491
Morropón, 389
Mosna, river, 266, 268
Motupe, 65, 224, 225, 229, 483, 491
Moyobamba, 25, 73, 287, 434, 436, 493, 494
Muquiyauyo, 502
Muruhuay, Santuario de, 441

Nanay, 286, 289, 292
Naplo, 514
Napo, river, 292, 295
Naranjo, hill, 229
Naranjos, 494
Narihualá, 389
Nasca, 25, 28, 48, 73, 79, 80, 83, 278, 283, 285, 359-367, 371, 512, 518, 519, 520, 532
Nauta, 292
Negra, Cordillera, 259, 260, 263, 264, 477, 496, 497
Negro Mayo, pass, 535
Nepeña, valley, 477
Neshuya, 511
Ninacaca, 508
Ninamarca, 29, 546
Ninash, 330
Ninaybamba, hacienda, 533
Nonura, bay, 388
Nusiniscato, river, 544

Ñapique, lake, 486
Ñaupe, 483

Obrajillo, 329

Occe-Occe, pass, 533
Ocongate, 64, 174, 542, 543
Ocoña, 110, 522
Ocopa, convent, 244, 245, 247, 502
Ocros (Áncash), 476
Ocros (Ayacucho), 530
Ocucaje, 282, 518
Olaechea, 540, 544
Olmos, 229, 483, 491, 492
Ollantaytambo, 189, 190, 345
Ollape, 208
Óndores, 255, 508
Orcococha, lake, 530
Orconcocha, lake, 271
Orcototo, 328
Orcotuna, 502
Oropesa, 536, 538
Otuzco, 61, 148, 152, 447
Oxapampa, 65, 75, 214, 216, 217, 218, 219, 506, 508
Oyón, 475

Paca, lake, 245, 502
Pacamayo, river, 348
Pacanguilla, 482
Pacaraos, 471
Pacaritambo, 173
Pacasmayo, 25, 482, 489
Pacaya–Samiria, National Reserve, 46, 292, 293, 297
Paccha, 504, 507
Pacific, ocean, 19, 20, 58, 260, 264, 324, 496, 497, 501
Pacucha, 65, 103, 105
Pachacallo, 501
Pachacámac, 244, 300, 325, 326, 513
Pachachaca, 94, 531, 533
Pachacoto, 265, 269, 497
Pachía, 428, 527
Paiján, 455, 482
Paita, 25, 379, 380, 382, 383, 486, 487
Pajaritos, Quebrada, 487
Pala Cala, waterfall, 500
Palca, 427, 428, 504, 505, 527

Palcamayo, 438, 441, 504
Palomino, island, 87, 320
Palpa, 74, 518
Pallanchacra, 509
Pallasca, 478
Pampa de los Arrieros, 156
Pampa del Confital, 156
Pampa Galeras/Bárbara d'Achille, National
    Reserve, 48, 364, 519, 532
Pampa Hermosa, 215
Pampamarca, 121
Pámpano, 516, 530
Pampas, 29, 128, 138, 528, 530
Pampas de Heath, 402, 405
Pampas de Hospital, 463
Pampas del Sacramento, 511
Pañamarca, 477
Pao Caño, channel, 395
Paracas, National Reserve, 20, 33, 48, 79,
    83, 87, 282, 283, 368-377, 516,
    517, 523
Parachique, 486
Paraíso, 474
Paramonga, 476
Pardo de Miguel, pass, 494
Paredones, 364
Pariacoto, 259
Pariahuanca, 503
Parón, lake, 272
Paruro, province, 175
Pasamayo, 471
Pasco, department of, 46, 508
Paso de la Concordia, see Concordia
Pastoruri, mount, 265, 266, 269, 497
Patahuasi, 156, 534, 535
Patascache, 416
Pataz, 447
Pativilca, 258, 470, 475, 476, 495, 496
Pato, Cañón del, 259, 264, 478, 497
Patria, 547
Paucará, stone forest, 236
Paucarcolla, 408, 541
Paucarpata (Arequipa), 117
Paucarpata (Puno), 419

Paucartambo, 60, 62, 65, 177, 194, 195,
    356, 537, 545, 546
Paullo, 515
Pedro Ruiz, 491, 493, 494
Perené, river, 506
Phuyupatamarca, 348, 349
Picota, 510
Pichanaki, 506
Pichu Pichu, volcano, 107, 108
Pikimachay, 27, 128
Pilcomayo, 502
Pilcomoso, hill, 249, 253
Pilcopata, 547
Pilpichaca, 530
Pillahuata, 547
Pillco, 249, 253
Pimentel, 221, 222, 228, 482
Pinchollo, 161, 164
Piquillacta, 193
Pirámide Garcilaso, mount, 272
Pirca, 471
Písac, 188, 189, 193, 195, 537, 546
Pisco, 25, 48, 73, 79, 368, 369, 376, 377,
    516, 517, 523, 528, 529, 530
Piscobamba, 264,
Pitusiray, mount, 188, 192
Piura, 25, 31, 46, 56, 76, 79, 80, 82,
    378-391, 483, 485, 486, 491
– department of, 46, 65, 82, 89, 371, 465,
    492
– region, 41, 128
– river, 378
Piuray, river, 192
Planchón, 544
Plateros, 463
Playa Blanca, 514
Playa Chica, 474
Playa Hermosa, 214
Playón, 375
Pocpa, 259, 273
Pojpojquella, 540
Poma, forest, 227
Pomabamba, 264, 478
Pomacochas, 494

Pomalca, 482
Pomata, 412, 416, 417, 418, 419, 541
Pompey, 270
Porcón, 64, 143, 144, 151
Porculla, pass, 492
Poroy, 534
Pozo de Las Lisas, 526
Pozo Santo, 282, 517
Pozuzo, 64, 214, 216, 217, 218, 219, 506
Primavera, 522
Puca Pucara, 187
Pucallpa, 25, 73, 79, 82, 87, 392-398, 501, 506, 510, 511
Pucará (Cajamarca), 492
Pucará (Junín), 242, 528
Pucará (Puno), 410, 418, 541
Pucayacu, 509
Pucusana, 514
Pueblo Viejo (Áncash), 269
Pueblo Viejo (Lambayeque), 482
Puente Inambari, 544
Puente Paucartambo, 506, 508
Puente Ruinas, 345, 346
Puerto Bermúdez, 216, 505, 511
Puerto Callao, 395
Puerto Chicama, 482
Puerto Chiple, 492
Puerto Eten, 385, 482
Puerto Fiel, 515
Puerto Inca (Arequipa), 521
Puerto Inca (Huánuco), 511
Puerto Maldonado, 25, 48, 75, 82, 87, 399-405, 539, 541, 542, 544, 545
Puerto Mori, 455, 479
Puerto Pardo, 402
Puerto Pizarro, 459, 461, 488
Puerto Rico, 387
Puerto San Martín, 371
Puerto Viejo, 522
Puinahua, channel, 292-293
Puma Sillo, see Wakay Willca, mount
Pumapashimi, 269
Pumunuta, 170
Punchana, 289

Puno, 25, 48, 56, 59, 64, 65, 70, 79, 85, 86, 87, 88, 193, 194, 201, 406-422, 423, 527, 536, 537, 540, 541, 542, 544, 546
– department of, 48, 65, 82, 400, 401, 408, 409, 413, 415, 540
Punta Aguja, 387
Punta Arquillo, 370
Punta Bapo, 387
Punta Bermejo, 476
Punta Caballas, 518
Punta Callán, 259, 477
Punta Camarón, 460, 463
Punta Coles, 526
Punta Colorado, 476
Punta Culebras, 476
Punta El Huaro, 477
Punta Hermosa (Lima), 324, 513
Punta Hermosa (San Martín), 495
Punta Hornillos, 523
Punta Las Zorras, 476
Punta Mero, 488
Punta Muñi, 476
Punta Negra, 513
Punta Nonura, 387
Punta Olímpica, pass, 270
Punta Pejerrey, 371
Punta Rocas, 324, 514
Punta Sal, 460, 464, 465, 466, 487, 488
Punta San Juan de Marcona, see Marcona
Punta Shode, see Punta Nonura
Punta Tric-Trac, 387
Pupuja, 418
Puquio, 360, 364, 519, 532
Purcay, hacienda, 533
Purgatorio, hill, 227
Puruchuco, 329
Puruña, 155

Qenko, 187
Qorihuayrachina, 345, 347, 349
Qoyllur Ritt'i, 61, 176, 177, 195, 542
Quebrada de la Huaca,
    see Puerto Inca (Arequipa)
Quebrada Fernández, 465

Quebrada Juliana, 402
Quebrada Verde, 326
Querecotillo, 487
Querobamba, 533
Querococha, lake, 268, 269
Quicacán, hacienda, 253, 509
Quilca, 522, 523
Quilcayhuanca, canyon, 265
Quillabamba, 85, 201, 345, 347
Quincemil, 542, 543
Quinua, 131, 132, 137
– Pampa de la, 34, 136
Quiquijana, 536, 539
Quiroz, see Huancabamba, river
Quispicanchis, province of, 177
Quistococha, 292

Ramón, lake, 484, 486
Raqchi, 536, 540
Rataquenua, 259, 273
Raura, Cordillera, 330, 476, 497
Ranrahirca, 497
Recuay, 259, 262, 263, 268, 269, 497
Rentema, 493
Repartición (Arequipa), 523
Repartición (Lima), 328
Reque, river, 482
Requena, 293, 398
Reventazón, 387
Ricardo Palma, 499
Rímac, 305, 308, 317-319
– river, 299, 300, 308, 313, 328, 329, 500
Río Abiseo, National Park, 46
Río Seco, 330, 474
Rioja, 84, 494
Rosaspata, 541
Rumichaca, 530
Rumisapa, 495
Runtur Cochas, 475
Runturacay, 348
Rúpac, 471

Sabancaya, volcano, 156, 164
Sabandía, 109, 117, 118

Sacaco, 520
Sacsarayoc, mount, 533
Sacsayhuamán, 186, 187, 345
Sachabamba, plain, 138
Sachapite, stone forest, 236
Sahuanay, Reservoire, 99
Salalá, 389
Salaverry, 445, 479
Salcantay, mount, 533
Salinas, lake, 119, 156
Salinas de Otuma, 374, 375
Salinas y Aguada Blanca, National Reserve, 48, 119, 155, 535
Salvación, 547
Sama, river, 526, 527
Samanco, 477, 478
Samiria, river, 293
San Alejandro, 511
San Andrés (Huánuco), 509
San Andrés (Ica), 377, 516
San Andrés, mount, 500
San Antonio, 435
San Antonio de Cumbaza, 435
San Bartolo, 324, 514
San Bartolomé, 499
San Blas, 178, 179, 181, 182, 202
San Clemente, 516, 529
San Cristóbal (Huancavelica), 235
San Cristóbal (San Martín), 495
San Cristóbal, hill, 303, 305, 318, 319
San Francisco (Áncash), 476
San Francisco (Lima), 471
San Francisco (Ucayali), 394, 395
San Gabán, 544
San Gallán, island, 375
San Ignacio, 492
San Isidro, 300, 305, 308, 321, 331, 520
San Jerónimo (Apurímac), 103, 104, 531
San Jerónimo (Cusco), 537, 546
San Jerónimo de Surco, 499, 500
San Jerónimo de Tunán, 241, 242, 502
San José (Arequipa), 523
San José (La Libertad), 478
San José (La Libertad), 482

San José (Lambayeque), 482
San José (San Martín), 433
San José, hacienda house, 516
San José (Ica), plain, 361, 518
San José (La Libertad), plain, 482
San José de Quero, 503
San José del Moro, 482
San Juan, 152, 490
– river, 516
San Juan del Oro, 416
San Lorenzo (Cusco), 543
San Lorenzo (Madre de Dios), 545
San Lorenzo, island, 320
San Luis, 264, 271
San Luis de Shuaro, 506
San Marcos, 149
San Martín, department of, 46, 82, 431,
    436, 495
San Mateo, 500
San Miguel, 259
– waterfall, 509
San Miguel de Pallaques, 489
San Pablo, 489-490
San Pedro, mangrove swamps, 486
– beach, 516
San Pedro de Cajas, 240, 241, 441, 442,
    504, 507
San Pedro de Casta, 330
San Pedro de Lloc, 447, 482, 489
San Pedro de Pari, 508
San Rafael, 509
San Ramón, 25, 73, 79, 212, 213, 214,
    215, 217, 219, 220, 442, 504, 505
San Roque, 143
San Sebastián, 537, 546
San Vicente, 515
Sandia, 416
Sandoval, lake, 403, 404
Santa, 259, 478, 497
– river, 258, 259, 260, 261, 263, 264, 268,
    478, 496, 497
Santa Ana, 132
Santa Apolonia, hill, 144
Santa Bárbara, mine, 232, 233

Santa Clara (Loreto), 292
Santa Clara (Ucayali), 396
Santa Cruz, 518
Santa Eulalia, 330, 500
Santa Inés, 530
Santa María, 324, 514
Santa Rosa (Apurímac), 533
Santa Rosa (Lambayeque), 482
Santa Rosa (Lima), 471
Santa Rosa (Loreto), 294
Santa Rosa (Madre de Dios), 544
Santa Rosa (Puno), 540
Santa Rosa (Ucayali), 395
Santa Rosa, border complex, 527
Santa Rosa de Frías, 389
Santa Rosa de Quives, 62, 329
Santiago de Chuco, 447
Santo Domingo de los Olleros, 328
Santo Tomás, 288, 289, 292
Sapallanga, 241
Saposoa, 435
Sarapampa, 324, 515
Sarasara, volcano, 120
Sarhua, 129, 132
Satipo, 246, 502, 506
Sauce, lake, 433
Sawasiray, mount, 188, 192
Sayacmarca, 348
Sayán, 474, 475
Saylla, 536, 537, 546
Saywite, 97, 98, 533
Sechín, 477
Sechura, 74, 387, 483, 491
– desert, 378, 379, 486
Señoritas, 324, 513
Sequión, 368, 375
Serjali, river, 352
Shalacoto, 441
Shanao, 495
Shauro, 496
Shelby, 508
Shilcayo, 431, 435
Shintuya, 195, 355, 356, 545, 547
Shipata, 209

Sibayo, 158, 169, 170
Sicaya, 502
Sicuani, 29, 536, 540
Siete Pozos, lake, 389
Sihuas, 120, 264, 478, 522
Silaka, 521
Sillustani, 415, 541
Simbilá, 381
Sinakara, valley, 177
Sincos, 502
Sipán, 28, 37-42, 221, 222, 225, 226, 227
Sipia, 120
Socosani, 118
Socsi, 515
Sol, Huaca del, 453, 454, 479
Sol (Bolivia), island, 407, 420
Solimana, 120
Sóndor, 105
Soraccocha, 530
Subtanjalla, 517
Sucre, 497
Sucsunya, 245
Suches, lake, 527
Sullana, 25, 76, 378, 380, 388, 487
Sumbay, 27, 121, 155, 524
Sunchubamba, mount, 188-189
Sunicancha, 328
Supe, 475

Tabalosos, 495
Tablachaca, 528
Tacalá, 379
Tacama, hacienda, 281
Tacna, 25, 34, 65, 76, 79, 82, 423-430, 512, 523, 526, 527, 541
– department of, 82
– region of, 128
Tahuamanu, river, 545
Talara, 76, 80, 82, 487
Talavera, 531
Talpo, 282
Tamarindo, 463
Tambillo, 522
Tambo, river, 523

Tambo Colorado, 516, 529
Tambo de Mora, 233, 516
Tambo de Viso, 500
Tambopata, river, 399, 401, 402, 404, 405
Tambopata–Candamo, Reserved Area, 48, 400, 401, 402, 404, 405
Tamborero, 476
Tambomachay, 187
Tanaka, 74, 521
Tangarana, pass, 494
Tangarará, 379
Tapay, 161, 165
Taquile, island, 65, 88, 410, 414, 415
Taquitiza, 493
Taraco, 407, 410
Tarapoto, 25, 82, 431-437, 491, 494, 495, 510
Tarata, 527, 541
Tarma, 25, 46, 56, 64, 73, 79, 438-443, 501, 503, 504, 507
Tarmatambo, 439, 442
Taruca, 509
Tayakome, 353
Tembladera, 489
Tempón, hill, 229
Terijway, mount, 188
Tiawanaco (Bolivia), 419, 420
Ticapampa, 269, 497
Ticlio, pass, 498, 500, 503, 506
Ticrapo, 530
Tinajani, canyon, 540
Tinajas, canyon, 328
Tingo (Amazonas), 206, 208, 211, 494
Tingo (Arequipa), 523
Tingo María, 25, 73, 79, 255, 256, 501, 506, 509, 510
– National Park, 256
Tinqui, 542
Tinta, 536, 540
Tintacayoc, 138
Tintaya, 536
Tinyahuarco, 508
Tipón, 194, 536, 537
Tiquina, strait, 417, 419

Tisco, 165
Titancayoc, 138
Titicaca (Bolivia), island, *see* Sol, island
Titicaca, lago, 29, 88, 116, 173, 406, 407, 410, 411, 412, 541
– National Reserve, 48, 413
Tocache, 510
Toccto, 138
Toccyac, 236
Tocra, 155, 156
Tomas, 503
Tomayquichua, 253, 509
Toquepala, 526
Tornamesa, 85, 86
Toro Muerto, rock carvings, 121, 522
Torre Torre, 246
Tortuga, 486
Tortugas, 477
Totoritas, 516
Tres Cruces, 195, 546, 547
Tres Hermanas, 526
Trujillo, 25, 29, 46, 56, 64, 65, 76, 79, 82, 222, 322, 432, 444-458, 470, 478, 479, 481, 488, 489
Túcume, 75, 224, 227, 229, 483, 491
Tulumayo, 505
Tumán, 482
Tumbes, 25, 46, 79, 82, 459-468, 470, 486, 488
– department of, 46, 82, 79, 460, 461
– río, 459, 460, 461-462, 463, 488
– National Sanctuary Manglares de, 46, 461, 468
– Reserved Area, 46, 461, 463, 464, 468
Tumshucayco, 272
Tungasuca, 32
Tununtunumba, waterfall, 431, 435
Tuquillo, 476
Tuti, 169

Ucayali, department of, 82, 87, 89, 393, 510
– river, 292, 352, 392, 396, 398, 493

Uchiza, 509
Uchumayo, 523
Ulta, 270
Umayo, lake, 415
Uracuza, 492
Urcos, 194, 536, 538, 539, 542
Uripa, 530
Uros, 49, 88, 413
Urricape, plain, 482
Urubamba, 49, 187, 188, 191, 192, 193, 197, 340, 341, 345, 347, 534, 536, 537, 546
Uspacocha, lake, 98
Utcubamba, 204, 206, 208, 493
Uyu-Uyu, 170

Valencia, lake, 403
Valley of Chanchamayo, *see* Chanchamayo
Valley of the Pyramids, *see* Túcume
Valley of the Volcanoes, 120
Valley of Colca, *see* Colca
Valley (Sacred) of the Incas, *see* Urubamba
Vaquería, pass, 271
Végueta, 474
Velo del Ángel, 256
Venecia, lake, 435
Ventanilla, 471
Verónica, *see* Wakay Willca, mount
Vesique, 478
Vicco, 255, 508
Viconga, lake, 272, 273
Vicos, 270
Vichaycoto, hacienda, 253
Vichayito, 487
Vila Vila, 526
Vilca, 501, 515
Vilcabamba, 102, 128, 129, 190, 193, 533
Vilcamayo, river, 536
Vilcanota, mountain range, 189, 534
– river, 188, 340, 536, 539, 546
Vilcashuamán, 128, 138, 530
Villa, Reserved Area Pantanos de, 46, 325, 513

Villa Rica, 216, 218, 219, 506, 511
Villacurí, 277, 517
Vinzos, 259, 497
Virrilá, estuary, 387, 486
Virú, valley, 478
Viscachani, 535
Vischongo, 139
Vista Alegre, hacienda, 282
Vitoc, 505
Vítor, 522
Viviate, 381

Wakay Willca, mount, 188
Wari, 28, 128, 137
Warmiwañuska, pass, 347, 348
Wayo, lake, 330
Waywaka, 105
Willcahuaín, 273
Willcamayu, see Urubamba, river
Wiñay Wayna, 348, 349

Yajirhua, mount, 157
Yálape, 209
Yanacocha, lake, 239
Yanachaga–Chemillén, National Park, 216
Yanahuara, 111, 113
Yanamate, 508
Yanque, 157, 158, 159, 160, 161, 162, 163, 170, 171, 534
Yarinacocha, 393, 394, 395, 396, 397, 398

Yasila, 383, 486
Yauca, 520, 521
Yauli, 500
Yauri, 534, 536, 540
Yaurihuiri, 533
Yaután, 259
Yauyos, 503
Yaverija, river, 545
Yerupajá, mount, 272
Yesu, waterfall, 216
Yucay, 193
Yulpa, 493
Yumagual, 152
Yumaque, 283
Yungay, 260, 261, 262, 263, 265, 270, 271, 274
Yunguyo, 416, 417, 419, 541
Yura, 118, 119, 155, 534
Yuracmarca, 497
Yuracyacu, river, 510
Yurimaguas, 82, 87, 433, 435, 495

Zaña, 221, 226, 228, 229, 482
Zapallal, 471
Zárate, Bosque de, 499
Zarumilla, 461, 462, 488
Zepita, 416, 417, 418
Zorritos, 460, 461, 462, 463, 464, 466, 488

24 de Julio, see Corral Quemado, bridge

Index of Maps

Arequipa, city map, 112
– access and bypass routes, 524-525
Ayacucho, city map, 133
Cajamarca, excursion map, 149
– city map, 145
Colca Valley, the, 166-167
Cusco, city map, 180-181
– access and bypass routes, 538-539
Chachapoyas, excursion map, 207
Chanchamayo, excursion map, 215
Chiclayo, excursion map, 226
– city map, 223
– access and bypass routes, 483
Huancayo, excursion map, 243
Huaylas, el Callejón de, 266-267
Ica, excursion map, p. 281
Iquitos, city map, 290

Lima, city map, 306-307
– access and bypass routes, 472-473
Machu Picchu, the citadel of, 342-343
Nasca, excursion map, 363
Paracas, National Reserve, 372-373
Perú, physical map, 581
– political map, 580
– principal protected natural areas, 44
Piura excursion map, 384-385
– city map, 381
– access and bypass routes, 484-485
Puno, excursion map, p. 412
Tarapoto, excursion map, 434
Trujillo, city map, 449
– access and bypass routes, 480-481
Urubamba Valley, the, 190-191

Route Maps

Index map, 583
Route map 1, 584-585
Route map 2, 586-587
Route map 3, 588-589
Route map 4, 590-591
Route map 5, 592-593
Route map 6, 594-595

Route map 7, 596-597
Route map 8, 598-599
Route map 9, 600-601
Route map 10, 602-603
Route map 11, 604-605
Route map 12, 606-607

Sources

Instituto Geográfico Nacional (IGN)
Ministerio de Transportes y Comunicaciones (MTC)
Field work by the *Inca Guide to Peru* team

Index of Photographs

10 (WW); 11 (Arch. *Cosas*); 17 (WW); 20 (WW); 21: 1, 2 (WW); 23 (Arch. PEISA); 27 (WW); 28 (Arch. PEISA); 29 (WW); 30: 1, 2 (WW); 31 (Arch. PEISA); 32: 1, 2 (Arch. PEISA); 33 (Arch. PEISA); 35 (Arch. *Caretas*); 36: 1 (Arch. *Caretas*), 2 (AB); 38 (WW); 39: 1, 2 (WW); 40 (WW); 41 (WW); 42 (WW); 45: 1, 2 (WW), 3 (WL/PEISA); 48: 1, 2 (WW); 49: 1, 2 (WW); 50 (WW); 51 (Md'A); 52 (Md'A); 53 (Md'A); 54 (WW); 55 (WW); 56 (Md'A); 57: 1, 2 (WW); 58 (RU); 59 (RU); 60 (WW); 61: 1, 2 (WW); 62 (WW); 65 (Arch. PEISA); 69 (WW); 71: 1, 2 (WW); 74 (WW); 75: 1, 2, 3 (WW); 76 (WW); 82 (AB); 84 (WW); 85 (AB); 87 (WW); 88 (WW); 89: 1 (WW), 2 (JM), 3 (WW); 93 (WW); 94 (WW); 97: 1, 2 (WW); 98: 1 (JP), 2, 3 (WW); 99 (WW); 101 (WW); 102 (WW); 104: 1, 2 (WW); 105: 1, 2, 3 (WW); 107 (Arch. PEISA); 109 (RU); 110 (Md'A); 111 (Arch. PEISA); 113 (Md'A); 114: 1 (Arch. PEISA), 2 (Md'A), 3 (Arch. PEISA); 115 (Md'A); 116 (Md'A); 117: 1 (AB), 2 (WW); 118: 1 (WW), 2 (AV); 119: 1, 2 (WW); 120: 1 (WW), 2 (MT); 121 (AB); 127 (WW); 128 (RU); 129 (WW); 130 (AB); 131: 1 (WW), 2, 3 (Arch. PEISA); 132 (Md'A); 134: 1 (WW), 2 (Md'A); 135 (AB); 137 (RU); 138: 1 (CS), 2 (WW); 141 (JM); 142 (RU); 144: 1, 2 (RU); 146 (MT); 147: 1 (Md'A), 2 (RU); 149: 1, 2 (WW); 150 (JM); 151: 1 (WW), 2 (JM); 155 (RU); 156: 1, 2, 3 (WW); 157: 1 (WW), 2 (JP), 3 (WW); 158 (RU); 159: 1 (RU), 2 (JP); 160 (WW); 161 (RU); 162 (JP); 163 (JP); 164 (WW); 165 (RU); 169: 1 (JP), 2 (WW); 170: 1 (WW), 2 (LP); 172 (WW); 174: 1, 2, 3 (WW); 176 (Arch. PEISA); 177: 1, 2 (WW); 178: 1 (Arch. PEISA), 2 (WW), 3 (AB); 179: 1 (AB), 2 (WW); 181: 1 (WW), 2 (RU); 182: 1, 2 (WW); 183: 1 (Arch. PEISA), 2 (RU); 184 (DG); 185 (WW); 186: 1, 2 (WW); 187: 1, 2, 3 (WW); 188: 1, 2 (WW); 189 (AB); 192 (MT); 193: 1, 2 (WW); 194: 1, 2, 3, 4 (WW); 195 (WW); 203 (RU); 204 (WW); 205 (JP); 206: 1, 2 (WW); 208: 1, 2 (WW); 209 (WW); 210 (WW); 214: 1 (JP), 2 (WW); 216: 1 (WW), 2 (JP); 217: 1, 2 (JP); 221 (Arch. PEISA); 223 (WW); 224 (Arch. PEISA); 225 (WW); 226 (WW); 227: 1 (RU), 2 (AB), 3 (WW); 228: 1, 2 (Arch. PEISA); 229 (WW); 232 (WW); 233 (WW); 234 (Arch. PEISA); 235: 1 (Arch. PEISA), 2 (WW); 236 (WW); 238 (Arch. PEISA); 240: 1 (Md'A), 2 (Arch. PEISA), 3 (Md'A); 241 (Arch. PEISA); 244 (Md'A); 245: 1 (Md'A), 2, 3 (WW); 246: 1 (Md'A), 2 (WW); 249 (JP); 251 (WW); 252: 1 (WW), 2 (JP); 253: 1, 2 (JP); 254 (JP); 255: 1, 2 (WW); 256 (WW); 258 (WW); 259: 1 (JP), 2 (WW); 260 (WW); 261: 1 (Arch. PEISA), 2 (WW); 262 (WW); 263 (WW); 264 (WW); 265: 1, 2, 3 (WW); 267 (Arch. PEISA); 268 (HP); 269: 1, 2 (WW); 270 (WW); 271: 1 (WW), 2 (JP); 272 (WW); 273 (JP); 277 (AB); 278: 1, 2 (WW); 279 (WW); 281 (Arch. PEISA); 282: 1, 2, 3 (WW); 286 (WW); 287 (AB); 288: 1 (RU), 2 (Arch. PEISA), 3 (SP); 289 (WW); 291: 1 (AB), 2 (SP); 292: 1, (WW), 2 (RU); 293 (WW); 294 (WL/PEISA); 299 (MT); 300: 1 (Arch. PEI-

SA), 2 (JP); **301**: 1 (JP), 2 (WW); **302**: 1 (RU), 2 (JP); **303** (RU); **304**: 1 (JP), 2 (WW); **305**: 1 (Arch. PEISA), 2 (JP); **308**: 1 (WW), 2 (JP); **309**: 1, 2 (WW), 3 (MT); **310** (Md'A); **311** (Md'A); **312**: 1, 2 (JP); **313**: 1 (JP), 2 (RU); **314**: 1 (Arch. PEISA), 2 (JP); **315** (JP); **316** (JP); **317** (JP); **318**: 1, 2 (JP); **319**: 1, 2 (RU), 3 (JP); **320**: 1 (JP), 2, 3 (RU); **321** (RU); **322** (Arch. PEISA); **324**: 1 (MT), 2 (JP); **325** (MT); **327** (MT); **328** (WW); **329** (WW); **330**: 1 (RU), 2, 3 (Md'A); **340** (WW); **342** (WW); **343** (WW); **344** (WW); **345** (WW); **346**: 1, 2 (WW); **347**: 1, 2 (WW); **348**: 1, 2 (RB); **349** (RB); **351** (WW); **353**: 1, 2, 3 (WW); **354**: 1, 2 (WW); **355** (WW); **356** (WW); **357** (WW); **359** (WW); **360** (AB); **361** (WL /PEISA); **362** (WW); **364** (MT); **365** (WW); **368** (WW); **370**: 1 (MV&CM), 2 (WW); **371** (WW); **373**: 1, 2 (WW); **374**: 1, 2 (WW); **375**: 1, 2, 3 (WW); **378** (WW); **379**: 1, 2 (WW); **380** (WW); **382**: 1 (WW), 2 (MT), 3 (WW); **383** (WW); **385**: 1, 2 (AB); **386** (WW); **387**: 1, 2 (WW); **388**: 1, 2 (WW); **392** (WW); **393**: 1, 2 (WW); **394** (MT); **395** (WW); **396**: 1, 2 (WW); **398** (WW); **399** (WW); **400**: 1, 2 (WW); **401** (WW); **402**: 1, 2 (WW); **403**: 1, 2 (WW); **404** (WW); **406** (WW); **407**: 1, 2 (WW); **408**: 1, 2 (WW); **409** (WW); **410** (WW); **411** (WW); **412** (WW); **413**: 1, 2 (WW); **414** (WW); **415**: 1, 2 (WW); **416**: 1, 2 (WW); **417** (WW); **418** (Arch. PEISA); **419** (WW); **423** (MT); **424** (Arch. PEISA); **426**: 1, 2, 3 (MT); **427** (MT); **428**: 1, 2 (WW); **431** (WW); **432** (WW); **433**: 1, 2 (WW); **434** (RU); **435**: 1, 2, 3 (WW); **436** (WW); **438** (WW); **439**: 1, 2 (WW); **440** (AB); **441**: 1, 2 (WW); **442**: 1 (WW), 2 (Md'A); **444** (MT); **445**: 1 (WW), 2 (Md'A); **446** (MT); **448**: 1 (RU), 2 (WW); **450**: 1, 2 (Md'A); **451**: 1, 2 (Md'A); **452** (Md'A); **453**: 1, 2 (MT); **454** (MT); **455** (MT); **459** (MT); **460**: 1, 2 (WW); **461** (WW); **462** (WW); **463**: 1, 2, 3 (WW); **464**: 1, 2 (WW); **465**: 1, 2 (WW); **469** (WW); **471** (MT); **474** (WW); **475** (WW); **476** (WW); **477** (WW); **478** (WW); **479** (AB); **480**: 1 (Md'A), 2 (WW); **484**: 1 (WW), 2 (WW); **486** (AB); **487**: 1, 2 (AB); **488** (WW); **489** (WW); **490** (WW); **492** (WW); **493** (WW); **494**: 1, 2 (WW); **496**: 1, 2 (WW); **497** (WW); **498** (WW); **499** (WW); **500** (WW); **501** (WW); **502** (WW); **504**: 1, 2 (WW); **505** (WW); **507** (WW); **508**: 1, 2 (WW); **510** (WW); **511** (WW); **513** (WW); **514** (WW); **515** (WW); **516** (WW); **517** (WW); **518** (WW); **519** (WW); **520** (WW); **521** (WW); **522** (WW); **524**: 1 (RU), 2 (WW); **526**: 1, 2 (WW); **528**: 1, 2 (WW); **529** (WW); **530** (WW); **531** (WW); **532** (WW); **533**: 1, 2 (WW); **535**: 1, 2 (WW); **536** (WW); **537** (WW); **540** (WW); **541** (WW); **543** (WW); **544** (WW); **545** (WW); **546** (WW); **547** (WW); **549** (WW); **579** (WW).

Md'A: Mylene d'Auriol
AB: Alejandro Balaguer/Biósfera
RB: Ricardo Balarezo
DG: Daniel Giannoni
WL: Wilfredo Loayza/PEISA
JM: Jaime Marimón
SP: Sengo Pérez/Biósfera
LP: Luis Pilares
HP: Heinz Plenge

JP: Juan Puelles
CS: Carlos Sala
MT: Michael Tweddle
RU: Renzo Uccelli
AV: Antonio Valdivia
MV&CM: M. Valqui & C. Munn
/Inka Natura
WW: Walter H. Wust

Modelo 2002   Diseñada por Pininfarina

MITSUBISHI
MONTE

Pragma D'Arcy

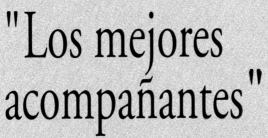

"Los mejores acompañantes"

BEST COMPANIONS

SanCor
CALIDAD LÁCTEA INTERNACIONAL

BRAEDT
Embutidos
Desde 1885

HACCP
Hazard Analysis of Critical Control Points

Certificación Internacional
de Calidad en Alimentos

**En Repsol YPF nos preocupamos por la conservación
y preservación del medio ambiente.**

*In Repsol YPF we are concerned about the preservation
of the environment.*

AREA
PROTEGIDA

Para disfrutar del Perú...

National *Car Rental*® tiene para Ud. el vehículo ideal

Costa, Sierra o Selva; Ud. elija el destino... ¡Nosotros le damos las llaves!

- Las mejores tarifas en autos y camionetas
- Tarifas con kilometraje libre
- Entrega y recojo a domicilio sin recargo
- Servicio de chofer y celular a solicitud

- Traslados y recojos al/del aeropuerto
- City Tours y Servicios Matrimoniales
- Reservaciones en todo el mundo

**Servicio de Alquiler de vehículos y Remisse Ejecutivo.
Atención personalizada las 24 horas**

- **LIMA:** Av. España 449. Telf.:433-3750 e-mail: national@terra.com.pe
  WEB SITE: http//:nationalcar.dnet.com.pe
- **SAN ISIDRO:** Hotel Los Delfines, Los Eucaliptos 555. Telf.:222-1010
- **AEROPUERTO:** (Atención las 24 horas). Telf.: 575-1111
- **TALARA:** Av. Angamos 176. Telf.: (074) 38-2752

6

ROUTE MAPS
In which the roads, places, towns and innes
of this singular kingdom are
meticulously illustrated.

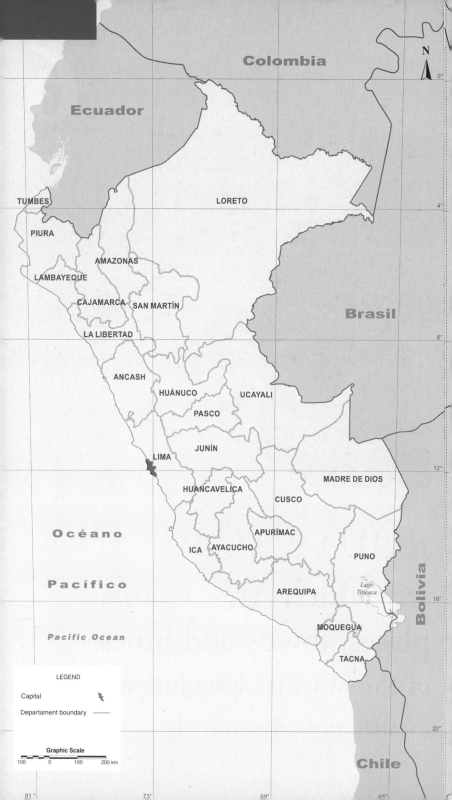

ROUTE MAP LEGENDS

ROAD MAP

═══════	Multi-lane highway
▬▬▬▬▬	Paved, national N-S road
▬▬▬▬▬	Unpaved, national N-S road
─────	Paved, national E-W road
▬▬▬▬▬	Unpaved, national E-W road
─────	Paved local road
─────	Unpaved local road
- - - - - - - -	Railway
↓ 10 ↓	Total distance in kilometers
(1N)	National N-S road number

AREA OF INTEREST

/////////	Protected natural area
🛉	Area of interest to travelers
⚓	Beach resort
∿∿∿	Surfing
⚑	Windsurfing
⚜	Hot springs
♟	Archeological site

POLITICAL DIVISION

▬▬▬▬▬	International boundary
▬▬▬▬	Department boundary
⬗	Department capital
◉	Provincial capital
●	District capital
○	Town

SERVICES

●	Restaurant
⛽	Service stations
🛢	Fuel sold from drums
◈	All services
✈	Airport
✗	Airstrip
A P	Customs / tollbooth
🚓	Highway police
🐟	Fishing village
✷	Lighthouse
⚓	Seaport
➤	River port

GEOGRAPHICAL FEATURES

──────	Primary river	⬜ Lake, dam	
──────	River, stream	◤ Estuary, lowlands	
──────	Dry streambed	→ ←	Pass or high point

Altitudes

4000 to 5000 masl
3000 to 4000 masl
2000 to 3000 masl
1000 to 2000 masl
0 to 1000 masl

Some roads in Peru are so winding, it is impossible to reproduce their exact path. Consequently, roads on the map may not reflect the exact length in kilometers.

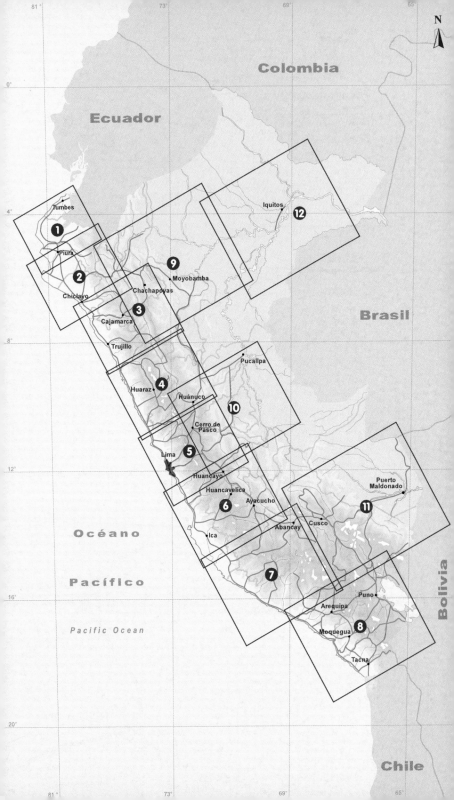

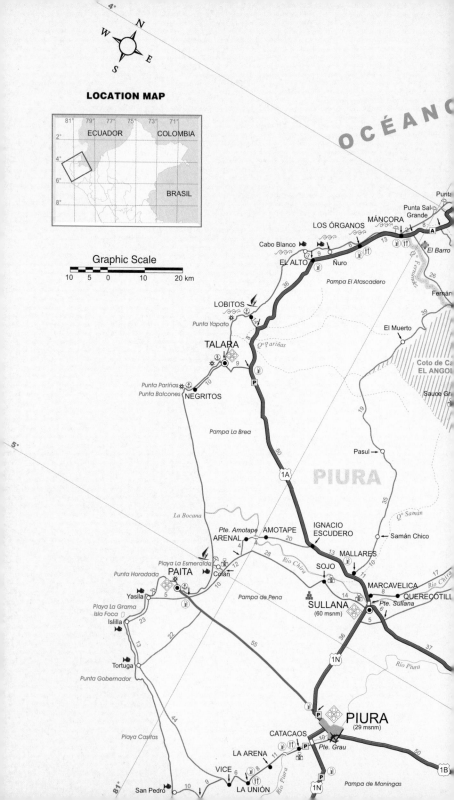

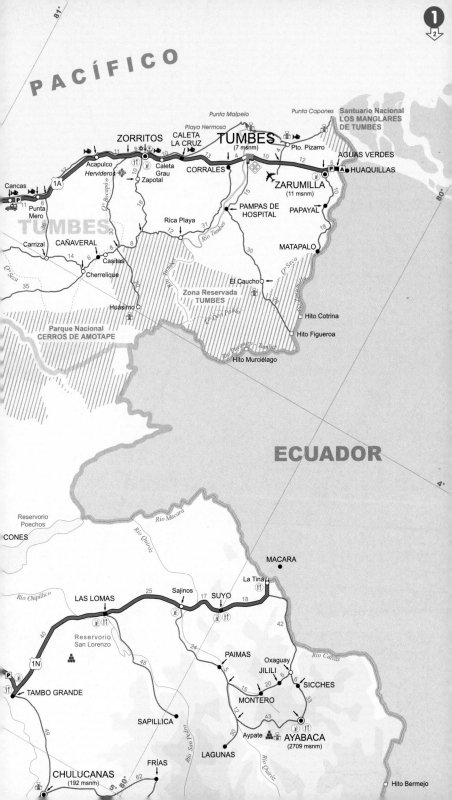

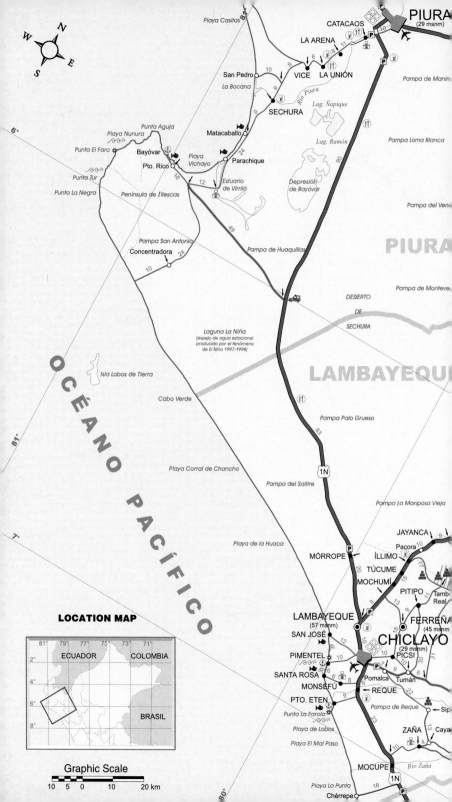

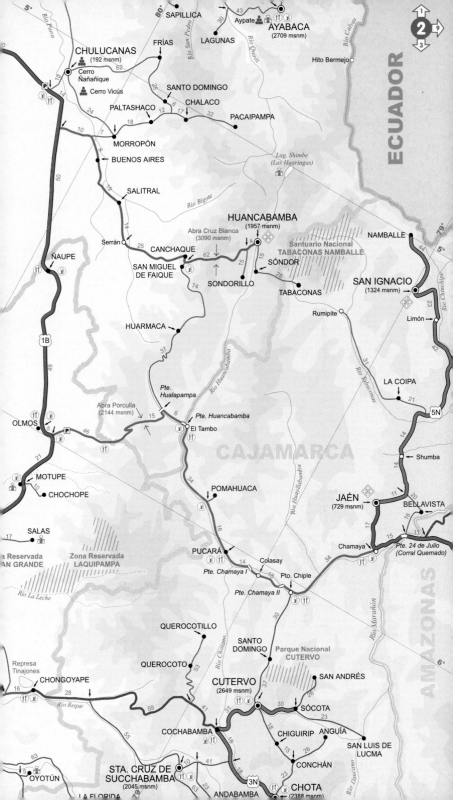

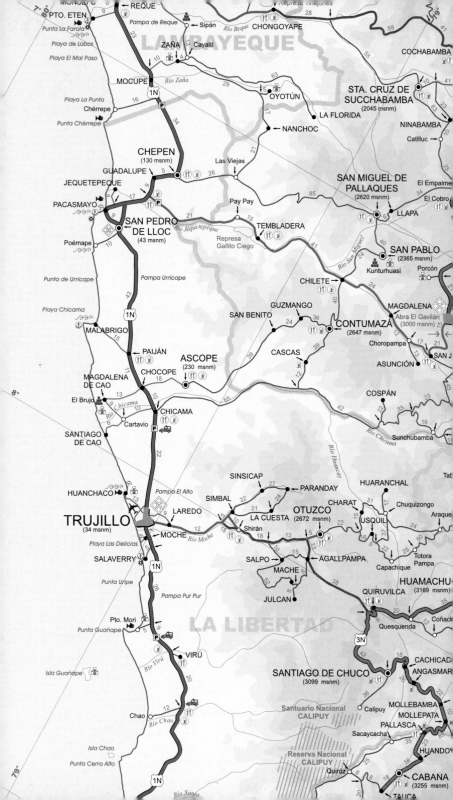

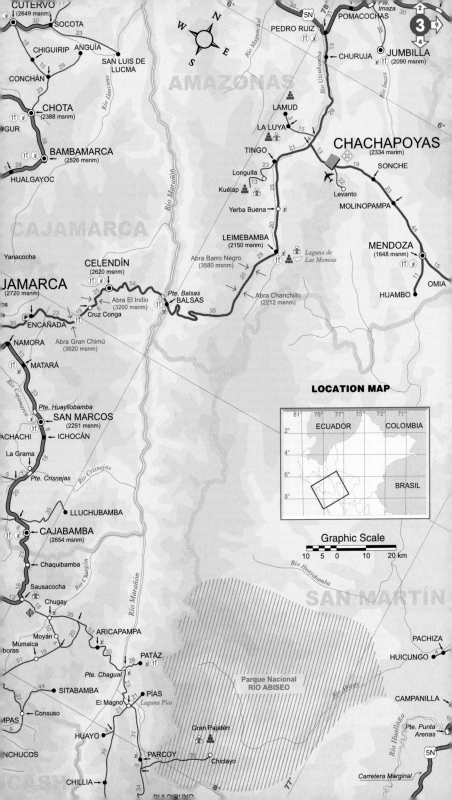

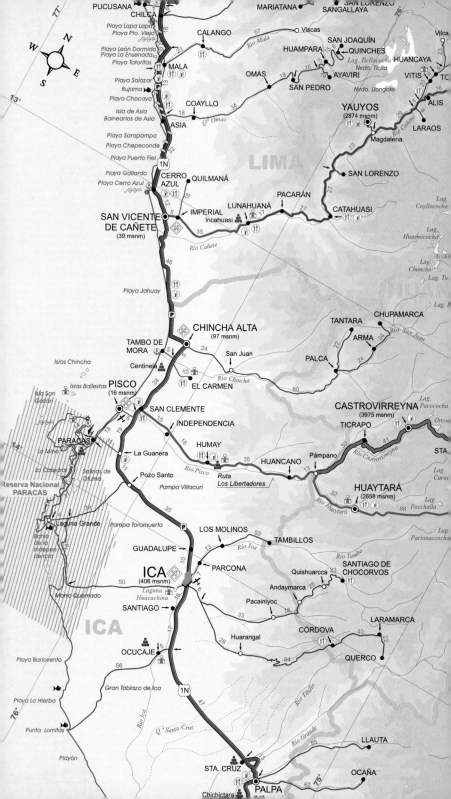

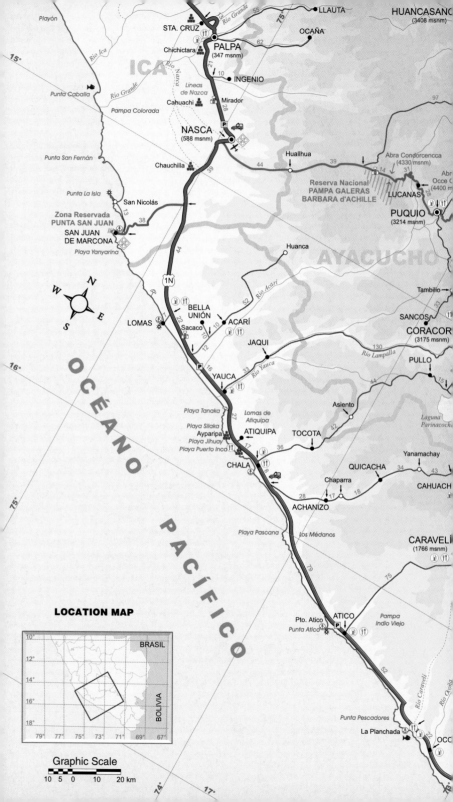

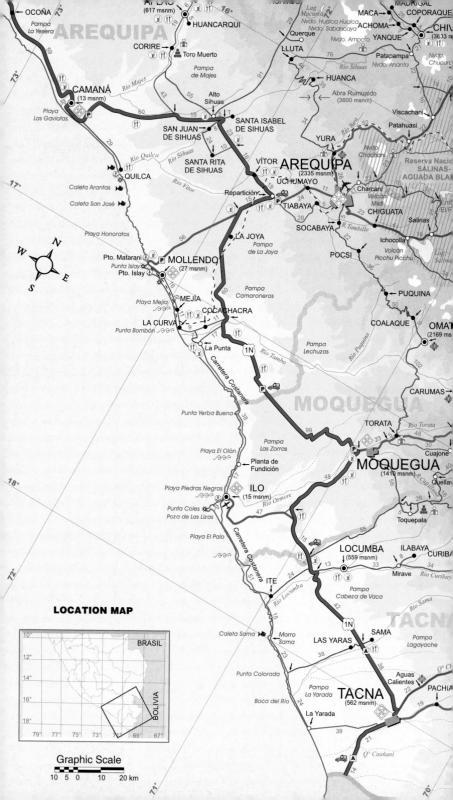

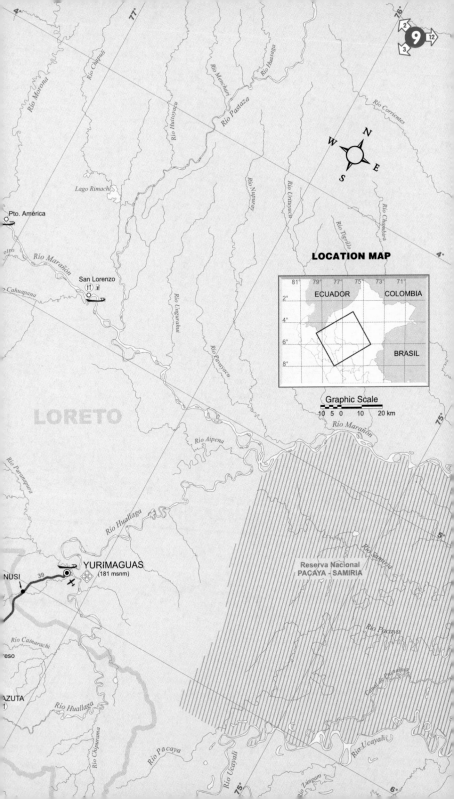

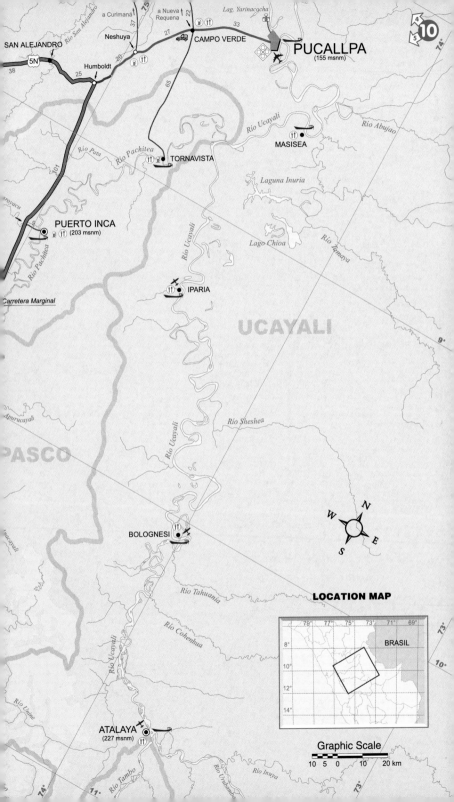

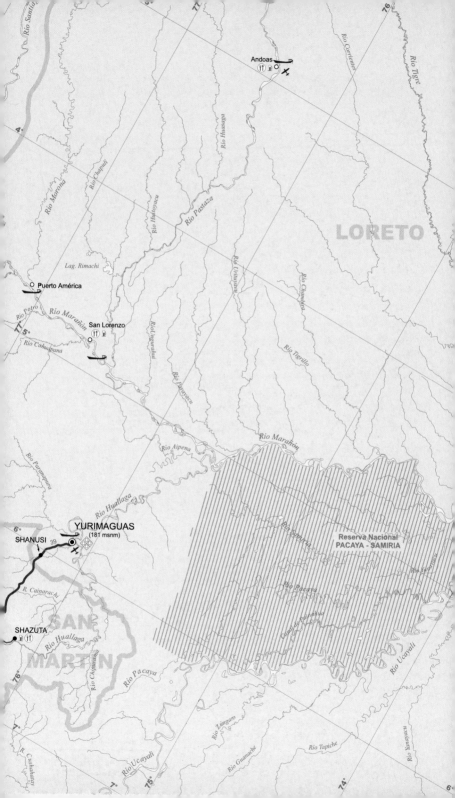

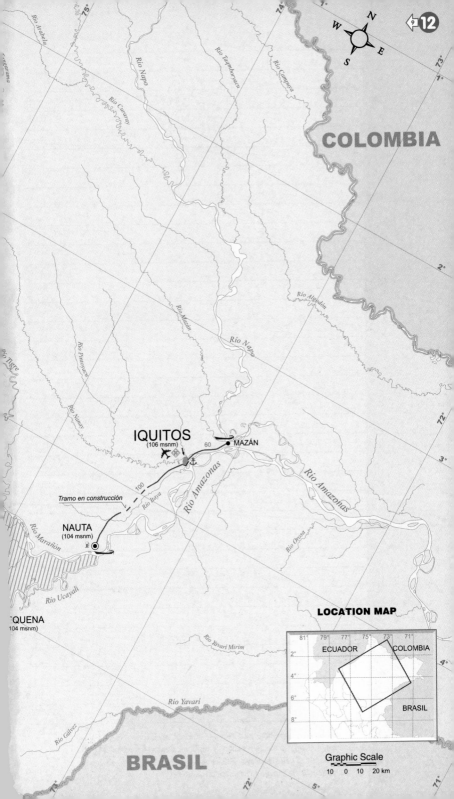

NOTES

_____

We would greatly appreciate your letting us know of any error,
omission or change in the information in this book. Contact the editors at:
Ediciones PEISA, Av. Dos de Mayo 1285, Lima 27 • Tel 221 5988
E-mail: peisa@terra.com.pe • whwust@terra.com.pe